The Origins
of Socialism
in Cuba

The Origins of Socialism in Cuba

JAMES O'CONNOR

Cornell University Press

ITHACA AND LONDON

First published 1970

Standard Book Number 8014-0542-4

Library of Congress Catalog Card Number 75-87007

PRINTED IN THE UNITED STATES OF AMERICA
BY VAIL-BALLOU PRESS, INC.

For Daniel
and Steven

Preface

The research for this book and the first draft were completed in early 1964. I wanted to visit Cuba in 1968 to gather data to bring certain parts of the story up to date, but I was unable to obtain State Department permission. The observations in the Postscript are therefore based on secondhand material, impressions of friends who have been in Cuba recently, and the press. In the five years since I was there much has happened in Cuba, but nothing that leads me to change any of my basic theses.

A number of friends and scholars read parts of the manuscript in various stages of completion and offered valuable criticisms and suggestions. I would like especially to thank Mr. Saul Landau, Professors Maurice Zeitlin, Albert O. Hirschman, Alexander Erlich, and Evsey Domar, and Mr. Martin Kenner.

I also want to acknowledge the help of Mr. Thomas Carroll, who kindly made available to me the Inter-American Development Bank's library on Cuban agrarian reform. The staffs of the libraries of Columbia University, Yale University, Harvard Business School, and Stanford University's Hispanic-American Institute extended unfailing courtesy and aid. The same can be said about the personnel of the National Library of Cuba in the course of my three visits to the island in 1960, 1961, and 1963.

I cannot begin to name the dozens of Cubans and non-Cubans working in Cuba who courteously afforded me help and without whom I could not have done this study. They gladly submitted to interviews, supplied materials, and engaged in correspondence. My debt is particularly great since they were (and are) the busiest group of men and women I have ever encountered, and their time was (and is) very valuable.

Much of the material in this study has appeared in different form in journals and periodicals. I wish to thank the editors of the following publications for permission to use this material: "On Cuban Political Economy," *Political Science Quarterly*, 79, No. 2 (June, 1964); "The Foundations of Cuban Socialism," *Studies on the Left*, 4, No. 4 (Fall, 1964); "The Organized Working Class in the Cuba Revolution," *Studies on the Left*, 6, No. 2 (March–April, 1966); "Industrial Organization in the Old and New Cubas," *Science and Society*, 30, No. 2 (Spring, 1966); "The Labour Force, Employment, and Unemployment in Cuba, 1957–1961," *Social and Economic Studies*, 15, No. 2 (June, 1966); "Agrarian Reforms in Cuba, 1959–1963," *Science and Society*, 32, No. 2 (Spring, 1968); "Political Change in Cuba, 1959–1965," *Social Research*, 35, No. 2 (Summer, 1968).

Of course, responsibility for the general interpretations offered in this study and whatever errors and inconsistencies it contains is mine alone.

JAMES O'CONNOR

San Francisco
May 1969

Contents

Preface   vii

[1] Introduction   1

[2] Economic and Political Background:
The Permanent Crisis   12

[3] Economic and Political Background:
Castro's Rise to Power   37

[4] The Mismanaged Economy:
Prerevolutionary Agriculture   55

[5] The Agrarian Revolution   90

[6] The Nationalization of Industry   135

[7] Organized Labor before and
after the Revolution   177

[8] Agricultural Planning   214

[9] Industrial Planning   240

[10] The Political Economy of
Cuban Socialism   279

[11] Postscript   315

Appendixes

A: The Statistics of Rural Revolution   319

B: The Labor Force, Employment, and Unemployment in Cuba, 1957–1961   328

Index   337

The Origins
of Socialism
in Cuba

[1]

Introduction

[1]

The origins of socialism in Cuba remain to this day clouded and confused. On the eve of the Revolution of 1959, Cuba was one of the most prosperous countries in Latin America. Cubans owned more automobiles, appliances, and television sets per capita than the citizens of any other Latin country. There were a large number of moderately well-to-do businessmen, most farm tenants enjoyed secure tenure rights, the peasantry was relatively small and isolated, and employees in the large government bureaucracy were relatively well paid. The proportion of the island's labor force in the organized labor movement was one of the largest in the world. In many branches of production, wages and salaries approached Western European and Canadian standards.

Coca-Cola, baseball, Standard Oil, American tourists, abstract-expressionist painting, United Fruit, and Madison Avenue advertizing techniques seemed to have submerged the once powerful social and political force of Cuban nationalism. The United States' economic, political, and cultural relations with Cuba were more intimate than those with any other major country or territory, excepting Puerto Rico. During the six decades following political independence from Spain, Cuba imported not only investments, consumer commodities, food, technology, and business methods from the United States, but also much of its culture, including many of the ideas that Cuba held about itself. In Havana, at least, a unique Cuban identity and mode of life was filed away in the memories of a few Cuban anthropologists and historians.

Working-class militancy and radicalism, prominent in the explosive early decades of the century, seemed to belong to another, more romantic era. This makes Cuban socialism even more perplexing. The Cuban Communist party, which dominated the labor movement during most of the 1940's, was divided and discredited in the 1950's. No organized, disciplined, mass-based revolutionary movement existed. Only a handful of lawyers and other professionals, intellectuals, labor leaders and students originally opposed the dictatorship of Fulgencio Batista, who seized power in 1952 with the backing of the army, ending Cuba's last, short-lived experiment with constitutional democracy.

The final incongruity arose in 1958. The United States withdrew most of its military support from Batista when it became clear that Castro's Rebel Army was defeating the regular armed forces, and that the political consensus between business, labor, and the farmers, which the dictator tried to strengthen to consolidate his rule, was in ruins. Far from shoring up the dictator with arms, military advisers, and money, the United States abandoned him to his fate. Previously the United States had not been blind to the real or imagined threat of revolution to its economic and political interests. One only need recall Guatemala and Iran.

The fact is that the State Department had little reason to believe that the Cuban Revolution posed any danger to the United States. United States policy-makers were taken completely by surprise when the revolutionary leadership launched a program of deepgoing economic and social reform, pressed on with it in the face of State Department and Congressional opposition, nationalized industry and agriculture, tore the island away from the world market system, and transformed a national, democratic revolution into a socialist revolution.

Was the establishment of Cuban socialism true drama—the product of a complex interplay of social, economic, and political forces which no one, not even Castro himself, planned or even foresaw? Or melodrama—a conspiracy of a few secretive Communist or crypto-Communist revolutionaries? Or, alternatively, a drama of the absurd—an emotional, irrational process triggered by the feud between Castro and the United States government?

Was the Cuban Revolution a "historical process running on from one inevitable conclusion to another, down to the outcome, hidden from the actors in the drama"?[1] Was it a conspiracy in the grand style, staged and directed by a handful of plotters who concealed their real motives from friends and enemies alike? Or was it merely a product of the blow-for-blow economic and diplomatic war with the United States?

Who really betrayed the revolution? The middle-class liberals and reformers who broke with Castro over the issues of agrarian reform, nationalization of industry, communism, and relations with the United States and the Soviet Union? Castro himself? Or no one?

[2]

As these questions suggest, there are two contending schools of thought about Cuban socialism: the "revolution betrayed" and "conspiracy" thesis, and the theory that what happened in Cuba was largely a response to United States opposition to the revolution. The two theses are contradictory; neither can encompass the other. The first is profoundly wrong, the second subject to serious correction. A third thesis is put forward in this book. It holds that the rise of Cuban socialism was true drama, not melodrama or farce.

The first thesis comes in two versions and adopts the central idea that Castro betrayed the revolution. The crude, backwoods version is that the Castro brothers and their immediate aides were Communists all along; that they planned from the start to deliver Cuba to the Soviet Union; that they wanted to clamp a tight yoke on the Cuban people in order to exercise unlimited personal power and fulfill their bottomless personal ambitions.[2] Castro is seen as a man of great intelligence and charisma, but also as a pathological liar or, in

[1] Pieter Geyle, *Debates with Historians* (New York, 1958), p. 268.

[2] Nathaniel Weyl, *Red Star Over Cuba* (New York, 1961) and Daniel James, *Cuba: The First Soviet Satellite in the Americas* (New York, 1961). Some other writers could not make up their minds about Castro. Irving Pflaum in *Tragic Island: How Communism Came to Cuba* (Englewood Cliffs, N.J., 1961) wrote that Castro was both a "shrewd, foresighted creator of an [Communist] epoch" and a "creature of forces he couldn't control and possibly couldn't always comprehend . . . an unstable person who had been hoodwinked."

some versions, a psychotic. Working furiously against time, Castro fooled nearly the entire Cuban population, exiling, imprisoning, or murdering those who saw him for what he really was. United States power was immobilized by politically blind, personally timid men in the State Department. Under Castro the Cuban economy steadily deteriorates, the people are more and more impoverished, the farmer is a slave of the state. Revolt against Castro's rule is imminent, frustrated only by the blind obedience and devotion of a terroristic, well-armed militia and secret police.

This variation of the "revolution betrayed" thesis, only slightly caricatured, need not detain us for long. It offers no firsthand observations and relies on the dubious testimony of disenchanted exiles (many of them Batistianos who fled for their lives early in 1959) and the files of Batista's secret police. It also offends common sense and reason and displays an attitude toward the Cuban people bordering on contempt.

The sophisticated version of the "revolution betrayed" thesis, a more intelligent, less hysterical variation,[3] is based on three major propositions: first, that Castro was a highly competent revolutionary politician and personally ambitious man who brilliantly exploited the wait-and-see attitude of the United States toward the revolution for his own ends; second, that most of the social and economic reforms introduced during the first few months of the revolution were sensible and practical, but that their effectiveness was quickly eliminated by Castro's alliance with the Cuban Communists, his demagogic nationalism, and his eagerness to polarize the revolution against the middle classes, who were chiefly responsible for the victory against Batista. Cuba's unreadiness for socialism, it is claimed, was evidenced by the lack of interest of the people in socialist planning, inefficiencies in the operation of industry and agriculture, and the general failure of the economy to perform up to prerevolutionary standards.

The third proposition is that Castro deliberately initiated the economic and diplomatic war against the United States that culmi-

[3] Theodore Draper, *Castro's Revolution: Myths and Realities* (New York, 1962).

nated in the complete rupture of relations between the two countries in 1961. In brief, the argument is that Cuba needed reform, not
revolution; an honest, practical, liberal democratic political leader
(with whom the United States would have been prepared to work),
not a revolutionary. This variation is at least credible and merits detailed examination.

Similarly, the second school of thought on Cuban socialism,
which includes most writers who are (or were) sympathetic to the
revolution, cannot be dismissed out of hand. At heart it is a rebound
theory, crediting the State Department with the emergence of
Cuban socialism, or at least those aspects of socialism which most
North Americans find distasteful.[4] Writing in mid-1961, two of its
defenders concluded that "if, in Cuba today, the chances for political
democracy are slim, if Cuba accepts and imitates Soviet methods
uncritically, and comes increasingly under Communist influences, if
there now be an end to civil liberties for some time to come, it is a
result of our government's policies." Elsewhere the authors hedge
somewhat, writing that "infatuation with the Soviet example" was
"probably inevitable as a result of American policies." [5]

The basic failure of this school is its unwillingness or inability to
probe those forces at work *within* Cuba that resulted in socialism.
The authors cited above rightly argue that Castro was "prepared to
take whatever steps [he] deemed necessary to assure the people of a
rising material and cultural standard of living." But nowhere do
they explain why socialism with central economic planning was necessary or at the least a viable alternative to a reformed capitalism.
Until this question receives a satisfactory answer, the "revolution
betrayed" theory will continue to go basically unchallenged.

[3]

This book is a rebuttal of the first school of thought and a correction of the second. We contend that Cuban socialism can be understood only in the context of the old economy and the old social and

---

[4] Maurice Zeitlin and Robert Scheer, *Cuba: Tragedy in Our Hemisphere*
(New York, 1963), pp. 207, 221.
[5] *Ibid.*, pp. 207, 221.

political structure, not as the bitter fruit of some "abnormality" or "conspiracy" nor as the product of a series of mistaken judgments by Cuban liberals and reformers and United States policy-makers.

The heart of the argument is that Cuban socialism was inevitable in the sense that it was necessary if the island was to be rescued from permanent economic stagnation, social backwardness and degradation, and political do-nothingism and corruption. The main points of our argument are:

1. From an early date Cuba displayed the main structural features of a capitalist economy. At the end of the nineteenth century, two of every three farmers and farm workers worked in the cultivation of cash crops. By the 1950's subsistence farming was nearly eclipsed by specialized agricultural production for export and home consumption. Meanwhile, foreign capital—exploiting opportunities for the large-scale production of sugar cane and corporate, absentee ownership—transformed propertied farmers into tenants and farm laborers. The sugar, mining, utility, and other industries were increasingly dependent upon foreign banks; manufacturing, commerce, and service industries were more integrated into the structure of foreign companies based in the United States.

At the same time there was a growing cartelization and monopolization of Cuba's agricultural production. Output restrictions, pegged prices, and other monopolistic practices blanketed the livestock industry and sugar, tobacco, rice, potato, and coffee farming. Partly the result of economic forces and partly the product of the development of powerful associations of sugar mill owners, of cane farmers and other cultivators, and of sugar workers, monopolistic policies and practices limited the pace of agricultural development. They inhibited the improvement of crop yields, wasted land and labor, reduced labor productivity, prevented the wide introduction of a mixed, scientific agriculture, and in general hindered the ability of the economy to mobilize and utilize Cuba's abundant economic resources fully and efficiently.

Similar conclusions can be drawn about industrial and labor organizations. By the 1950's there were more than 150 employers' associations of one kind or another, many of them exercising wide powers over their members. Compulsory producers' associations dominated sugar and tobacco manufacture, for example, and all the great public utilities had clear monopolies in their fields. Powerful labor unions and a well-paid "labor aristocracy" sealed off important labor markets from outside competition and shared responsibility for the extraordinarily low relationship between labor productivity and wage rates.

The old Cuban economy consisted of a series of economic baronies, well organized, special-interest minded, corporate oriented, and unwilling to sacrifice local or special privileges for total economic and social development. State economic policy—including tax, expenditure, and loan and subsidy policies—emerged from the interplay of pressures from the interest and industry groups, hardening the prevailing pattern of economic resource utilization. Government interference in the economy took on a redistributive, rather than productive, character. Private and state monopolistic practices sprang up in the soil of a market economy. Restrictions in the rural economy were not of the type ordinarily associated with traditional agricultural systems, controls in industry and labor markets were not those customary in mercantile or neomercantile systems. Cuba's economic institutions were industrial capitalist institutions, historically specific to Cuba.

2. The second part of the argument follows from the first and concerns the nature of the political rebellion (1953–1959) and the social revolution (1959–1963). Few groups or classes failed to be represented in or identified with *both* the Batista consensus *and* the political struggle against the consensus. Prerevolutionary economic policy and protection benefited some businessmen, some workers, and some farmers, and abandoned others to the vicissitudes of the marketplace. Control and influence over the means of administration—the Ministry of Labor, the Sugar Stabilization Board, and the Agricultural and Industrial Development Bank, to cite three examples—were more important than control of the means of production. One of the supreme ironies of the revolution is that the social and economic programs of the Batista government closely resembled those of Castro's 26th of July Movement: both focused on structural

problems of the economy, and both held out promises to nearly every socioeconomic group in Cuba. Political divisions cut sharply across class lines; nearly every organized economic class was divided against itself.

This is why the dedication of a handful of young revolutionaries was the decisive influence in the political rebellion. Neither the farmers nor the workers grasped the political initiative at any point in the struggle. Ernesto Guevara, with Raúl Castro, Fidel's closest *compañero,* accurately described the poor farmers in the Sierra Maestre as the revolution's "invisible collaborators." Organized labor put up even less resistance to Batista, offered little open or surreptitious aid to the rebels. The general strike called in April, 1958, was a failure. Only in January, 1959, after the regular armed forces had succumbed to the Rebel Army's final blows, did the working classes shut down Havana's industry and commerce. Organized professional, educational, and business groups protested the dictatorship but officially struck a wait-and-see attitude.

Similarly, Castro's ruling group initiated each of the stages of the social revolution. The poorer farmers did not seize and cultivate idle lands; they even failed to claim the small fields in which they labored until the Revolutionary Government formally turned these tracts over to them. Nor did the urban workers or sugar mill laborers independently occupy the factories, in sharp contrast to the spontaneous creation of workers' soviets during the abortive social revolution of 1933. Rebel Army or militia units, at the direction of the central government, took possession of the island's farmland and factories. Owners and managers of economic enterprises put up little or no resistance.

These two events, the exclusive, individualistic character of the political revolution and the peaceful, bloodless social revolution, were intimately connected. The social revolution was peaceful and orderly because the political revolution transferred economic power from one small group of men to another—the Rebel Army, taught by its guerrilla experience how to make hard decisions, take risks, and lead men—and because the nationalization of agriculture and industry won the consent and support of the majority of the Cuban people.

Class warfare—reactive, controlled, and mainly fought with words, not guns—inevitably emerged as the Revolutionary Government cut progressively deeper into the old system of privilege and profit. Economic and social reform increasingly discriminated against the urban and rural middle classes and in favor of the working classes and small farmers. This was reflected in government propaganda, in the speeches by the revolution's leaders, which systematically polarized attitudes on the issues of reform, elections, political parties, and relations with the United States. According to the "revolution betrayed" thesis, class-oriented reform and forced polarization of opinion provide prima-facie evidence that Castro betrayed the original spirit and aims of the revolution: the flowering of economic, social, and political life in Cuba.

But Castro's early postvictory support was nearly universal and extremely heterogeneous. Any policy would seem a betrayal to someone; no policy would be considered a betrayal by everyone. Few reform measures, and no significant ones, could be universally popular; every measure would heighten the loyalty, bind more closely, some of Castro's supporters. "To stop, to obstruct or constrain a revolutionary process," Castro said in 1961, "would be tantamount to betraying it." Thoroughgoing reform, political polarization, and the deepening and widening of the revolutionary process were the logical consequences of a sincere, intelligent, and uncompromising attempt to bring to fruition the revolution's original general aims.

3. The final part of the argument concerns the personalities who dominated the revolution from the incipient stages of the rebellion to the consolidation of socialist power. Lawyers, doctors, journalists, students—most of these men came from the nonbusiness middle classes. They were supremely practical, nonideological: "This is the first time—ever, anywhere," Leo Huberman and Paul Sweezy wrote, "that a genuine socialist revolution has been made by noncommunists." [6]

They were also highly individualistic and devoted to improving the social and economic condition of Cuba. Castro's personality in

[6] Leo Huberman and Paul M. Sweezy, *Cuba: Anatomy of a Revolution* (New York, 1960).

particular gives the revolution a special flavor. In the summer of 1960, at the time the United States acted to bar Cuban sugar from the mainland market, Castro promised that "in each cooperative we are going to build a town . . . with or without the [sugar] quota. Each little town will have a school for the children of the members of the cooperative, with or without the quota. . . ." [7] His boundless optimism was apparent as early as the famous "History Will Absolve Me" speech in 1953, and it invariably impressed friends and enemies alike. In his speeches and declarations, the images of defeat or even retreat rarely, and then reluctantly, appear. Castro's limitless confidence undoubtedly gave the revolution a powerful sense of anticipation, buoyancy, and faith in itself. He had (and has) a deep-rooted faith in the Cuban people.

He also had faith in his own perceptions. These originally non-Communist—and in some cases anti-Communist—revolutionaries more or less rapidly perceived that social and economic development required the abolition of capitalist institutions and the introduction of socialist institutions. Their ideas, including their conception of their own role in the revolution, were shaped by their practical experience in the reconstruction of Cuban society. There were two distinct aspects to their ideology. First, they saw the institutions of the old society as forces of economic retardation and social reaction, and the social revolution was increasingly oriented by this perception. Second, they learned later that new, progressive institutions had to be rooted in the Cuban reality, shaped by Cuban conditions. Some institutional forms that were imported from other socialist countries and others that had sprung up in the heads of the revolutionaries but were out of touch with actual Cuban conditions had to be abandoned.

It was one of the triumphs of revolutionary ideology that the Cuban leaders were able to separate the question of retardative institutions from that of progressive institutions. Abolishing the former does not provide a formula for the latter; if the Cuban revolutionaries at first had some mistaken ideas of what to put in the place of the old institutions, they were right to eliminate these institu-

[7] Quoted in *Trabajo Cuba*, No. 3 (July, 1960), p. 3.

tions. It is not proof of the irrationality of Cuban socialism, as is claimed by those who assert that Castro "betrayed" the revolution, that the leadership sometimes failed to hit upon new, practical institutional forms.

[4]

This, in brief outline, is our answer to the two prevailing schools of thought about Cuban socialism. In the next chapter we will sketch in the background for a detailed analysis of the origins of socialism in Cuba. This background description will arouse more interest if the main outlines of the argument are kept firmly in mind. First, the political economy of the old society was not traditional, feudal, or mercantile, but capitalist, a variety of industrial capitalism, highly integrated into another, more powerful capitalist economy, the United States. Second, Cuban capitalism was a particularly regressive kind of monopoly capitalism; in the classic Marxist idiom, the relations and organization of production stifled the further development of the forces of production. Third, the political ideologists (broadly speaking, the leadership of the Cuban Communist party) failed to have the political initiative at any time. Fourth, Castro and his closest comrades were practical revolutionaries, in the sense that they took every measure they considered necessary to get the old economy and society off dead center. In the context of the old political economy this meant that the revolutionary leadership, as well as the revolution itself, was progressively radicalized. Fifth, these men were able to forge socialism in Cuba comparatively peacefully, with a minimum of opposition, violence, and bloodshed. The socialist revolution, including all the mistakes it inevitably entailed, was accepted and supported by the majority of Cuban people. Last, Cuban socialism was not an ideological product, nor a betrayal of the Cuban people, nor mainly the effect of the United States hostility and intervention. Rather, it was an expression of hard economic, social and political reality, as understood and acted upon by men whose guerrilla experience conditioned them to act as revolutionaries as well as realists to stay alive.

[2]

Economic and Political Background: The Permanent Crisis

[1]

Cuba is the largest of the Caribbean islands. To its discoverer, Columbus, it was a place of breathtaking beauty. To Imperial Spain it was a thorn in the side. To United States history it is a footnote. But it is also an idea, a rallying cry, a hope, and an example. Above all, Cuba is sugar: *"Sin azúcar, no hay país."* The history of Cuba is the history of sugar.

Sugar was the star of a play within a play enacted in Cuba during the tumultuous pageant of world economic expansion in the nineteenth and early twentieth centuries. Frenzied capital accumulation, massive inflows of foreign investments, the opening up of all available land, abrupt technological changes, and large-scale immigration all combined to revolutionize Cuba's economy, social structure, and political life. Cubans and resident Spaniards and North Americans transformed Cuba into the sugar bowl of Europe and the United States. Under Spanish mercantilist impulses until 1900, under the wing of the United States until 1959, Cuba was part of the system of international specialization and division of labor. But world capitalism—which enriched England, the United States, and other advanced capitalist societies—reduced Cuba to overwhelming dependence on sugar cane and to chronic economic stagnation.

Cuba's fertile soils are especially nutritive to sugar cane, and the reasonably stable rainfall and warm climate also favor its cultivation. Less than a day from the United States by ship, Cuban sugar was guaranteed a market in the booming mainland economy. Until the mid-nineteenth century there were few cane planters, large-

12

scale sugar mills, farm laborers, or investment funds, but Spain, the United States, and other regions in the Caribbean rapidly made up these deficiencies.

The way was opened for United States economic penetration of Cuba by technological advances in sugar manufacturing and transportation during the last half of the nineteenth century. High profits through large-scale, low-cost production encouraged the first wave of United States investments before Cuban independence from Spain; from 1890 to 1895 crude sugar production rose from 600,000 tons to more than 1 million tons, of which United States-owned mills produced over 10 per cent. The War of Independence cleared away the tangled undergrowth of Spanish mercantilist policy in Cuba and left sugar mills and improved lands in ruins, offering even greater opportunities for North American investors. Meanwhile, an undernourished domestic money market, obstacles to the mobilization of capital, and perpetually rising overhead costs curbed Cuban access to cane cultivation and manufacture. By 1926 foreign-owned sugar mills ground over 70 per cent of the island's cane. The rapid expansion of the sugar industry was also the major impulse for labor immigration during the first quarter of the twentieth century, when a large shortage of cheap, unskilled labor developed. Attrition sharply reduced the black ex-slave labor force, and Mexican and Chinese contract labor proved unsatisfactory. The great sugar companies therefore turned to Haiti and Jamaica. Of total immigration from 1902 to 1932—which equaled the natural increase in population during this period—black workers accounted for nearly one-third. The rest of the immigrants were mainly Spanish, many encouraged by immigrant subsidies the Cuban government granted in 1906 and 1911. While Spaniards were welcome to remain permanently, the sugar companies were authorized to import blacks on a seasonal basis only. But the great majority of the black immigrants stayed in Cuba and became permanent fixtures of the labor force. In these ways Cuba was outfitted for the role of sugar exporter. From Europe and North America came capital, techniques, professional managers; Spain, Haiti, and Jamaica furnished farmers and laborers.

[2]

The Cuban sugar economy passed through two stages during the twentieth century and obeyed two different laws of economic growth and development. Between 1905 and 1927 foreign investments expanded more rapidly than the labor force, the return to capital rose, and thus profits seized a larger share of total national income,[1] helping to thwart the development of the domestic market. First, the well-to-do sugar farmers, the mill owners, the local business and commercial classes, and foreign managers, bankers, and technicians disposed of the mass of available purchasing power. Consumer demand was channeled into imports of luxury commodities, and imports in relation to total domestic consumption increased markedly. In 1912, for example, 70 per cent of total imports was consumer goods, and their value came to nearly $84 million, or roughly one-fourth of total consumption.[2] The local bougeoisie and resident Spaniards and North Americans confined their expenditures in the local market to housing, food, domestic servants, and little else. Perhaps as much as one-third of total consumer spending was expended on personal services during the first decade of the century.[3]

Second, repatriated profits on foreign investments (and remit-

[1] There are no data on labor and capital's relative share of income during this period. The above conclusion is based on the following estimates: The sugar labor force grew at a maximum rate of 6 per cent annually (over twice the rate of growth of population) from 1905 to 1927. In 1905, U.S. mills produced 21 per cent of Cuba's sugar; in 1906, U.S. investors had $30 million in sugar. Assuming U.S. mills were capitalized neither more nor less than Cuban mills and other foreign properties, total sugar investment came to $150 million. Applying the same method to 1927, total sugar investment is estimated at $1 billion. The apparent increase in capital was 25 per cent annually. Appreciation of assets during this period inflates the rate of growth of real capital, to be sure. Supposing a nearly 200 per cent appreciation, however, the rate of growth of real capital still was greater than that of the labor force.

[2] National income in 1912 was an estimated $397 million (Julien Alienes y Urosa, *Características fundamentales de la economía cubana* [Havana, 1950], Table 17, p. 52). Import data are given in *ibid.*, p. 330. We assume that the ratio of consumption to national income was .8.

[3] Domestic and personal servants made up *one-half* of the urban labor force in 1899. Supposing that labor productivity in this sector was one-half that in other sectors, one-third of the value of consumption consisted of services.

tances of wage income by immigrants) also deprived the domestic market of purchasing power. Finally, Cuba's deep-water ports, proximity to the United States, and commercial agreements that discriminated against European suppliers cheapened imports from the north, limiting opportunities for Cuban businessmen to exploit the local market. Thus, during the first quarter of the century the very definition of economic growth was the expansion of cane cultivation and sugar manufacture.

During the next thirty years the Cuban economy went through a second stage. On the one side, the rhythm of economic activity at home was increasingly determined by fluctuations in the price and volume of sugar exports. On the other side, the economy began to accumulate capital in other branches of production.

There were three reasons for these seemingly contradictory developments. In the first place, more and more land was planted in cane: at the turn of the century half of Cuba's cultivated land was under cane; in the 1950's about 60 per cent. Meanwhile, total land under cultivation increased fivefold, from 3 per cent to 15 per cent.[4] Second and third, local capital increasingly replaced foreign capital, and there was a growing substitution of Cuban labor for immigrant workers. By 1926 immigration from Haiti and Jamaica came to an end, workers' remittances abroad declined, the demand for locally produced wage goods increased. During the 1930's foreign corporations and banks sold cane fields and sugar mills to Cuban nationals, and repatriated profits fell off in absolute terms and in relation to

---

[4] At the turn of the century, about two-thirds of land under cultivation was systematically cultivated for export. This proportion remained the same in the 1950's; 60 per cent was under sugar, and about 6 per cent under tobacco, fruits, and other minor export crops. Thus, Cuba as a total primary exporter (setting aside other export commodities) did become more specialized until the mid-fifties. There were, of course, wide fluctuations in the proportion of cane exports to total exports; in 1908, for instance, the figure was only 54.4 per cent; in 1919, 88.6 per cent. Compared with the 1920's, when the percentage averaged over 80 per cent, Cuba in the 1950's was somewhat less dependent on sugar. Roughly 70 per cent of Cuba's exports were sugar and sugar products in the more recent decade. See Leonard Wood et al., *Opportunities in the Colonies and Cuba* (New York, 1902), p. 140; and my Chapter Four. On the question of the (declining) importance of repatriated profits, see note at end of chapter.

total dollar spending outside of Cuba. For these reasons a larger share of the island's income was retained by Cubans and expended in the home market, and local economic activity became increasingly sensitive to changes in the value of sugar exports.

The mechanics of the prerevolutionary economy were simple. Exports were ordinarily one-third to two-fifths of national income and two or three times greater than total investment. Proceeds from exports of sugar and sugar products fluctuated between 70 and 85 per cent of total export earnings. The seasonal and cyclical ups and downs of the local economy and the main thrust of economic growth were determined by the world sugar market and U.S. sugar policy, factors not of Cuba's making.[5]

The major source of expansion of Cuban national income and, during the second stage of growth, local consumption and investment expenditures was an increase in sugar exports. Increases in consumption, generated by rising national income, in turn induced new investment spending. The rise in liquidity and bank credit brought about by export booms also encouraged new capital expenditures. Finally, investments were directly induced in the sugar industry itself.

Compared with the expansionary effects of a rise in expenditures in more balanced economies, however, export booms generated relatively little spending at home; roughly 25 per cent of total income was expended on imports of consumer and investment commodities. Yet Cuba's export trade yielded adequate, if not spectacular, average rates of new capital formation, which in turn reduced the island's reliance on imported consumer goods. The ratio of new investment to (net) national product averaged about 10 per cent between 1950 and 1958, only slightly lower than the rate of capital formation in the United Kingdom, France, and Belgium, reaching a high of nearly 15 per cent in 1957. At the same time imports of capital goods and raw materials expanded more rapidly than imports of food, clothing, and other consumer items.[6] Cuba's total stock of cap-

---

[5] Details of the operation of Cuba's export economy are given in the note at the end of this chapter.

[6] Consumer good imports in 1927, 1949, and 1957 were $167.5, $213.5, and $287.8 million, respectively. Fixed capital good imports rose from 15.4 per cent

ital thus grew at a slow, although unstable and unspectacular, rate, and the island became more self-sufficient in the production of many basic consumer commodities.

[3]

Yet production and incomes were nearly at a standstill. This is a central mystery surrounding the performance of the old Cuban economy. By the single standard of average income, the island's economy stagnated during the entire sixty years leading up to the 1959 revolution. Income per head (in constant prices) averaged $201 annually in 1903–1906, $216 per year in 1945–1948, and about $200 in 1956–1958.[7] Between 1950 and 1958 total production increased at an annual rate of only 1.8 per cent while population growth was 2.1 per cent per year. Hence, average income declined every year by 0.3 per cent.[8]

These averages obscure large ups and downs in the movement of

---

of total imports in 1912 to 26.7 per cent in 1957. Raw material and fuel imports jumped from 30 per cent of the total in 1912 to 62.8 per cent in 1957 (Alienes y Urosa, *op. cit.*, p. 330; Banco Nacional de Cuba, *Revista* [October, 1958], p. 470).

[7] For data for the first two periods, see Alienes y Urosa, *op. cit.*, Table 17, p. 58. He deflated his income series (which ends in 1948) with 1926 U.S. wholesale prices. We have adjusted money income figures for 1956–1958, using the same set of prices.

[8] Had the volume of sugar exports remained at their high 1951 level, the level of investment and the growth of production would undoubtedly have been higher. On the other hand, the sugar crisis of 1952 compelled the new Batista regime to develop an extensive program to encourage the growth of industry and agriculture. Thus, in the absence of this special stimulation of the economy, Cuba's growth certainly would have dropped below the recorded rate. It is difficult to weigh the importance of these two offsetting developments, but it appears likely that government stimulation of the economy more than compensated for the decline in sugar earnings. From 1952 to 1956, $612 million was invested in economic development and $149 million in public works (Cuba, National Bank of Cuba, *Economic Development Program, Progress Report No. 1* [Havana, September, 1956], p. 27). Much of this investment would have taken place in the absence of a public development program, but a sizable, although unknown, amount would not have. Meanwhile, cane production fell by one-third from 1952 to 1953, remained stable until 1955, and in 1957 underwent a sharp expansion. Thus, it is likely that the "natural" rate of growth was probably closer to 1 per cent annually than the actual rate of 1.8 per cent.

per capita income. During the first quarter of the century income followed a steady upward curve, but the gains of this period were wiped out during the depression of the 1930's, when wages and income plummeted to unprecedented depths. During World War II the island prospered, but over the thirteen postwar years the trend was stable. Four years of war were required to recover the gains stolen by the Great Depression; postwar Cuba operated at levels achieved fifty years earlier.[9]

The general economic reasons are twofold. In the first place, Cuba's investment booms depended on high levels of export activity, which invariably had a temporary character. In the absence of a permanent expansion of Cuba's sugar exports, the rate of capital formation in the home economy was bound to be very uneven. Secondly, the productivity of investments in Cuba was unusually low, reaching barely one-third of the level of capital productivity in most advanced capitalist countries.[10] One of the reasons was that commercial and public construction took a relatively large share of total

[9] To be sure, there were many improvements in the quality of Cuba's social economy that the income figures do not reveal. The mass of Cubans ate better, went to school longer, and lived more years. They received better medical care, owned more consumer goods, traveled faster and cheaper, wrote more letters, and generally communicated with each other more often. But the source of these changes lay mainly in the systematic redistribution of income and public services brought about by the Grau government of 1933 and all subsequent regimes; "structural" changes were nonexistent or minor. There were two aspects to this redistribution: first, the decline in the share of total income going to foreigners, and second, a shift of income from upper-class Cubans to workers and small farmers. We will see later that the emphasis Cuban governments consistently placed on "redistributive" economic policies (as contrasted to those which would provide incentives to expand production) was unfortunately an important cause of the long-run tendency of the Cuban economy to stagnate.

[10] Official data actually underestimate the net investment ratio, since the rate of depreciation is overestimated. Almost 6 per cent of net national product was charged to depreciation in the old national income accounts, a figure borrowed from Puerto Rico, where the structure of the economy was somewhat similar, so that the longevity of the two countries' assets might be considered comparable. This is mistaken, however, since Puerto Rico grew far more rapidly than did Cuba during the 1950's. This means that the Cuban depreciation rate ought to be lower.

In connection with capital productivity, the figure for Cuba was roughly

capital outlays; also, an inordinate amount of investment funds were expended in trade and commerce and in consumer-goods industry. The main reason, however, was the underutilization and misuse of investments in industries where they were in fact employed. More specifically, Cuba's investment resources were integrated into the structure of large United States corporations and the United States economy as a whole, not into the Cuban economy itself. The underemployment and misallocation of investment and other resources also prevented the ratio of savings and income (and investment and income) from rising above the barely adequate level reached in the 1950's.

[4]

On the surface, the permanent crisis of Cuba's sugar economy—high-level stagnation—appeared to be the result of the "natural" play of market forces. Nothing could be further from the truth. Stagnation and underdevelopment were at root political, not economic, problems. They were the result of the interpenetration of political decisions made by organized economic classes and groups inside and outside Cuba, and by successive United States and

---

1/10 over the period 1950–1958, measured as follows:

Increase per year, Gross Domestic National Product ÷ GDNP
———————————————————————————————————
Domestic Capital Formation ÷ GDNP

The question arises, Was the level of real savings sufficient to finance this high rate of investment? Given the absence of inflation, the answer is, by and large, yes. Batista did drain Cuba's foreign exchange reserves as one source of financing, but in the twenty years prior to 1959 a number of changes had come about which generated a more satisfactory level of domestic savings. In the first place, although average income did not rise, income per urban family had increased, owing mainly to the reduction in the average size of the Cuban family. Second, the 1940's and 1950's had given birth to an active capital market; branch banking in savings was an important offspring of the latter decade. Perhaps most important, Cubanization of industry and the labor force meant that a larger proportion of the island's surplus was retained within the home country. Available data on personal savings show that families in Havana earning an average of $200 monthly saved nearly 5 per cent of their incomes. Families earning an average of $350 monthly saved nearly 15 per cent of their incomes. Nearly one-quarter of the first group and over one-third of the second group were not savers (Cuba, Consejo Nacional de Economía, "El presupuesto familiar cubano" [Havana, August 13, 1951]).

Cuban governments. No one wanted a dormant economy; nearly everyone wanted Cuba to move off dead center. But the interplay of political forces rendered this impossible.

The crucial political decisions, however, were not made in a vacuum. Economics and politics are, after all, labels attached to different aspects of the same phenomena: the acquisition of wealth and power by the few, the attempt to meet basic needs and to acquire a modicum of human dignity by the many. The distinction between economics and politics is thus a matter of convenience, not necessity. Keeping this in mind, we can examine the basic points of interpenetration between economic and political developments in prerevolutionary Cuba under two general headings: United States policy toward Cuba, and Cuban nationalism, including its policy toward the United States.

The historical bases of United States influence in the Cuban political economy were geographical proximity, including the geopolitical significance of the island for United States hegemony in the Caribbean; the attempts by the slave states to bring Cuba into the Union; American intervention in the Cuban War of Independence; and the planned complementarity of the two economies.

More specifically, United States investments in Cuba were for the most part direct, not portfolio, investments. For the island this meant foreign management, investment policies that were at odds with Cuba's needs, and a partial community of interests between domestic and foreign capital. During the 1950's an important port of entry for North American interests was the economic development banks and other agencies established by the Batista government. United States influence and control also fanned out from established beachheads in sugar, cattle ranching, commerce, banking, and utilities into new branches of manufacturing and mineral production and processing. Forging a complex but flexible system of interlocking directorates and bank control, North Americans managed and directed a number of "native" enterprises.[11] In these sectors overhead costs and economies of large-scale production were unu-

[11] Don Villajero, "American Investment in Cuba," *New University Thought*, 1, No. 1 (Spring, 1960), Tables V and VI, pp. 84–87. Prior to World War I, European capital made up the majority of foreign investments; Europe's and

sually large, and capital requirements were out of reach of most Cuban investors.

More social and economic influences were introduced into Cuba by the island's dependence on imports from the United States, which averaged about four-fifths of total imports. This dependency was the consequence of special United States trade preferences, intensive advertising, after-scale service of machinery, rapidity of deliveries, the purchase of United States commodities by U.S.-controlled businesses and technicians trained abroad, and the absence of foreign exchange controls.

For the United States, the "Cuban problem" had two major facets. The first was the problem of maintaining political stability in order to protect investments amounting in 1958 to more than a billion dollars. Before the revolution the United States oriented the island's foreign policy and many aspects of domestic policy.[12] The United States government, North American business firms operating in Cuba, and business interests with important Cuban ties regularly interfered directly and indirectly in Cuban affairs, ordinarily to resolve various issues favorable to foreign interests. Long catalogues of charges of United States interference and intervention in Cuba have been drawn up by a number of historians and other writers, and it is not necessary to reproduce them here.[13]

The second problem was related to the first. The United States wanted to maintain Cuba as a profitable market for United States

---

North America's roles were reversed during the war. During the 1920's railroad investments expanded as rapidly as sugar investments; for the most part the railroads serviced the sugar sector. World War II encouraged mining investments. U.S. oil refineries in Cuba were constructed during the 1950's.

[12] "Whenever I asked President Batista for Cuba's vote to support the United States in the United Nations, he would instruct his Foreign Minister to have the Cuban delegation vote in accordance with the U.S. delegate and to give full support to the American delegate at the U.N." (Earl Smith, *The Fourth Floor* [New York, 1963], p. 55).

[13] Robert F. Smith, *The United States and Cuba, Business and Diplomacy, 1917–1960* (New York, 1960), pp. 19, 46–48, 51, 81, 98, 102, 121, 163, 201–221; Benjamin H. Williams, *Economic Foreign Policy of the United States* (New York, 1929), pp. 56, 169, 201–202; Leland Jenks, *Our Cuban Colony* (New York, 1928), *passim; INRA*, 1, No. 1 (December, 1960), pp. 36–37; Juan Noyola, "Principales objectivos de nuestra Plan Económico hasta 1963," *Cuba Socialista*, 2, No. 13 (September, 1962), *passim.*

exports and a source of crude sugar supplies that could be relied on to balance mainland and offshore production. The United States thus deprived Cuba of any autonomy the island might have enjoyed in a world of free international commerce and mutual respect for national sovereignty.

Until the Castro revolution the United States felt confident that the "Cuban problem" was well in hand. In the first place, economic penetration by the United States early in the century nearly eliminated the independent, property-owning rural middle class, which might have resisted North American domination of agriculture. Second, United States hegemony in Cuba largely transformed the urban middle classes into a dependent, *comprador* stratum of foreign business interests. Let us examine these two developments in turn with an eye to their importance for Cuban economic and political sovereignty.

United States investments in the first quarter of the century resulted in the polarization of the rural class structure, even though a cursory glance at the census data fails to reveal any important objective changes in the composition of economic classes. By 1907 the island's social economy already featured a typically capitalist class structure. The rural proletariat was (statistically) well developed; according to the census of that year, of roughly 770,000 Cuban wage workers, about 40 per cent, or 310,000 laborers, were farm workers. Also included in the agricultural labor force were 40,000 tenant farmers and 17,000 farm owners. Forty years later, the proportion of farm owners to tenants, rural wage workers to urban laborers, and farm owners to the total rural labor force all remained unchanged.

Nevertheless, there were sharp alterations in the composition of the owner and tenant classes which the aggregate data obscure. Thousands of independent tobacco and sugar growers lost their farms during the crises of the late 1920's and 1930's and were transformed into tenants and sharecroppers.[14] Replacing them in the

[14] The independent tobacco farmer, like the sugar grower before him, was the victim of large-scale capital. The mechanization of cigarette and some cigar production diverted foreign capital into the manufacturing branch of the

owner column were marginal subsistence farmers and small coffee and other growers who passed on increasingly fragmented plots from generation to generation. Thus, the remnants of the rural petty bourgeoisie were to a large degree erased by large-scale foreign investments in sugar cultivation and manufacture and replaced by large administrator-operator plantations or transformed into dependent tenants. By mid-century there were relatively few well-to-do farm owners and a large absolute and relative increase in the number of small, dependent tenants.

The second general reason that the United States did not worry excessively about the "Cuban problem" was that the urban middle class was also largely transformed into a dependent stratum. The Cuban urban bourgeoisie lacked a sense of power, a sense of themselves as agents of progress. Some segments of the middle class were demoralized by their inability to compete effectively with efficient foreign enterprise and privileged imports from the United States. Elsewhere in the urban economy foreign investment "took the form of the establishment of subsidiaries by United States companies with participation by local Cuban capital. . . . Cuban capital was thus invested not in competition but in collaboration with United States capital. The result was the structural integration of the Cuban bourgeoisie within the economy of the alien capitalism." [15]

---

tobacco industry. Fluctuating leaf prices introduced an element of unpredictability into the cost calculations of the manufacturers, turning their attention to tobacco cultivation itself. If they could have effective control over supplies of leaf, they realized, costs could be stabilized. But once the manufacturers moved into tobacco cultivation they had to do so on the largest possible scale, for the product of each grower varied from year to year in quality. Only when the manufacturers owned extensive producing lands were they assured of a consistently similar product from one season to the next. What is more, by the late 1920's and early 1930's land could be purchased at rock-bottom prices. In this way, Partagas, the giant English-owned firm, came to own 18,000 acres of the finest tobacco lands in Cuba. From 1925 to 1940, the number of independent growers fell from over 11,000 to 3,000.

[15] Robin Blackburn, "Prologue to the Cuban Revolution," *New Left Review*, No. 21 (October, 1963). Blackburn's statement that Cuba lacked any (or nearly any) national bourgeoisie is too extreme. He gives as one "proof" the fact that many Cuban industrialists were naturalized Cubans; but this does not make them any the less independent or semi-independent of imperialist con-

There was also a tendency for the middle classes (particularly those of recent Spanish origin) to adopt the social, cultural, and ideological standards of the old landed wealth, their consumption patterns in particular. These old standards were mixed liberally with modern business attitudes imported from the United States, together with specifically Cuban attitudes conditioned by the tight networks of market controls, the all-pervasive atmosphere of artificial economic scarcity, and the speculative ups and downs in the sugar market. Yet in some sectors of the economy—notably in urban construction—this mixture was overwhelmed by accepted standards that emphasized the rapid turnover of capital and quick profit-taking. In this light, the sources of middle-class ideology, business outlook, morale, and sense of identity are difficult to trace and define with any precision. Clearly, whatever the exact sources, the Cuban bourgeoisie lacked a progressive, optimistic, creative ideology of its own making and, in fact, assumed a dependent status.

Nor were the middle classes as important quantitatively (and hence as potentially independent politically) as they would have been in the absence of United States penetration and control of large sectors of the local economy. Large-scale foreign enterprise created few new satellite industries, few opportunities for small-scale investments. Investment opportunities in industries supplying raw materials, semifinished goods, transportation, packaging, and distribution facilities to the sugar industry were limited by foreign control. Satellite and secondary industries, which in other circumstances would have sprung up on Cuban soil, holding out promises of wealth and power to the middle classes, were located in the United States.

Perhaps the best illustration is sugar refining. United States duties on refined sugar were always higher than those on crude, and in 1934 Congress placed physical limits on imports of the refined prod-

trol. For another thing, "much of [upper-class] capital was invested abroad or in foreign-controlled interests in Cuba, with the result that the upper class appeared to many other Cubans partly foreign in composition and largely foreign in the orientation of its social and economic interests (Wyatt Mac-Gaffey and Clifford R. Barnett, *Twentieth Century Cuba* [New York, 1965] p. 56).

uct from Cuba.[16] In relation to the island's total sugar quota in the mainland market, a maximum of 22 per cent was permitted to enter as refined sugar, a ratio that remained roughly the same until 1960, when Cuba was deprived of United States sales altogether. North American commercial policy also contributed to the "export" of the Cuban manufactured tobacco industry. High tariffs on manufactured products encouraged the American Cigar Company and other foreign firms partly to shift operations to the mainland, although militant wage and antimechanization policies by the tobacco workers' union also contributed to the transfer of capital to the United States. Caught between United States commercial policy and union militancy, foreign capital tried (and failed) before World War II to reduce the industry to its purely agricultural phase. Similarly, in mining industries foreign control deprived Cuba of many processing and finishing activities. And in the more modern branches of manufacturing, final stage assembly, packaging, and distribution were largely monopolized by North Americans.

[5]

The economic, social, and cultural dependency of the Cuban middle classes on the United States reinforced Cuba's political dependency, forced upon the island early in the century. In the course of nearly sixty years of commercial and other negotiations with Cuba, the United States rarely hesitated to use its superior bargaining power. In return for limited Cuban access to the mainland sugar market, United States commodity imports enjoyed wide tariff preferences, which were an obstacle to Cuban industrialization and effective trade bargaining with other countries. But this did not stop Washington from unilaterally reducing Cuba's sugar quota when it was expedient to do so.

Of the many negotiations between the two countries, the Recipro-

[16] Smith, op. cit., pp. 66, 160. Had the Hershey Company not produced about 50 per cent of Cuba's refined sugar, the island's refined quota would no doubt have been lower. The northern refining interests were pleased with the legislation. According to Earl Babst of the American Sugar Refining Company, the two pieces of legislation were "a step in the direction of a sound Colonial policy" (quoted in ibid., p. 161).

cal Trade Agreement of 1934 was perhaps the most prejudicial to Cuba's interests. Cuba left the bargaining table with modest cuts in United States duties on crude sugar, tobacco, and some other agricultural products, thus slightly increasing potential foreign exchange earnings. In return, Cuba raised United States tariff preferentials by wide margins, agreed to refrain from increasing duties on a large number of mainland products and to reduce or abolish internal taxes on many American products, and accepted a ban on quantitative restrictions of any item receiving the benefit of tariff reductions.[17]

During the twenty-five years before the 1959 revolution, "the single most important decision to the Cuban economy," as a world's leading sugar authority has written, "the size of the American sugar quota, [was] determined by legislative authorities with whom Cuba [had] no official standing. The affront to national sovereignty inherent in this statellitic relationship should be . . . obvious." [18] In the hands of the United States were placed life-and-death decisions over the Cuban economy. The Sugar Act of 1948, for instance, gave the Secretary of Agriculture power "to withhold or withdraw any increase in the share of the domestic consumption requirement provided for (a country which the Secretary of State found to deny fair and equitable treatment to nationals of the United States, its commerce, navigation, or industry)." [19] The effects were far-reaching: the Sugar Act of 1951, for example, reduced Cuba's quota for 1952–1956 and led to a fall in world sugar prices and a decline in Cuba's national income.

[6]

Nevertheless, the United States did not have a completely free field for investment and commercial activity; foreign corporations, the Department of State, and Congress were compelled to adjust to rising nationalist sentiments in order to secure political stability.[20]

[17] *Ibid.*, pp. 158–159.
[18] Boris Swerling, "Sugar and Sympathy," *The Nation*, 190, No. 7 (February 13, 1960), pp. 142–143.
[19] U. S. Statutes at Large, 61 Stat., 80th Congress, 1st Session, Ch. 519 (August 8, 1948), p. 195.
[20] Smith, *op. cit.*, p. 113.

Originally the product of the long and arduous struggle against Spain, Cuban nationalism received fresh impetus during the late 1920's and 1930's, the period of crisis in the world sugar market. In turn, nationalist economic policy began to change the character and behavior of the Cuban economy itself.

The first important benchmark was in the mid-1920's. Businessmen acquired influence and power with the ascension of Gerardo Machado to the presidency, a victory achieved at the expense of the Conservative party, the instrument of the wealthy landowners. Neither the workers nor the farmers were organized economically or politically until the next decade; thus, Machado and the national bourgeoisie could safely court United States disapproval with semi-independent, nationalist economic policies. The new "businessmen's government" forced through measures that kept Cuba's income at home, channeled consumption and investment spending into the local economy, and provided opportunities for native capital. The 1927 tariff encouraged local manufactures at the expense of United States exports and was an authentic expression of Cuban nationalism,[21] even though the favorable effects of the tariff on investment, production, and income were overwhelmed by the decline in total demand and income caused by the Great Depression.

Meanwhile the Cubanization of the sugar industry was getting under way. Hopes for the revival of the industry (the prospects for which were gloomy after 1925) were crushed by the depression; foreign owners began to liquidate their holdings, Cuban businessmen and bankers began to purchase mortgages obtained by the foreign banks during preceding crises. The share of total production accounted for by United States mills dropped to little more than 55 per cent in 1939. By 1951 the share was 43 per cent and in 1958 only 37 per cent. The number of United States-owned mills decreased from 66 in 1939 to 36 in 1958, and the amount of foreign-owned cane land fell from 1.7 million hectares in 1946 to 1.2 million hectares in 1958. The small farmers grew only 9 per cent of Cuba's cane in

---

[21] Smith (*ibid.*, p. 51) argues that Machado was compelled to suspend sugar production and market controls introduced in 1927 the following year after protests by American producers and banks. On the surface, Machado was bowing to United States interests pure and simple; in fact, his policies conformed to Cuban industrial interests as well.

1932, but by 1958 their share was well over 50 per cent. The Cubanization of the industry, together with restrictions on labor immigration that inhibited the decline of wage income, as we have seen, channeled demand into the home market.

The second important milestone was in the late 1930's. Politically, the island's workers and farmers took center stage during and after the 1933 revolution that overthrew Machado, whose nationalist policies the depression rendered impotent. No subsequent government could afford to ignore the pressing demands of the working classes and the poorer and middle farmers or fail to attempt to mobilize resources for national economic development.

The reason was simple: Cuban workers and farmers acquired a sense of class consciousness and class loyalty as a result of the fluctuations of the sugar economy. At the beginning of the century it was possible to describe the rural worker as a "peaceful, temperate and hard working man, as a rule. . . . The Spanish laborer expects little." [22] If anything, the class consciousness of black agricultural workers was less developed; black laborers had always been the victims, not the makers, of Cuban history. By 1933 the extreme deterioration of the rural and urban economies, intensive union organizational work, the decline of the landed oligarchy in the late 1920's, and the economic and political bankruptcy of the propertied classes worked a profound change in the outlook of the average worker. Union organizational work was aided by a number of new developments. The ban on immigration from Haiti and Jamaica stabilized the labor force, the depression attracted hundreds of urban revolutionaries and political activists into the ranks of the professional labor organizers, and the concentration of capital in cane farming meant that labor was hired in increasingly large units—all facilitating the task of agitation and organization. Attracted by a tradition of militant struggle and fast-developing organizations, even many of the smaller sugar growers identified more with the rural workers than with their own class. [23]

---

[22] According to the British consul-general in Havana at the time.

[23] Charles Page, "The Development of Organized Labor in Cuba" (Ph.D. dissertation, University of California, 1950), p. 204.

Organized labor thus constituted a potential threat to both the domestic and foreign business and commercial classes. The threat was neutralized by a newcomer to the political scene: Fulgencio Batista. Originally a sergeant in the Cuban Army, Batista seized power in 1934 after leading a successful revolt against the officers. He restored stability to Cuban politics on the basis of a corporatist conception of social and political organization. In brief, he enticed organized labor into a national consensus in which the unions refrained from independent political action in exchange for a free hand economically. Protective legislation—including minimum wage laws, union security legislation, and Cubanization decrees, which required employers to hire definite numbers of Cuban workers—kept organized labor firmly in the developing corporatist consensus.

Parallel developments in the political awareness, orientation, and organization of Cuba's small and middle farmers, in particular the cane growers, took place in the 1930's. The basic reason was the same: the crisis in sugar, which underlined their dependent status in relation to the sugar mills, plantations, and banks. The loss of political power by the landed oligarchy, the lack of markets, common economic need, farmer revolts during the early 1930's, and, later, government protection, all played a role in the development of growers' associations which quickly acquired political influence and power, winning favorable tenure arrangements and contractual agreements with the sugar mills and other important economic gains. The small and middle farmers also became part of the consensus.

The final step in the development of Cuban nationalism was the 1950's, when the island embarked on an industrialization program. But this was doomed by the complex of political alliances and entanglements that Batista inherited after his coup of 1952. In brief, Batista attempted to revive his corporatist ideas and policies not in the guise of the "savior" of Cuba and Cuban nationalism (as in the 1930's), but in the role of usurper of constitutional democracy and dictator. He tried to maintain a delicate balance between workers and farmers, propertied and nonpropertied, foreign businessmen and Cuban industrialists.

He approved wage increases in the private sector and wage decreases in the public sector. He guaranteed the incomes of some farmers, removed existing guarantees for others. He tried to diversify agriculture—with American capital. He put forth what for Cuba was a revolutionary industrialization program, stressed the importance of the participation of Cuban businessmen—and offered large-scale concessions to American capital. He won United States agreement to alleviate the economic crisis that threatened at the close of the Korean War by purchasing large stocks of surplus sugar —and granted more concessions to North American corporations. His advisers wrote endless national economic development plans— while he refused to employ the most elementary instruments of national economic policy.

Batista was caught in an enormous contradiction, one which he had helped to create twenty years earlier. Unlike economic *growth* (a rise in per capita income), economic *development* required national autonomy; political stability, the precondition for foreign investment, required dependence on Washington. Economic development required an independent monetary system and monetary autonomy; political stability required that Cuba be secured against inflation, the scourge of United States operations in many other Latin American economies. Economic development required that Cuba be able to postpone, adjust, and modify her international payments; political stability required prompt, full payments: in 1957–1958, 70 per cent of United States credit collections were termed "prompt," and 90 per cent were paid within thirty days. Economic development required that Cuba seize the advantages of established instruments of economic and commercial policy: exchange controls, multiple exchange rates, import quotas, controls over profit remittances, and so on; political stability required that the island's international economic relations be arranged in the interests of North Americans. Economic development required that Cuba liberate herself from the sugar quota system; political stability required that the island's fate be linked to the interests expressed in the United States Congress and Executive.

There was no conceivable way for Batista to keep up the juggling act for longer than a few years. Cuban nationalism was frustrated, turned back, distorted, betrayed. Cuban industrialization, which aimed to reduce the island's dependence on sugar, was a failure. Structural changes in the economy continued to be elusive: the proportion of the employed labor force in primary, secondary, and tertiary activities was about 42, 20, and 38 per cent, respectively, in both the immediate prewar period and in the late 1950's. The economy continued to stagnate. Thus, "Cubans tended to view the material benefits of economic activity as fixed quantities, incapable of expansion, and available to individuals and groups through political rather than economic effort." [24] Political, rather than economic forces continued to be the main determinants of the distribution of income.

[7]

The near total failure of Cuban nationalism, originally a powerful and positive force, went hand in hand with economic underdevelopment, dependency on the United States, corporatist-minded political leadership, and the lack of a viable constitutional democracy. But this failure itself needs an explanation; one link in the chain is still missing: the nature of the prerevolutionary Cuban state.

The old state can be characterized as bureaucratic, opportunistic, redistributive, classless. Until the mid-1920's, national political leadership was in the hands of men who gained prominence in the War of Independence and whose main goal was to seize the spoils of office. Later, both elected governments (1940–1952) and governments formed on the basis of armed revolt and coup (1933–1939 and 1953–1958) drew their support from all of the major economic classes, representatives of which were located in key decision-making positions. These included labor leaders "bound by personal, official, and financial ties to the members of the Batista regime." [25] Also included were representatives of the rural associations of ten-

[24] MacGaffey and Garnett, op. cit., p. 70.

[25] Maurice Zeitlin and Robert Scheer, Cuba: Tragedy in Our Hemisphere (New York, 1963), p. 23. The authors go on to say that labor officials "cooperated with [Batista's regime] and served its ends." This is overly simplified; Batista was also compelled to serve the (economic) ends of organized labor.

ants and landlords, who answered largely to the most prosperous of the island's farmers, and deputies of the mill owners, ranchers, manufacturing, commercial, and financial interests, and professional classes. Batista even retained a number of Communists in high technical posts in the old government. Lacking a solid class base, old governments rose to power on whatever support they could obtain, anywhere it was available. The balance of class forces—taking into account quantitative, organizational, and ideological considerations —created a political nexus in which no class had the political initiative. To be sure, "sugar dominate[d] the economic policy of the country, and other interests [had to] stand aside in the interest of sugar." [26] But all major economic groups were enmeshed in the fortunes of the sugar industry.

Cuba was therefore governed by men who had no class interests in governing efficiently or honestly. In the 1950's the collection of opportunists willing to support the dictator were by and large neither for nor against capital or labor or the farmers or United States economic interests either on principle or from the standpoint of their own class interests. Instead, they were very much out for themselves.

There were, of course, many honorable men in the ranks of the civil services, the financial institutions, the armed forces, and other state agencies who deplored not only the excesses of the Batista dictatorship but the very principles of the Cuban polity. But the men who stood on the commanding heights of the public economy—the operators, the in-group, those who knew who to see about loans, a labor problem, a price increase—these men were in the game to maximize income and power for themselves. If the competitive, individualistic market mentality was largely absent in the cartelized private sector of the economy, it dominated the public sector.

Because few in government believed that what was being done was in Cuba's best interest; because few were willing or able to put together honest, progressive administrations by excluding from the middle and lower ranks timeservers, incompetents, and thieves; because few resisted the trend toward a mushrooming, unproductive

[26] Wallich, *op. cit.*, p. 12.

state bureaucracy; ultimately, because political power was not rooted in national economic power, an intelligent, effective nationalist policy could not be formulated or implemented. The nationalist option was simply not open, because there was no powerful national middle class to employ state power for its own ends.

The small, fragmented, independent national bourgeoisie was unable to free Cuba from the United States, nor was it able to control the farmers and workers. The United States hesitated to allow the national middle class to walk on its own power, even though in principle United States policy-makers (and the World Bank and other international agencies) continually stressed the need for widening the horizons of the middle class by creating investment and other economic opportunities. Thus, a durable, stable, progressive politics and a fragmented, demoralized bourgeoisie were necessarily incompatible social forms in the old Cuban capitalist society.

This was why Batista faltered and floundered in his final years, at first trying to please everyone, and finally, driven to the wall, having to suppress everyone.

Note on the Operation of Cuba's Export Economy

For theoretical orientation I have borrowed freely but not uncritically from: Alienes y Urosa, *op. cit.*, *passim;* Henry C. Wallich, *Monetary Problems of an Export Economy: The Cuban Experience, 1914–1917* (Cambridge, Mass., 1950), *passim;* Jonathan V. Levin, *The Export Economies: Their Pattern of Development in Historical Perspective* (Cambridge, Mass.), 1950, *passim.*

In studies of balanced capitalist economies, emphasis is ordinarily given autonomous investment as the source of economic fluctuations and growth. Some models also stress limits placed on induced investment (dependent on income via consumption) by ceilings on factor availabilities and/or real consumption at full employment. In the old Cuban economy, autonomous changes in exports replaced investment as the main source of fluctuations and growth.

In 1958 total exports came to $733.5 million, while national income (at factor cost) was $2,209.6 million. (National income data: Cuba, Ministerio de Hacienda, *Informe al Consejo de Ministerios* [Havana, 1959], p. 97. Export data: Cuba, Banco Nacional de Cuba, *Memoria, 1958–59* [Havana, 1959], p. 185.) An independent study of Cuba's national income in 1953 concludes that the Banco Nacional underestimated income (Harry T. Oshima, "The National Income and Product of Cuba in 1953," *Food Research Institute Studies,* 2, No.

3, November, 1961). In absolute terms, then, Cuba's 1958 income was probably greater than shown above; relative to exports, though, our conclusions are undoubtedly correct. Proceeds from sugar exports (including sugar products) fluctuated between 70 and 85 per cent of total export earnings. Exports were independent of national income; a rise in Cuba's income and imports failed to affect significantly the total exports, income, and hence imports of the United States, the island's chief trading partner (two-thirds of Cuba's exports in 1958 were destined for the United States).

It will be instructive to analyze the effects of an autonomous expansion of Cuban exports on national income and investment; wherever possible, these effects are roughly quantified. A rise in Cuban exports, in the first place, increased national income by an amount equal to the rise in exports. The expansion of income raised domestic spending by roughly 25 per cent less than the rise in income itself. The propensity to import consumer goods was about 15 per cent; another 10 per cent of income was channeled away from the stream of domestic spending into savings. Consumer good imports and savings were thus the major "first-round" spending leakages. Both the import and savings functions were unusually stable. Relative price changes (independent of those associated with changes in national income itself) did little to disturb the import function because elasticities of substitution between foreign and domestic goods were so low. Also contributing to the stability of the function was the fact that the higher the level of Cuban national income, the more evenly income was distributed; wages were flexible upward and relatively inflexible downward (income by factor shares for the 1950's is shown in *Memoria, 1958–1959*, Table 1.2, p. 96).

As for the savings function: Cuba's price level remained remarkably stable over most of the decade; there were no sharp fluctuations in consumer durable purchases, which destabilize the function in an affluent capitalist society. Finally, corporate savings were to a degree less disturbing than in a creditor country; foreign corporations accumulated or paid out earnings without affecting spending in Cuba.

Prior to the 1930's, and to a lesser degree, the 1940's, repatriated earnings and personal remittances turned more spending away from the local market. Repatriated profits on direct investments as a proportion of total imports averaged about 15 per cent during the 1920's (Henry C. Wallich, "Cuban Monetary Experience, 1914–1942" [Ph.D. dissertation, Harvard University, 1943], p. 333). The World Bank reported for the latter years of the 1940's that 30 per cent of Cuba's total savings went into the reduction of foreign obligations and the acquisition of foreign assets. But in the 1950's this picture changed dramatically, showing, incidentally, that there is no basis for the theory that Cuba's stagnation was attributable to the drain on the island's investable surplus by U.S. corporations; repatriated earnings as a percentage of gross receipts on current account averaged less than 4 per cent annually in the 1950's, by my estimate. In 1958, for example, dividends paid to foreigners amounted to only $36 million, while receipts exceeded the $1 billion mark.

On the basis of the above analysis, the value of the after-tax multiplier can be estimated at between two and three; the propensity to pay out additional income as taxes has been estimated at roughly 15 per cent (see Cuba, Banco Nacional de Cuba, *La economía Cubana en 1955–56* [Havana, 1957], p. 48). Tax evasion was widespread in Cuba, and this figure should be taken with a grain of salt. Thus, one would expect an export boom to generate some induced investment, but not so much as in a balanced economy enjoying a comparable increase in autonomous investment or government spending.

Induced investment was but one—albeit the most important—source of investment encouraged by an export boom. Theoretically, some investment will be directly induced in the export sector by an expansion of demand for the export commodity. This mechanism had little practical importance in Cuba. Fixed plant and equipment in the sugar sector were sufficient for all export booms in recent Cuban history. Since the 1920's no sugar mill had been built on the island. One study of those Cuban mills producing 25 per cent of total output in the late 1940's showed that 60 per cent of gross investment was replacement investment, and 40 per cent new capital formation, most of the latter modernization, not expansion, investment. As for the agricultural branch of the industry, capital formation was minimal; sugar grows like a weed on the island, and, besides, as we will see in Chapter Four, monopoly controls inhibited investment in land improvement.

Lastly, Cuba's positive balance of payments during periods favoring sugar exports increased liquidity and bank credit and might have been expected to encourage more new investment. In recent years, however, both foreign and Cuban banks tended to be overcautious in extending credit created by an expected temporary favorable balance of payments. The great crash of sugar prices in 1920–21 had first aroused their caution; subsequent crises confirmed their pessimism.

Turning from theory to Cuba's actual experience, movements in investment in the 1950's tend to confirm the above analysis. From 1950 to 1951 (a good year for sugar exports) net capital formation in relation to national income rose from 6.5 per cent to 8.8 per cent; from 11.2 per cent in 1955 to 14.8 per cent in 1957 (another favorable year). To refine the analysis somewhat, over the years 1950–1958, total imports and fixed capital good imports as a proportion of total imports moved together fairly closely. There was also a positive correlation between raw material imports as a proportion of total imports, and the total volume of imports.

More interesting results are obtained when imports of investment goods are related directly to exports. There was a positive correlation between fixed capital good imports as a proportion of total imports in one year and total exports in the preceding year (had data been available, one would expect a tighter relationship with a six-month lag). As would be expected from the theoretical analysis, the relationship between fixed capital good imports in relation to total imports, and exports of processed foods (mainly sugar)—again lagged one year—was closest of all (*Memoria, 1958–59*, Table 1.7, p. 98 for data on capital good imports; Table 1.11, p. 101 for investment and national income data; because national income accounting procedures were drastically revised in 1950, it is impossible to extend our computations back to earlier periods).

From these empirical relationships, viewed in the context of the rough model developed above, it is clear that capital formation in Cuba was normally linked to exports of sugar. Had the expansion of exports persisted, the encouragement given investment would have had a more permanent character, raising the rate of growth of national income. And the fact that a rising proportion of total investment induced by the export booms went into productive investment (and relatively less into residential construction) reinforced the relationship between sugar exports and real output.

At the end of the boom, when exports fell off, given leakages into savings, consumer good imports, and repatriated earnings, the whole system contracted sharply. (Before the system of production controls was introduced in the 1930's, the supply of sugar for decreases in price was highly inelastic, as was the demand for sugar. Meanwhile, the income elasticity of demand was relatively high. And developments in other sugar-producing countries, together with changes imposed on the demand for Cuban sugar by the actions of the U.S. Congress—the Hawley-Smoot Tariff of 1930 and the 1934 quota are two examples—meant that the demand for Cuban sugar fluctuated a great deal. As a consequence, sugar prices and the incomes of sugar producers [and indirectly the incomes of all Cubans] were highly unstable. For rises in prices supplies were also inelastic because of limits on the size of the labor force and the fact that sugar requires an eighteen-month growing period. After the restriction schemes were introduced, price fluctuations were reduced because there were so many unused resources, including reserve stands of cane, thus making supplies more elastic for increases in demand.) Because Cuba's rural subsistence sector was relatively small (reducing alternative employment opportunities), a drop in the sugar market would, in the absence of government controls, cut sharply into real wages. As it was, employment was hard hit; the level of employment where leakages into savings and imports became zero was much lower than in a typical balanced economy. A number of other factors worsened the effect on the local economy of an export crisis. First, monopoly restrictions in sugar growing reduced mobility of farmers and capital. Furthermore, until the 1950's little agricultural credit was available outside the export sector. For another thing, unlike other farmers (cultivators of grain, for example), sugar growers were unable to shift from market to subsistence agriculture; inventories of sugar could hardly be consumed on the farm itself.

So far the discussion has been conducted on the assumption that the spending effects of new investment were felt entirely within the domestic economy. This was not at all the case; roughly one-half of total investment spending (excluding changes in inventories) went abroad, raising the total spending leakage. For this reason, like the simple export multiplier, Cuba's super-multiplier fell considerably below that associated with the ordinary balanced economy. Every dollar of new export spending generated no more than two dollars of new consumption and investment spending. This was one reason why there were rarely inflationary pressures in the old Cuban economy; with the exception of the World War II boom (when imports were in very short supply and financial savings were not matched by real resources), spending leakages were consistently high enough to help to inhibit significant price rises.

[3]

Economic and
Political Background:
Castro's Rise to Power

[1]

All nations, in some eras of their history, and some nations, in all eras of their history, unashamedly and uncritically idolize their revolutionary heroes. Cuba belongs in the second category. Conservatives as well as liberals and radicals worship the memory of José Martí. The heroic (and some not-so-heroic) leaders of the struggle against Spain automatically became the political chieftains of independent Cuba. The army enlisted men's hero, Batista, was a strong and hence popular executive before he began to rule by intimidation and terror. Side by side on the walls of *bohíos* in rural Cuba are pictures of Jesus Christ and Fidel Castro.

Castro has all the qualities and accomplishments required to endear him to the Cuban people as an authentic hero in the Cuban revolutionary tradition: victory in military struggle, the will and ability to be a strong leader, an uncanny capacity to establish empathy with individual workers, farmers, and students as well as with masses of people at a public rally, great oratorical prowess, unusual physical strength, integrity, *machismo*. That he is impatient with detail, sometimes fails to compromise when compromise would serve his aims, often makes unilateral decisions that take his colleagues by surprise, hates paper work, restlessly moves from place to place—these and other qualities authenticate him even more as a man among men.

But Castro's most "revolutionary" quality is his capacity, indeed his need, to lead, to take and keep initiatives and make far-reaching decisions with the utmost confidence of success. This is readily con-

37

firmed by a backward glance at the major steps of his rise to power. The first was in 1953 when Castro took up arms against Batista. A young lawyer, the son of a well-to-do cane grower, and a member of the Ortodoxo party's national assembly, Castro was a congressional candidate in the elections that Batista annulled after his seizure of power in March, 1952. Castro petitioned the Supreme Court to declare the Batista government unconstitutional. The petition was denied. The electoral road to power closed by Batista, the army, and the Court, Castro without hesitation turned to armed struggle.

He struck the first blow on July 26, 1953. At the head of a small column of young men, most of them student activists, Castro attacked the Moncada barracks at Santiago de Cuba and three minor targets. The rebels expected to hold the barracks until the Cuban people rose up against the illegal regime and restored constitutional democracy. But the rebellion was a military and political failure. The barracks put up a successful resistance, and Castro had grossly overestimated the Cuban people's antipathy for unconstitutional government.

The attack on the barracks and the political trials that followed made Fidel Castro's name a household word in Cuba. "Sentence me," Castro cried at the end of the now-famous five-hour speech in his defense. "It doesn't matter. History will absolve me." Released in May, 1955, in a general political amnesty, Castro returned triumphantly to Havana. His personal popularity was growing, his party, the Ortodoxos, was torn apart by factional struggles and personal rivalries, and within two months Castro decided once again to abandon conventional political struggle.

The second way station of Castro's political journey was his decision to go into exile in Mexico and plan another armed rebellion. He raised money from Cuban exiles in the United States and other countries, recruited and trained men for guerrilla warfare, made the friendship of Ernesto Guevara, an Argentine doctor and revolutionary. In December, 1956, Castro and his men reached Cuba in an old yacht. Of eighty-two rebels, only twelve survived to reach their destination—the remote, mountain forests of the Sierra Maestra. Fidel and Raúl Castro and Guevara were among the survivors.

For two years Castro's guerrillas attacked police posts and army patrols, built up a base among the local peasants, and transformed themselves into an experienced, effective guerrilla army. Partly inspired by the accomplishments of the guerrillas, partly as a result of parallel, independent efforts, an urban resistance movement grew swiftly. Student groups, business, church, and professional organizations, and factions within labor unions arrayed themselves against Batista. Many leaders of the established political parties opposed Batista, and some went into exile. There was a major split between moderates and activists. The former pressed for negotiations, new and honest elections, and peaceable change. The latter took up arms against the most immediate symbols of oppression: police stations, army posts, and other government buildings. Batista attempted to suppress all opposition, at times ignoring the moderates, at times not distinguishing them from the activists. He opposed counterrevolutionary terror to revolutionary terror. Isolated, demoralized, politically bankrupt, militarily on the defensive, Batista and his followers finally fled the island on January 1, 1959.

Forty-eight hours after Batista's flight, Castro's 26th of July Movement, now a loose coalition of oppositionist forces of all political shades and colorations, seized control of Havana. Castro stepped forward as the head of the Rebel Army and the undisputed leader of the movement. He had maintained his independence from the older, established anti-Batista politicians who had been jockeying for the leadership of the rebellion. He was the universally popular guerrilla leader, the man who had started the uprising.

The third step of Castro's rise to power was his determination in early 1959 not to let the political initiative slip from his grasp; most of the urban rebels and city politicians were unknown quantities, and he felt that he could trust only his closest companions. This decision had three profound implications. First, it meant that he would personally make the major political decisions for the foreseeable future. Second, it meant that the new government, in particular the Cabinet, would be little more than window dressing and that major policy decisions would be made behind the scenes. Third, it meant that Castro would eventually be compelled to confront the United States government, together with those groups within Cuba that were dependent upon United States-owned businesses or mainland trade or were otherwise in a subordinate position.

Thus, the Revolutionary Government's first and second presidents, Manuel Urrutia and Osvaldo Dorticós, were Castro's personal choices.

Thus, Castro personally ordered the political reforms of 1959: the postponement of elections; the dismissal of Congress; the purge of Batistianos from the judiciary, local government office, and the police; the discharge of over 3,000 government employees; and the total reorganization of the armed forces.

Thus, Castro's men wrote the revolution's basic economic and social law, the Agrarian Reform Law of May, 1959, behind the backs of the Cabinet.

Thus, Castro initiated most of the revolution's major economic and social policies during 1959–1962, in particular sugar policy, industrialization, and education planning.

Thus, Castro personally conducted the economic and diplomatic war with the United States which flared up in 1959–1960 and personally led the Rebel Army and militia against the invaders at the Bay of Pigs in April, 1961.

At first, contenders for power and seekers of special influence sprang up everywhere. Moderates, reformers, labor leaders, businessmen, farm organizations, Communists, the United States government, and, in different ways and for different reasons, the Soviet Union and China, all attempted to weaken Castro's authority or tamper with the autonomy of the revolution. In the end, they all failed. Cuba remains "Castro's Cuba" and Castro remains "Cuba's Fidel."

Half of the original Cabinet resigned in protest against the agrarian reform, to no avail. Leaders of the majority of the national labor unions opposed the revolution's "socialist" policies; Castro compelled them to resign. A popular Rebel Army commander, Huber

Matos, resisted what he considered to be growing Communist influence in the Rebel Army and opposed the speed of the agrarian reform; Castro personally arrested him. Political defections rose rapidly in 1960–1961; Castro called the defectors traitors and bid them good riddance.

Castro himself led the purge of Communist party members from the key positions in the revolutionary organizations in the spring and summer of 1962.[1]

And try as the State Department and CIA might, the United States failed to deflect the course of the revolution.

[2]

The Cuban Revolution went through two basic stages, one characterized by class harmony, the second by class antagonism and conflict. Needless to say, Castro guided the revolution through both stages.

In the last analysis, the 26th of July Movement originally consisted of diverse, potentially antagonistic elements, reflecting the contradictory character of the Batista regime. Castro opposed himself to a politics in which every major economic class was to one degree or another organized and entrenched in the state bureaucracy. The rebellion at first did not set class against class, but out-groups against in-groups, unorganized against organized, men who either did not want or could not acquire access to the public treasury against those who did, constitutionalists against anticonstitutionalists, youth against age, and, last but not least, idealists

[1] The role of the party in 1959 is described in Maurice Zeitlin and Robert Scheer, *Cuba, Tragedy of the Hemisphere* (New York, 1963). The situation in 1960 and 1961 is discussed in Theodore Draper, *Castro's Revolution: Myths and Realities* (New York, 1962). Cuban radio broadcasts and periodicals revealed that the purge had reached into the lowest levels of the main revolutionary organizations by midsummer, 1962. This was confirmed by the author in August, 1963, by another American, Maurice Zeitlin ("Castro and Cuba's Communists," *The Nation*, 195, No. 14 November 3, 1962), and by an anti-Castro writer in an article in *Cuba Nueva* ("Pero sigue la Purga," May 14, 1962). That the PSP never had important initiatives is unwittingly suggested by the leading exponent of the "revolution betrayed" thesis when he wrote that "if all had been going well in Cuba for the past year, the PSP's control might well have gone unchallenged" (Draper, *op. cit.*, p. 209).

against pragmatists and opportunists. Segments of each class stood to lose, while others could only gain, from the annihilation of the Batista regime. There was therefore no single revolutionary class that conducted, or at least gave momentum to, the political rebellion. There were no Cuban counterparts to the peasants in the Mexican and Chinese Revolutions, the urban working class in the Russian Revolution, or for that matter, the urban merchants in the American Revolution.

The Cuban Revolution was neither bourgeois revolution, lower-class rebellion, nor peasant uprising. "It has never been a revolution of the upper classes," Castro said in 1962. "Not a single representative of the upper class took part in the revolution, not a single rich man." [2] This is true—and unexceptional. "All the participants . . . were young men with a modest, working-class background; workers and peasants, the sons of working people, employees." This is not true; the kindest interpretation is that Castro was deliberately employing the language of the common man, whose social categories were normally confined to the "rich" and the "poor."

The analogy of the blind men and the elephant is not inappropriate. In Havana the rebellion resembled a middle-class democratic revolution with the aim of restoring constitutional government. In Santiago de Cuba the revolution seemed to be a working-class rising against a brutal state power and state administration. In the Sierra Maestra the rebellion appeared to be a peasant war against a combination of greedy landlords and corrupt state officials.

In the Havana area middle-class students, intellectuals, and professionals were the main protagonists. Employees in tourism, "privileged" workers in the labor "aristocracy," politically inexperienced recruits for the urban work force fresh from the countryside, domestic servants, and white-collar workers constituted the vast majority of the Havana working class. None of these groups had any overriding incentive to engage in hard, risky political struggle. Worker participation in the rebellion was also limited by the fact

[2] Radio interview of Fidel Castro with the Editors of *Pravda* and *Izvestia*, January 29, 1962.

that the top-heavy, conservative union bureaucracy was based in Havana.

Thus, even though there were rumblings of discontent in the Havana working classes as early as March, 1958, as recorded by Batista's labor chief himself,[3] the general strike called by Castro's 26th of July Movement for April, 1958, was a failure. The struggle in Havana was confined to student strikes, demonstrations, and terrorism and to vocal opposition on the part of professional, business, political, and other established groups, together with underground activity of all types organized by the 26th of July Movement and the Civic Resistance Movement. Even in conservative Havana, however, mass action was possible when there was no fear of reprisals. Castro himself claimed that the second general strike in January, 1959, actually consolidated the revolution.[4]

Cuba's second largest city, Santiago de Cuba, located at the other end of the island, was shut down by the April strike. Even earlier, in August, 1957, strikes spread out from Santiago as an aftermath to the assassination of two popular 26th of July leaders, Frank Pais and Raúl Pujol. In Santiago there were few labor "aristocrats" and *compradors*, unemployment was greater, employed workers were more exposed economically and less influential politically, and the working classes were generally more cohesive than in Havana. Thus anti-Batista sentiment was relatively strong.

The leading and decisive element in the struggle was the Rebel Army, which operated in the Sierra Maestra in Oriente Province. Castro's guerrilla forces were led and manned by the sons of middle-class families, with some recruits from the poorer farm districts. In southern Oriente Castro's main forces were maintained from the outside, as well as by isolated peasant families who were among the few subsistence farmers on the island. In northern Oriente Raúl Castro's group operated among the poorer coffee growers, as well as the subsistence farmers eking out a living in the mountains. At no time during the rebellion did the Rebel Army's base include Cuba's numerically strongest class, the sugar proletariat.

[3] Earl Smith, *The Fourth Floor* (New York, 1963), p. 27.
[4] Radio speech, June 13, 1960.

In town and country, revolutionary-minded intellectuals, students, and professionals constituted the leadership. They were outside the consensus politics and the system of patronage. They perceived more clearly than other groups the structural malformations of the Cuban economy and society. They were totally disenchanted with the established political process, including the farcical electoral process. And they understood that Cuba historically demanded of them a major role in the struggles for social, economic, and political progress.

[3]

The economic program of the 26th of July Movement reflected the contradictory forces at play during the political rebellion.[5] The program revealed that the movement lacked a unifying political theory or ideology and a coherent program of economic and social development. This was one "unprecedented hallmark of the revolution . . . the logical product of pre-revolutionary society." [6]

Central to movement policy was, in fact, an idea already seized and acted upon by Batista: the participation of all sectors and groups in economic planning. Undoubtedly this slogan was partly a tactic designed to consolidate one united front against another united front (the out-group against the in-group), but it was actually much more significant. The movement knew that it could profitably appeal to varied groups because the existing political economy thwarted in one way or another the realization of their interests. Had the dictatorship its own solid economic base, and had the movement its own, antagonistic base, the movement's appeal would have been unambiguously directed to the latter.

The authors of the program stressed two themes, one negative, the

[5] The official program of the movement is Felipe Pazos and Regino Boti's "Thesis of the Revolutionary Movement of July 26th," in *Political, Economic, and Social Thought of Fidel Castro* (Havana, 1959), pp. 119–166. Castro's views and opinions are in: Fidel Castro, "What Cuba's Rebels Want," *The Nation*, 185, No. 18 (November 30, 1957), a translation of an article appearing in *Cuba Libre*, a Costa Rican publication of the 26th of July Movement; and "Why We Fight," *Coronet*, 43, No. 2 (February, 1958).

[6] Robin Blackburn, "Prologue to the Cuban Revolution," *New Left Review*, No. 21 (October, 1963).

other positive. The negative theme was an attack on the state economic policy of the Batista government. The positive theme was the stress on mobilizing domestic capital and other resources for rapid economic development.[7] Both themes were shot through with contradictions.

In the first place, one part of the program condemned Batista's policy of restricting sugar production. In another section, the program called for strengthening the marginal cane farmers by raising minimum quotas, that is to say, by fortifying the system of production restrictions as a whole. Secondly, Batista came under attack for his policy of building highly mechanized plants at the expense of jobs for workers. Elsewhere, the program asserted that agriculture should be mechanized in order to raise productivity and incomes in the countryside.

Nor was the positive aspect of the program free of contradiction. On the one hand, the emphasis on channeling domestic savings into productive investments and granting more protection to manufacturing industries appealed to local business. On the other hand, a proposed profit-sharing plan that promised workers in nonagricultural enterprises 30 per cent of net income won support in some labor union circles. Clearly, these proposals also were highly incompatible.

The program also suffered from excessive vagueness. For one thing, Castro came out for the nationalization of the electric and telephone companies; then, on the eve of taking power, he changed

[7] The authors of the program made a detailed analysis of the amount of domestic savings required to finance a level of investment that in ten years would wipe out unemployment. Taking into account estimated existing capital: labor ratios in agriculture and industry, existing excess capacity, and the low productivity of social capital, they concluded that $200 million per year was required to do the job—an amount exactly the same as the then current volume of savings forthcoming with the given distribution of income. This equivalency suggests that there was some wishful thinking in their analysis, which, in point of fact, contained two serious errors. First, given that existing modes and organization of production placed sharp limits on capital efficiency, marginal capital: labor ratios were no doubt less than average ratios. Second, given that a reallocation of capital to more productive employments would affect the distribution of income, the volume of savings no doubt would have fallen. In short, their estimates had a mechanical, uncritical character.

his mind. For another, the movement called for ceilings on land-holdings, the distribution of excess acreage to small farmers, and the promotion of Western-European-style cooperatives. Not a word was said about the rural wage laborers whose traditional sources of employment would be eliminated. Who would employ them, and under what conditions, was left in doubt. Lastly, the movement's program was also silent on the disposition of the confiscated assets of grafters and embezzlers of state funds. Nowhere was it stated whether these assets would be turned over to honest businessmen, sold at auction, or managed by the state. All of these became highly important issues in 1959.

[4]

The second stage of the revolution, which was characterized by class antagonism and conflict, began around the middle of 1959. During the first five or six months of 1959, farmers, workers, and businessmen were all optimistic about the future economy and society. The large farmers and estate owners could not anticipate that the agrarian reform would wipe them out. The small farmers and peasants believed Castro's promise to "redeem" the countryside. The workers were asking, and getting, higher wages. United States capital "generally did not expect the change in Cuba's government to hamper their operations."[8] Many foreign and Cuban companies prepaid taxes to help Castro consolidate his new government or planned to accelerate investment programs temporarily postponed during the rebellion.[9] Business leaders who "as recently as one month ago were gravely concerned about the revolution" radically shifted their outlook.[10]

Interclass unity and the resulting political euphoria speedily gave

[8] *The Havana Post*, April 22, 1959. In a seminar at Princeton University held on April 21, 1959, Castro himself attributed this near unanimous support to his failure to carry out a specifically class war in 1957–1958 and to the people's universal fear and hatred of Batista's police.

[9] Textilera Ariguanabo and the Cuban Telephone Company, for example, made advanced payments on their profits taxes totaling $640,000 (*The Havana Post*, January 22, 1959).

[10] *The Wall Street Journal*, January 2, 1959.

way to doubts about Castro's intentions, to honest confusion over the disparity between Castro's promises of "democracy" and "constitutionalism" and Castro's role of "maximum leader," and to fears about the consequences of his economic policies, in particular, income distribution policies which favored the poorer workers and farmers over the middle classes. The real reasons for the developing class conflict lie in the process of radicalization of the revolution, which we will explore in detail in subsequent chapters. In brief, the original agrarian and urban reforms triggered a complex interplay between middle-class opinions and actions, United States attitudes and policies, and Cuban government policy toward private business, the middle classes, and the United States. No one could anticipate the speedy radicalization of the revolution nor the socialization of the island's economy, because no one "caused" them; rather, they were the product of the *relationships* between individuals, groups, and classes. But some things could have been anticipated. These concerned Castro the man and leader.

In the first place, middle-class Cuba and the propertied interests failed to understand that Castro was a revolutionary, a man conditioned by the guerrilla struggle to see people and events in sharp blacks and whites. Castro the guerrilla leader learned to make life-and-death decisions, when to attack and when to retreat and, above all, whom to trust and whom not to trust. The man who compromises and vacillates, the man who sees only shades of gray, did not belong in the guerrilla army. Thus, as 1959 wore on, Castro increasingly sharply marked off the "revolution" from the "counter-revolution" well before it was clear what either meant economically, socially, or politically. By early 1960 (months before the nationalization of industry) Castro completely polarized public opinions and attitudes. "To be a traitor to the revolution," he said, "is to be a traitor to the country. The destiny of our sovereignty is at stake." [11]

Second, and closely related to the above, the propertied interests failed to appreciate Castro's determination to transform Cuba economically and socially, no matter what the political consequences.

[11] Radio interview with Fidel Castro, reported in *The Havana Post*, January 19, 1960.

They made the mistake of believing that Castro was another "safe" politician because the content of his program did not greatly depart from the content of past economic and social programs. As early as 1908, for example, Charles Magoon, the provisional governor, proposed to the then powerful landed oligarchy that seasonally idle sugar workers be employed on agricultural diversification projects. In 1955, Gustavo Gutierrez, the head of Batista's National Economic Council, denounced Cuba's "structural deformations" and "colonial structure." [12] In May, 1958, Eusebio Mujal, Batista's labor chief, published a *National Plan for Strengthening and Developing the Economy of Cuba*. The plan called for agrarian reform, price ceilings, higher income taxes, the elimination of indirect taxes, a new protectionist tariff against United States exports of foods and light manufactured goods, "aggressive" trade policies to stimulate export diversification and the development of industries to replace imported commodities, and a vast housing program for workers and peasants. In 1959, even the "conservative" National Association of Cuban Industrialists presented to Castro a far-reaching *Plan for the Economic Development of Cuba*.

What distinguished Castro from Magoon, Gutierrez, Mujal, Batista, and the industrialists was less the specific economic solutions to Cuba's difficulties (nearly all of the measures to be found in Mujal's National Plan were implemented by the Revolutionary Government in 1959) than Castro's lack of fear of the political consequences that these economic changes would inevitably bring about. This in the last analysis saves Castro, but not the others, from the charge of opportunism.[13]

Thus, Castro pushed through reform after reform, yielding nothing

---

[12] *The Economic Program of Cuba*, Havana, March 1, 1955.

[13] In this connection, Lenin's experience is relevant. "When one has said that for Lenin," Maurice Dobb has written, "the economic problem was mainly a matter, not of applying principle, but of experiment, one has at once to modify it by admitting that all was not opportunism and that certain lines of the picture were, of course, drawn a priori. What is important is that these were lines of a general direction rather than a static, detailed diagram of formal structure" (*Russian Economic Development Since the Revolution* [London, 1929], p. 25).

to his opponents. Almost immediately he revealed his basic serious-ness by seizing the Cuban Electric Company, which had been the target of many accusations of inefficient operations and monopoly profits. During the first nine months of 1959, there were no less than 1500 decrees, laws, and resolutions.[14] Most of the early reforms were *capitalist* reforms in the area of rents, tariffs, taxes, money, and so on, although some reforms, in particular the collective aspects of the agrarian reform, contained a *socialist* bias. Despite the latter, all signs pointed to Castro's belief that a reformed Cuban capitalism (or a mixed economy) could perform in a satisfactory manner.

Nearly every measure, in particular those which affected the property system, deepened the commitment of some Cubans to the Revolutionary Government and antagonized others, leaving few in-different. At the very least, the major changes—some examples are the across-the-board rent reductions, the price-control laws, the seizure of the utilities, and the agrarian reform—touched on the day-to-day life of every Cuban, compelling him to question his economic and political beliefs. The most sweeping of these changes occasioned Cabinet crises, official resignations, arrests, and exile. The basis for the demand to choose sides—for or against the revolu-tion—was therefore laid by the Revolutionary Government's first economic measures.

[5]
To make such a demand required considerable confidence on Castro's part that the majority of Cubans would side with the Revo-lutionary Government. His decision to polarize opinion around the fundamental issues of Cuba's sovereignty and the government's eco-nomic and political programs was not the only path open to him. In-stead of isolating oppositional elements and branding them with the label "counterrevolutionary," he could have allowed them to form into functioning interest groups. These groups probably would have ranged from the "left-opposition" of the small Cuban Trotskyite

---

[14] Author's estimate based on *Primer Indice Anual de la Legislación Revo-lucionaria,* January 1 to December 31, 1959 (Havana, 1960).

movement all the way to the moderate right, consisting of the large sugar, cattle, banking, and commercial interests purged of their pro-Batista elements. Castro could have thwarted any majority coalition by playing one group against another, ceaselessly probing the weaknesses of each, and employing the tactics of divide and conquer.

The politics of divide and conquer are useful, indeed necessary, only when the ruling group fears the majority. Only a ruling elite that anticipates mass support and has the loyalty of the military can for long afford to alienate oppositional elements so thoroughly that they are compelled to try to form working alliances. The Castro government appeared to be well along this path by the summer of 1960, as the crisis with the United States was reaching its peak. This analysis suggests that the government's economic and political programs were like a giant whirlpool expelling the odd debris of the old middle class, the established bureaucrats, and the local partners of United States business firms, and simultaneously pulling in the mass of working class and rural Cubans.

There were four basic reasons why the Revolutionary Government was confident that its programs would win mass approval and alienate only a fraction of the Cuban people. In the first place, there was widespread recognition that "something had to be done" about the Cuban economy and that mild reforms were insufficient to get the economy off dead center. The Great Depression, war and postwar speculative booms and busts in sugar, and economic stagnation in the 1950's revealed to nearly everyone that development and prosperity required that the sugar economy undergo basic structural changes.

Increasingly, the rural workers and peasants were made aware by hunger and enforced idleness of the abundance of unused lands and badly cultivated fields; the teacher and doctor, by illiteracy and disease, of the backwardness of the education and health systems; the small businessman, by his sluggish profits, of state corruption and irrational labor, trade, and other laws; and the industrial worker, by his underemployment and lack of training, of inefficient operations and underutilized capacity in manufacturing and other industries.[15] "For fifty years," a well-to-do importer said in July, 1960, voicing the attitude of many Cubans, "Cuban society has been decrepit and decadent. Of course Castro has turned a popular movement into a dictatorship. I don't know, perhaps it is necessary now. But believe me when I say that a revolution was both desirable and inevitable." [16]

The second reason that the government's programs met with relatively weak opposition was that earlier government development schemes, in particular those of the Batista dictatorship, raised the expectations of the poorer classes, undermined respect for "free enterprise," and conditioned the average Cuban to accept a prominent role of the government in the economy. Related to this, the average Cuban understood the old electoral process to be totally corrupt, and hence there was little popular sentiment favoring a return to constitutional government.[17] Moreover, the 1940 Constitution was viewed less as a document that established a basis for parliamentary government than as authority for a strong executive committed to deep-going social and economic change.

Third, government policy toward property owners whose wealth and income were adversely affected by the new economic programs was designed to minimize opposition. Urban landlords, retailers, and the middle farmers received compensation under the laws taking over apartment houses and office buildings, small stores, and medium-sized farms. To be sure, plantation owners, sugar compa-

[15] This awareness of underdevelopment and stagnation was perhaps the most important difference between the situation in 1933 and that in 1957–1959. In the revolution of 1933, the most pressing need seemed to be to revive the market for Cuban sugar, and hence a quota agreement was negotiated with the United States. By 1959 it was clear to everyone that development and prosperity required that the sugar economy undergo fundamental structural change. In another sense the two revolutions were very similar; like Batista's rule, "the Machado dictatorship had been so ruthless . . . that it brought about a coalition of [opposing] heterogeneous forces" (Charles Page, "The Development of Organized Labor in Cuba," [Ph.D. dissertation, Berkeley, 1950], p. 71).

[16] James O'Connor, "Cuba's Counter-Revolution," *The Progressive*, 24, No. 12 (December, 1960), p. 8.

[17] Maurice Zeitlin, *Revolutionary Politics and the Cuban Working Class* (Princeton, 1967), p. 38.

nies, the large ranchers, and the big businessmen did not receive compensation, but these groups constituted only a tiny proportion of the island's propertied classes. Moreover, for reasons we have seen in the preceding chapter, these groups were not "permeated by a spirit of loyalty." In G. D. H. Cole's words, a man "will be able to act effectively in social matters only if he transfers his allegiance to some . . . group or class within which he can find like-minded collaborators. A class cannot be defined, when it is regarded as an active agent of social change, simply in terms of its common economic experience. It becomes fully a class, in this positive sense, only to the extent to which it is permeated by a spirit of loyalty." [18]

Finally, and perhaps of greatest significance, due to the intimate ties between Cuba and the United States, government programs were nationalist, as well as reformist or socialist, in character. Cuban nationalism was the strongest thread that ran through both the class harmony and class struggle phases of the revolution. Nationalism was one issue that bound together the diverse elements engaged in the struggle against Batista. The 26th of July Movement's heavy emphasis on the mobilization of domestic savings for investment and economic development reflected the rebels' unwillingness "to compromise our economic and political future with the importing of capital." [19] The fear of foreign influence and control was also reflected in the movement's stress on export diversification and the production of substitutes for imported commodities. Liberals and radicals, moderates and activists, reformers and revolutionaries—nearly every tendency within the 26th of July Movement was nationalist-minded.[20]

During the class-struggle phase of the revolution, nationalism, now transformed into anti-imperialism, bound together the workers and farmers not only against the United States but also against the local middle classes. The hostility of the United States to many of

---

[18] G. D. H. Cole, *The Meaning of Marxism* (London, 1950), pp. 37–38.

[19] Pazos and Boti, *op. cit.*

[20] Naturally, this included the radical wing after the seizure of power. In a speech to the Sociedad Nuestro Tiempo in January, 1959, for example, Guevara stressed that dependence on United States trade was dangerous for Cuba's autonomy (*The Havana Post,* January 28, 1959).

the Revolutionary Government's programs and policies, together with the strong nationalist character of these programs, transformed nationalism from a theoretical issue into a practical one. The liberals and reformers within the movement looked to the national middle class to simultaneously reconstruct Cuban capitalism on a reformed basis and withstand pressures from the United States. But they failed to understand the implications of the absence of a large, unified, progressive national bourgeoisie: the political initiative must inevitably shift to the left. In brief, the reformers in the movement who involved themselves in nationalist, anti-Yankee policies were unaware that they were playing with a loaded gun. The reformers and national middle class unwittingly helped the revolution along the path of socialism.

[6]
In the last two chapters we have accounted for the major economic and political developments in pre- and postrevolutionary Cuba. Our next task is to analyze these developments in detail, paying special attention to the agricultural and industrial economies and the labor situation before and after the revolution. The detail will take on meaning, however, only if the major landmarks of the political economy are kept firmly in mind.

First, twentieth-century Cuba was an example without equal of an export economy whose rhythm of development was determined by forces beyond the island's control. For the first quarter of the century the expansion of sugar production defined economic growth in Cuba. For the next thirty years the Cuban economy became more sensitive to changes in sugar exports but also experienced an accumulation of capital in manufacturing and other industries, owing mainly to the partial severing of economic ties with the United States during the depression and World War II, the retention of a larger share of sugar earnings by Cuban nationals, and active state interference in the economy.

Second, the Cuban economy stagnated despite the accumulation of industrial capital. The immediate reason was that a relatively large portion of Cuba's capital was channeled into unproductive branches of the economy, and the rest was underutilized or used inefficiently. The misallocation and underutilization of economic resources was the consequence of political and economic decisions made within and outside of Cuba, not the result of the "natural" play of market forces. Originally, the United States failed to encourage (and, at times, actively prevented) agricultural diversification, reduced dependence on sugar, and industrialization. This was partly a deliberate attempt to keep Cuba in an underdeveloped state and partly a result of the direct and indirect effects of the integration of the Cuban economy into the structure of the mainland economy. Later nationalist-oriented attempts to develop the economy were by and large a failure. Nationalist policies failed to break Cuba's dependency status, and nationalism made the local political economy even more irrational, mainly owing to the cartelization of agriculture, the monopolization of industry, and the redistributive character of state economic policies.

Also, Fidel Castro came to power as the leader of a united front against the Batista dictatorship. The immediate issues were political: Batista's suspension of the Constitution, censorship, police terror. The underlying issues were economic and social; that is, economic underdevelopment and stagnation and economic dependency on the United States. The economic and social program of the 26th of July Movement closely resembled programs put forth in the past; it promised something for nearly every economic group and thus reflected the classless character of the rebellion.

Finally, the revolution took on a class character because Castro pushed forward with a nationalist program of social and economic development despite opposition from the large landlords, the big ranchers, the more important industrialists, the *comprador* element, the state bureaucratic apparatus, the "economist"-minded labor leaders, and the United States government. Castro was successful because he carried the majority of Cubans with him and because the opposition was small and divided among itself.

[4]

The Mismanaged Economy: Prerevolutionary Agriculture

[1]

Rural Cuba before the revolution was an example without equal of a political economy made up, not of individuals, but of organized groups—earlier we described them as "economic baronies, well-organized, special-interest minded, corporate-oriented." Some of the groups were private, others public. Together they constituted a system of corporate economy: each was intent on acquiring its "fair" share of income and wealth; each professed a "responsibility" for the national well-being; each rejected the ideology of economic liberalism.

The private organizations included the Mill Owners' Association, the Colonos' (Cane Growers') Association, the Sugar Workers' Union, the Cattlemen's Association, and the various groupings of tobacco, coffee, rice, potato, and other growers. The public groups were state economic agencies. The Sugar Stabilization Institute, the Rice and Corn Stabilization Institutes, and the Coffee Purchase and Sale Administration were the most important.

The wealthiest, most powerful interests dominated both the private and public associations and agencies. Informal power relationships in the private economy were reproduced in the formal power relationships in the public economy. There was a "oneness" between private and public interests and the private and public economy.

Both the private associations and the public agencies perpetuated rural underdevelopment and economic stagnation by promoting policies that systematically underutilized and misused investments, labor, and land. Underdevelopment was not deliberately planned by any association or agency acting independently or in collaboration with others, but was rather the result of the interpenetration of the economic and political interests of these groups. Economic policies formed in both the economic and political arenas combined to harden the pattern of economic-resource utilization in inefficient, irrational molds.

[2]

Cuba stretches over seven hundred miles from end to end, 11.5 million hectares of plains, swamps, valleys, and mountains, 10 million hectares of farm or ranch lands. Before the revolution, 4.5 million hectares were natural pasture; 2.4 million hectares were under cane and other crops; the rest was overgrown with *marabú* and other weeds or otherwise unused.

One hundred seventy thousand farms dotted the countryside, each comprising an average of 60 hectares, each planting an average of 14 hectares in crops. Nevertheless, the typical farm was much smaller. At one extreme, there were 150,000 farms no larger than 16 hectares each; at the other extreme, there were 600 sugar plantations with an average size of 600 hectares and 1,000 cattle ranches with more than 1,000 hectares each. Most of the large farms and ranches were operated by hired managers; most of the small farms were cultivated by tenants, sharecroppers, and squatters.

Cuba's climate and soil are remarkably uniform, and sugar cane grows almost everywhere. Cultivation was extensive in character; cane was hand-cut all over the island. In 1959 about 60 per cent of total farm area cultivated was under cane, and about 53 per cent of total area harvested was planted in sugar (20 per cent of the island's cane was not cut in 1959).[1]

The harvest in 1958 was 5.8 million Spanish long tons, which was processed into about 13 per cent of the world's supply of crude sugar.[2] Most of the cane was grown by 68,000 *colonos*, independent

[1] Jacques Chonchol and others, *Proyecto de Plan Quinquenal para el desarrollo de la agricultura Cubana en 1961–1965* (Havana, March, 1961), Table 1, p. 14. Henceforth, this source will be called *Agricultural Plan.*

[2] The number of growers is given in *Anuario Azucarero de Cuba, 1959* (Havana, 1959), p. 79. In 1962 official Cuban sources placed the number of

cane growers and tenant farmers who leased land from the big sugar companies. No more than 20 per cent, and no less than 10 per cent, of the harvest was "administration cane," or cane grown by the sugar companies on plantations. One company, for example, controlled over 100,000 hectares of cane land and planted only 4,-000 hectares in administration cane; another 41,000-hectare company cultivated only 1,300 hectares.[3] About 400,000 wage hands brought in a peak harvest.

Cattle ranching was the island's second largest rural enterprise. In 1960 there were 5.1 million head of cattle on the island, or about .75 head per capita, one of the highest ratios in the world. Approximately 250 giant ranches, or *cebadores,* controlled the great mass of Cuba's 4.5 million hectares of natural pasture and owned about 43 per cent of the island's cattle, including nearly all of the 500,000 to 800,000 adult head slaughtered every year. Cattle ranching was concentrated in Camagüey and other eastern provinces.

The minor contours of Cuba's agriculture were tobacco, coffee, rice, corn cultivation, the root crops, tropical fruits, and other *frutas menores.*[4] Accounting for less than 40 per cent of the total value of agricultural production in 1958, the "minor crops" described two distinct regions, the "advanced sector" and the "backward sector." The advanced sector included tobacco, rice, potato, henequen, and

growers at 73,476, of which 67,238 operated farms containing less than five *caballerías* (Alfredo Menéndez Cruz, "Problemas de la industria azucarera," *Cuba Socialista,* 2, No. 12 [August, 1962], Table 1, pp. 1–2). Only a handful of *colonos* were mill employees; a few were owners, most were tenants and subtenants.

[3] Teresa Casuso, *Cuba and Castro* (New York, 1961), p. 197. In 1905 *colono* cane accounted for only 70 per cent of the total. (Thirty-seven per cent was grown on *colono*-owned land and 33 per cent on land rented from the mills. The government first discouraged administration cane in 1926. Quota allotments in 1933 discriminated further in favor of the *colonos.* In 1937 more restrictions were placed on the sugar companies (Boris Swerling, "Domestic Control of Cuban Sugar," *Journal of Farm Economics,* No. 3 [August, 1951], p. 351, note 21). By 1946, *colonos* produced 90 per cent of total output, and by 1952, 95 per cent. These figures are somewhat inflated because some mills grew administration cane in the name of one or more of their *colonos* to get around official restrictions on administration cane.

[4] *Agricultural Plan,* Table 1, p. 14. Nonbeef animal products came to 8 per cent, and nonsugar agricultural crops came to 31 per cent.

other cultivation. Rice farming was highly capitalized, tobacco farming highly skilled and specialized, and henequen cultivation employed modern techniques. In relation to the total number of farms, however, the advanced sector was small, including fewer than one-quarter of the island's farms that employed any wage labor.

The backward sector consisted chiefly of coffee, viands, corn, and *plátano* farming. Except during the coffee harvest, when the growers employed about 100,000 wage laborers, cultivation was carried on by the family unit. Farms were small, land was normally leased or sharecropped, techniques were backward, and incomes were low.

The backward and advanced (including sugar) sectors had one striking feature in common: both were ravaged by forced seasonal unemployment. In 1954, for instance, Cuba's 424,000 agricultural wage laborers averaged only 123 days of work; farm owners, tenants, and croppers fared little better, averaging but 135 days of employment. Low annual income due to seasonal unemployment was perhaps the most important explanation of the economic and social backwardness of the majority of rural Cubans. Forty-three per cent of the rural adult population could not read and write; 60 per cent of the island's rural families lived in dwellings with earth floors and roofs of palm leaves; two-thirds lived in houses without water closets or latrines; only one of every 14 families had electricity.

Poor housing was matched by deficient diets; only 4 per cent of all country families consumed meat regularly. Rice furnished 24 per cent of the average diet, kidney beans 23 per cent, and root crops 22 per cent. Bad diets and housing had terrible consequences for the health of rural Cubans. Thirteen per cent of the population had a history of typhoid, 14 per cent of tuberculosis, and over one-third had intestinal parasites.[5]

[5] These (rounded) data are from a study made by the Catholic University in 1956. A representative sample of 1,000 families distributed between Cuba's 126 municipalities was taken to represent a universe of roughly 400,000 families (Agrupación Católica Universitaria, *Por qué Reforma Agraria,* n.p., n.d., mimeographed). Although the categories are not exactly similar, the results of the full count of the island's 463,143 rural houses reported by the Population Census of 1953 roughly corresponds to the 1956 sample. According to the census, for example, 63.4 per cent of rural housing had palm leaf roofs and earthen floors, and 90.5 per cent lacked bath or shower either inside or outside.

Country people in Cuba consumed a tiny share of the island's social resources; their social development lagged well behind their economic and political development; there were clearly sharp limits to what the private and public associations and agencies could accomplish in prerevolutionary Cuba.

[3]

The organization and operation of the sugar industry was of central importance for the performance of the Cuban economy as a whole. Manufacturing, transport, banking, and commerce were heavily dependent on sugar. Crude sugar manufacture was the island's most important industry; the mills and growers were the railroads' biggest customers; the banks made from one-third to one-half of their loans to sugar growers and manufacturers; and crude sugar and sugar product exports made up more than 70 per cent of Cuba's foreign trade.

Cuba's key political economic organizations were the Mill Owners' Association, the Colonos Association, and the Sugar Stabilization Institute. The decisions of these groups determined how most of the island's economic resources were used. Cuba was like a hall of mirrors: wherever one turned, the predominance of sugar was inescapable.

The sugar industry was organized into an official cartel. A production quota was assigned to each cane grower, who was entitled to have his cane ground in proportion to his share in the total grinding of a specified mill in 1937.[6] Each sugar mill, in turn, was awarded two export quotas (one for the United States market, the other for the world market), a local consumption quota, and a quota for special reserves. Cuba's most important production restriction scheme dates back to the 1937 Law of Sugar Coordination, and while the details of the program have been changed from time to time, its general features were preserved until after the revolution, although the "free" harvest of World War II and the Korean War were excep-

[6] Swerling, *op. cit.*, p. 350. Thirty thousand *arrobas* was set as a minimum quota, even in the event that a *colono's* grinding factor prevented him from grinding that amount. As for growers who produced less than 30,000 *arrobas* in 1937, they were guaranteed a minimum quota equal to their 1937 production volume.

tions. The all-Cuba quota was set by presidential decree on the eve of the annual harvest and was subject to change during the harvest. The decreed level of production depended on the International Sugar Agreement and the United States Congress, which allocated the island quotas in the world and mainland markets, respectively. Of 1960's total harvest of 5.7 million tons, more than 1 million tons was destined for the world market and over 2.3 million tons was supposed to have been sold in the United States. The local market absorbed only 350,000 tons, and the greater part of the remainder was stored as reserve sugar.

Thus, the Cuban economy suffered a costly once-and-for-all burden of processed cane inventories, an important source of economic waste. A more significant source of waste was the enormous inventory of cane on the stalk (sugar is a perennial and in Cuba it has an average life of eight years or so). In 1959, for example, 1.4 million hectares was planted in cane, but only 1.1 million hectares was harvested. With over one-fifth of Cuba's cane land held in reserve, the quota system entailed the unproductive use of a sizable share of the island's agricultural wealth.

But these were relatively minor sources of waste. The quota system had more unfavorable economic implications owing to the special nature of the *colono* payments system and land tenure laws. Of the value of cane delivered to the mill, each *colono* received 48 per cent. From the standpoint of the grower whose marginal costs exceeded market prices at the level of production corresponding to his assigned quota, it would have paid to refrain from meeting his quota.[7] But this line of action was impractical; the Colonos Statutes

[7] This was the so-called *arrobaje*, which was fixed at a flat 48 per cent in 1949. From 1937 to 1949, the *arrobaje* was 47 per cent if the mill produced 12 to 13 tons of sugar from each 100 tons of cane, 46 per cent if yields were higher, and 48 per cent if yields were lower (Swerling, *op. cit.*, p. 352). The economic effects of this arrangement were: The mills were given a special incentive to raise productivity because their share of the total value of product varied directly with crude sugar yields. There was no incentive for the *colono* to raise the sucrose content of his cane because he shared in the average yield of *all* cane ground in the mill to which he was assigned. Moreover, his share declined as yields rose. The fixed *arrobaje* was aimed at reducing the monopsony power of the mills. This power arose because the grower depended on

and Sugar Coordination Law required that each *colono* fulfill his quota as a condition of permanent tenure.[8] Thus, when the market was especially poor, many high-cost growers temporarily produced at a loss. These "permanency rights" tended to freeze the pattern of land use. Few *colonos* shifted out of cane cultivation altogether.

From the standpoint of low-cost growers, the quota system clearly inhibited production and technical change. When sugar prices were high, the costs of many farmers fell considerably below prices at outputs corresponding to their quotas, although some efficient growers did expand production up to the point at which costs equalled prices in anticipation of a growth in the market that might compel the authorities to declare a "free" harvest. Indirect proof is the fact that many growers tended reserve cane fields year after year.

The quota system thus placed a protective umbrella over inefficient growers and prevented an expansion of production and sales by efficient farmers. Minister of Agriculture Humberto Sori Marin summed up the situation in February, 1959, when he referred to the "existing disadjustment in quotas." [9] He observed that some planters had large amounts of cane, but no quotas, while others lacked cane with which to fulfill their quotas. For the first group of growers prices were obviously in excess of costs, and for the latter prices fell well under costs.

The rigidly enforced quota system damaged Cuban agriculture in a number of ways. The all-Cuba quota artificially restricted the aggregate production of cane and needlessly inflated costs. *De facto* discrimination against low-cost growers and administration cane and protection of high-cost growers magnified the discrepancy be-

---

the mill for transportation and grinding facilities. Since cane must be cut before the rainy season begins, and since the stalk is not storable, the mill had considerable control over prices. In addition, the grower had to compete with the mill's own cane. Legislation in 1937 tied each *colono* to a specified mill. Had this legislation not introduced the fixed *arrobaje*, the monopsony power of the mills would have been further enhanced.

[8] R. G. F. Spitze and Gregorio Alfaro, "Property Rights, Tenancy Laws of Cuba, and Economic Power of Renters," *Land Economics*, 35, No. 3 (August, 1959), p. 280. These "permanency rights" were first established in 1937.

[9] Reported in *The Havana Post*, February 27, 1959.

tween actual and optimum costs.[10] The system also discouraged new investments, because few *colonos* could hope to profit by the introduction of cost-reducing technological changes so long as a decline in costs was contingent on an expansion of production. Nor were there strong incentives to raise yields per hectare or introduce new cane varieties; it was no accident that the most popular variety of cane in the old Cuba had been developed in Java in the 1920's.

From the standpoint of the development of the agricultural economy, however, the most serious consequence of the cartelization of sugar was the effect on the labor force. Specialization in sugar created its own "economic resource," an unskilled, untrained, backward labor force perpetuated by unchanging production techniques. Thus, it was less profitable to introduce and develop agricultural and industrial commodities requiring a trained, skilled labor force elsewhere in the economy.

[4]

To penetrate deeper into the irrationalities of Cuban cane cultivation requires a brief detour into economic theory. A rational agriculture means that both area under cultivation and yields per unit of cultivated area will approach an "optimum" in the sense that costs will be minimized. By no means, however, will either area cultivated or yields be maximized. Neither idle lands nor apparently "backward" modes of cultivation necessarily signify inefficient farming. In a rationally organized rural economy, foods and raw materials may be produced as cheaply as possible even though farmers fail to exploit arable lands or intensive methods of production technically available to them.

In practice, competition from other farmers, including those producing different commodities, compels each grower to estimate carefully the costs (in the form of outlays for fertilizer, irrigation equipment, and so on) of raising yields, and compare them with the costs

---

[10] In the world cane sugar industry, yields of plantation sugar are on the average twice as high as those realized by small growers (United Nations, Department of Economic Affairs, *Land Reform: Defects in Agrarian Structure as Obstacles to Economic Development* [New York, 1959], p. 22).

of buying (or renting) and cultivating new lands. If a farmer has planted too much land on which yields are too low (compared with the optimum), an expansion of demand and production will confirm that his costs are dangerously high compared with going prices. Free movement of capital into agriculture in search of maximum profits will oblige the farmer to reduce his cost structure, in this case by introducing yield-raising investments. There can be no competition, in the ordinary sense of the word, without rational choice, and in the absence of reliable information about alternative modes of production, there can be no rational choice.

In the old Cuba small and large farmers alike remained ignorant of the yield-raising potentialities of fertilizers and water control: "Not even the large foreign or Cuban [sugar] growers have taken the trouble to analyze their soils for specific deficiencies as a guide to the kinds of fertilizer needed." [11] It is also significant that the last completed professional study of Cuba's soils was made as long ago as 1928; perhaps it is more than symbolic that 1928 began the transformation from a competitive to monopolistic agriculture. Were cane cultivation competitive, economic necessity would have compelled farmers to explore the possibilities of untried techniques. Cuba's sugar growers failed to do so because the quota system cushioned them from competitive market forces.

Compared with other sugar-producing countries, yields per hectare were extremely low, less than one-half those in Indonesia and Hawaii, for example. From a technical standpoint, Cuba's sugar yields could have been doubled.[12] Technical optimums correspond to economic optimums, however, only when capital for yield-raising investments is costless. A closer examination of the industry is therefore necessary before we can attribute Cuba's low yields to the effects of the sugar cartel.

Such an examination discloses that the backwardness of the sugar industry can indeed be placed at the door of the cartel. For the av-

[11] International Bank for Reconstruction and Development, Economic and Technical Mission, *Report on Cuba* (Baltimore, 1951), p. 106.

[12] Antonio Portuondo, *Informe a la sección de Recursos de la Tierra del I Symposium Nacional de Recursos Naturales de Cuba* (Havana, February, 1958).

erage *colono*, irrigation would have raised yields by 50 to 100 per cent, but for water control to have paid for itself, production would have had to increase by 33 to 45 per cent.[13] Thus, the rationalization of sugar production would have required a fundamental readjustment of the quota system to allow efficient growers (or those cultivating especially good land or with ready access to financial capital) to sell nearly half again as much as they actually marketed. In this event, under a system of capitalist markets, uncounted thousands of sugar growers would have been put out of business. Politically, such a course would have been blocked by the powerful Colonos Association. No Cuban politician dared to tamper with the quota system and the cartelization of the industry.

Rises in demand would certainly have been met by an improvement in yields had the sugar industry not been handcuffed by monopoly restrictions. Under the quota system a rise in demand was shared more or less equally by low-cost and high-cost producers, and few growers were able to expand production enough to make investments in water control and fertilizers pay off. Moreover, there was little incentive to hire extra labor to weed the cane fields. It was not impossible, a British group pointed out a few years before the revolution, for growers to raise yields, but "in many areas the value of the increased output would probably be absorbed by increased costs." [14]

[13] *Report on Cuba*, p. 113. Fertilizer alone could raise cane yields from 10 to 50 per cent, depending on the quality of the soil and type of fertilizer employed (*ibid.*, p. 106). Recent experiments have shown that five tons of fertilizer can raise yields by 15 to 20 per cent, and that a well-irrigated, fertilized, and cared-for field can double the amount of cane grown.

[14] Great Britain, Board of Trade, Overseas Economic Surveys, *Cuba: Economic and Commercial Conditions in Cuba* (London, 1954), p. 45. It may be objected that sugar growers brought new lands under cultivation during periods of high demand (during the Korean War, for example), indicating that no less costly path to a rise in production was possible. This is circular reasoning. Given rural monopoly, an increase in cultivated area was the only economical way to raise production.

In 1959, there were well over one million hectares of idle sugar lands. Small *colonos* cultivated a larger proportion of their land than large growers, who cultivated a bigger share than the plantations. As we will see, it cannot be concluded a priori that good quality idle lands were the product of rural

The backwardness of production modes in Cuba is also revealed by the tendency for yields to remain unchanged over long periods of time. Around the turn of the century, yields were actually somewhat higher than in 1958 (about 20 tons of cane per acre compared with roughly 19 tons in the latter year).[15] Nor was there any improvement in the sucrose content of the cane, indicating that little improvement was made in the *quality* of Cuban sugar cane.[16] Thus, the dramatic expansion of sugar production during the first quarter of this century was based largely on increases in land under cultivation. Half a century ago the industry was not organized into a cartel, suggesting that extensive modes of production were at one time efficient. As late as 1925, average costs of production were actually lower than in the Hawaiian Islands, Puerto Rico, Louisiana, and other cane-producing areas, confirming this view.[17] Extensive cultivation meant low costs because Cuba's rainfall was satisfactory, labor was scarce relative to good land, and commodities that competed with sugar for land and other resources lacked important domestic or export markets. With the introduction of the quota sys-

monopoly. This is a standard error in the Cuba literature (see, for example, Severo Aguirre, "Ante el Tercer Aniversario de la Reforma Agraria," *Cuba Socialista*, 2, No. 9 [1962], p. 9). A cruder analysis places idle land (and low yields and underemployment) at the feet of "monoculture" (Marco Antonio Durán, "La reforma agraria en Cuba," *El Trimestre Económico*, 27, No. 107 [July–September, 1960], p. 421).

[15] Leonard Wood, *et al.*, *Opportunities in the Colonies and Cuba* (New York, 1902), pp. 154–162. Yields were estimated at 1.25–1.5 million pounds per *caballería*. Scanty data on costs suggest that average costs rose during the period. Around the turn of the century, the first cut cost $1,200 per *caballería*, of which the cost of cultivation alone was $383. This latter figure would be roughly equal to the cost of the second cut. In the late 1940's, it was estimated that the cost per *caballería* of the first cut was $1,700, and for later cuts, $360 each (Julián Alienes y Urosa, *Características Fundamentales de la Economía Cubana* [Havana, 1950], p. 112). It is interesting to note that these data imply real wages over the period remained unchanged, given no important changes in field production techniques.

[16] At the turn of the century, the sugar content of cane was 11 per cent, according to one estimate, and 13 per cent (December cuts) to 18 per cent (March–April cuts), according to another (Wood, *op. cit.*). In 1961, the sugar content of the cane was an average of 12.6 per cent.

[17] United States, Tariff Commission, *Sugar, Report of the U.S. Tariff Commission to the President of the U.S.* (Washington, 1926), p. 92.

tem in the 1930's, however, extensive cultivation became increasingly inefficient. The cartelization of the industry preserved the old methods of production by sealing off sugar growers from competitive pressures emanating from both within and without the island, and thus Cuba paid heavily in the form of wasted land, labor, and capital.

[5]

Our next task is to examine the economically irrational roles of rents and profits within the sugar sector. Land rents in a competitive agricultural economy have two functions. For the landowners and tenants they indicate the most profitable ways to utilize land. Changes in the demand for foods and raw materials will be reflected in changes in the structure of commodity prices, which in turn will determine the structure of rents. A rise in the price of corn, for example, will raise rents on wheat land, signaling owners and tenants to shift to the higher-priced commodity. From the standpoint of society as a whole, rents are a pure "surplus," or monopoly return.

In the Cuban sugar economy, land rents came to 5 per cent of milled output *regardless of cane prices*.[18] For this reason a rise in the price of a commodity competing with sugar for land failed to influence in the slightest rents on cane lands. Although at first glance it would seem that a really striking price increase would tempt landowners to shift land into new, more profitable uses, the sugar *colonos* retained permanent tenure—so long as they met their quotas and paid their rents. For the growers there clearly was little incentive to shift out of sugar and into the more profitable crop since such a course of action would threaten their own hard-won security. For these reasons rents failed to serve any useful role in the alloca-

[18] This was true on land planted in cane in 1937 (so-called Area A land). On additional land planted in cane (Area B land), rents varied with the price of sugar (Law of Sugar Coordination, cited by Gregorio Alfaro, "The Land Tenure Situation in Cuba" [San José, Costa Rica, November, 1957], mimeographed, p. 6). Until 1950, when Area B rents were abolished, this legislation helped to explain why the mills favored restricted outputs and higher prices.

tion of agricultural resources. Quite the contrary, they inhibited, even if slightly, economic development, since their only significance was as unearned landlord income.

However irrational the structure of rents in the sugar industry, the profit structure had a greater adverse effect on the level of efficiency in agriculture. In a competitive rural economy the commodity that commands the highest rate of profit will occupy the most productive land. In the early development of the Cuban sugar industry there were no important alternative uses for the island's richest and most productive soils. From 300,000 tons of sugar in 1850, production rose to over 1 million tons in 1894 and shot up to 4 million tons in 1920. High-yield land went under the plow, and soils easily subject to erosion, difficult to clear hilly grounds, and swamplands were bypassed.

Decades after the industry's period of the great expansion, it still could be written that "the land in sugar cane is generally the best land on the island." [19] Even sharply declining markets failed to dislodge the ever present cane; monopoly control held up the rate of profit and discouraged the diversification and expansion of other branches of agriculture. The net annual rate of return of eight large sugar companies operating twenty-one mills was 23 per cent from 1937 to 1957, an extraordinary record considering that eight of these years were crisis periods (1937–1941 and 1954–1956). The Cuban-Atlantic Sugar Company, to cite an extreme case, earned an after-tax income of $78.5 million on an average capital investment of $7.2 million during the period 1935–1957.[20]

In the 1940's and 1950's the *colonos* also took out monopoly profits. The quota system sealed off the growers from outside competition, and legislation that promoted their interests against the mills

[19] Lowery Nelson, *Rural Cuba* (Minneapolis, 1950), p. 49. In the manufacturing end of the industry, economies of large-scale production were very large. In 1877, there were 1,190 sugar mills, only 207 in 1899, and but 170 in 1920. For a profound exposition of the complex, early development of the sugar industry, see Ramiro Guerra y Sánchez, *Azucar y Población en las Antillas* (Havana, 1961), pp. 80–110.

[20] Antonio Núñez Jiménez, "Las realizaciones del INRA," *Divulgación*, 1, No. 6 (1959), p. 21.

guaranteed them a fixed share of sugar earnings. The value of production per hectare planted in sugar cane exceeded that in all other branches of agriculture except tobacco farming, where labor inputs were far greater. Cane farming required less labor and capital than the average Cuban farming operation; thus, profits per hectare under cultivation were significantly higher in the sugar sector than in other branches of the island's agriculture.[21]

There were thus few incentives to cultivate other cash crops, even when the market for Cuban sugar was weak. Instead, sugar lands reverted to pasture or were held in reserve as insurance against a possible future rise in the market or possible agrarian reform.[22] Land hoarding was also encouraged by the lack of a rural real estate tax corresponding to the productive value of the soil. Moreover, the level and distribution of income discouraged an expansion of food and raw materials production, particularly in those sectors requiring skilled farm labor.

Politically unable to attack the problem at its roots, Cuban governments on several occasions indirectly attempted to encourage the cultivation of reserve and pasture lands. The Sugar Coordination Law of 1937 required the mills to furnish land rent free to employees for the cultivation of subsistence crops during the dead season. Prior to this time it was often forbidden to plant subsistence crops at all. Although the law encouraged some new cultivation, the over-all impact on Cuban agriculture was slight because no complementary technical aid or capital was provided and the lands made available were often of poor quality. A further step was taken in 1942 when the government obliged the mills themselves to plant

[21] Deduced from data given in Francisco Dorta-Duque, "Justificando una reforma agraria," Instituto de Ciencias Sociales, Pontíficia Universidad Gregoriana (Rome, n.d.), pp. 24, 28. The data are for 1945, when the sugar market was especially buoyant, producing an unusually high value of output. The war boom also made the cultivation of other crops unusually profitable. Moreover, the island failed to profit as much as it would have under competitive conditions because the United States placed a ceiling price on Cuban sugar. Sugar employed the most unskilled labor in the rural labor force, and, in comparison with crops such as rice, tomatoes, henequen, and potatoes, capital inputs per unit of output were low. Thus our assumption is probably not too wide of the mark.

[22] Robert B. Batchelder, "The Evolution of Cuban Land Tenure," *The Southwestern Social Science Quarterly*, No. 3 (December, 1952), p. 244.

subsidiary crops—significantly termed *frutas menores*—on their idle lands and required that employers pay the same wage rates off season as the sugar workers earned during the *zafra*. These measures were the product of the new, post-1933 configuration of political forces and were consistent from a strictly political standpoint; they were designed to raise the material condition of the rural proletariat and simultaneously cheapen foodstuffs in the city. From an economic standpoint, however, they formed a contradiction. The mills simply could not profit from the cultivation of subsidiary crops, and few companies heeded the law; in fact, one of the demands of the sugar workers in 1959 was for unused lands for garden plots. Thus, one condition for an advanced and diversified agriculture was a rational wage policy together with effective government control of the sugar companies. In this sense political solutions to Cuba's economic problems in cane cultivation were necessary as a preliminary to technical or economic solutions.

That Cuba's sugar problem was fundamentally political is stressed by the lines of analysis developed above. Sugar cane blanketed the island's most productive lands; the quota system reinforced and hardened this pattern of land use, reduced yields per hectare, and inhibited the introduction of yield-raising technical innovations and changes. From the standpoint of the Cuban economy as a whole, it would have been more efficient to produce the same amount of cane with less land and higher yields, and it would have paid to wipe out seasonal unemployment. Clearly, any Cuban government seriously committed to the development of agriculture would be compelled to shift a sizable portion of the island's cane land to food and industrial crops, cultivated with the help of seasonally unemployed labor, and to raise yields on the remaining fields in order to maintain the volume of cane production. This course, however, required that the government reduce or eliminate the independent economic and political power of the mill owners, the *colonos*, and other interests dependent upon the *status quo*.

[6]

Like cane cultivation, cattle ranching in Cuba was highly inefficient and characterized by technological stagnation. In the mid-

nineteenth century, before one hundred years of poor land management despoiled Cuba's natural pasture, the ratio of cattle to pasture
land was roughly 1.5 head per hectare. By the turn of the century
the ratio stood at 1.0; in 1960, at 1.1. Cuba's best land was under
sugar, and there were few incentives to raise yields by using artificial grasses.

Also, like cane cultivation, cattle ranching was highly monopolized. The industry was organized in a pyramidal structure. Thousands of small ranchers grazed and fattened calves on the island's
poorest pasture land for sale to a smaller number of medium-sized
ranchers, or *mejoradores*. The *mejoradores*, in turn, sold their yearlings to a few giant *cebadores*.[23]

The largest ranches exercised considerable monopoly power over
both the smaller ranchers and the slaughterhouses.[24] Faced with
hardly any competitive pressures, the big ranchers had few incentives to rationalize their operations. This was the basic reason that
these ranches were too big for efficient management. The second
reason was that many Cubans from both the old oligarchy and the
sugar-rich middle classes still considered "ownership of vast tracts

---

[23] According to the 1952 cattle census, there were 89,934 "cattle farms" on
the island. The principal source of income of only a minority, however, was
cattle. The 1946 Agricultural Census reported only 28,836 farms whose chief
business was cattle. In 1952, there were about 75,000 farms with less than
fifty head each. Most were not small ranchers, however. Many were dairy
farmers, sugar planters, and other growers who owned a few oxen and other
draft animals.

It is even more difficult to estimate the number of medium-sized ranches.
According to an INRA survey in 1959, there were 8,919 cattle ranches comprising more than 30 *caballerías* (Aurleliana Sánchez Arango, "Situación de
los campesinos y obreros dentro de la reforma agraria," *Cuadernos*, No. 47
[Paris, 1961], p. 39). Many of these farms, however, were *cebadores*, the very
largest ranches, which purchased yearlings from the *mejoradores*. Others were
larger farms that specialized in food or industrial crops and kept a few head
of cattle. As for the number of *cebadores*, the 1952 census reported 2,817 farms
on which more than 250 head of cattle grazed. Fewer than 100 ranches
dominated this group.

[24] Durán, *op. cit.*, pp. 422–424. The favorable market position of the large
ranchers acquired much political significance in 1959–1960 when a crisis of
demand forced the government to seize many ranches that it had originally
intended to leave in private hands.

of land [to be] . . . a distinctive sign of class superiority." [25] The
Infante family, for example, grazed 80,000 head of cattle on nearly
half a million acres. These Texas methods, basically unchanged
since the nineteenth century, were totally unsuitable in a country
where population density was up to 50 times as great, and where
rainfall was four or five times heavier.

The third reason for the failure to rationalize the industry was the
lack of local demand for high-quality beef owing to the low level
and unequal distribution of income within Cuba. Controlled pasturing, for example, would have improved the quality of Cuban herds,
but the extra costs probably would not have been absorbed by increased revenue. [26]

The backwardness of Cuban ranching revealed itself in many
ways. With an almost complete absence of controlled pasturing, the
island's cattle were left to fend for themselves and put on weight
only during the seven-month wet season. Half-starved during the
dry season, cattle required a three-year growing period. Trampled
by the free herds, much fodder was lost, and the shortage of feed
during the dry season was aggravated by the lack of any real effort
to cut and store fodder. Cattlemen held their herds off the market
during the lean months in order to fatten them during the wet season, so Cuba suffered persistent seasonal shortages of beef. For the
island as a whole, deaths and loss of weight and milk during the
dry season cost upwards of $160 million each year. [27]

---

[25] Batchelder, *op. cit.*, p. 244.

[26] Until the mid-1950's, a standard official price for beef on the hoof also
encouraged ranchers to raise poor grades of cattle (*Report on Cuba*, p. 180).
When price restrictions were lifted, there was some improvement in forage
feeding and an increase in grain feeding (The American Chamber of Commerce of Cuba, *Cuba: Facts and Figures* ([Havana, April, 1957], p. 207).

[27] Severo Aguirre, "Problemas fundamentales de la producción pecuaria,"
Cuba Socialista, 3, No. 21 (May, 1963), p. 36, citing an INRA study. This is
an overestimate. To derive the true "loss," the costs of improved organization
and cattle management should be deducted. Since these costs would be for
the most part once-and-for-all outlays, they would not weigh very heavily
against the benefits over a long period of time. The wet-season all-Cuba average
for milk yields was three to four liters daily, double the dry-season average.
These data illustrate the absence of a mixed agriculture along the lines of

Another consequence of the monopoly organization of the industry and insufficient demand for beef products was the absence of artificial grasses, systematic techniques of artificial insemination, and a concerted effort to wipe out widespread cattle diseases. It was not until the Revolutionary Government came to power in 1959 that a beginning was made to eliminate these and other irrationalities and sources of waste.

Again like cane cultivation, the fundamental problem was political. The small but weighty Cuban Cattlemen's Association wielded much political power and influence. Any serious attempt to rationalize the use of the island's pasture land would necessarily have to be based on a policy of moderating or breaking the independent political power of this group.

Actually the situation was more complicated than appears at first glance. The interests of the cattlemen merged with those of the giant sugar mills, and on many issues the combined weight of the two groups was irresistible. The tie-in of interests sprang from the fact that when the sugar market was poor, cane lands were allowed to revert to pasture. Some of the sugar companies actually operated their own ranches; in 1958–1959, for example, the Francisco Sugar Company's 23,000-acre El Indio ranch earned nearly one-half of the corporation's income. Another instance was the 40,000 acre Compañía Ganadera Becerra, one-half of which was owned by the King Ranch and the other half by the Manati Sugar Company. When the sugar market was poor, ranching thus received a kind of land "bonus" which inhibited even more the introduction of land-saving innovations and techniques, such as controlled pasturing and artificial grasses. Rational from the standpoint of the individual ranch or sugar company, from the point of view of total agricultural development, these "gifts" reduced the rate of capital investment and braked technological change in ranching.

[7]

In other branches of the rural economy, many of the conclusions

---

dairy farming in north central United States, where yields were six times those in Cuba.

drawn for cane cultivation and cattle ranching do not apply without serious modification or qualification. Common to both major and minor agriculture, however, were inefficient techniques and modes of production. According to a 1957 conference of agronomists, only black beans and sweet potatoes in the backward sector were grown efficiently, probably because these items were staples in the Cuban diet and enjoyed a wide market. Elsewhere in the backward sector, disparities between optimum and actual yields ran as high as four to one in coffee farming, and nearly seven to one in the case of onions. Including land under sugar cane, well over 70 per cent of the island's cultivated land was therefore used unproductively, and if grazing land is added, the figure exceeded 90 per cent.

Statistics of crop yields, however, fail to convey a truly accurate picture of agricultural efficiency, particularly in the advanced sector. A brief analysis of some key minor branches of the rural economy is instructive. In rice farming, on superficial examination an efficient industry, yields could have been augmented by 100 to 200 per cent had varieties more suitable to Cuba's soils been planted.[28] The Revolutionary Government's first Five-Year Agricultural Plan actually envisioned (albeit unrealistically at the time) a doubling of yields through better soil preparation, double cropping, more efficient control of pests, and the use of fertilizer. Few corners of Cuban agriculture were free from monopoly controls and irrationalities, and rice cultivation was no exception. A very special configuration of market forces made it profitable to introduce and expand rice production in the 1950's: the United States exported rice to Cuba at high mainland prices under a quota system that gave foreign producers a sizable share of the Cuban market. Cuban growers flourished under this umbrella of high prices and were sheltered from thoroughgoing competitive pressures. Rice farmers were also the largest single recipients of the cheap agricultural credit provided by the new state investment banks created by the Batista dictatorship.

[28] Dr. Jukyo Cho, head of a Japanese rice mission to Cuba in 1960 (*The Havana Post*, May 29, 1960). The 1957 conference of agronomists claimed that actual yields were about two-thirds of optimum yields.

Elsewhere in the advanced sector, the experts who drew up the Five-Year Plan maintained that better control of crop diseases and selection of seed could raise potato yields by over one-third. As for fruit growing, costs of production were unnecessarily high; a modern mixed agriculture was a rarity in the old Cuba, and the island's fruit trees served neither as shade for cattle nor windbreaks for other crops. Although there were only fourteen henequen farms in Cuba, this valuable industrial crop was grown efficiently, as were tomatoes and the island's high-quality tobacco, although tenure relationships in the latter sector probably discouraged long-term capital improvements.[29]

In the backward sector a mixture of traditional methods of production and monopolistic controls combined to inhibit productivity and production. To the vast majority of Cuba's small farmers, crop rotation, soil conservation, the use of artificial seeds, and other modern farming techniques were almost completely unknown. Nearly 90 per cent of Cuba's coffee, for example, was grown by about 20,000 small farmers in the mountains of northern Oriente Province with the use of crude production methods. Unlike sugar cultivation, there were no profitable economies of large-scale production to attract foreign capital into this sector. Coffee growers, moreover, had attachments to the land which stemmed from noneconomic factors; this was perhaps the main reason why the size of the average Cuban coffee farm fell far below optimum. Early in the 1950's the government made a stab at improving yields, and the industry was given high tariff protection. The possibility of augmenting yields and production was thus raised, but monopoly controls in the form of quotas and fixed prices cancelled many of the potential advantages of tariff protection. During the record crop year of 1955–1956, for example, the new Coffee Purchase and Sale Administration was compelled to buy over fifteen million pounds of beans; fixed prices insured the survival of many inefficient producers, contributing to the maintenance of low yields and rigid patterns of land use.

[29] Production was efficient even with regulation and controls because Cuban tobacco requires much specialized hand labor and careful management, and if farmers fail to cultivate correctly, there is little profit in cultivating at all.

The production of other minor crops was by and large very inefficient; tenure arrangements, a scarcity of capital, inadequate markets, untrained growers and workers: all of these factors combined to produce technological backwardness. Modern, scientific farming was a rarity in potentially one of the richest agricultural countries in the entire world.

[8]

Our economic analysis of the specific branches of the rural economy completed, we will next examine briefly the effects of tenure arrangements on agricultural efficiency. About two-thirds of Cuba's farmers, and a larger proportion of the island's small growers in the backward sector, were tenants, sharecroppers, or squatters. Relations with landlords were defined by the 1948 Land Lease and Sharecropping Law, together with legislation in 1952 and 1954 which "guaranteed" secure tenancy to small farmers. As we know, prior legislation granted the same rights to the *colonos*. Particularly in the later years of the Batista dictatorship, however, the more recent laws were often honored more in the breach. In his futile efforts to bring down the Castro military forces in 1957–1958, for example, Batista ordered the evacuation of entire communities from some areas in Oriente Province.

Contract periods were fixed by law: six years for ranchers and cultivators of tobacco, rice, cocoa, beans; three years for fruit, grains, and vegetable growers. Tenants were able to prolong their contracts indefinitely so long as they remained up to date on rental obligations; in this way tendencies to immobilize labor and capital were reinforced: "All rural Cubans seem to be less mobile than farm people in the United States. . . ."[30] Legal maximum rents were 5

---

[30] Nelson, *op. cit.*, p. 171. This statement is confirmed by 1946 census data. In 1945, 36.1 per cent of all proprietors had worked their farms more than 25 years. The proportions were 20.9 per cent, 17.8 per cent, 16.0 per cent, and 10.7 per cent for administrator-operated farms, renters, subrenters, and squatters, respectively. On the other hand, only 17.9 per cent of all proprietors had been on their farms for less than five years; 21.1 per cent of all renters; 21.0 per cent of all subrenters; and 34.8 per cent of all squatters. Legislation protecting tenancy, fixed prices, quota systems, and informal monopoly controls all played a role in inhibiting mobility.

per cent and 6 per cent of the value of farm properties under and over five *caballerías,* respectively, and values were determined by government officials. But between the officials and the landlords there was often an "understanding," and where the tenants lacked solid organization the law was open to many abuses. Nor were "wash sales" uncommon; land values were raised artificially and tenants were compelled to pay exorbitant rents; some of Oriente's coffee farmers, for example, paid up to 40 per cent of the value of their crops in rents.[31]

The coffee growers suffered most at the hands of the landlords. They were dependent on landowners for the processing of beans and often for transportation services, and it was not unusual for them to be systematically overcharged. Partly for these reasons, Cuba's coffee farmers supported Castro when he organized and expanded the Rebel Army in Oriente Province in 1957 and 1958. Elsewhere on the island, in the dominant sugar sector and in tobacco farming, where tenure and rent laws were enforced more rigorously, the social base for the liberation army was much narrower.

The exploitation of Cuba's small tenant farmers was not confined to illegally high rents and exorbitant prices for needed services. Even outside of the coffee sector it was common to find in small rural communities so-called "tick shops" (*tiendas de raya*) from which farmers drew foods and supplies on the security of future crops, which in turn were purchased by the *tiendas* at low prices and short weights. Where the hold of these rural middlemen over tenant farmers was especially strong it was difficult or impossible for small farmers to accumulate anything but debts.

Another important piece of rural legislation was more rigidly enforced than the rent laws, even in the more remote corners of the mountains of northern Oriente where the most technologically backward of the coffee farmers lived and worked. In the event that a landlord improved his property, only 5 per cent of the value of the improvement could be added to the rent, stretching out the amorti-

---

[31] Universidad Popular, *Economía y Planificación* (*segunda parte*) (Havana, 1961), p. 23. International Labour Office, *The Landless Farmer in Latin America* (Geneva, 1957), p. 65.

zation period to twenty years. Because few Cuban landowners had any interest in improving or modernizing their properties under any circumstances, it was rarely necessary to enforce the law. It did, however, undoubtedly discourage Cuba's few innovating landlords. Like most important rural legislation, this law was irrational because it hindered the full and efficient utilization of the island's agricultural resources.

[9]

We have finally to describe and evaluate the agricultural policies of successive Cuban governments, placing greatest emphasis on the innovations of the Batista regime during the 1950's. The first important step to encourage the expansion of the rural economy by reducing Cuba's dependence on sugar exports and promoting local production of imported foods and raw materials was in 1927, when a wide range of commodities was given the protection of high tariffs. Although total imports dropped from nearly $300 million in 1925 to just over $50 million in 1932, local supplies, with few exceptions, failed to increase. Imports were cut back by the rise in prices accompanying the new tariff schedules, together with the decline in incomes brought about by the Great Depression. Minor revisions were made in tariffs in the 1930's and 1940's, but few other steps were taken to raise production. From the 1930's onward most emphasis was placed on the redistribution of income in the countryside. As we have seen, the instruments of redistribution included production and sales quotas, guaranteed prices and incomes, permanent tenure arrangements, minimum wages, and the Cubanization of the sugar industry.

Two related events in the early 1950's started Cuba once more on the path of agricultural expansion and diversification. First, the end of the raw materials boom following the stalemate in Korea produced a crisis of major proportions in the international sugar market. Second, Batista attempted to win a broad national consensus for his new government (which had come to power through the *coup d'état* of March, 1952) by expanding and diversifying the Cuban economy.

Although the dictatorship's major stress was on industry, new agricultural development received more attention than ever before. To be sure, the new regime continued to starve the Ministry of Agriculture of funds.[32] Private bankers, however, were encouraged to expand loans to farmers; before 1952 little credit was available outside the sugar, tobacco, and cattle sectors. Pressed to inspire popular support for his government, Batista also accelerated the activity of existing public and quasi-public organisms concerned with the rural economy and created new organizations with the task of reconstructing Cuban agriculture.

In the first category was the Agriculture and Industrial Development Bank (BANFAIC), organized in 1951 to provide cheap credit for Cuba's farmers and new industries. Up to this time low-cost credits were available only to producers for export, and the masses of Cuba's small farmers were compelled to pay interest rates ranging from 12 to 30 per cent annually.[33] Real rates of interest were still higher; in order to liquidate their loans, farmers were forced to sell their crops at harvesttime when market prices were lowest. Until 1953, BANFAIC's portfolio was modest: in 1952 it held less than $720,000 in outstanding loans. From 1953 to 1956, however, its portfolio expanded from $5 million to over $14 million.[34] Interest rates on both working capital and capital investment credits averaged 8 per cent. In 1956 the bank had $350,000 in loans with the new rural credit associations set up under the law that established BANFAIC. The associations in turn held $11 million in farmer obligations.

In the category of new lending agencies were the Cuban Bank for Foreign Commerce, which was founded in 1954 and specialized

[32] Of the total 1957–1958 budget, the Ministry of Agriculture received only $4.6 million, or about 2 per cent (Cuba, Consejo Nacional de Economía, *Boletín Informativo*, 10, No. 1 [July, 1958], p. 16).

[33] Digby Solomon Espinosa, "Agricultural Credit in Cuba," *Proceedings of the International Conference on Agriculture and Cooperative Credit*, August 4–October 2, 1952 (University of California, Berkeley), pp. 649–652. See also A. Rochac y M. Monzón, "La tenencia de la tierra y crédito agrícola en Cuba," *Problemas Agrícolas e Industriales de México*, 6, No. 1 (1954), *passim*.

[34] Cuba, Banco Nacional de Cuba, Progress Report No. 3 (Havana, October, 1957), Table 7, p. 24. The largest beneficiaries were big farmers (*Hoy*, August 10, 1963).

in financing Cuban exports, in particular coffee exports, and the Economic and Social Development Bank (BANDES), created in 1955 to finance the other public institutions and extend loans to private companies for the construction of plants to process raw materials.

Combined public and rural credit association loans totalled nearly $7 million in 1952, of which $2.8 million were extended to farmers. By 1956, the total volume of loans jumped to $212 million, $15 million of which were in agriculture. The Batista government clearly had great hopes that abundant, cheap credit would stimulate the rural economy.

Other new institutions incorporated during the 1950's included three organizations in the old tradition of "redistributive" economic policy, the Rice and Corn Stabilization Institutes and the Coffee Purchase and Sale Administration. Their task was to maintain minimum prices and farmer income by purchasing surplus commodities. Two other new organizations were more production oriented, while the character of a third was mixed. In the first group were the National Executive Committee of Farms and Mining Cooperatives (1954), which established a number of production and processing cooperatives, and the Cuban Institute of Technical Investigations (1955), which began a few studies in agricultural productivity. The third public corporation cushioned market forces by buying surplus beans, potatoes, onions, and tobacco and also initiated some plans for the processing and distribution of farm products.

The new agencies and institutions helped to expand farm production by 8 per cent per year from 1953 to 1956.[35] Rice cultivation held top priority. Total area planted nearly doubled between 1950 and 1954, and production rose by over 150 per cent.[36] The state encouraged rice farming in every conceivable way. In 1953–1954, for example, over a third of BANFAIC's portfolio was in rice loans. Poultry and eggs, cereals, dairy products, beans, and other commodities imported from the United States also received help. Although

[35] Cuba, Banco Nacional de Cuba, *Memoria, 1957–1958* (Havana, 1959).
[36] United Nations, Department of Economic and Social Affairs, *Economic Survey of Latin America* (New York, 1954) Chapter IV, p. 163.

total food imports remained roughly the same between 1952 and 1958 ($163 and $159 million, respectively), food imports in relation to total imports fell off sharply, from 26.7 per cent in 1952 to 20.4 per cent in 1958.[37] Batista's National Bank estimated that between 1954 and 1956 the development of import substitutes saved $70 million to $119 million in foreign exchange. State subsidies and guaranteed markets and prices clearly had a positive, if modest, effect on agricultural production.

In its program of export diversification, the Batista regime met with total failure. From 1952 to 1956 total farm exports fell from $629 million to $600 million; sugar and sugar products (excepting high-tested molasses and some minor cane derivatives) dropped from $573 million to $502 million. An expansion of coffee exports from almost nothing in 1952 to $21.5 million in 1956, together with a rise in molasses exports, prevented total exports from falling to the same degree as sugar exports. The composition of total exports remained fundamentally unaltered; in 1958 sugar exports still made up 80 per cent of total sales. The rhythm of foreign trade and the development of the internal market continued to be intimately linked to the ups and downs in the market for Cuban sugar.

On the positive side, the composition of agricultural production was more sensitive to changes in the structure of commodity prices and incomes, technological breakthroughs, and other market conditions, particularly those brought about by government subsidies and other public economic policies. Moreover, Cuban agriculture became more intensive in character. Although more land was brought under cultivation during the two decades prior to the 1959 revolution, and although there was an expansion of the total rural labor force, the rate of growth of capital (in the form of land improvement investments, agricultural machinery, and so forth) outpaced both the growth of new land and the labor force.[38]

[37] Cuba, Ministerio de Hacienda, Dirección General de Estadísticas, *Comercio Exterior* (Havana, 1951–1952; 1952–1953; 1953–1954; 1954–1955; 1955–1956; 1956–1957; 1957–1958).

[38] From 1935–1939 to 1958, total agricultural output rose by nearly 35 per cent. Excluding sugar production, output rose by almost 40 per cent (Leon G. Mears, "Cuba's Agriculture: Four Years Under the Revolutionary Regime,"

The chief historical significance of Batista's agricultural development programs, however, was not confined to the 1950's. Their real importance was that they conditioned the Cuban people to accept a more prominent government role in the island's economy and, at the same time, raised the expectations of the rural masses. Their main impact was subjective, on consciousness and attitudes. In addition, deepening involvement of the state in the private economy placed an increasingly larger share of the island's economic assets in the hands of the public and quasi-public institutions. This provided one basis for the rapid movement into socialism in 1959–1961.

[10]

Limitations on the effectiveness of Batista's agricultural development program stemmed from the modes of agricultural organization and the rural social class and political structures. These limitations appeared to be of three kinds, the first economic and the last two political, but the first is also reducible to a political limitation.

Foreign Agriculture [January 1, 1963], p. 4). Agricultural growth was due to an expansion of the rural labor force, the stock of capital available to farmers, the amount of land under cultivation, and the quality of employed capital.

Total area under cultivation rose from about 1.8 million hectares in 1931 to roughly 2.3 million hectares in 1958, an increase of about 30 per cent. Labor inputs increased by about 18 per cent; in 1931, the agricultural labor force consisted of 728,000 persons, and in 1958, of 860,000 workers. Estimates of capital inputs are completely lacking. On the basis of very partial data, however, one can safely conclude that the stock of capital rose by at least as much as the expansion of the labor force.

For example, in 1945 there were only 1,888 tractors in Cuba. By 1957, imports had raised the total to 19,700 tractors (Dorta-Duque, *op. cit.*, Table 26, p. 73). With regard to trucks and other agricultural equipment, the order of magnitude of change was probably more or less similar. From 1949 to 1958, a period during which imports were expanding, the proportion of fixed capital good imports employed in agriculture to total fixed capital good imports remained unchanged at about 6 per cent (*Memoria, 1957–1958*).

These data make it clear that Cuban agriculture was becoming more intensive over time, in the sense that more labor and capital were employed per hectare under cultivation. There may also have been some substitution of capital for labor during this period. At the very least, the stress on rice cultivation altered somewhat the composition of output in favor of capital-intensive farming.

Since there are no reliable data on the factor share of income originating in

The economic limitation springs from the cartelization of the industry, monopoly controls in cattle ranching, and various irrationalities in the cultivation of other crops. These rigidified prevailing mode of production and hardened the pattern of land use. They slowed down the process of replacing imports with home-produced commodities and prevented the diversification of exports altogether, thus linking the fortunes of Cuban society more closely to the world market for Cuban sugar. Sugar cultivation retained the largest corner of cultivated farmland and the major share of the expanding area under crops. In absolute terms, sugar cultivation expanded from 1940 to 1958; in relative terms, it held its own. Moreover, there was no significant change in the proportion of national income orginating in the sugar sector, which averaged slightly less than 25 per cent after the period of World War II. Faster economic progress could be made in a planned economy in which other branches of the economy could be sealed off from the effects of short-run fluc-

---

agriculture, it is impossible to estimate the marginal product of each factor. Since the percentage increase in land (30 per cent) and the rise in labor inputs (18 per cent)—although probably not the rate of growth of capital—were less than the rate of growth of output (35 per cent), there may have been increasing returns to scale. Also, the expansion of output may have partly resulted from superior capital, management, and labor inputs. Some evidence suggests that this was indeed the case. Had Cuban agriculture been subject to increasing returns to scale, it is likely that the average-size Cuban farm, together with the average-size area under cultivation, would have been larger in 1958 than in 1931. In fact, the trend was in the opposite direction. Area in farms rose by about 53 per cent and area under cultivation rose by roughly 33 per cent. Meanwhile, the number of farms nearly doubled (Dorta-Duque, *op. cit.*, Table 5, p. 20). In 1931, there were 87,396 farms, probably an underestimate since many farms in remote Oriente Province were not counted. In 1958, there were about 170,000 farms. The size of the average Cuban farm fell from 75.9 hectares in 1931 to 59.2 hectares in 1958.

Actually, these over-all averages lose much of their significance once it is recalled that landholding patterns were polarized in the twentieth century. Thus, some sectors may have benefited from increasing returns, while others may not have. In 1899, the average Cuban farm comprised 58 hectares, nearly the same as the 1958 figure (United States War Department, Office, Director of the Census of Cuba, *Report on the Census of Cuba, 1899* [Washington, 1900], p. 14). In the first quarter of the century, increasing returns in cane cultivation encouraged the growth of the sugar latifundium and widened the disparity between large and small farms. Meanwhile, inheritance laws splin-

tuations in sugar exports, or which was guaranteed stable sugar sales overseas at fixed prices.

Another economic limitation and source of backwardness was "superspecialization" in the export sectors. International demand, at times seemingly unlimited in the past, promoted a far-reaching division of labor in sugar and tobacco, destroyed the mixed agriculture of the nineteenth century, and ruled out a new and advanced mixed agriculture in the present century. From the standpoint of the individual or corporate grower, superspecialization was rational and profitable; from that of the society as a whole, it was prodigiously wasteful. Land and labor were utilized badly; sugar workers remained prisoners of their technical backwardness; compared with a mixed agriculture there was little possibility for widening and generalizing labor skills, and less opportunity to conserve foreign ex-

---

tered smaller farms, especially those of tenants. From 1931 to 1956, for example, there was an increase in the number of tenants of about 100 per cent. Total area cultivated by tenants, however, remained the same. Nor was the process of fragmentation confined to the tobacco sector, where tenancy predominated; Nelson cites an example of a coffee farm comprising 1,650 acres which was divided among twelve heirs (*op. cit.*, p. 128). Whether or not landholding patterns polarized further between 1945 and 1958 is unknown. Inheritance laws probably continued to fragment the smaller farms, but there is no evidence that the sugar or cattle latifundium expanded further after the 1930's.

The fact that Cuban farmers employed more fertilizers and irrigation facilities confirms our conclusion that the island's agriculture tended to be more intensive over time. In 1945, only 3 per cent of cultivated land was irrigated. The great drought of that year generated large investments in water control, a trend that was checked by satisfactory rainfalls in 1946 and 1947. Nevertheless, by 1959, 10 per cent of cultivated land was irrigated (Dorta-Duque, *op. cit.*, Table 5, p. 20; and author's interview with Jacques Chonchol, United Nations representative in Cuba June, 13, 1960). Moreover, fertilizer sales doubled between 1954 and 1957. Most of the increased use of fertilizer was in cane cultivation, where there was an attempt to reduce high-cost labor requirements, chiefly on the plantations.

Not only was there a tendency for Cuban farming to become more intensive, there was also some flexibility regarding the composition of output. The cross-elasticities of supply between cane land and grazing land, on the one hand, and other crops, on the other, was quite low. But in other branches of production, cross-elasticities were relatively high. These were all relatively weak tendencies, however, and failed to help Cuba raise per capita income or per capita output of agricultural commodities.

change for industrialization. Thus, the social costs of superspecialization far exceeded the costs borne by individual farmers and
rural corporations.[39]

Superspecialization, the absence of a mixed agriculture, and rural
backwardness were mirrored in the retardation of agricultural research, education, and extension facilities. "Little progress has been
made in agriculture in [these] basic fields. Six Provincial agricultural schools have a variable enrollment that seldom exceeds 100 in
any one school. Funds and equipment are scarce." [40] In the only
real agricultural research center on the island, activity was often in-
terrupted by lack of funds and administrative changes. The so-
called Sugar Cane Experiment Station in Matanzas cultivated ordinary cane to pay its operating expenses and grew little else. At the
university level there were two faculties of agriculture offering five
years of courses, only one of which covered the important area of
agricultural economics. Cuba's backwardness in these fields was
chiefly due to the rural cartels and the system of monopoly controls,
which limited the demand for output-increasing innovations and
technologies and, to a lesser degree, cost-reducing technical
changes. But scanty technical knowledge and a shortage of well-
trained agronomists and technicians had in turn an independent,
adverse effect on the development of the rural economy.

Beside these economic limitations on the realization of Cuba's agricultural potential must be placed other limits that stemmed from
the structure of the island's economic classes and were manifested
on the level of national politics. As we have seen, the structure of
classes in rural Cuba was due to the penetration of foreign capital,
the concentration of wealth, and the development of an agricultural
export economy. Owners and tenants slowly developed their own

[39] Farm operators in the export sector were not interested in a mixed agriculture. Over 85 per cent of the incomes of cane planters was earned by sales
of cane. Tobacco farmers obtained 75 per cent of their incomes by tobacco
sales. These proportions were lower in other branches of the rural economy. The
division of labor and specialization was far less developed in branches of farming producing for home consumption.

[40] United States, Department of Commerce, Bureau of Foreign Commerce,
Investment in Cuba (Washington, 1956), p. 30.

organizations, which were partly economic and partly political in character. The big landowners and sugar companies also had their own organizations. Whether or not the leaders of these organizations were openly allied with the government in power, after the mid-1930's the latter was compelled to throw important economic benefits their way or court serious political trouble. This was the chief reason why Cuban governments laid great stress on "redistributive" economic policies, as opposed to policies that would create incentives to expand and diversify agricultural production. Seen in this light, the quota systems, guaranteed prices, and so on were *political* phenomena. These redistributive policies had unfavorable economic implications which were not susceptible to economic solutions. The solutions to the problems of Cuba's rural economy were therefore first and foremost political in character.

Within the framework of the complex net of redistributive public policy, however, big capital had more or less its own way. Political initiative was largely in the hands of the large banks, the sugar companies, the cattle barons, and the very largest *colonos*. The Cuban Sugar Stabilization Institute (ICEA), which made key economic decisions for the entire island regarding quotas, sales, reserves, and prices, was dominated by the spokesmen of the sugar companies and the larger *colonos*.[41] Following the Batista coup in 1952, ICEA consolidated its position by seizing control of the Ministry of Agriculture, which it then systematically weakened. In a position to manipulate artificially reserve stocks of sugar in the classic monopolistic pattern, ICEA was operated strictly in the interests of the big landowners and speculators. Speculators also used the Coffee Stabilization Institute to earn windfall profits. ICEA perhaps damaged the Cuban economy most decisively by constantly reinforcing the memory of the great speculative sugar booms of 1917–1920 and 1939–1948; psychologically there was no break from the speculative pattern of the past. Combined with other limitations on rural development, this explains why the island's physical and technical infrastructure continued to be oriented toward the sugar industry, and

[41] Raúl Cepero Bonilla, *Política Azucarera* (*1952–1958*) (México D.F., 1958), p. 15. For a description of the operation of ICEA, see pp. 34–35, p. 73.

why there were no important structural changes in transport, marketing facilities, storage depots, and electrical power distribution.

The third general limitation on the expansion of Cuban agriculture was derived from the special nature of the island's relations with the United States. The ICEA, the Mill Owners' Association, the Cattlemen's Association, the banks, and other private and public economic organizations and agencies with United States representatives or members were points of entry into Cuba for North American interests.

The significance of this was twofold: first, the Cuban economy was fragmented internally and integrated into the structure of United States agricultural (and also manufacturing, mining, and financial) corporations. Economic resources were thus immobile between branches of the Cuban economy. Second, the United States was Cuba's main trading partner; the pattern of trade and indirectly the composition of production generally remained oriented to United States-Cuban political-economic relations. We have seen that the volume of sugar sales to the United States was determined unilaterally by the United States Congress; the island was thus prevented from competing in its largest market.[42]

---

[42] Owners of United States mills and land in Cuba had some say in the determination of the quota, and thus Cuban producers (whose interests largely coincided with United States owners) had informal "representatives" in Congress. On the issue of the quota, Cubans also had allies in United States exporters, in whose interests it was to raise incomes and thus demand in Cuba. That this alliance ordinarily failed to win over the combined interests of domestic beet sugar producers, other offshore producers of cane sugar, and others interested in restricting Cuban imports is easily shown. The Hawley-Smoot Tariff of 1930 raised tariffs on Cuban sugar, worsening the island's situation. The Jones-Costigan Law of 1934 introduced the quota system. To determine Cuba's share of the market, an average of any three years over the period 1925–1933 was to be chosen. The United States chose the years 1931–1933, the period when Cuba's share was lowest. Once again, in 1948 Cuban exports to the United States were reduced when the United States gave the island only 28 per cent of total supply, together with 98 per cent of any unexpected increases. In 1953, Cuban exports fell again when offshore suppliers were handed increased quotas at Cuba's expense. Finally, in 1956, Cuba's participation in increases in consumption was reduced from 98 per cent to 30 per cent. Historically, the real importance of Cuba for the United States was not merely as a sugar supplier, but as a source from which deliveries could be adjusted in maintain price stability in the United States.

Although Cuban sugar entered the United States market at a premium price, except during brief periods when the world market price exceeded the government-supported domestic United States price, it is likely that free access to the mainland market would have meant a much larger volume of sales, and therefore a larger volume of total sugar earnings. Cuban sugar was potentially able to outcompete mainland and other offshore supplies. Under a system of free trade, an expansion in the volume of exports would probably have more than offset a decline in sugar prices.

Whether or not Cuba's sugar earnings would have been greater under free trade as compared with the existing quota system, the mere fact that the United States unilaterally determined sugar sales in the mainland market had highly unfavorable consequences for Cuba's agriculture. First, we have seen that a large portion of Cuba's cultivated land was held as reserve cane against sudden and unexpected changes in the United States demand for the island's sugar. To be sure, if there had been a competitive market for sugar, some lands would have been held in reserve against ordinary market fluctuations. United States control, however, substantially increased the degree of market uncertainty, and thus more land was retained in reserve cane than was necessary. Cuba's reserve cane land entailed much economic waste, a large part of which can be placed at the doorstep of the United States government.

Secondly, as we have also seen, the United States government alone decided the amount of refined sugar that Cuba was allowed to sell in its northern market. This imposed on Cuba a large economic loss in the form of income and employment opportunities. That it would have paid Cuba to refine her own sugar is borne out by nearly all the evidence: transport costs would have minimized because sugar is a "weight-loser" in higher stages of production; plant space and shipping and transportation facilities would have been economized; and power capacity would have been more fully utilized.[43]

---

[43] It can be argued that continental refining rationed scarce Cuban capital. But was this efficient? The only study available showed that there was no significant difference between refining costs in Cuba and the United States (United States, Tariff Commission, *Report to the President on Sugar,* Report

Thirdly, restrictions on crude sugar exports reinforced the traditional pattern of agriculture which yielded low returns to the Cuban economy. In the domestic economy the quota system profoundly inhibited economic efficiency and growth; the United States quota further hardened the pattern of land use, discouraged new investments and innovations, and thwarted the introduction of a scientific, mixed agriculture. This was the indirect, inevitable outcome of the system of market controls imposed from within and without. Until the 1930's, United States policy deliberately discouraged the diversification of Cuban agriculture in order to maintain a favorable market for United States food and raw materials exports.[44] After the 1930's, the quota system inhibited agricultural diversification; the effects were induced, but no less significant. Finally, the short-run needs of the United States also conditioned its Cuban policy. To take an example, with the materialization of a large shortage of jute supplies during World War II, the United States helped to establish in Cuba the Cooperative Fiber Commission to expand the production of a substitute commodity, kenaf. When jute supplies were normalized after the war, the United States lost all interest in the incipient industry. In the early 1950's, however, when underdeveloped countries were again receiving attention from the United States, Point Four aid was granted to Cuban kenaf producers.

Viewed in the context of these political-economic limitations on agricultural development, it is not difficult to understand why pre-1959 solutions to the "agricultural problem" were timid and conservative. Invariably, economic rather than political solutions were proposed and applied; invariably, these failed to "solve" the problem. There was, for example, the "all-out" attack on the problem of seasonal unemployment mounted in the early 1950's. The National Economic Board put together a catalogue of plans: public works, new

No. 73, second series [Washington, 1934], p. 109). In 1960, of the island's 160 mills, only 20 had refineries. There were also two small independent refineries, but total capacity was only 7,800 metric tons daily ("Hay que modernizar la industria azucarera," *Divulgación*, 1, No. 6 [1960], pp. 48–49).

[44] William Appleton Williams, *Cuba, Castro, and the United States* (New York, 1962), p. 15, citing a Cordell Hull memorandum.

rural housing, the promotion of national tourism, and a wide range of employment-creating investments.[45] Nowhere in the so-called Minimum Economic Program, however, was there mention of the obvious and highly efficient possibilities of raising sugar yields to release cane land and pasture for a diversified agriculture. The reason is apparent: such a line of action would conflict with powerful, well-organized, and highly articulate rural interests.

Despite moderately successful attempts to diversify Cuban agriculture and the construction of some cold storage plants and processing mills, despite the early construction of the central highway and tariff protection and subsidies, despite all of the "economic" solutions to the rural problem, despite the rhetoric of generations of ambitious Cuban politicians, public policy altogether failed to come to grips with the question of land reform, rural monopoly in its varied forms, political relations with the United States, and, indeed, the entire political structure of the island.

[45] Cuba, Junta Nacional de Economía, *Programa económico mínimo* (Havana, May 13, 1952), p. 52.

[5]

The Agrarian Revolution

[1]

During the first four years of Fidel Castro's rule there was a deep-going, irreversible agrarian revolution in Cuba. It was partly the consequence of the application of policies put forth in the past, not only by Castro, but also by politicians, administrators, and technicians associated with the old regime. It was partly a supervention, or the response to the day-to-day exigencies arising in the context of general revolutionary upheaval. Whatever the exact combination of reasons, the agrarian revolution was above all a process, a development, not an episode or event.

The "problems concerning land" headed the catalogue of burning economic questions and issues that Castro drew up in his speech during the Moncada trial.[1] As we have seen, agrarian reform figured importantly in the program of the 26th of July Movement. More significantly, Castro underlined the importance of rural reform and development by designating the Agrarian Reform Law of May, 1959, as the revolution's "basic law."[2] And a few weeks after the agrarian reform was passed, Castro formulated his "ten points of peasant redemption," which included promises of land ownership, low interest charges, guaranteed prices, new housing, nonprofit stores, and farm-to-market roads.

Actions as well as words pointed up the central place of agrarian reform in the revolution. More than two months before Castro

---

[1] Fidel Castro, *History Will Absolve Me* (New York, 1959), *passim*.

[2] *Ley de la Reforma Agraria,* Article 18 in *Gaceta Oficial de la República de Cuba,* Edición extraordinaria especial, June 3, 1959.

seized power, the Rebel Army decreed the first agrarian reform law, Law Number Three.[3] One article of the law promised all farm operators cultivating fewer than 27.2 hectares a plot of land of at least that size free of charge, a provision incorporated into the Agrarian Reform Law of May, 1959. The law also stated the intentions of the Revolutionary Government to limit the maximum size farm holdings controlled by one man or corporation. In practice, some land was distributed to small farmers in the territories occupied by the Rebel Army in 1958. In 1959, after the seizure of power, the Rebel Army also turned over to small peasants a portion of the 350,000 hectares of prime farmland taken from key Batista supporters and collaborators.

Until the last half of 1959, however, the vast reaches of Cuba's sugar, cattle, rice, and tobacco lands remained under traditional private ownership and control. Few Cubans were able to anticipate how far-reaching the May, 1959, law would be until its exact provisions were published. Public debate was avoided, and the law was drafted by men close to Castro, but who did not have Cabinet positions in the first revolutionary government. When the law was finally disclosed, a storm broke over the island and the revolution quickly began to polarize. The agrarian reform was the first and most important "class issue" of the revolution. It was the immediate reason for the resignation of many Cabinet members, an indirect cause of the purge of the traditional labor union leadership, and the first important issue to divide Cuba and the United States. In nearly every respect a revolutionary measure, the agrarian reform had ramifications that no one could possibly have foreseen at the time.

[2]

For the functionaries of the new National Institute of Agrarian Reform (INRA), most of whom were drawn from the officer corps and ranks of the Rebel Army, the law was less a mandate than a challenge. At INRA headquarters in Havana and the field offices of the twenty-eight agricultural development zones set up under the

---

[3] *Ley No. 3 de 10 oct. 1958,* Departamento Legal, Sección Asesoría de Las Delegaciones de Zonas Reforma Agraria (Havana, 1959).

law, little was known of the existing division of farmland, and dependable records of land rights and rental values were nonexistent. The 1946 Agricultural Census was out of date, and the form in which the statistics were available rendered them useless for practical purposes; the unit of enumeration, the *finca*, was an operational not an ownership unit. Aerial surveys undertaken by the old Development Bank in 1955 had completely mapped only one province, and even as late as 1961, fewer than one-third of Cuba's farms had been photographed from the air.[4] The absence of statistics and maps slowed down the distribution of expropriated farmland, but not the pace of expropriation itself. A conference between small tenants and INRA officials in July, 1960, at the institute's headquarters in Matanzas, at which the author was present, prefigured many similar meetings. With the help of a new aerial map, land allotments were studied and debated, although the properties to be disposed of had been purchased or seized many months before.

To obtain usable information about the size and tenure distribution of Cuba's farms, the law ordered all landlords subject to expropriation under the law to disclose the extent and division of their holdings. As a check against these disclosures, INRA asked tenants to submit boundary information. Landowners presumably were to be guided by Articles 1, 2, and 6. The first article proscribed properties in excess of 30 *caballerías*, or 402.6 hectares; Article 2 made exceptions in cases of especially productive land. On sugar cane and rice lands, the article placed a 100-*caballería* limit, provided that yields were at least 50 per cent greater than the national average. INRA could make exceptions for other farms as well. Later, INRA's Legal Department disclosed that 2,873 proprietors owned 3,602 farms comprising more than 30 *caballerías* each.[5]

But from a political standpoint perhaps Article 6 was the most important of all, though at first it was the least known. This article au-

---

[4] Casto Feragut, "Algunos comentarios sobre determinados puntos del informe provisional del equipo Latino-americano de Reforma Agraria" (La Paz, Bolivia, November, 1960), p. 5 (manuscript). Antonio Núñez Jiménez, *Informe sobre dos años de reforma agraria* (Havana, May 17, 1961), p. 7.

[5] Jacques Chonchol, "La reforma agraria Cubana (I parte)," *Panorama Económico* (Santiago de Chile), 15, No. 227 (January, 1962), p. 18.

thorized the expropriation of any property occupied by a tenant, sharecropper, or squatter cultivating less than five *caballerías*. The political implications of Article 6 were far-reaching. Nearly 28,000 property owners leased land to small farmers, and every one of these landlords was a potential target. But the article was not enforced systematically at the time. If it had been, an alliance between the large and middle landlords might have been forged that would have included over 30,000 rural families, or more than one-half of the island's farm-property owners. Such an alliance might have been powerful enough to place the future of the Reform Law itself in doubt.[6] A number of demonstrations did take place before the government clarified its position, including a protest in May, 1959, staged by five hundred small and middle property owners in Pinar del Río. Many of these protesters were members of the National Association of Tobacco Growers, which supported the general lines of the Reform Law before and after its passage.[7]

INRA failed to enforce Article 6 systematically, partly for political reasons and partly for economic reasons. Over 2 million hectares, or 20 per cent of Cuba's farmland and probably 4 per cent of the island's cultivated land, would have been expropriated, placing on the Reform Institute an intolerable administrative burden and putting into doubt the first optimistic forecasts of agricultural production. About 6 million hectares were actually confiscated, expropriated, or purchased by INRA from mid-1959 to mid-1963, much less than the 8.5 million hectares theoretically subject to expropriation.[8] Relatively few small- and medium-sized farms were attached,

[6] The 1946 Census of Agriculture reported 48,792 owner-operated and 9,342 administrator-operated farms. The latter figure grossly overestimated the number of owners; for example, only 83 corporations and individuals owned 3,129 sugar farms. On the other hand, there were a number of absentee owners who leased their properties and who do not show up in either statistic. A rough estimate would place the number of Cuban landowners in 1946 at about 50,000. The expansion of owner-operated farms was probably somewhat less than proportional to the expansion of the total number of farms during the years 1946–1959. I estimate the number of owners in 1959 at 60,000.

[7] The demonstrators warned that they would face execution before surrendering their land (*The Havana Post*, May 27, 1959; July 10, 1959).

[8] See Appendix A.

and almost 400,000 hectares in holdings of more than 30 *caballerías* remained in private hands.[9]

No one, however, was left with more than 50 *caballerías*, despite the statute's clear intent to the contrary. Only in the case of sugar cane farming was there an obvious reason for this limitation. Cuba's best cane land was in large plantations, and their yields raised the national average. Only 116 farms between 30 and 100 *caballerías* in size, none of them larger than 50 *caballerías*, surpassed this average by 50 per cent and, by way of Article 2, escaped expropriation.

INRA provincial and zone administrators encountered little serious political resistance on the part of owners and farm managers to the "interventions" (seizures) and expropriations of agricultural properties. In the first place, less than 5 per cent of the island's landowners were actually divested of their properties. For another thing, there was little of the intense land hunger that exploded during the Mexican, Russian, and Chinese revolutions. Only a "few impatient peasants attempted to invade some large landed estates" during the early months of 1959,[10] although the government, to be on the safe side, decreed in February that titles would be denied any peasant who had seized land without authorization after January 1, 1959. Another check on spontaneous land appropriations was the isolation of many tenants and squatters and the absence of contiguous properties belonging to the doomed estates.

The fate of the Cuban countryside in this period was literally in the hands of the INRA provincial and zone leadership. The Communist party was counseling moderation, besides being under attack by important Fidelistas, and did not figure importantly in any stage of the reform.[11] The revolutionary leadership also lacked confidence in existing state organisms, and granted the old Ministry of Agriculture little autonomy. Moreover, INRA headquarters in Havana was understaffed in an attempt to avoid an urban-based bureaucracy. The central government neglected to supervise the actions of local officials in a coherent and systematic manner. Thus,

[9] *Ibid.*

[10] *Revolución*, March 26, 1961, reporting speech by Fidel Castro.

[11] Author's interview with Felipe Pazos, Washington, D.C., June 6, 1962.

the speed and character of the reform was uneven, varying from province to province and zone to zone, depending on how the official in charge personally evaluated the situation. Yet, despite some "confusion uncertainty, and over-militancy" on the part of INRA cadres,[12] everywhere there was "extraordinary tranquility." [13]

Although the landlords, many of them residents of Havana or the provincial cities, failed to offer any physical resistance to the agrarian reform, many groups were highly vocal against some or all of its provisions. The cattlemen pledged a "fight to the death" against the agrarian reform, but there is no case known to the author of physical violence accompanying an act of land seizure. Other groups that protested the law in whole or in part were the National Association of Cuban Rice Growers, the sugar mill operators, and the *colonos*.

More important than these immediate and somewhat feeble protests was the economic resistance to the reform. Cuban landlords waged an economic war against INRA on many and varied fronts. In the cattle industry, there was a crisis of demand and a step-up in the rate of slaughter. Few large tobacco farmers prepared the land for the following year's crop, and many cane farms operated by the mills failed to plant new seedlings. There was a general shortage of private credit created by the uncertainty of future owner-tenant relations, and many larger owners began to neglect their 1959–1960 crops.[14]

These economic considerations helped to shape INRA's "over-militancy." In the context of the "ever-present fear that something [would] prevent the completion of land reform (cf. Puerto Rico since 1950)" which "motivated the administrators of INRA to make

[12] Author's interview with Ernesto Guevara, Havana, September 4, 1961.
[13] Author's interview with Jacques Chonchol, Havana, July 10, 1960. A letter from Chonchol (United Nations agricultural adviser to Cuba from the beginning of the agrarian reform until the end of 1961) to Thomas Carroll (who was with the FAO at the time) stressed the extent of the authority of local INRA personnel (February 9, 1960). This observation, and that the social revolution in Cuba had a peaceful character, were confirmed by the author's impressions during his travels through Cuba in the summer of 1960.
[14] One of the reasons INRA became the giant organization that it did by the end of 1959 was that it had to provide working capital to thousands of private farmers, most of them tenants.

daring promises and launch out on even more daring experiments," [15] the approaching agricultural crisis compelled INRA leaders to put aside any fears and doubts of the viability of the law that they may have entertained earlier. The reform which Castro had said would take three years to accomplish was in its main outlines completed within twelve months.

[3]

Cattle ranchers in large, sparsely settled Camaguey Province were the first to surrender their land to the government. Economic forces gave over-all direction to Cuban agrarian reform, and nowhere was this more true than in the island's extensive ranching business.

The Agrarian Reform Law, the large cattlemen asserted, would do "irreparable damage to our country." [16] In an extraordinary session called by the Cattlemen's Association on May 31, 1959, nearly one thousand ranchers voiced sharp protests against the law. They claimed that it would discourage foreign investment, annul free enterprise, and destroy the private property system. They also blamed the law for the growing crisis in the cattle industry.

The crisis was one of demand. Almost overnight the large ranchers suspended their purchases of yearlings and calves, although some sales did occur at unofficial rock-bottom prices.[17] The medium-sized ranchers, who bought calves from the smaller ranchers and sold yearlings to the giant cattle farms, suddenly were deprived of their customary markets. The demand for calves fell accordingly, putting the small ranchers into a bind. With fixed official prices, the market for more than one million yearlings and calves, well over one-half of Cuba's total stock, completely dried up.[18] Simulta-

---

[15] Thomas Mathews, "The Agrarian Reform in Cuba and Puerto Rico," *Revista de Ciencias Sociales, Número Especial sobre el Caribe,* 4, No. 1 (March, 1960), p. 122.

[16] Cited in *The Havana Post,* May 26, 1959.

[17] *Ibid.,* June 24, 1959.

[18] In 1952, there were more than 1.6 million yearlings and calves in Cuba, but a large number of these animals, possibly as many as 600,000, were owned by the large ranchers themselves.

neously, the giant ranches hurriedly liquidated their assets, pushing up the slaughter rate of three-year-olds to an unprecedented level.

The government could not step into the market because INRA did not have any land on which to fatten the animals. In a sweeping resolution authorized in late June, INRA therefore ordered its provincial chief in Camaguey to seize all cattle ranches of more than 100 *caballerías*. By November, few ranches in excess of 50 *caballerías* remained in private hands. This was the first major expression of "over-militancy" by local INRA officials.

Had the institute not moved rapidly against the ranchers, INRA would have been compelled to regain their confidence, possibly by ceding them secure tenure rights or other guarantees. In this event, the political initiative would have shifted away from the Revolutionary Government, and the Agrarian Reform Law, which proscribed the latifundio and was held to be the cornerstone of economic reform by the revolutionary leadership, would have been seriously discredited. At the very least, the government may have feared that such a course might undermine its popular support. The big ranchers might also have been partially disarmed by offers of prompt and handsome compensation for lands and cattle which might be seized under the law. Such offers would have probably reduced the rate of slaughter, but they clearly would not have tempted the cattlemen to step up their purchases of young cows.

The demand crisis probably worried the government more than anything else. INRA was not overly concerned with the rising rate of slaughter and even passively encouraged an expansion of beef production and consumption in order to deliver immediate economic benefits to the Cuban population and help to consolidate the new government's political position. In 1958, only 850,000 older yearlings and three-year-olds were butchered. In 1959, the total jumped to 950,000, not including an estimated 65,000 cows, reflecting the ranchers' desire to reduce their herds. In the following two years, total production rose to 2 million animals, although in 1961 less beef reached the market than in 1960.[19] Meanwhile, the aver-

[19] From 1959 to 1961, 200,000 cows were killed, and we assume that an equal number were killed each year (Felipe Torres, "Algunas Cuestiones sobre

age weight per slaughtered animal dropped by more than 10 per cent, indicating that more younger animals were butchered. The government failed to halt the reduction of the island's herds until the fall of 1961, when a representative from the new Integrated Revolutionary Organizations (ORI) was assigned to each slaughterhouse to stop the killing of cows.[20]

It is true that INRA attempted to limit beef production early in 1960, but the institute's new orders were not overly restrictive. In February, for example, INRA merely clamped down on the slaughter of yearlings under thirty months of age, and the statistics of animal weights given above indicate that the new policy met with little success. Beside the relatively weak attempts to reduce production must be placed two facts. First, as we shall see, many ranchers escaped the INRA's attention until well into 1960. Second, as late as the spring of 1961, private slaughterhouses accounted for two-thirds of Cuba's meat production.[21] These units could have been absorbed by the institute's Consolidated Meat Enterprise, a state organism set up the year before. Thus, both the buyers' and sellers' side of the market remained largely private in character, and for this reason, government controls were easily circumvented. Even later on, during the first quarter of 1961, when all or nearly all of the large ranches were under INRA's control, the number of slaughtered animals was double that during the first quarter of 1959.[22]

For these reasons, it is difficult to resist the conclusion that the

---

el desarrollo de la ganadería en Camaguey," *Cuba Socialista*, 2, No. 8 [April, 1962], p. 43). Two million head of all types were slaughtered in 1960–1961. Unpublished INRA estimates showed that one million yearlings and three-year-olds alone (excluding cows and calves) were killed in 1960, indicating that beef production was somewhat lower in 1961 than in 1960.

[20] "Discusión del Discurso de Fidel Castro sobre la ganadería," *Cuba Socialista*, 2, No. 6 (February 1963), p. 136. Ranchers who were left with some animals and from thirty to fifty *caballerías* of pasture were also encouraged to liquidate their stocks because they sometimes lost their buildings and equipment to INRA and were left with uneconomic units.

[21] "Ganaremos," *Trabajo Cuba*, 2, No. 3 (March, 1961), p. 69.

[22] This is true at least in the two provinces for which data are available. In the first quarter of 1959, cattle production was 17,174 head and 22,899 head in Las Villas and Oriente Provinces, respectively. In the first quarter of 1961, production was 40,692 head and 49,603 head, respectively.

new government as a matter of policy encouraged the expansion of beef production, risking damaging reductions in the stock of cattle.[23] At least it is certain that vigorous measures were taken neither against the private ranchers nor the slaughterhouses until well into 1961. If INRA was less concerned about the production and consumption of beef than the problem of the demand crisis, its reluctance to guarantee large compensation awards is readily explicable. Unwilling to compromise the authority of the new government by modifying the Reform Law to suit the ranchers, INRA was compelled to pursue the radical policy of seizing direct control over more pasture land than was originally intended.

By July, 1959, 400 of Cuba's largest ranches, owned by forty U.S. and Cuban companies, were seized. By the end of the year, another 50 or so ranches had fallen under INRA's direction.[24] One year later, the institute's Cattle Administration occupied a total of 900 ranches, the vast majority of the over 1,050 ranches comprising more than five hundred head each (reported 1952 cattle census), and covering well over one million hectares. At least one-half of Cuba's largest ranches were retained by their owners until 1960.[25]

The seizures of 1959 went far beyond the provisions of the Reform Law in order to resolve the market crisis that followed the announcement of the law itself. The expropriations of 1960 were motivated by new developments: by the summer of 1960 it was clear that a planned agriculture was incompatible with private ownership of the remaining key sectors of the industry.

[23] INRA was aware that small ranchers held many of their cattle off the market at the prevailing low prices. However, because these ranchers, who expected to retain and in fact held on to their lands, owned relatively few three-year-olds, the effect of their actions on the aggregate rate of slaughter was minimal.

[24] One source estimates that 475 farms were seized or bought in 1959 (*Revista*, Banco Nacional de Cuba [November–December, 1959], p. 1,210).

[25] This conclusion is confirmed by the fact that in May, 1960, only 605,000 head of cattle had been assigned to either the new cane cooperatives or to what were called the directly administered farms of INRA (later to become people's farms) organized on the old cattle ranches. One year later, the public sector owned 1,154,428 head, or nearly double the amount owned in mid-1960.

[4]

That some kind of planned rural economy was favored by the revolutionary leadership was made apparent by INRA's policy concerning Cuba's sugar lands. From the earliest days of the revolution, great stress was given economic development in general, and the expansion and diversification of agriculture in particular. In the minds of many planners, the sugar lands were the key to this plan because they comprised so much of Cuba's productive soils and were used so irrationally, and because a large supply of seasonally unemployed labor was available to work them.

On July 5, 1959, Castro explained that neither money nor personnel were available at that time to follow through on those provisions of the Reform Law that would affect the lands of the sugar companies, but that INRA would take over these properties in 1960 after the harvest was in.[26] Apparently the delay temporarily calmed the fears of the National Association of Sugar Mill Owners, because after lodging a number of protests with the Revolutionary Government over the feasibility and equity of the law, the group seemed to fall into line by mid-July, when it admitted that "agrarian reform was indispensable for industrialization." [27] Many association members failed to plant new seedlings, however, and much "administration cane" was cultivated more poorly than ever.

By early 1960, progovernment newspapers began to anticipate the expropriation of the sugar *latifundio,* and in February about 65,000 *cabillerías* of U.S. sugar land was in the process of being legally taken over. The formation of the General Administration of Cane Cooperatives on March 3, 1960, provided an adminstration basis for the collectivization of the sugar lands. Detailed General Regulations for the cooperatives were hammered out in discussions between INRA and the National Federation of Sugar Workers (FNTA) and guided the formation of many cooperatives in the first half of 1960.[28] The Revolutionary Government also anticipated being cut

[26] *The Havana Post,* July 7, 1959.

[27] *Ibid.,* July 11, 1959.

[28] Cuba's first cane cooperatives were formed in February, 1960, on the old San Ramon properties in Oriente, which had produced about 10 million *arrobas* of "administration cane" annually (*ibid.,* February 18, 1960). Twenty-six

off from the mainland market by accelerating shipments of sugar to the United States during the first months of 1960.[29] Thus, while the immediate cause of Law 890, which authorized the expropriation of North American sugar properties on July 6, 1960, was the withdrawal by the United States on July 5 of the Cuban quota for the remainder of 1960, the groundwork for the expropriation was laid much earlier. It is obvious that the nationalization of United States sugar properties cannot be attributed to United States action against Cuba, except with respect to the precise timing of the seizures. Prepared long before President Eisenhower barred Cuban sugar from the United States, the expropriations were either ideologically motivated or economically necessary or both, and would have been carried out had Eisenhower's order never been signed.

Neither the mill owners nor the cane planters fully accepted the Agrarian Reform Law. Each group pleaded for its own special interests and, guided by the principles of the prerevolutionary special interest politics, attempted to push the advantages won under past governments one step further. The portion of the Reform Law that proscribed the *latifundio* naturally met with bitter objections from the mill owners, most of whom were large landlords themselves. They attacked the law from two directions: on practical grounds, they asserted that the agrarian reform would have "serious economic consequences on the national economy in general and the sugar industry in particular." [30] It was clear that they were referring to the potential effects of the law on new investments, particularly the flow of new foreign investments into Cuba. From an ideological standpoint, they protested that the new law did not limit itself to giving property a "social function," but rather that it deprived owners of their legitimate rights.[31] In both respects their interests and attitudes corresponded with those of the cattle ranchers.

---

cooperatives were begun on nearly 111,000 hectares of old United Fruit Company land two and one-half weeks after Eisenhower barred Cuban sugar from the United States market, but these lands were expropriated in April.

[29] Felipe Pazos, "The Economics of a Revolution: Cuba, 1959–1960," July 14, 1960, pp. 16–17 (manuscript).

[30] *The Havana Post*, May 23, 1959.

[31] *Ibid.*, June 5, 1959.

Instead of taking over all farm units comprising more than thirty *caballerías,* they proposed that agrarian reform begin with idle, untilled land and properties already owned by the Cuban government. As our analysis in the last chapter disclosed, these measures would not even have scratched the surface of the Cuban agricultural problem. The mill owners put forth painless technical solutions where political solutions were necessary.

The *colonos* also made public an alternative plan, which corresponded in part to government policy. They favored the expropriation of the sugar mill properties and supported that section of the law designed to enlarge the size of every Cuban farm to the so-called basic minimum of two *caballerías.* They also wanted the chance to purchase the land that they cultivated, but this was a less important demand; ownership rights concerned tenant cane farmers less than did opportunities to bring more land under cultivation.[32]

Fundamental to their program were two demands the agrarian reform failed to meet, one of which was in the program of the 26th of July movement. The planters called for an increase in the "permanent grinding factor" (on which grower production quotas were based) from 30,000 to 40,000 *arrobas,* and they also wanted inefficient, low-income growers relocated to the expropriated sugar mill lands. They were clearly wedded to the existing quota system and its paraphernalia of controls. As could be expected, the formation of the cane cooperatives on the old "administration cane" or plantation lands in the following year failed to win their support. Because they supported the inefficient quota system and failed to pose an alternative solution to the profound problems of low yields, inefficient techniques, and idle land, the cane growers' program also did not really come to grips with the industry's basic difficulties. Understandably, their primary interest was to enlarge their *share* of total industry earnings by further discriminating against relatively low-cost "administration cane," by enlarging their quotas, and by carving up the mill lands into uneconomic units.

There were only a handful of mill owners, and they lacked politi-

---

[32] The reason was probably that rented farms actually appeared to be more profitable than owner-operated units in sugar (Gregorio Alfaro, "The Land Tenure Situation in Cuba," November, 1959, p. 43 [manuscript]).

cal authority and stature because they had long been identified with foreign interests. Thus, the revolution could safely ignore their demands. The *colonos,* on the other hand, were a sizable class, and while INRA failed to comply with their key demands, they granted a number of benefits. First, in July, 1960, INRA abolished rents on farms of less than thirty-three hectares.[33] Second, farmers cultivating between two to five *caballerías* were allowed to purchase more land. Of the 2.8 million hectares of expropriated sugar land (much of it plains that had reverted to pasture land after 1952), about 475,000 hectares were distributed to these farmers.[34] Third, many smaller planters were brought up to the "basic minimum" of two *caballerías.* Looked at from a negative viewpoint, there was no attempt to collectivize the planters forcibly, although the largest *colonos* did balk at the agrarian reform. The Colonos Association of Cuba, whose antigovernment agitation was climaxed by an extraordinary general assembly in August, 1960, and which was dominated by the big planters, was dissolved in January, 1961.

The rural proletariat was the real key to the consolidation of the regime's power and, at least in a passive sense, gave direction to the agrarian reform. Cuba's agricultural workers, particularly the sugar workers, who outnumbered the *colonos* about five to one, were—and are—the revolution's favored class. Their main demand was for better material conditions: more employment, higher wages, schools, hospitals, recreational facilities, and so on. The vast majority were indifferent to owning their own land. Most helped to form the cane cooperatives, although the sugar workers who lived in the provincial towns and cities (perhaps one-fifth of the total) were not as "collective-minded" as the back-country workers. According to Regino Boti, Minister of Economy, in a conversation with the author, they "thought like capitalists," although, by and large, they did not want their *own* land.

While meeting the demands of the "economism" of the rural proletariat, INRA was able to turn Cuba's large-scale seasonal unem-

---

[33] As we have seen in Chapter Four, this made good economic, as well as political, sense. On farms of from two to five *caballerías,* two *caballerías* were exempted from rent (*Gaceta Oficial,* No. 135, July 14, 1960).
[34] See Appendix A.

ployment into a political advantage for the new government. Most sugar workers eagerly joined the new cane cooperatives and people's farms, which supplied off-season jobs cultivating expropriated lands, and which could, therefore, raise annual incomes of the workers without significant increases in daily wages. To the degree to which production failed to keep pace with employment, this was an inflationary policy, but it did allow the government to meet the needs of large numbers of rural workers without touching off demands for higher wages elsewhere in the economy. Wage demands and wage increases did occur in other sectors, but not as a result of agitation inspired by a high wage policy in agriculture.

INRA's sugar and cattle lands policy was clearly politically feasible, and no less important, the expropriations provided a solid foundation for the rational exploitation of the island's productive resources. By the end of 1960, the institute controlled Cuba's most productive farmland, or nearly 4 million hectares of sugar and grazing land and over 2 million hectares of rice, tobacco, and other properties. Of the island's 10 million hectares of farmland, about 6 million hectares, or 60 per cent of the total, thus changed hands. Almost 1 million hectares comprising "administration cane" land and the properties of a few large *colonos* was incorporated into the cane cooperatives, which were transformed into cane farms (state farms) in the fall of 1962. Over 2.8 million hectares of grazing land and old rice, tobacco, tomato, potato, and other properties were transferred to the Granjas del Pueblo (people's farms or state farms). Of the remainder, which amounted to about 2.3 million hectares, 400,000 hectares were given to Cuba's smallest farmers and, as we have seen, about 475,000 hectares were purchased by the medium-sized *colonos*. The rest, about 1,425,000 hectares, most of it sugar and pasture land, remained in private hands. Rents were abolished and tenants became *de facto* owners.

By controlling Cuba's most arable farmlands, which had been used badly or not at all, INRA was in an extremely favorable position. The institute could attempt to raise yields, labor productivity, and efficiency in general by large-scale investments in human and physical capital, in order to maintain or even raise the volume of sugar production, while simultaneously raising land for other crops.

This is of primary significance because Cuba would have to nearly *double* the amount of land cultivated (given 1958 yields) to be self-sufficient in foodstuffs. What is more, with its control of the mills (won in the fall of 1960), and as monopoly supplier of working capital, technical aid, and other resources, INRA was in a position to wield considerable influence over the masses of *colonos* and other small farmers.

It is for these reasons that a collectivized agriculture had the air of inevitability, and it is difficult to see how any government determined to accelerate Cuba's economic development could have escaped the general land politics INRA was compelled to follow. These were not doctrinaire expropriations that satisfied the tenets of some grand historical abstraction at the expense of political and economic wisdom and human needs and desires. Rather, they were grounded in very practical and sometimes obvious considerations. If INRA later erred in its investment and production policies, its land distribution policies were beyond major criticism.

[5]

In accordance with the original program of the 26th of July Movement, the Revolutionary Government attempted to organize cooperatives on many of the cattle, sugar, and other farm properties taken over under the Agrarian Reform Law. The law created the National Agrarian Reform Institute (INRA) and directed it to "promote agrarian cooperatives . . . whenever possible." The institute was invested with broad authority and great autonomy. INRA was empowered to appoint cooperative administrators "during the initial stages . . . and until greater autonomy is granted by the law." The law also said that the institute "shall see to it that . . . [the cooperatives] are willing to accept aid and follow the guidance of the said Institute in technical matters." [35] "Technical matters" was left undefined and presumably could include production and investment decisions.

Late in July, 1959, a high INRA official announced that twenty cooperatives had been formed,[36] and in August ten more were

[35] Articles 43 and 44.
[36] Oscar Pino Santos, quoted in *The Havana Post*, July 31, 1959.

added. Through the fall and winter dozens of others sprang up throughout the island on properties confiscated by modifications to Article 24 of the Constitution, farms purchased or donated to INRA, and lands expropriated under the law itself. By March of 1960, INRA had organized 539 agricultural cooperatives, and 199 mixed agricultural and cattle, 8 agricultural, and 7 charcoal cooperatives. The burst of activity in the winter months slackened during the spring; from March to May the institute created only 37 additional units.[37] The reason was twofold. First, the *zafra* turned the government's attention to the sugar harvest. Second, by late 1959, INRA had seized and collectivized or distributed to small farmers nearly all of the land that was confiscated under the modifications to Article 24. Therefore, until the summer, most available land was disposed of. Meanwhile, on the large cattle ranches INRA had created 494 directly administered farms (*de facto* state farms), and on other farmlands, 11 more.

The institute claimed that by May, 1960, approximately 25,000 families were associated with the cooperatives, but the membership of the individual units was in constant state of flux, and the records of the provincial and regional offices of INRA and those of the cooperatives themselves rarely tallied. INRA's estimate was very imprecise and, what is more, failed to disclose the number of workers and former tenant farmers employed as wage laborers by the cooperatives. It was not unusual for two or more members of Cuba's rural families to hire out temporarily for wages; thus, total employment on the cooperatives probably exceeded 50,000.

The early cooperatives did not have definitive organization or administration procedures, and there was very little coordination of plans drawn up for each individual unit. Invariably enthusiastic and imbued with high revolutionary spirits, most of the zone chiefs and many of the local administrators lacked technical experience and an awareness of the administrative and operational problems of the Reform Law. What is more, in order to avoid the creation of a do-nothing, urban-based bureaucracy, the Revolutionary Government

[37] Antonio Núñez Jiménez, *Report*, March 17, 1960 (mimeographed); *Un Año de liberación agraria*, Edición Especial para la Sexta Conferencia Interamericana de Agricultura de la OEA (México, August 8–10, 1960), p. 14.

failed to supply INRA headquarters in Havana with sufficient technical and administrative personnel. Thus, the main features of the first cooperative movement were local autonomy and experimentation. On some of the cooperatives, the workers and ex-tenants had a collective voice in cooperative affairs; in others, the members played only an advisory role; and in the remainder, the administrator had absolute authority.

All of the cooperatives retained the wages system. In those cooperatives where labor productivity was comfortably high, the surplus over wage and material costs was plowed back into the construction of houses, schools, health clinics, and other social overhead capital investments. Few cooperatives, however, survived without INRA's help. The construction programs of even the most profitable units were financed partly by INRA subsidies. The cooperatives also depended on INRA for seeds and credits and machinery, and in 1959–1960, Rebel Army units were at work on dozens of construction projects and operated a number of new, small factories producing brick, tile, hand-assembled stoves, and other materials and equipment for new rural housing.

These first cooperatives were short-lived. The handful specializing in sugar were transformed into cane cooperatives in mid-1960. Many of the remaining cooperative farms were disbanded, in part or in whole, while others became credit or service cooperatives. Reflecting INRA's bias in favor of large units, the shortage of able agricultural technicians and administrators, the lack of interest of the workers in management problems, the need for tighter controls over food supplies, and the need for coordination and control in rural planning, the cooperatives were consolidated into *granjas del pueblo* (peoples' farms) beginning in December, 1960. By the following spring, the last of the cooperatives had been reorganized or disposed of in one way or another.[38]

[6]

The second attempt to reorganize agriculture along cooperative

[38] It is difficult to estimate how many cooperatives were actually disbanded, compared with the number consolidated into *granjas*. In Oriente, the big cotton cooperative "Malagueta," which comprised 1,517 *caballerías*, and the

lines began during the 1960 sugar harvest. *Cooperativas cañeras* (cane cooperatives) were formed on lands on which the sugar mills had previously grown "administration cane" and on the nationalized properties of the large *colonos*. There was no attempt made to bring the masses of small and middle sugar growers into the cane cooperatives. By May, 1961, of Cuba's approximately 225,000 regular cane field workers, over 45,000 and 122,000 workers were temporary and permanent cooperative members, respectively.[39] The remainder, more than 50,000 workers, continued to hire out as wage labor to the remaining larger *colonos*.

In mid-1961 there were 622 cooperatives, incorporated into 46 *agrupaciones* (groups), each of which comprised the properties controlled by a given mill. Most of the cooperatives were formed by subdividing the properties of the larger mills, and in many cases, cooperative property consisted of scattered and isolated strips of cane land. There was no significant change in the size or distribution of producing units. The temptation to break large farms up into uneconomic units was avoided.

Formally, to quote an ex-director of INRA, "the members of the Cane Cooperatives received from INRA absolute rights to the lands, and they are the absolute owners of them."[40] These rights were theoretically reflected in the mode of control on the level of the cooperative itself. The cooperative membership comprised a general assembly, which elected a *consejo de dirección* (directing council), consisting of a coordinator and six other officials in charge of in-

---

rice cooperatives "Camilo Ciefuegos" (650 *caballerías*), "Limones" (500 *caballerías*), and "La Tanquera" (204 *caballerías*) were transformed into *granjas*. So were the huge mixed cooperatives "Providencia" and "Yateritas," containing 2,712 and 2,500 *caballerías*, respectively, and other large units throughout the island. Probably one hundred or so small cooperatives were broken up, the properties distributed to local tenants or allowed to revert back to their owners.

[39] "La reforma agraria Cubana (III parte)," p. 101.

[40] Materials on cooperative organization were drawn from the following sources: *Cooperativas Cañeras, Orientación y Reglamento*, La Administración General de Cooperativas Cañeras (Havana, October, 1960); *Informe sobre dos años de reforma agraria*, pp. 10–12; *Trabajo Cuba*, 1, No. 8 (December, 1960), p. 39; 2, No. 5 (May, 1961); *Obra Revolucionaria*, No. 21 (May 29, 1961); *Revolución*, December 30, 1961.

struction, supplies, machinery, housing, production, and personnel. Sharing the direction of the cooperative and allowed to speak but not to vote at council meetings was an administrator appointed by INRA's General Administration of Cane Cooperatives. In practice, INRA often appointed the coordinator and administrator, and often the two functions were merged into one. From the cooperative membership it was often difficult to find competent personnel, and INRA's zone chiefs were compelled to recommend outsiders for management jobs. The fundamental reason that the General Administration statutes were not fully implemented was the low technical level of the vast majority of Cuba's sugar workers. The nature of the work in sugar farming failed to provide opportunities for the development of individual technical and administrative capacities. On the other hand, past labor union and political activity had prepared the workers to participate in general assembly meetings. For these reasons, the general assemblies often played active but not leading roles in the management of the cooperatives.

Central direction was also reflected in income and wages policies. Members received in advance the equivalent of current day wages for nonmembers against 20 per cent of future net income. INRA itself decided to use the remaining 80 per cent to finance the construction of housing for a period of at least five years. Fifty pesos per member was distributed in October, 1961, but there is no record of other payments (apart from wages) having been made. Where workers' housing projects were begun, the recipient paid for the construction costs at the rate of 10 per cent of his monthly income. Other member rights, most of them fixed by the central authority, included aid in case of sickness or accident; benefits equal to total earnings during the preceding five-year period in case of total incapacitation or death (in which case the benefits would be paid to the worker's wife); free medical and dental services; free education; the right to leave the cooperative voluntarily or transfer (but not sell) membership; and the right to buy at the local *tienda del pueblo* (people's store).

At the Cane Cooperatives Congress of August, 1962, local delegates voted almost unanimously to reorganize the cooperatives as *granjas cañeras* (cane farms or state farms). Dissatisfaction with the cooperatives had been made public late in the year before. A "bureaucratic spirit" had developed in the directing councils. The coordinators were accused of having failed to hold regular meetings, either for council functionaries or with the members themselves. Regular lines of communications were never established in many units, and no systematic attempt to integrate the workers into the administration of the cooperatives was undertaken. Meanwhile, the workers —as *cooperativistas*—had been deprived of their unions. With little or no voice in the management of the cooperatives, and with no trade union representation, worker interests were often bypassed. The temptation to ignore these interests for the sake of administrative expediency was evidently too great to pass up. In addition, frictions and tensions developed between the *cooperativistas* and the *eventuales* (nonmember, temporary workers). The latter, termed "second-class citizens" by Castro, performed the same tasks as the former but, as outsiders, were less privileged economically and socially.[41]

There were two basic reasons that INRA decided to transform the cane cooperative into *granjas cañeras*. The first requires some background explanation. If the *cooperativistas* were in a privileged position vis à vis the *eventuales*, they were unfavorably situated compared with employees on the new people's farms (discussed below). The crop expansion and diversification programs were developing at a snail's pace on the cane cooperatives, while on the people's farms new opportunities for year-round employment were rapidly opening up. INRA was pouring resources into the latter and discriminating against the former, on the grounds that the benefits of investments in the people's farms accrued to the entire population, while those in the latter redounded to only the *cooperativistas*. Cooperative workers, meanwhile, harvested much less cane in 1962, compared with 1961, and the cooperatives were in no position to fi-

[41] "Conversión de las Cooperativas en Granjas del Pueblo Cañeras," *Trimestre* (*de Finanzas al Día*), *suplemento del directorio financiero*, Instituto de Estudios Financieros, Ministerio de Hacienda No. 2 (Havana, April–June, 1962), p. 111.

nance large-scale investment projects by themselves. What is more, average wages on the *granjas* were somewhat higher than on the cooperatives, and because little cane was grown on the former, working conditions there were considerably better (backbreaking sugar-harvesting work was confined to the cooperatives).[42] For these reasons, there was a steady flow of labor from the cooperatives to the *granjas* in 1961 and 1962, complicating the job of cooperative administration.

A number of other factors added to the difficulties. Competent personnel were very scarce on the service level; an average of only seventeen repair shop employees serviced each *agrupación,* which incorporated an average of over fourteen cane cooperatives. Moreover, the diversification program of 1961 strained the abilities of local administrators, and many cooperative members turned their attention to their private plots and neglected collective work. To be sure, Castro had argued in the summer of 1961 that the cooperative form of organization would strengthen incentives to work and save.[43] These incentives never materialized, however, because the shortage of able local personnel compelled INRA to administer the cooperatives directly, the allocation of cooperative income was determined by the central authority, and the work force was in a highly fluid state. Workers had few incentives to throw themselves into a collective effort. As long as the members were employees of INRA, the "cooperative" label was only an inconvenient fiction.

The second reason was related to the over-all development of the island's political economy. When the cane cooperatives were conceived and first organized in 1960, the Cuban economy was still basically a market economy. The majority of industry and domestic commerce remained in private hands, and, within a complex network of indirect and direct economic controls, the allocation of economic resources and the composition of commodity production was still guided by the structure of market prices. By mid-1961, after the sweeping nationalization decrees in the fall of 1960, the new Cen-

---

[42] *Obra Revolucionaria,* No. 17 (May 25, 1962), reporting a Castro speech of May 14.

[43] *Ibid.,* No. 21 (May 29, 1961).

tral Planning Board had introduced the rudiments of direct physical planning. In this new context, the government viewed the cane cooperatives in an entirely different light. The cooperatives comprised the most productive 10 per cent of Cuba's total farmland, and a higher proportion of the island's cultivated land. With the development of the crisis in food supplies in late 1961 and 1962—attributable mainly to the lack of success (and interest) in integrating private agriculture into the structure of the reformed rural economy, and the mistakes made in the diversification program—the planners were especially eager to extend direct physical planning throughout the public sector.[44]

There was no attempt to enlarge the size of the cooperatives' producing units. From the standpoints of exploiting economies of large-scale production and possibilities for mechanization and efficient administrative controls, the size of most of the cooperatives was adequate. The average cooperative comprised between 1,000 and 1,500 hectares of farmland; thus, the ratio of land to labor was neither strikingly high nor low, averaging between 3.9 hectares per worker in Oriente to 6.5 hectares per worker in Matanzas.[45]

INRA thus experimented unsuccessfully with a cooperative agriculture in all branches of the rural economy except one: cattle ranching. From late 1959 to late 1960, Cuba's large ranches were managed by INRA as directly administered farms, and in the first half of 1961, these properties were reorganized as *granjas del pueblos* (people's farms), or state farms. Cooperatives were not organized on the ranches, because labor:land ratios were very small, about one worker per 55 hectares, compared with the all-Cuba ratio

[44] *Hablan para el Instituto Popular de Chile*, p. 66.

[45] See Appendix A. Within each province and within each *agrupación*, however, there was considerable variation between the largest and smallest cooperatives, so far as the average number of workers was concerned. The average cooperative in Oriente had twice as many workers compared with the average Matanzas cooperative. Within *agrupación* "Sandino" in Pinar del Río, for example, the smallest unit employed 145 members and *eventuales*, while 332 workers labored on the largest. As a general rule, however, where the work force was small, the amount of land comprising the cooperative was small as well. For this reason, there was considerably less variation with regard to average hectares per worker, compared with average size of the work force.

of one to 13. The handful of ranch workers would thus have been able to constitute themselves as a new rural labor aristocracy. Raising the level of employment on the ranches, without long-range diversification programs and heavy investments of complementary resources (including social overhead capital), would have been costly and useless.

In conclusion, it should be stressed that most of the cooperatives, the cane cooperatives, and the directly administered farms were administered in the same way, and since the INRA administrator nearly everywhere had absolute authority, names and labels meant very little. In fact, INRA never systematically attempted to build rural economy cooperatives. The institute was influenced by the role of large-scale agriculture in North America, the socialist countries, and, last but not least, Cuban history itself. INRA also wanted to exploit administrative and production economies of scale and, perhaps most important, desired direct control over rural investments and agricultural production. Thus, the early "cooperatives" lacked a legal and administrative basis as cooperatives in the usual sense of the word; by and large, they were run as state farms by the central government, which also administered the expropriated ranches. It is for this reason that one cannot really speak of a "cooperative stage" in the development of the Cuban agrarian revolution.

[7]

We have seen that most of the early cooperatives were consolidated and converted into people's farms beginning in the late fall of 1960. In 1961, INRA's Cattle Administration, which had been operating Cuba's 900 largest cattle ranches, turned its properties over to the new General Administration of People's Farms, created in January, 1961. Counting the nearly 800 first cooperatives, the new administration thus controlled about 1,700 farm units. By May, 1961, these had been consolidated into 266 people's farms, employing over 27,000 permanent workers and nearly 70,000 part-time employees. Workers on the people's farms were salaried state employees, entitled to free housing, utilities, medical care, education, and recreational facilities. All were formerly landless members of the rural proletariat. Many of the state farms' part-time employees were tenant farm operators who sought wage work during slack periods.

The people's farms and the cooperatives differed in a number of ways. In the first place, the structure of the General Administration of the former was a simplified version of that of the latter. There were no *agrupaciones* of people's farms. Between the farms themselves and the Havana-based General Administration in the hierarchy were INRA's provincial chiefs. Informally, the degree of centralization was even more extreme. The INRA-appointed *granja* administrator and accountant often received their orders directly from Havana.

Second, the *granja* administrative unit was on the average nearly ten times as big as the cooperative administrative unit.[46] Provincial averages ranged from about 7,500 hectares in Havana to over 12,000 hectares in Camaguey. Third, although the size-distribution of units of both were extremely wide (in Oriente, for example, the smallest *granja* comprised about 4,000 hectares, while the two largest made up about 67,000 hectares each), unlike the cane cooperatives, average hectares per *granja* worker varied widely between provinces. Production was most land intensive in Camaguey, where farms comprised an average of 57.8 hectares per worker. This was particularly significant because, in an effort to avoid *granja* bureaucracies, each unit was understaffed, and besides, there were no parallel worker groups to help administer the farms. This was later recognized and corrected; in the words of one INRA administrator: "Where there are eight people, when only five are needed, that's bureaucracy; but where to avoid bureaucracy there are only one or two people, when four are needed, that's self-defeating, uneconomical, and inefficient."

Lastly, average hectares per worker in absolute terms were considerably higher on the *granjas*. Farmland per permanent worker came to 89.1 hectares, compared with a mere 6.6 hectares on the cooperatives. Including temporary workers, the ratios were to 25.2 and 4.8 hectares, respectively. These differences were due mainly to the fact that cane cultivation was relatively labor intensive, while

[46] See Appendix A.

the old ranches, the core of many of the *granjas*, employed relatively few wage workers.

Many of the people's farms, particularly in the central and western provinces, each incorporated a number of the early "cooperatives," enlarging the size of the administrative unit, but leaving the size of the producing unit unchanged. In these cases, INRA was able to exploit administrative and service economies or large-scale production at the risk, however, of inefficiencies due to rural gigantism. The *granja* "Camilo Cienfuegos" in Matanzas, for example, comprised 372 *caballerías*, broken up into three separate units.[47] Before the people's farm movement got under way, there had been two large rice "cooperatives" in the same municipality; one was 177 *caballerías* in size, employing 60 families; the second extended over 148 *caballerías* on which 56 families worked.[48] These "cooperatives" made up two of the *granjas* three units and, between them, accounted for 325 *caballerías*. The third unit of 47 *caballerías* was composed of the lands of one or more of four other smaller "cooperatives" in the same municipality, whose sizes ranged from 24 to 81 *caballerías*. On "Camilo Cienfuegos" production expanded as idle land and local labor were put to work: in 1960 the "cooperatives" employed less than 200 families; one year later, the consolidated *granja* hired over 500 families.

Another *granja* in this category was "Raúl Gomez García" in Havana Province, which employed 450 families on 857 *caballerías*. This unit had been formed from two "cooperatives" of 413 and 200 *caballerías*, with which 150 and eight families respectively had been associated, and two or three other smaller cooperatives.[49] Employment on this unit had jumped by at least 50 per cent in one year.

On these farms, typical of the *granjas* in the western provinces, an expansion of employment meant that production became more labor intensive without any appreciable change in the size of the

[47] *Viviendas Campesinas*, Organo Oficial del Departamento de Vivendas Campesinas del INRA, 2, No. 5 (1961).

[48] Unless noted otherwise, all data used in this section are drawn from *Un año de liberación agraria*, *passim*.

[49] L. McBeath, "Todo florece en las grandes llanuras cultivadas," *Verde Olivo*, 2, No. 32 (August 20, 1961), pp. 12–15.

producing unit. Labor productivity thus fell somewhat less than proportionately until fertilizer, insecticide, irrigation, and other yield-raising investments were made. Compared with farms in the east, these *granjas* lacked a surplus of good idle land to exploit, although there were some opportunities for double cropping.

In the eastern provinces, many of the ranches consolidated into individual *granjas* were contiguous, and the land had been by no means fully utilized. For these reasons, there were more opportunities for raising production by increasing employment and exploiting economies of large-scale production. To illustrate, one *granja* in Oriente Province consisted of two former privately owned ranches, both of which had been entirely in pasture. Between them they had employed four or five cowboys.[50] By the fall of 1961, the *granja* had 210 permanent members and 150 temporary workers on its rolls and had planted 15 *caballerías* of previously unused lands, with plans to cultivate 30 *caballerías* more. Since the majority of the workers were seasonally unemployed for a number of months each year before the *granja* was organized, and since the land had been idle or badly utilized as pasture, production costs were limited to necessary outlays for seeds, machinery, and other supplies and equipment.

On both the western and eastern ends of the island, the vast majority of the new *granjas* consisted of a number of centrally administered properties not geographically contiguous, which were often very extensive in size. Administration was extremely difficult; INRA's head in 1962 said that many *granjas* administered up to twelve dispersed farms each. But perhaps the most striking example was "Unidad," a people's farm located in Havana Province. With 265 *caballerías* distributed in forty-nine small, scattered farms (previously worked by wage labor under professional management), each more or less specialized, efficient communication and control within the *granja* were highly elusive.[51]

Aside from the administrative difficulties inherent in the opera-

[50] "Un domingo in la Granja", *Verde Olivo*, 2, 38 (September 24, 1961), pp. 30–34.

[51] *Hablan para el Instituto Popular de Chile*, p. 66; "Unidad: de latifundio a granja del pueblo," *Trabajo Cuba*, 3, No. 6 (March, 1962), pp. 58–61.

tion of rural organizations composed of dispersed units, the sheer size of some of the *granjas* posed serious problems. Up to 60 kilometers separated operating units on some people's farms,[52] and distances of 20 or 30 kilometers between *granja* headquarters and fields were very common. Another problem stemmed from the "anti-bureaucratic" mentality of the INRA directors: the National General Administration of People's Farms employed only twenty-four inspectors, who spent an average of only two days each month on each *granja*.

Inefficiencies arising from overcentralized decision making, together with a shortage of qualified personnel aggravated by a tendency to place politically reliable people in top administrative posts even when they lacked technical skills, led to some decentralization in 1961 and the actual breakup of some of the largest *granjas* in mid-1962. To take one example, the giant 3,500-*caballería* "Granma" in Oriente was transformed into so-called *agrupación básica,* which bore a similarity to the *agrupación* of the Cane Cooperative Administration. This tendency toward reorganization and decentralization was more characteristic in the large cattle-raising eastern provinces, and INRA hoped that it would allow more local autonomy within a tightened and better coordinated planning structure. Other attempts to rationalize the administration of the *granjas* came in the form of a six-month training course for accountants and the creation of technical councils of *granja* workers, with authority to "advise" the INRA-appointed administration.

Administrative and other problems aside, the new people's farms yielded two big advantages to Cuban planners. First, INRA acquired direct control over economic resources and, by equalizing wages on rich and poor farms alike, insured itself against worker opposition to the cultivation of crops required by agricultural development but which commanded relatively low prices in the domestic or international market. Moreover, by placing over-all *granja* budgets on a purely accounting basis, there was no need for each unit to "pay" for itself. In this way INRA was in a position to seize the ad-

[52] René Saladrigas, "Criterios para una reestructuración político-administrativa de Cuba," *Cuba Socialista,* 3, No. 7 (January, 1963), p. 47.

vantages of external economies of large-scale production which can be exploited in a growing economy undergoing fundamental structural changes.

The second advantage of the people's farms was related to the question of income distribution. Political and social tensions had been created by the uncomfortable existence of "rich cooperatives" (prominent in the tobacco sector) and "poor cooperatives" side by side. The new *granjas* made it possible to reduce these tensions by equalizing wage rates (at a standard $3 per day, plus special incentives) and, as much as possible, general living conditions. INRA's new policy of redistributing rural incomes, however, had two drawbacks, one more apparent than real. INRA's leveling policy clearly ruled out the use of wage differentials to allocate labor between *granjas*. Until 1964, at least, this had no important repercussions for the planning of labor needs, since the people's farms drew their work force from the cane cooperatives, which were starved for capital and had much "invisible" unemployment, and from the unemployed.

More serious was the fact that, because wage rates bore little or no relationship to labor productivity and *granja* income, there were few incentives for workers to engage wholeheartedly in a collective effort. The discipline of the marketplace was replaced by a guaranteed wage and income, and for this reason, INRA was compelled to turn to "emulation" campaigns, sanctions against malingerers, and volunteer labor, and openly discussed possibilities of modifying the "equalization" policy by plowing back some *granja* profits into social investments.[53]

[8]
The major events in the agrarian revolution were the expropriation of the sugar and cattle lands and the substitution of "cooperatives" and state farms for the old capitalist agriculture. Of less significance, in terms of both the amount of land and number of people affected, were the changes that the revolution brought about in the condition of the small farmer.

We have seen that Castro's "ten points of peasant redemption" in-

[53] *Hablan para el Instituto Popular de Chile*, p. 68.

cluded ownership of the land by the individual peasant cultivator. Castro kept his promise. All of Cuba's 125,000 small tenants, share-croppers, and squatters became owners of the land on which they labored. The Agrarian Reform Law provided that the farm of every small cultivator be increased in size to two *caballerías*. The law was not fully implemented; only 32,000 of Cuba's small farmers were actually given land.[54] The reason was threefold.

First, many farms were not expanded to the "basic minimum" of two *caballerías* because optimum-size producing units are smaller. In tobacco cultivation, for example, although some aspects of production lend themselves to collective exploitation (drying the leaf, for instance), given the limited supply of skilled wage labor, Cuba's 20,000 small tobacco farms could not be efficiently enlarged without a deterioration of the quality of the leaf.

For another thing, there was often no available land contiguous to the properties of the small growers: [55] for example, most of Cuba's 20,000 coffee farms and other farms in mountainous and isolated territories. Most of the land expropriated under Article 1 that was not already occupied needed to be improved and colonized.[56] Land that could have been made available under Article 6 belonged to middle farmers. We have seen that INRA decided not to strengthen the small growers at their expense. Finally, in some cases where land was available, it was Castro's view that dividing up the estates would have a "negative effect on production," and by 1961, it was the explicit policy of the government to prevent the development of a new class of middle-sized farmers.[57]

[54] The number of titles is reported in "La reforma agraria Cubana (II parte)," p. 41.

[55] Feragut, *op. cit.*, p. 6. Castro pointed this out in a speech to the National Congress of Cane Cooperatives, August 18, 1962.

[56] Jacques Chonchol, "Memorándum sobre el proceso de la reforma agraria en Cuba," *Cuadernos Latinoamericanos de Economía Humana*, 3, No. 7 (Montevideo, January–April, 1960), p. 44.

[57] Castro quote from radio interview, January 29, 1962. In August, 1962, before the National Conference of Cane Cooperatives, Castro elaborated this view by arguing that large production units were necessary for mechanizing agriculture, growing rice efficiently, training agricultural workers in new skills, and rationally allocating social investments.

The basic problem facing INRA, however, was not the distribution of land but the organization of the small farmers. On the one hand, forced collectivization was rejected both in words and action.[58] Castro pledged that small holdings would never be expropriated at the 1961 and 1963 conventions of the National Association of Small Farmers. INRA explicitly barred small-farm owners from membership in the people's farms. On the other hand, the government increasingly encouraged small farmers to enter into INRA-sponsored cooperative arrangements.[59] The organization of a single, island-wide small farmers association was the first step.

As we know, in prerevolutionary Cuba the vast majority of the island's 165,000 private farmers were members of one or more of thirty different agricultural organizations. The Colonos Association was the largest and continued to function more or less normally after the revolution. INRA requested that the *colonos* elect delegates to the National Sugar Meeting scheduled for December, 1960 to plan the first "people's *zafra*." The larger growers who dominated

---

The slow pace of land redistribution supports the view that there was a shortage of conveniently located land that was formerly the property of the large estates. Only 1,750 land titles were passed out in 1959. One year was required to distribute the first 16,000 titles. In September and October of 1960, 4,000 more titles were granted, and during the following two months the pace of the redistribution accelerated and nearly 9,500 titles were given out (letter, Jacques Chonchol to Thomas Carroll). Under the Reform Law itself, the first titles (41 in number) were not granted until September, 1959. Informal land redistribution began in March, 1959, when deeds were granted to 340 farmers in Pinar del Río; involved were 746 *caballerías* purchased by BANFAIC through a local credit association with a Cabinet appropriation of $430,000.

[58] Castro radio interview, January 29, 1962. See also Fidel Castro, "Discurso en la Plenaria de la ANAP," *Obra Revolucionaria*, No. 21 (May 29, 1961); *Hoy*, August 10, 1963, reporting Castro's speech to the Second ANAP Congress. At the latter meeting, it was also pointed out that many farmers cultivating more than two *caballerías* must be considered "small farmers" from the standpoint of incomes, use of wage labor, etc.

[59] Typical propaganda in favor of production cooperatives can be found in Antero Regaldo, "La producción agropecuaria y los pequeños propietarios," *Economía y Planificación, Segunda Parte*, Universidad Popular, Séptimo Ciclo (June 1961), pp. 97–98. Examples of material incentives held out to the peasants are given by the director of INRA in a speech quoted in *Hoy* (August 10, 1963.

the association refused to participate in the conference. INRA undercut the authority of the old leadership by organizing an election, which picked a new set of representatives, drawn mainly from the large class of small *colonos*. The new leaders asked the government to change the name of the association and withdraw recognition from the old leadership.[60] Six months later, all the remaining associations had fallen into line and merged into the new National Association of Small Farmers (ANAP).

At the sugar meeting itself, Castro called on the small farmers to abandon their specialized associations and enlist in ANAP, where he promised that their common interest would be represented. Within a brief period, membership in ANAP, which still lacked formal organization and structure, stood at about 50,000. In May, 1961, 3,800 delegates met at ANAP's first national meeting and from a single slate elected a national executive board; two weeks later, INRA published the association's general regulations. By then an estimated 40,000 *colonos,* 20,000 coffee farmers, 4,000 potato farmers, 20,000 tobacco growers, and an equal number of coffee planters had been organized into the new association.[61] The more than 30,000 new titleholders were included in these groups. Membership was nominally restricted to farmers whose properties did not comprise more than five *caballerías,* but did not exclude others who were considered active revolutionaries.[62] From a membership of about 85,-000 in mid-1961, ANAP rapidly grew until it finally included nearly all of Cuba's more than 150,000 farmers whose properties fell under the five *caballería* limit.[63]

It was ANAP's stated purpose "to organize, unite, and orient" small farmers in the application of the revolution's agrarian program. In the view of the revolution's leadership in 1962, ANAP was

[60] *Revolución,* May 17, 1961. Locally, many of the associations had been reorganized under the guidance of the Rebel Army in 1958 (*Obra Revolucionaria,* No. 21 (May 29, 1961).

[61] *Economía y Planificación, Segunda Parte,* Eduardo Santos Rios, p. 22.

[62] Or large farms worked in common by large families without benefit of wage labor (*Hoy,* August 10, 1963, citing Castro speech to Second ANAP Congress.)

[63] See Appendix A.

a "step toward socialism," and its task was to "lead farmers through gradual transition to the organization of great mechanized production." [64] But Cuba's small farmers were continually reassured that cooperatives would be voluntary and that the government would continue to respect the desire of Cuba's growers to remain independent farmers, although INRA increasingly made it clear that small farmers who joined cooperatives would be able to obtain credits on easier terms, regular technical help, subsidized housing, and other benefits claimed for a system of collective agriculture.

At the same time, INRA realized that a far-reaching, voluntary cooperative movement would be stalled until the *granjas* learned how to utilize modern agricultural technology to impress the advantages of collective agriculture on the private farmers, and until increased productivity in the state sector raised production and lowered prices, placing independent growers in an unfavorable competitive position. Cuba's 13,000 "rich peasants," farmers cultivating more than five *caballerías,* were excluded from this future of voluntary cooperatives and, until their lands were nationalized in late 1963, operated independently.

ANAP's first important practical role was in the sphere of rural credit. Before the association's Credit Department was even formally set up in May, 1961, ANAP had made over 22,000 different loans, most of them for working capital to finance the cultivation of new crops (like cattle corn), although many were for ox teams, plows, and other fixed capital investments.[65] With the creation of the Credit Department, the National Bank loaned 20 million pesos to ANAP and transferred to the association all fourteen branches of the prerevolutionary credit associations, which until 1960 were affiliated with BANFAIC, in this way furnishing ANAP with experienced personnel. The National Bank grant was to be applied against a planned volume of 35 million pesos in eighty thousand

[64] Quotes from *Hablan para el Instituto Popular de Chile,* p. 69, and radio broadcast of December 15, 1962.

[65] See the speech by ANAP's head, Pepe Ramírez, *Obra Revolucionaria,* No. 21.

separate loans during 1961. ANAP in turn extended credits to its base organizations, and to a special plan to develop Oriente's coffee and cocoa industry. Working capital loans up to 60 to 80 per cent of the value of production and long-term loans for new cultivations were authorized.

ANAP credits quickly developed into the single most important link between private farmers and INRA's agricultural plan. The Agrarian Reform Institute withheld credits for crops that held a low priority in the plan and expanded loans for the cultivation of crops that Cuba lacked but needed badly. Other, less effective techniques for integrating the private sector into the planning mechanism were not ignored. In a strictly advisory capacity, ANAP guided the production plans of private farmers and provided personnel to help organize and direct the base organizations. The association also intervened in the official market for farm products in order to guarantee that members received a "just price."

ANAP's general regulations provided for three types of base organizations: credit and service cooperatives, peasant associations, and production cooperatives. From each base group, a representative was elected to ANAP's municipal groups, which sent delegates to the provincial organizations, which were themselves represented on the national board. Democratic principles, the most important of which were free elections, majority rule, and the subordination of inferior to superior level organisms, were laid down, although in practice they were often honored only in the breach. As late as August, 1963, the organizational secretary of ANAP condemned some local delegates for failing to make ANAP meetings true general assemblies.[66]

As it happened, the base units evolved into two well-defined modes of organization, and a third more or less *ad hoc* form of cooperation. Far and away the most popular, the credit and service cooperatives (CCS) were organized in mid-1961 around the old rural credit associations, about which there had been many complaints of failure to acquire farm machinery and create collective social investments and market transport facilities. By late 1961 fewer

[66] Antero Regaldo to the Second ANAP Congress (*Hoy*, August 10, 1963).

than three hundred credit cooperatives had been formed, most of them in the tobacco regions of Pinar del Río and Las Villas provinces. In December, 1962, INRA began to reorganize them with particular attention to their financial structure, and by the fall of 1963, the number of cooperatives was doubled, and over 46,000 farmers were enrolled. This number represented less than one-third of all ANAP farmers, but almost 60 per cent of Cuba's small farmers who planted crops other than sugar. The latter figure is more significant, because the *colonos* still received working capital from the mills, and because the sugar growers had their own Delegations of Cane Cultivators, made up of all those farmers who sold cane to a given mill. As a basis for constructing a collective agriculture, however, the delegations were totally inadequate because many growers associated with a particular mill were widely scattered and out of contact with each other. The tobacco sector continued to be the best organized; in Las Villas, for example, of 239 credit cooperatives, 195 were organized around the tobacco growers,[67] although some small rice, bean, coffee, and viand farmers also belonged to credit cooperatives.

The cooperatives' main task was to extend working credits and long-term (up to ten year) loans, and they provided services of one kind or another as well. In tobacco, they have accomplished some machine-planting and helped to rationalize the use of expensive hand labor in harvesting and grading operations. Their greatest potential lay in the area of investments in social overhead capital. Members turned over 4 per cent of the value of their crops—a large proportion of which were sold collectively to INRA purchasing organisms—to their cooperatives, which placed the moneys into a social fund to finance irrigation projects, small-scale reclamation work, and other investments.

In this way INRA, through its influence in ANAP, began to foster a collective consciousness on the part of small farmers, and it was generally assumed that INRA planned to develop these cooperatives

[67] Arnaldo Millán, "Las Cooperativas Campesinas de Créditos y Servicios en Las Villas," *Cuba Socialista*, 3, No. 12 (May 1963), p. 51.

into "higher" forms of collective activity in the future. It was perhaps this aspect of the cooperatives, together with a lack of attention to democratic decision-making (publicly criticized throughout 1963), which opened the way here and there to counterrevolutionary sentiment and, finally, a more *laissez-faire* attitude on the part of INRA.

The credit cooperatives were in fact being guided in the direction of the second unique form of small farmer organization, the *sociedades agropecuarias,* which were pure production cooperatives. Land was worked and animals were raised in common. In the summer of 1963, 4,400 farmers belonged to 358 *sociedades,* many of which, including over one-half of the groups in Las Villas, had developed from the credit cooperatives themselves.[68] In order to discourage the employment of wage labor by private farmers, a ceiling of fifteen *caballerías* was placed on the *sociedades,* and partly for this reason, the *sociedades,* like the credit cooperatives, were composed of the island's smallest farmers.

Over 60 per cent of Cuba's nonsugar farms were incorporated into either the credit cooperatives or *sociedades,* but these farms cultivated only 35 per cent of total ANAP land (again excluding land under sugar).[69] In the "unorganized" nonsugar sector of ANAP were about 840,000 hectares, and farms exceeding five *caballerías* in size (on which crops other than sugar were cultivated), which were excluded from both organizations, accounted for about 3,376,000 hectares. The *granjas del pueblo* and henequen farms together incorporated about 2,450,000 hectares.

Thus, until the Second Agrarian Reform of August, 1963, of a total of 7.2 million hectares, 4.2 million hectares, or about 58 per cent, belonged to farmers who remained outside of the planned rural economy. Excluding the more than 1 million hectares of pasture in the public sector (and land under sugar) about 43,000 small and middle private, "unorganized" farmers held close to 70 per cent of the island's farmland (actually somewhat less since some pasture

[68] *Hoy,* August 6, 1963.
[69] See Appendix A, from which all estimates below are made.

land remained in private hands).[70] *One-quarter of Cuba's farmers cultivating nearly three-quarters of the island's food crops thus remained outside the planned agriculture.*

To allocate economic resources in the largest corner of the island's agriculture, Cuban planners were compelled to rely almost exclusively on their control over the structure of commodity prices. That so much of Cuba's agricultural wealth lay outside INRA's direct or indirect control (through ANAP's base organisms) was a fundamental drawback to an efficiently planned agriculture. Making matters worse, the political and economic climate of 1960–1963 —the growing fear of expropriation, substantial reductions in imports of consumer goods, and irrational pricing policies—had very unfavorable effects on private farm investment and new plantings, and increased autoconsumption and liquidity.

Other difficulties arose from the new organization of private agriculture. For one thing, there was very little coordination between the policies of local ANAP groups, on the one hand, and those of the cane farms and people's farms, on the other. This was not so much owing to inadequate personnel as to a structural defect in the agricultural organization as a whole. The economic problems and needs of the private sector spilled over into the public sector, and vice versa. The same soil conditions, irrigation potential, insect life, and so on that characterized the lands and agriculture of a given *granja* also typified the surrounding private lands. The former was directly administered by one state organism, while the latter was only indirectly influenced by another.

One attack on this problem was made in August, 1963, at ANAP's Second Congress. Extensive discussion about the nature and role of ANAP redefined the association as strictly a "mass, political organization." Most of ANAP's administrative functions—machine service and purchasing and sales divisions—were handed over to INRA. This was a step in the right direction, yet the credit cooperatives re-

[70] Some tobacco farmers in neither the credit coops nor the *sociedades* belonged to the so-called *cooperativas intermedias,* in which one or two tasks (mainly sowing seed) were accomplished collectively. These cooperatives were, however, quantitatively insignificant.

tained their authority and would have to continue to consult nearly perpetually with local *granja* and cane farm personnel on questions ranging from common reclamation projects to common use of public transport.

For another thing, within the ANAP structure the artificial separation of the credit cooperatives and *sociedades* handicapped rational and coordinated agricultural planning. There was a considerable overlap in the membership of the two groups; farmers from both organizations attended the same functions and educational programs and served in the same militia units. For these reasons, delegates to the Second ANAP Congress discussed the possibility of consolidating the two organizations at great length; action was reserved for a later date.

The organization of the *sociedades* themselves left much to be desired. Few groups had developed systems of cost controls, and fewer still had practical sets of work norms. At least until the end of 1963, some *sociedades* were using ANAP credit to cultivate for autoconsumption. But, most serious, they were too diversified (given the size of producing units) and failed to exploit available economies of scale. Beginning in 1963, an attempt was made to correct these problems; INRA worked up plans to build pilot *sociedades,* on which other groups could model their organization, in each province. The question remained whether or not these and other "partial" solutions to rural Cuba's new problems of organization could be worked out in the absence of an over-all rationalization of the Agrarian Reform Institute itself.

[9]

Unlike the role of the small farmers in the agrarian revolution, that of the middle farmers—Cuba's 13,000 ranchers, *colonos,* and other growers who held between 5 and 30 *caballerías* of land— was at first confused and uncertain, although the government's position on the "kulaks" progressively hardened between 1959 and 1963. In June, 1959, Castro promised the middle farmers that they would be able to purchase land up to the 30 *caballería* limit. Between mid-1959 and 1961, when the revolution rapidly polarized, INRA's attitude became increasingly cautious and noncommittal. On the one hand, the middle farmers were expanding production, partly because they were more skilled in adjusting production policies to changes in demand, and partly because they feared that the government would seize their land in the event that they did not increase supplies to meet the expansion of the market. On the other hand, the middle farmers were politically hostile to the revolution and resisted becoming a part of the developing "worker-peasant alliance."

INRA's caution vis à vis the middle farmers was reflected in two ways. First, they were barred from membership in ANAP, unless they were able to prove that they were truly "revolutionary." Second, there was no serious attempt to integrate them into the structure of the reformed agriculture with regard to the acquisition of credit, materials, and machinery and the disposal of output. Moreover, the middle farmers faced a labor shortage when year-round employment became increasingly available on the state farms. Thus, there was a noticeable deterioration of the economic performance of the "kulaks" in 1961 and 1962, which was reflected in a rise in autoconsumption, greater barter sales, and a decline in production and deliveries to INRA's purchasing agencies. In late 1961, local INRA cadres indiscriminately seized the properties of many farmers who were hoarding foodstuffs or reducing production.

By April, 1962, food and raw material shortages were Cuba's single most troublesome economic problem, and INRA reversed its line on the "kulaks." Much of the land that had been expropriated in the preceding months was given back to its owners,[71] although INRA retained many farms because the owners reportedly neglected or abandoned their fields.[72] In May, 1962, Castro announced that all but the largest farms would be returned to their owners if INRA "had to" in order to maintain production.[73] Next month, Carlos Ra-

---

[71] In 1959 and 1960, INRA zone chiefs and local leaders took the initiative in returning some lands seized by overeager cadres (Lisandro Otero, *Cuba: Zona de Desarrollo Agrario* [Havana, Casa de las Américas, 1960], p. 48). On the later period see Blas Roca, "Discursos en la cuarta reunión de las Escuelas de Instrucción Revolucionaria," *Hoy*, July 26, 1962.

[72] *Hablan para el Instituto Popular de Chile*, p. 70.

[73] Speech on May 10, 1962, monitored radio.

fael Rodríguez, the head of INRA, assured middle farmers who put idle land under the plow that they would receive "guarantees" against expropriation.[74]

Toward the end of 1962, when the food situation improved slightly, it became increasingly clear that the middle farmers had received only a temporary respite. In the first place, many farmers were involved in counterrevolutionary activities, particularly in the region of the Escambray Mountains. Rafael Rodríguez wrote in 1963 that the middle farmers were completely at odds with the revolution politically.[75]

Second, the new agricultural policy introduced in 1963, which emphasized sugar and cattle production at the expense of rapid diversification, compelled INRA to re-evaluate the role of the middle farmers who cultivated nearly one-quarter of the island's cane land. Under a system of physical planning, the division of the cane fields between the private and public sector placed a number of hurdles in the way of programming the harvest, chief among which was the rational utilization of the cane labor force. A labor shortage developed during the last half of the 1961 harvest and became successively more severe in 1962 and 1963. With no important incentives to reinvest current earnings and declining opportunities to use incomes for current consumption or financial investments, the middle *colonos* were able to offer relatively high wage rates and bid labor away from the state cane farms. Another compelling factor in the situation was INRA's inability to plan irrigation and other investments rationally where cane land and *colonos* properties were contiguous and fundamentally one and the same economic resource.

For these reasons, the government decreed a second Agrarian Reform Law in October, 1963.[76] INRA took over approximately 10,000

[74] Speech on June 19, 1962, monitored radio.

[75] Carlos Rafael Rodríguez, "El nuevo camino de la agricultura Cubana," *Cuba Socialista*, 3, No. 27 (November, 1963), p. 73.

[76] Ley de Nacionalización, *Gaceta Oficial Extraordinaria*, October 3, 1963. Compensation equal to $15 per expropriated *caballería* per month (with a $100 monthly minimum and a $250 monthly maximum) payable for ten years was granted those who lost their land, in the event they were working the land directly or indirectly via an administrator. In the event that they were not work-

farms incorporating over 130,000 *caballerías*, or almost 20 per cent of Cuba's farmland. An estimated 3,000 farms escaped nationalization because they were owned or administered by more than one member of the same family, or because they were especially well managed. INRA thus enlarged the state sector of the agricultural economy to well over 70 per cent of Cuba's total farmland. The Second Reform placed the nationalized properties under a new organization set up on the provincial level, the Nationalized Farm Enterprises. This phase of the agrarian revolution thus came to a close, and socialism replaced capitalism in rural Cuba.

[10]

We have finally to consider the role of the National Institute of Agrarian Reform in the agrarian revolution. With the aid of hindsight it is easy to understand how INRA came to be the cornerstone of the new rural economy. The institute was staffed by the officers of the Rebel Army, the same men who had been in charge of the unplanned and informal reform movement in occupied Cuba in 1958 and during the first half of 1959. These men were given broad authority and sweeping, vaguely defined tasks to accomplish. They were also taught the rudiments of the causes and cures of Cuba's backwardness. But most of these men were not administrators or technicians, and when, during the abortive Communist "take over" of the mass revolutionary organizations in 1961 and early 1962, some of them resisted the introduction of rational administrative procedures, technical questions became confused with political questions, to the benefit of the old-line Communists.

A number of new Rebel Army departments were set up in 1959 to facilitate the work of the guerrillas turned agrarian reformers. The most important of these were the Departments for the Organization of Cooperatives (created in February, 1959), Peasant Cultural, Material, and Technical Assistance (formed two months later), and

---

ing the land at all, payment was set at $10 monthly. In November, a compensation fund was created with an original capital of $6 million (Resolución No. 1188 del Ministerio de Hacienda, *Gaceta Oficial*, November 21, 1963).

Peasant Housing Construction, organized in June.[77] These new groupings were given money, personnel, and physical resources by existing government organisms, private businesses, and private individuals, and most of their early work was in the field of investments in social overhead capital. Army units erected schools, clinics, and rural housing, completed farm-to-market roads, and here and there supplied farm labor and management to small cooperatives. INRA, during its first months, was in a real sense a branch of the Rebel Army. The institute's director and nearly all its provincial and zone chiefs were army officers, and Rebel Army soldiers continued to be used in local rural construction work throughout 1959 and 1960.

Until early 1960 the work of three INRA departments was most prominent. To the Legal Department fell the jobs of instituting expropriations proceedings, title revisions, and adjudications under the Reform Law, while the Department of Land distributed properties, organized, administered, and developed the early cooperatives, and in July created the Zones of Agricultural Development, which were meant to be planning areas, but whose main function was the redistribution of land.[78] The Department of Production and Foreign Commerce, which quickly became INRA's most powerful division before the year ended, was responsible for planning rural investments and diversification programs, and providing credit, technical help, and other resources to execute these programs. During the following three years, INRA expanded in all directions; new departments were created and old ones were enlarged; existing autonomous agencies were incorporated into the institute; the process of expropriation and the emergence of fresh economic and political problems compelled INRA's chiefs to constantly modify the organization's structure.

[77] There were four others concerned with Reforestation (a task later given to the Ministry of Agriculture), Assistance to War Victims, Construction and Organization of School Cities, and People's Beaches.

[78] There were twenty-six ZDA's at first; consolidation and addition of new zones led to an expansion to twenty-eight. In January, 1961, they had outlived their usefulness and were abolished and replaced by the General Administrations of the People's Farms and Cane Cooperatives.

The Production Department underwent perhaps the most far-reaching modifications. Before 1959 was out, it acquired the Agricultural Production Committee of the old Tobacco Stabilization Fund, together with the direction of the fund itself. In 1959 and 1960 the Institutes of Coffee Stabilization and Purchase and Sales of Coffee, the Cuban Sugar Stabilization Institute, and other, smaller bodies fell under its control. In 1961 the General Rice Administration, created in October, 1960, was placed under the Production Department, whose Supply Section, broken down into three administrations (seeds, fertilizers, and insecticides) rapidly extended over Cuba's rural landscape and by mid-1961 maintained ten regional and dozens of local storehouses.

A change of major proportions was ushered in during November, 1959, when INRA created its Industrialization Division to manage the growing number of enterprises related directly or indirectly to agriculture that it was operating. The new Ministry of Industries almost immediately took over these plants, however, and, as the land reform proceeded, other divisions, notably the Legal and Land Departments, receded to minor importance. At the same time, existing institutions touching on various aspects of Cuban agriculture were absorbed into the INRA structure. The most important of these was BANFAIC, which INRA took over in March, 1960; INRA's credit division and the moderates in BANFAIC had an uncomfortable working arrangement and failed to see eye to eye on policy matters.

Thus, INRA reached into nearly every corner of Cuban agriculture. By late 1963, INRA's structure had become so complex and uncoordinated that Rafael Rodríguez spoke openly of the need to reorganize the institute from top to bottom. From the outset the institute had seized the initiative away from the old state organisms, particularly the Ministry of Agriculture, which (before it was abolished in January, 1961) had been handed such minor tasks as reforestation.[79] Given a key role by the Agrarian Reform Law, INRA enlarged its domain when the cattle land's were seized, and when it took on the job of administering confiscated properties and, in August, 1959, all state, provincial, and municipal lands. The expropria-

[79] *The Havana Post,* January 21, 1960.

tion and transfer of the sugar lands ratified INRA's central role, while the failure of the banks and large landlords to provide credits in 1959–1960 opened up new doors to the institute. Once INRA was established, it was the logical candidate to administer the various farm-related enterprises that before the revolution were owned by the National Bank and BANFAIC itself. Moreover, INRA was naturally drawn into the business of supplying machinery, fertilizers, credits, and so on to the early cooperatives and state farms, and it was compelled more and more to engage in direct agricultural planning. It is probably attributing too much foresight to the new government to assert that "the Agrarian Reform Law recognized these implications by stipulating that INRA should be independent and its rulings final regarding land redistribution, and implementation of agricultural development plans," although it is true that "once having assumed responsibility for the land, INRA would then have to assume responsibility for all aspects of land reform operation and financing." [80]

More generally, INRA expanded and prospered because the social revolution in Cuba was first and foremost in agriculture, where the expropriation and collectivization of land were the preconditions for accelerating the rhythm of economic development and *in and of themselves* helped to consolidate the new government's power. The Agrarian Reform Law of 1959 turned fewer than 5 per cent of Cuba's landlords against the government but won the support of the rural masses and simultaneously opened up the path to the rational planned utilization of Cuba's soils. The Second Agrarian Reform affected less than 10 per cent of the island's remaining farmers and helped the revolutionary government a little farther along that path.[81]

[80] Maurice Zeitlin and Robert Scheer, *Cuba: Tragedy in Our Hemisphere* (New York, 1963), pp. 89–90.

[81] A discussion of Cuba's new rural organization would be incomplete without at least brief mention of a number of minor associations that sprang up between 1960 and 1963. Prominent among these were the island's eleven henequen cooperatives created on Cuba's fourteen privately owned henequen farms, which INRA purchased in January, 1960. These cooperatives had three thousand members and extended over about twenty thousand *caballerías*. Until 1962, when they were transformed into state farms, cooperative manage-

ment more or less paralleled that in the cane cooperatives. A managing council, elected by a general assembly of each cooperative, worked hand in hand with an INRA-appointed administrator. Another mode of organization was the cooperative in which members had few fixed assets, selling little more than their labor: the Cooperative of Yarey Weavers in Trinidad, organized in March, 1960, by the National Tourist Institute, which counted over one thousand members, fell into this category, as did some of the early, more backward carbon cooperatives. There was also the kind of cooperative set up to mutually assist widely scattered small producers; the Agriculture Cooperative of Cuba, formed in February, 1960, and consisting of only seventy small farmers, can be placed under this heading. Finally, a number of consumer cooperatives sprang up in 1960–1962, most of them, evidently, located in Las Villas. All of these new associations were pragmatic in character and aimed to simultaneously rationalize production methods and raise output, and improve the material standards of living of their members.

[6]

The Nationalization
of Industry

[1]

Like most branches of Cuban agriculture, the organization of industry before the revolution was monopolistic, price-fixing was widespread, productive investment opportunities were limited, production was generally inefficient, and productivity was low. Cartelization of industry and monopolistic practices were attributable to three broad factors. First, high overhead costs and economies of large-scale production in many spheres of industry limited investment opportunities to a handful of enterprises, each of which enjoyed considerable market power. Particularly in the high-technology, modern industries dominated by United States capital, such as chemicals and rubber, one or two enterprises were sufficient to supply the entire Cuban market.

Second, the Cuban government extended exclusive rights, special privileges, high tariff protection, and financial and other subsidies to most branches of industry, including subsidiaries of United States corporations. State protection and subsidies sheltered high-cost, inefficient enterprises, inflated profit margins of low-cost, high-productivity firms, and constituted an important source of state corruption.

Third, subsidiaries of United States corporations in manufacturing, mining, financial, and other spheres were integrated into the structure of the United States economy, not the local economy. The policies of the three corporations were "determined by their parent companies . . . and not by the local need to integrate industries and to increase inter-dependence between different sectors of the

135

economy." Many sectors of the local economy were therefore "hardly more than a locus of production made up of a number of fragments held tenuously together largely by government controls —themselves often borrowed from elsewhere." [1]

Also, as in agriculture, monopolistic industrial organization and an absence of local economic integration constituted the main impediment to industrial growth and development. Contributing factors included the backwardness of the agricultural sector, which failed to supply a strong demand for industrial goods, the underdevelopment of the mineral sector, the absence of widespread technical education, and restrictive practices of the trade unions.

Similarities between agriculture and industry also highlighted the postrevolutionary period. In the first place, the nationalization of industry afforded the Revolutionary Government direct control over industrial enterprise and resources, and hence was the basic precondition for the reorganization of industry. Second, the reorganization of industry was the fundamental prerequisite for the elimination of inefficiencies and waste inherited from the old regime.

[2]

An examination of Table 1 discloses the main contours of the prerevolutionary nonagricultural economy. Most startling was the unproductive allocation of labor. Three economic sectors employing nearly 500,000 workers, or roughly one-quarter of the labor force, contributed little or nothing to economic growth. Personal services (chiefly domestic servants) were important because of Cuba's highly stratified society and unequal income distribution. Wholesale and retail commerce thrived because of the central role of the island's export trade. The deep penetration of the state in the economy required an unproductive state bureaucracy. Manufacturing itself employed less than 17 per cent of Cuba's workers, nearly one-third of whom were sugar mill workers.

Crude sugar production suffered from a debilitating measure of cartelization. Ownership of the island's 161 mills was concentrated

[1] Lloyd Best, "Size and Survival," *New World,* Guyana Independence Issue (Guyana, 1966), p. 61.

Table 1. Industrial distribution of economically active population, 1953

Industry	Total workers	Percentage of total
Agriculture and related	818,706	41.5
Agricultural livestock	801,707	
Other	16,999	
Mining	9,618	1.4
Manufacturing	327,208	16.6
Food products	117,642	
Clothes and footwear	47,127	
Tobacco products	36,468	
Wood and cork products	29,408	
Machinery (exclud. elec.)	18,298	
Beverage	10,139	
Printing and publishing	10,027	
Textiles	9,707	
Other	48,392	
Construction	65,292	3.3
Public utilities	8,493	1.4
Commerce	232,323	11.7
Wholesale and retail	213,859	
Other	18,464	
Transportation and related	104,003	5.2
Transportation	94,845	
Other	9,158	
Services and related	395,904	20.1
Government	96,073	
Business services	104,083	
Personal services	178,504	
Other	17,244	
Other	10,773	1.4
Total	1,972,266	100.0

Source: Cuba, Oficina Nacional de los Censos Demográfico y Electoral, *Censos de Población, Vivienda y Electoral, 1953, Informe General* (Havana, 1953), p. 195.

in the hands of eighty-three individuals and corporations, roughly one-half North Americans and one-half Cubans. The aim of both foreign and domestic corporations was to enlarge the share of the United States market allotted to Cuban sugar, maximize speculative profits through the manipulation of sugar stocks destined for the international market, and maintain the local economic *status quo*. Between local and foreign capital there were no important conflicts of interest. Both groups were dependent on political decisions made unilaterally by the United States with regard to the sugar quota and thus controlled resources that were in reality "mere protrusions from the United States." [2] Moreover, there were extensive financial interlocks between the two groups.

Sources of raw cane supplies, market controls, and fixed prices were not left to the chance operation of a private ring. The Cuban government assigned a fixed supply of cane and fixed production quotas to each mill and established controlled prices. Awarded fixed quotas, there was little incentive for the mills to introduce cost-reducing, output-increasing innovations. Permanent employment rights at regulated wage rates granted by the government to the mill workers inhibited the introduction of labor-saving technical changes. Most capital expenditures in the mills were replacement outlays and capital-saving, modernization investments financed largely out of retained profits.

There was a large amount of excess capacity in the industry. Capital tied up in sugar milling was highly specialized and lay idle for six or seven months each year during the dead season. Only one mill had a vegetable-oil-extraction plant, and a small refinery was attached to but one other. Sugar by-products were the traditional commodities, molasses and rum, and a handful of newer activities such as paper products. A chemical industry based on modern sugar-processing techniques remained the dream of a handful of visionaries and the pipe dream of the entire society.

Finally, there were too many mills in operation, each too small in scale. The rationalization of the industry came to an end during the

[2] Boris Swerling, "Domestic Control of Cuba Sugar," *Journal of Farm Economics*, 33, No. 3 (1951), p. 347. The Tarafa Law of 1923 prohibited the construction of new private ports. The depression, however, improved the competitive position of United States mills (United States companies were mostly multiplant operations and closed down high-cost plants and worked low-cost plants to full capacity) and thus reinforced the existing distortions in the structure of social overhead.

1920's, which saw the number of mills reduced by more than 90 per cent from the mid-nineteenth-century high as a result of economies of large-scale production in milling and technological advances that reduced the costs of transportation. Despite further reductions in cost and technical developments that pointed toward larger and more efficient and integrated units, the number of mills remained almost fixed for three decades. The quota system which guaranteed each mill a fixed output and stable profit obstructed the further rationalization of the industry, even though a few large units equipped to process other foodstuffs and raw materials during the dead season would have been more efficient.

Two monopolies dominated the public utilities sector, where public regulation was virtually nonexistent. Although the telephone monopoly had been declaring a 6 per cent annual dividend, it refused to act on nearly 40,000 new phone applications in 1954 in the absence of a rate increase. In 1957, Batista granted the raise and received his famous gold telephone in return. The company raised dividends from 6 to 8 per cent and received a $17.5 million expansion loan from the government. Similar monopolistic pricing policies prevailed in electric power production and distribution, where rates were considerably higher than those in developed capitalist economies. Many firms established their own generators because official prices were out of reach.

Industrial organization was equally irrational in other leading branches of industry. Outside of the sugar and utilities sectors, three main types of industrial structures coexisted side by side. Between these sectors there was little capital or labor mobility; nor did technological advances and improvements in administrative and management techniques spill over from one sector to the other.

The most characteristic industrial structure consisted of a handful of dominant firms coexisting with a large number of tiny, backward enterprises, that is, oligopoly with a large fringe. In the footwear industry there were seven relatively large factories, a few out-of-date, middle-sized workshops, and over a thousand small sweatshops dominated by the tanneries and big retailers. In cigar and cigarette manufacture there were three large, mechanized factories and an uncounted number of small shops. Only 9,000 workers were engaged in factory production, while over 26,000 workers were employed in small-scale, mainly home, industry.[3] In the wood and wood products industry over 25,000 of 32,000 employed workers were located outside the factor sector. There were three large-scale, efficient meat-packing plants side by side with over thirty small, inefficient units producing low quality products. One large corporation produced most of Cuba's textile products, although there were dozens of smaller firms. Cuban capital controlled nearly all of the enterprises in the industries comprising this sector, with the exception of pharmaceuticals, which was dominated by three United States-owned corporations coexisting with a large number of small Cuban firms.

The second major type of industrial structure was organized almost altogether along classic putting-out and home industry lines. These industries were highly competitive, but labor productivity was abysmally low, mechanization was nonexistent, and product quality was inferior. Moreover, there was a great deal of overcrowding. Taken together with the inflated middlemen profits, this meant that costs and prices were much higher than necessary and that profit margins were tiny. Cuba's second largest industry, clothing and footwear, belonged in this category. Thus, in Cuba's three largest industries (excepting sugar milling)—clothes and footwear, tobacco products, and wood and cork products—the "typical" workman was a home or sweatshop worker.

The third type of industrial structure was pure oligopoly, that is, industries comprising two or three relatively large-scale modern enterprises with few or no small firms. Examples were rubber products, sulfuric acid and inorganic chemical products, oil refining, glass products, and cement. Subsidiaries of United States corporations established control in most of these industries, mainly on the basis of advanced technology, modern management, and controls of

[3] This calculation is based on the assumption that the nine thousand workers employed by firms nationalized in 1962 were in the "factory" sector, and that workers in units not nationalized were in the putting-out, sweatshop, and home industry sectors.

supplies.[4] Opportunities for local enterprise in this sector were few.

In Cuban manufacturing industry as a whole, one out of every three workers remained outside the factory sector. Even in factory industry, few workers were employed in efficient, modern production units. All in all, 1,333 production units in forty-two manufacturing industries were called "factories" or "mills." The average size plant thus employed only 126 workers. In twelve industries the average plant employed 50 or less workers; in thirteen industries, employment in the average plant was between 51 to 100 workers; in six industries (paper, minerals, artificial wood, matches, ferrous metals, and glass) between 101 to 200 workers were employed in the average plant; in nine industries, between 201 to 500 (these industries were, in order of importance, sugar milling, beer and malt, yarn and plain fabrics, petroleum refining, rubber, cigarettes, metal containers, cement and cigars). Finally, one unit producing synthetic fibers employed 920 workers, and three nickel-processing units employed an average of 1,138 workers (see Table 2).

[3]

Only a handful of Cuba's modern manufacturing plants spontaneously sprang up from the soil of "free enterprise." The majority of the island's large-scale production units enjoyed direct or indirect state subsidies. Cuba's four largest units outside of the sugar sector, each employing more than 1,000 workers, fall into this category: two nickel-processing centers, an electrical plant, and a textile center. Similarly, nearly all of the twenty-one production units that employed between 500 and 999 workers were built in part with state funds, besides enjoying tax and other advantages of various kinds.

The origins of state protection for home industry go back to 1927,

---

[4] As a rule, United States corporate branch plants and subsidiaries in Cuba did not buy and sell from each other; they imported intermediate goods, capital, etc., and sold final products in the Cuban market. Thus, technological advances in one industry had little or no impact on other industries, precisely because foreign-owned industry was not integrated into the Cuban economy. Similarly, a rise in commodity demand in one industry led to an expansion of demand *in the United States*, not Cuba, because most industries in the oligopolistic sector purchased most of their inputs from abroad.

Table 2. Cuban industries by number of plants, employment, and average size of plant in Cuba's "factory" sector, 1962

Industry	No. plants	Employment (Industrias) [a]	Employment (Educacion) [b]	Average size [a]
Group A				
Nickel	3	3,413	3,940	1,138
Synthetic fibers	1	920	964	920
Sugar	177	76,597	102,434	433
Beer and malt	6	2,104	2,297	351
Yarn/plain fabrics	28	9,026	9,668	322
Petroleum refining	3	956	2,708	319
Rubber	7	1,946	1,884	279
Cigarettes	10	2,786	3,149	279
Metal containers	6	1,424	1,777	237
Cement	4	893	1,583	223
Group B				
Cigars	42	8,901	7,172	212
Paper	8	1,327	1,295	166
Minerals	22	3,456	5,024	157
Artificial wood	5	713	646	143
Matches	9	1,064	906	118
Ferrous metals	6	704	2,070	117
Glass	5	529	596	106
Group C				
Gas	4	362	352	91
Recovery of raw materials	5	428	353	86
Natural fibers	7	586	575	84
Paper products	27	2,248	2,469	83
Leather products	73	5,950	6,270	82
Ceramics	6	478	420	80
Machinery	62	4,913	2,523	79
Soap and perfume	20	1,331	1,539	66
Knit goods fabrics	52	3,254	2,578	62
Paint	4	247	304	62
Basic chemicals	8	487	558	61
Plain textiles (readymades)	179	10,991	9,340	58
Plastics	12	628	788	52

Industry	No. plants	Employment (Industrias)[a]	Employment (Educacion)[b]	Average size[a]
Mineral water, soft drinks	33	1,662	1,675	50
Group D				
Fertilizer	22	1,053	961	48
Electricity	90	4,176	5,140	46
Non-ferrous metals	22	994	1,269	45
Wood products	71	3,134	2,412	44
Salt	15	575	478	38
Flour	117	4,258	6,768	36
Electrical equipment	6	168	346	28
Tanneries	37	1,015	1,023	27
Automotive	10	222	233	22
Liquors and wines	36	753	602	21
Pharmaceutical products	73	1,489	2,128	20
Total[c]	1,333	168,263	199,217	126

[a] Cuba, Ministerio de Industrias, Dirección de Trabajo y Salarios, "Total de obreros de las Empresas Consolidadas," n.p. (January 31, 1962), mimeographed.

[b] Cuba, Ministerio de Educación, "Censos de obreros en la Ministerio de Industrias," n.p. (July, 1962), mimeographed.

[c] There are a number of reasons why the two totals do not correspond. First, the Ministry of Education count was taken over six months after the Ministry of Industries census, and there were increases and decreases in employment in the interim. Second, with regard to employment in the sugar industry, roughly 25,000 workers in the Ministry of Education census failed to show up in the other count, because the latter was not taken during the *zafra*. Third, more often than not, the Ministry of Education census includes more "workers" than does the other census; the former includes foremen and supervisory and technical personnel, whereas the latter does not. It should be noted that included in the Ministry of Industries census were three supply "plants," employing 141 workers and 34 units consolidated by Province, and employing 2,151 workers. In the Ministry of Education census, these provincial units employed 1,262 workers.

when a reversal in Cuban tariff policy resulted in a reduction in tariffs on industrial raw materials and fuels and an increase in rates on the finished commodities Cuba was able to produce. Prior to the 1927 tariff, from which consumer durable and nondurable goods industries profited most, the rate structure was by and large fiscal in character and reflected the old Spanish colonial policy, which favored imports of manufactured goods and discriminated against raw materials. The General Agreement on Tariffs and Trade (1947) and other modifications made from time to time in the rate structure failed to depart significantly from the 1927 tariff.

By the mid-1950's about 10 per cent of the island's imports entered duty free, and tariffs on a larger proportion were quite low. Apart from their role as an instrument of national economic development, tariffs were used to promote Cuban exports. Tariff policy discriminated against countries whose imports from Cuba were a small proportion of their exports to the island. Finally, United States exporters received preferential treatment under the Cuban tariff structure. This was the price Cuba paid for the sugar quota.

Not until 1952 was a serious attempt made to rationalize the relationship between the Cuban state and the new domestic and foreign manufacturing interests. This development was the outgrowth of the new anticolonialist spirit that had exploded in Bolivia and other Latin American countries, the end of the Korean War, which threatened the Cuban economy with a severe crisis of exports, a fresh interest in manufacturing investments abroad on the part of United States capital, and the desire by Batista to consolidate his newly regained political power by promoting national economic development. Directly after his coup, Batista brought together Cuba's best-known economic and financial specialists (except those who had gone over to the opposition), and they drew up a National Program of Economic Action. Subsequently modified by industrial, agricultural, and labor groups, the program became the main guide for the dictator's economic goals.[5] Problems of market organization and monopoly were played down, except relationships between labor and capital, which the program's architects maintained required rationalizing. Major emphasis was given the expansion of the island's infrastructure and the stimulation of new manufactures.

To this end, United States tariff preferences were slightly modi-

[5] Cuba, Consejo Nacional de Economía, *El Programa Económico de Cuba* (Havana, 1955), pp. 39–42.

fied and important concessions were granted new industries.[6] Batista also expanded Cuba's public works construction. Under what finally came to be called the Economic and Social Development Program, the Cuban government granted itself authority to issue bonds up to a total of $350 million. Meanwhile, $74 million in outstanding public debt came due, and bondholders were given the option of liquidating their holdings or turning them in for new issues paying a 2 per cent premium. Only $1 million was taken in cash. The government had insured itself against an unfavorable outcome of the transactions. United States banks on the island were ready with a $50 million credit in the event that Cuba's investing classes should reject the new issues. The foreign interests were thus willing to underwrite the development program. From the standpoint of the foreign banks it was important that the dictatorship be stabilized.

Between 1953 and 1956, $145 million in new bonds were issued by the new quasi-public development banks.[7] From 1952 to 1957 the Cuban national debt rose from $240 million to an estimated $850 million, and, according to some reports, to over $1 billion. Inflation was avoided by tapping domestic savings (debt service was satisfactory) and allowing foreign exchange reserves to fall from over $500 million in the boom year of 1951 to less than $100 million in 1958. Also, large commercial bank cash reserves (which fluctuated between 30 per cent to 50 per cent of deposit liabilities) are evidence of the supercautious attitude of Cuba's private bankers. Thus, by the time of Batista's ouster, sources of noninflationary fi-

[6] Capital exports were exempted from taxes (if said capital had previously entered the country to be invested). There was a three-year exemption from levies on imports of machinery and equipment; from other taxes on the export of money; from fiscal taxes on property transfers in connection with the installation of industry. From levies on the import of raw materials, profits and excess profits taxes, up to 10 per cent of paid-in capital, and any tax specifically affecting raw materials produced in Cuba, there were ten-year exemptions. These and other exemptions were designed to encourage the exploitation of domestic raw materials, the import of raw materials for new industries, and new investment in manufacturing in general. Also, antidumping measures against export subsidies and exchange rate manipulation (as a form of subsidy) by foreign governments were promulgated in 1958.

[7] Cuba, Banco Nacional, *Economic Development Program, Progress Report No. 1* (Havana, September 1956), p. 15.

nance were nearly used up. This would have placed serious limits on the development program in the event that Batista had retained power and might have been a factor in the general demoralization of the government toward the end of 1958.

Excluding agriculture, total investments by the new development institutions jumped from $1.3 million in 1952 to $181.6 million in 1956, of which $80 million was in industry. The rapidly growing importance of the state in Cuba's economic development was reflected in the dramatic jump in capital formation by the public sector. In 1949 state investments accounted for a mere 14 per cent of total investment, but by 1957 the government's share had risen to 40 per cent.

Tax concessions, subsidies and loans, guarantees against expropriation, favorable price agreements, and other policies induced many domestic and foreign firms to construct new plants and expand old units. In this period the very largest investments were in power, mining, and oil refining, the sectors dominated by foreign capital; new small-scale investments in manufacturing were shared by Cuban and outside interests.[8] Meanwhile, the island's railroad network was rehabilitated with a $30 million capital outlay, and heavy expenditures were made on dock facilities, road improvements, and other transportation overhead. In 1957 tentative agreements with four British firms to develop Cuba's shipping were signed and a joint Cuban-British corporation was formed. Two years earlier Batista had legalized gambling to open the way for new hotel construction under a scheme whereby the government matched foreign investments dollar for dollar.

These new experiments in state capitalism raised the rate of growth of manufacturing output to an average of about 5 per cent during the dictatorship, and the development program succeeded in offsetting the worst effects of the post-Korean War sugar crisis. From the standpoint of multiplying available jobs, generating a

[8] From 1950 to 1958, United States investment in petroleum expanded from $24 million to $90 million; in mining, from $15 million to $180 million; in manufacturing, from $54 million to $80 million; in public services, from $271 million to $344 million; in commerce, from $21 million to $35 million. United States investments in agriculture remained the same.

wide range of import substitutes, diversifying exports, and laying a permanent foundation for steady economic growth, all of which would require a thorough overhaul of the manufacturing sector and the rationalization of Cuba's most important industries, the program was a total failure. Progress in the development of import substitutes was limited to certain branches of textiles and food processing. There were no breakthroughs in raw materials production or processing, nor was Cuba's dependence on fixed capital goods imports and foreign supplies of consumer goods lessened. (The decline in the ratio of imported consumer goods to total national production in the 1930's and 1940's was due less to government development programs than to depression- and war-induced shortages of consumer inputs, which made it highly profitable to produce input substitutes.) The structure of the economy remained fundamentally unchanged. The alliance between domestic and foreign capital merely superimposed a handful of more production units on an antiquated industrial structure. Labor productivity remained low and costs high. The failure to attack the problem of industrial organization sharply limited the island's industrial development. Yet Batista's program put the spotlight on economic development and undoubtedly made it easier for the post-1959 government to reintroduce and intensify the theme.

[4]

Batista's industrialization program failed for a number of interrelated reasons, most of them attributable to the limits on economic growth placed by the structure and organization of the Cuban economy. First and foremost, the emphasis given sugar production, together with the organization of the industry, sharply limited industrial development by distorting the structure of the island's social overhead capital and infrastructure, thus raising costs for producers in other branches of the economy. Ports, railroads, roads, storage facilities, and the distribution system were all oriented toward sugar production.

Second, the stagnation of the agricultural economy, including the sugar industry, limited the production of foods and raw materials and hence the development of food canning and other industries integral to agriculture. Suppliers of agricultural equipment were also faced with sluggish markets, in particular the iron and steel foundries producing heavy equipment for the sugar mills. In addition, large seasonal and other fluctuations in the incomes of farmers and farm workers generated sharp fluctuations in commodity demand, increasing risk and uncertainty, enlarging excess productive capacity, and rendering rational investment policies difficult.

Third, Cuban–United States economic relations limited the development of home industry. About two-thirds of all United States exports entered Cuba at a tariff rate of 16 per cent or less. Eighty per cent of United States exports to Cuba enjoyed tariff preferences of 30 per cent and up and were especially high on items that European and other suppliers were able to sell at competitive prices. Tariff preferences were in force after 1902 and conditioned Cuban importers to consider the United States as the only source of supplies. Undercapitalized, small-scale industry was too weak to compete with privileged imports on the basis of either price or quality. This was a major weakness in the textile and milk products industries,[9] as well as other branches of production. To be sure, a new Tariff Reform Commission was created in 1955 in order to study existing tariff laws, and although a new, more complex tariff schedule was worked out by early 1958, Batista postponed negotiations with the United States until it was too late.

Of more significance, the harmonization of investment, production, pricing, product, and other decisions by subsidiaries of United States corporations with similar decisions by Cuban firms was impossible. The parent corporations dictated policy to their subsidiaries within the frame of reference of the corporation's interests as a whole, not the interests of the individual subsidiary, still less the local economy.[10] In addition, Cuba's lack of monetary autonomy

[9] Carlos Quintana y Octavio A. Martínez, *El Desarrollo de la Industria Textil Cubana* (Havana, January, 1960), mimeographed (we will refer to this work as *Textil*); Great Britain, Board of Trade, Overseas Economic Survey, *Cuba; Economic and Commercial Conditions in Cuba* (London, 1954), p. 50.

[10] It has been asserted that the backward sector remained backward *because* the modern sector was controlled by foreigners (Juan Noyola, "Aspectos

restricted business loans (in 1957, 60 per cent of all bank credits were channeled into short-term sugar and import loans) and ruled out inflation-financed accumulation altogether.

Finally, widespread, systematic corruption limited investment opportunities, or at the very least narrowed the field of investment activity. Cuban capitalists had no important source of private long-term financing and were compelled to seek funds from the state, where the price of investment capital was frequently quite simply the investor's integrity. Political influence, personal access to the Presidential Palace, a well-placed bribe, and a pliable conscience counted far more than a well-planned project. Many Cubans and foreigners met one or more of these qualifications and acquired extraordinarily cheap credit and favorable terms. It was possible, for example, for a group of speculators to obtain 50 per cent equity in a projected enterprise on the basis of outlay amounting to no more than 5 per cent to 10 per cent of total capital requirements. Thus large-scale subsidies in effect eliminated the entrepreneurial function of Cuban capitalists, reinforcing prevailing short-term, easy-profit, opportunistic attitudes.

The corruption system was sustained by a variety of other factors, including the lack of opportunities in a stagnating economy, the all-pervasive gambling mentality which conditioned the outlook of urban Cubans and which was rooted in the island's over-all dependence on the volatile international sugar market, and restrictions specifically associated with the ways in which labor, capital, and product markets were organized. With the monopolization and cartelization of markets, supply-and-demand prices bore little or no relationship to one another, and thus opened the way for a flourishing system of bribery. On the most elementary and mechanical level, this involved a pay-off by a job-seeking worker to the corrupt union boss or employer's personnel agent. Frequently, one condition for a state

económicos de la Revolucion Cubana," *Cuadernos de Ciencias Sociales y Económicas,* Comisión Nacional Cubana de la UNESCO, No. 1 [1961], *passim*). In Cuba there is little empirical support for this proposition. The gap between the backward and modern sectors of industries not owned by United States capital (e.g., textiles) was as great or greater than in those industries dominated by United States capital (e.g., pharmaceuticals).

loan was that Batista men be given posts in the personnel offices of the new firm. In such cases, it would be the height of naïveté for a worker subsequently to expect to obtain employment without a large bribe. In the housing market, a combination of shortages and official rent ceilings gave incentives to landlords to bribe building inspectors in order to get tenements condemned. Tenants were then dispossessed and readmitted at higher rents. On a more rarefied level, "entrepreneurs" transferred vast sums to government officials for scarce public contracts and public funds. The official family itself was expert at getting something for nothing: parking meter revenues yielded the personal allowance of Batista's wife, and the dictator himself amassed a huge fortune from stolen public funds. The tax system itself consisted of, in Castro's words, "paying off the revenue collector instead of paying the state." [11]

The corruption system was basically a symptom of the island's backwardness. This is confirmed by the fact that it was wiped out in a few months by the Revolutionary Government. But it was also a "second order" cause of industrial underdevelopment, because it diverted the attention and energies of the population from acquiring physical and human assets and discouraged productive employment. In brief, corruption thrived because of the absence of opportunities in the private marketplace, which led to large-scale stealing from the public purse.

Under Batista's last government, the corruption system was extended, elaborated, and elevated to an everyday system of business. A confidential business report service described the system:

The "collector" is an important man on the island. Everybody doing business, from the cabbie to a hole-in-the-wall shop must pay to the regime's and the machine's ambulatory cash register. Veritable scales have been set for anything from street vendors to big businessmen . . . [graft] probably has never risen to such heights (or dropped to such depths), nor has it ever been so efficient as under Batista. In such areas as Santiago, many a small businessman has been ruined . . . be-

[11] Fidel Castro, "Why We Fight," *Coronet*, 43, No. 4 (February, 1958), p. 58.

cause he could no longer "deliver" the share demanded from him by his "protector." [12]

In higher circles in the public economy, about one-quarter of total state expenditures was paid out in graft, according to one experienced banker who financed a number of Batista's projects.[13] This corresponds to the estimate of another Cuban in a position to grasp the extent of official corruption: "In the years preceding the revolution, the average amount of graft in public works (alone) cost as much as the works themselves." [14] About three-fifths of the budget of the Public Health Ministry and roughly one-third of the Education Ministry budget were stolen.[15]

Nor was the National Lottery immune from the grasp of government officials, both high and low. Over $200 million worth of tickets were sold during Batista's last reign. Winning tickets collected $114 million, expenses came to about $9 million, and the rest was stolen.[16] A close student of Cuban affairs depicted the results of the lottery as "the further economic degradation of the poor . . . [and] the most potent enemy of any program designed to promote thrift among the population." [17]

Had the Cuban state been weak and poor, state corruption would not have significantly affected industrial growth. Next to the sugar industry, however, the Cuban government was the island's largest employer, and state institutions partially or wholly owned many industrial enterprises. Thus, public corruption had a large quantitative impact on Cuba's all-around economic performance.

[12] S. J. Rundt and Associates, *Rundt's Market Reports*, No. 199 (February 14, 1959), p. 22.

[13] Irving Pflaum, "Fidelista Finance," *Reports Service, Mexico and the Caribbean Service* (American Universities Field Staff), 5, No. 8 (August, 1960), p. 9.

[14] Felipe Pazos, "The Economy," *Cambridge Opinion*, 32 (February, 1963), p. 13.

[15] Speech by Fidel Castro to Second Congress of National Association of Small Farmers, reported in *Hoy*, August 10, 1963.

[16] Cuba, Instituto Nacional de Ahorro y Vivienda, *Revista*, November 1, 1959.

[17] Lowry Nelson, *Rural Cuba* (Minneapolis, 1950), p. 218.

[5]

The fundamental behavior characteristics of Cuban industry were due to monopolistic organization and the related phenomena of dependence on sugar, agricultural stagnation, subservience to the economic interests of the United States and foreign corporations, and widespread corruption. These characteristics were threefold.

First, and most important, as in many other Latin American economies, there was large-scale excess productive capacity in Cuban industry. The immediate reasons were the lack of domestic markets, seasonal and other fluctuations in sugar production and exports, the availability and popularity of United States products,[18] restrictive labor practices, and overcrowding in small-scale industry owing to the pressure of large enterprises.[19] Idle plant and equipment therefore ran as high as 50 per cent of total capacity in some industries.[20] According to one study, nearly one-third of Cuba's industrial workers were employed less than six months annually, and about 45 per cent were at work less than nine months per year.[21] In 1956–1957, total idle capacity mounted to an estimated $1,200 per worker.[22]

[18] For example, in 1958 9 of Cuba's 24 cigarette manufacturing firms were inoperative because Cubans chose United States brands (Wyatt MacGaffey and Clifford R. Barnett, *Twentieth Century Cuba* [New York, 1965], p. 95). After World War II, many new factories were closed because United States supplies were again available (*ibid.*, p. 88).

[19] Ernesto Guevara, speech on June 18, 1960, *Obra Revolucionaria*, No. 11 (1960).

[20] Oscar D. Domech, "Los Industrias Cubanas," *Humanismo*, 8 (January–April, 1959), pp. 199–200. See also "La reforma agraria en Cuba," *Cuba 1960*, 1, No. 1 (1960), p. 22.

[21] Maurice Zeitlin, *Revolutionary Politics and the Cuban Working Class* (Princeton, 1967), Table 2.1, p. 51.

[22] Estimated from the following data found in the 26th of July economic program, written by two of Cuba's best economists, Regino Boti (until 1964 Minister of Economy) and Felipe Pazos (head of the National Bank for most of 1959, now in exile). There was $8,000 in capital per man in manufacturing and $2,800 per man in agriculture, services, etc. To employ 20,000 workers per year in manufacturing and 80,000 workers in agriculture, annual investments of $320 million would be required. According to the authors, given existing idle capacity, only $200 million was needed. Deducing, there must have been about $1,200 in idle capacity per worker.

Second, price fixing, price leadership, marketing quotas, and other monopolistic practices blanketed Cuban industry. High-cost, low-volume outputs meant high, rigid prices, sanctioned by the government, in industries such as brick, match, shoes, and textile production. Many enterprises acquired tariff protection not to undersell foreign rivals but rather to raise prices, and thus they "lost the tariff advantage, and then requested still higher tariffs to protect their business." [23]

Third, Cuban capitalists were content to maintain their historic shares of commodity markets and hence failed to improve product quality, aggressively introduce new products, and generally follow policies that would expand their share of the market. Thus, Cuban oligopolistic industries lacked the growth potential and dynamism of their counterparts in the advanced capitalist countries.

Industrial backwardness and stagnation independently thwarted the development of other branches of the economy, in particular the mining industry. The sluggish rate of growth of industrial output and foreign ownership of the mines and reserves reduced the demand for minerals to a minimum. Cuban industry (except construction, which profited from the island's abundant clay and asphalt deposits) utilized hardly any local minerals. United States mining corporations restricted the level of production to the volume of materials usable in the United States, in the context of the availability of alternative supplies controlled by the parent corporations in other countries. From the standpoint of over-all Cuban economic development, mineral production therefore failed to reach optimum levels.

Thus, in a country in which iron deposits have been estimated at 3.5 billion tons, over 25 per cent of total Latin American reserves, and nickel reserves are among the highest in the world,[24] and

[23] MacGaffey and Barnett, op. cit., p. 102.

[24] Luís Emiro Valencia, Realidad y Perspectivas de la Revolución Cubana (Havana, 1961), p. 13. These are high-cost deposits, however, because they are either scattered and require small-scale mining operations or because they are contaminated by nickel, cobalt, and chrome. Moa Bay Mining Company, a subsidiary of the United States-owned Freeport Sulphur Company, was engaged in separating nickel and cobalt from the other metals. This ore was refined into two separate metals in the United States, and iron and chrome remained married in the laterites. Low-cost iron was available elsewhere in

which was the fourth largest copper producer in the hemisphere and had extensive deposits of manganese, chromium, and tungsten, the value of total mineral output from 1902 to 1950 was no more than that of one year's average sugar crop.[25] The budget of the Bureau of Mines and Forests, a division of the Ministry of Agriculture, came to less than $10,000 annually, and a single employee wrote Cuba's geologic reports. Under Cuban law, an individual or corporation was entitled to hold a claim indefinitely without working it, and mining and export taxes were insignificant. Thus, no penalties attached to withholding resources, and no claims were made on the resources exploited.

In mining, as well as manufacturing and other branches of the Cuban economy, a thoroughgoing reorganization and rationalization of industry was long overdue. In general, what Cuba required was the consolidation of small, backward firms in the major industries in order to lower costs, reduce middlemen's profits, and improve product quality; the expansion of home demand by reducing inequalities in the distribution of income and other methods; the integration of the manufacturing, mineral, and agricultural sectors; the diversification of capital tied up in sugar milling; the rationalization of the tariff structure; monetary independence from the United States; the integration of foreign companies into the local economy; the elimination of the system of subsidies to political favorites and corrupt investors; and the planned allocation of investment funds on the basis of the needs of the island as a whole.

The reorganizations of manufacturing, agriculture, and mining were clearly mutually interdependent. The development of the internal market required an increase in rural incomes by the elimination of seasonal unemployment. The solution to seasonal unemployment depended on raising the demand for food and industrial crops by expanding manufacturing industries. Mineral production clearly was determined by the rhythm of industrial output, which, in turn, depended on the availability of low-cost materials. In these and

---

Latin America, and it did not pay the foreign mining companies to make the necessary outlays to discover the secret of cheap Cuban iron.

[25] MacGaffey and Barnett, *op. cit.*, p. 90.

other ways the fortunes of all branches of the economy were bound up with those of industry. And the solutions to the problems in all branches were hidden in the matrix of the island's politics.

[6]

Like the agrarian revolution, the nationalization of Cuban industry during the first two turbulent years of the revolution was immediately motivated by three general factors. First, the Cuban state acquired many industrial assets that "belonged" to businessmen closely involved with the Batista regime. Many of Batista's associates fled the country in early 1959, relinquished their "equity" in enterprises financed largely by the state, and hence by default gave up their assets to the National Bank, the development banks, and other state organs. A large segment of the Cuban economy literally fell into the hands of the government in 1959. Moreover, the government was compelled to initiate the reorganization of many firms that had wasted or stolen state funds.[26] The seizure and ultimate nationalization of assets belonging to active collaborators of the dictator was partly motivated by political or ideological factors, and partly by the need to maintain and expand production.

Second, the active hostility of many businessmen to the revolution forced the government to take over many industrial enterprises faced with financial bankruptcy, labor strife, or the lack of supplies, any of which threatened to make the enterprises inoperative. Last, the government purchased or seized many key sectors of the economy in order to exercise direct control over production, investment, prices, and supplies.

The first seizures of nonagricultural businesses were "ideological" (broadly speaking, not based on economic criteria) confiscations authorized by three decrees in 1959 and another in 1961. The government then moved against many firms for more or less strictly economic reasons under a number of laws and resolutions giving the Ministry of Labor wide powers of seizure, or "intervention." The oil war between Cuba and the foreign oil companies in the summer of 1960 inaugurated the great nationalization decrees of August and

[26] Ernesto Guevara, speech on June 18, 1960.

October of that year, which placed the main physical resources of the Cuban economy in the hands of the state. From 1961 to the present, the main purpose of nationalization has been to widen the area of national planning and consolidate the central government's economic rule. This process of widening and deepening state ownership or control must be seen in the light of the fact that a sizable proportion of Cuba's productive assets were already in public hands before the 1959 revolution. BANFAIC and BANDES operated four and seventeen firms, respectively, while the National Bank owned controlling shares in many firms. The important railroads and many utilities and shipping companies were also operated by the state before the revolution.

Article 24 of the 1940 Constitution flatly prohibited the confiscation of private property, and for a few days after Fidel Castro's triumph in January, 1959, protected the assets of ex-dictator Batista and his collaborators. The Constitutional Reform Law of January 10 authorized the seizure of these assets, together with those of any Cuban who had misappropriated public funds, and one month later, the Reform Law of February 7 widened the government's range of action by authorizing the confiscation of properties of anyone who had "enriched their estate, taking advantage of their public office." [27] These were the first of a total of four modifications of Article 24.

Both changes commanded broad support on the basis of simple social justice and were decreed by the Revolutionary Government's original "moderate," reformist-minded Cabinet. They were somewhat analogous to the expropriations of the properties of Frenchmen who had collaborated with the Nazis during World War II, in that they had a classless and "apolitical" character and did not carry with them either a free enterprise or collectivist bias.

Of the millions of dollars of assets acquired by the state under these two decrees, a few examples will show the nature of the acquisitions. From January to April, 1959, the Ministry for the Recov-

[27] The two decrees were published in the *Gaceta Oficial* (*Extraordinaria*), February 7, 1959, and the *Gaceta Oficial*, January 14, 1959.

ery of Stolen State Property seized 236 enterprises in Havana Province alone. Of these firms, 90 were construction companies that had obtained "illicit gains" under the Batista regime, and were turned over to the reorganized Public Works Ministry to be reopened and temporarily operated by the government. Manufacturing, agricultural, commercial, and transportation enterprises were also included. In May, the MRSSP intervened in Cuba's four airlines: Cubana and Aerovias Q, which were passenger lines, and two cargo companies. Many other assets, including bank accounts, safe-deposit boxes, empty urban lots, and hidden caches of dollars, were taken over by the ministry in the course of 1959.[28]

Two further modifications of Article 24 had a somewhat different character. The Constitutional Reform Law of December 22, 1959, legalized the confiscation of properties belonging to Cubans convicted of "counterrevolutionary" activities abroad. A final decree, the Reform Law of January 4, 1961, broadened the scope of the government's authority still further by authorizing confiscations "to counteract counterrevolutionary activities."[29]

Like the first two laws, these reforms were political in character; economic efficiency or the strategic position of the enterprise in the national economy did not motivate them. They differ from the earlier laws because they aim at the real or imagined new enemies of the Revolutionary Government, rather than at the defeated Batistianos. The revolution had acquired a distinct class character by the end of 1959, and these measures clearly mirrored the political struggles created by other economic and social measures taken by the new government.

By the summer of 1960, an estimated 200 million pesos of assets had been recovered by the MRSSP. Key sectors of some of Cuba's most important industries passed from private to public ownership, including 24 of the country's 161 sugar mills, the island's largest tex-

[28] *The Havana Post,* April 4, 1959; May 14, 1959; May 24, 1959; December 19, 1959. The *Gaceta Oficial,* August 26, 1959, lists many firms and individuals whose assets had been confiscated.

[29] The two decrees were published in the *Gaceta Oficial* (*Extraordinaria*), December 22, 1959 and January 4, 1961, respectively.

tile mill, 10 firms that made up the so-called "match trust," and many other enterprises in other branches of the economy.[30] Undoubtedly, many of these seizures, particularly of some construction firms and dairy farms in the Havana milk shed, were "doctrinaire" and wasteful. Some of these businesses were small in size, Cuban-owned, earned little profit, cooperated with the revolution, and employed a work force that had not agitated for expropriation. In these cases, the revolution suffered a loss of organizational and technical skills with no clear economic or political gain.

A second series of laws and resolutions authorized the intervention in enterprises by the Ministry of Labor. During the early months of the revolution intervention meant state management of private property and was sometimes, but by no means always, the prelude to nationalization. Seizures under these decrees seemed to be nearly always economically justified; the firms taken over were crippled by labor disputes, financially unsound, abandoned by their owners, or otherwise not functioning.

Of these decrees, Law No. 647, promulgated in November, 1959, was far and away the most important. Its premise was that the government had the obligation to "mobilize resources" to meet economic crises in work centers, specifically, to maintain production.[31] Lockouts, mass discharges, and noncompliance with Labor Ministry laws and resolutions were legal grounds for intervention, which was limited to six months, but could be extended another six months by the ministry's Intervention Division, established in June, 1960.[32] The division's cadres were rarely idle, particularly in the latter half of 1959 before the unit was formally organized: the hostility of the middle classes to the Agrarian Reform Law, new monetary controls, an accelerating capital flight, militant trade union wage policies, and new foreign trade controls that complicated the acquisition of raw materials and other supplies, all contributed to the disorganization of normal production schedules. Moreover, the enormous cutback in private construction following the rent reduction law (com-

---

[30] *The Havana Post,* February 7, 1960; March 11, 1960.
[31] *Gaceta Oficial,* November 25, 1959.
[32] Ministry of Labor, Resolución No. 5302, June 17, 1960.

bined with the fact that many major public construction programs did not really get underway until 1960) compelled many firms to attempt mass layoffs. Ministry personnel were given more scope by a decree promulgated in January, 1960, which authorized actions against firms "when circumstances make it advisable," and by an order in March, 1960, which permitted the seizure of firms abandoned by their owners, whether or not professional managers remained on the job.[33]

The precise number and kind of interventions under these four authorities are not known. According to one estimate, fifty-one firms were taken over by March, 1960, all of them under Law No. 647.[34] The majority of these seizures were ordered in the latter half of 1959 and 1960, when growing hostility to the government threatened to throw the national economy out of balance. The government's first major action was aimed at the Cuban Telephone Company, which Castro at one time had promised to nationalize, and which the government intervened in March, 1959, following which, local rates were reduced from ten to five cents. With the announcement of the agrarian reform in May, 1959, more and more complaints flooded the Labor Ministry. Firms were taken over for refusing to comply with union wage demands, threatening to close their doors, refusing to reinstate workers who had been previously discharged for political reasons, and failure to live up to new work contracts. Four private frozen fish companies were placed under government control in February, 1960, in order "to restore normalcy to the production of sea-food for national consumption and export . . . the companies were working only one or two days a week." Protests over poor service and maintenance leveled at the Matanzas Bus Company by the Transport Ministry caused the company to be taken over in March. In April, Havana's twenty-four leather supply houses were seized, together with the electric company in Trinidad, on the grounds of "management irregularities."

There seemed to be a temporary letup during the late spring of

[33] Ley No. 696 (*Gaceta Oficial, Extraordinaria,* February 22, 1960) and Resolucion No. 554, March 30, 1960, respectively.

[34] *Trabajo Cuba,* 1, No. 1 (May 1960), p. 70.

1960. Cuba's attention was fastened on the sugar harvest, the unions were beginning to moderate their wage demands, and private business was beginning to learn how to operate within the framework of the new foreign trade, monetary, and raw materials controls. Early in the summer, however, three United States tire companies, which seemed to have anticipated the crisis in United States–Cuban relations during the months that followed, were seized at the request of the National Federation of Industrial Chemical Workers for "abandoning" their plants in a "frankly counterrevolutionary attitude." In July, after the oil war between Cuba and the foreign refineries had been resolved in favor of the former, the management of Cuban American Sugar Company mills reportedly withdrew from their posts, and the mills were occupied by militia units. Because their owners had "maneuvered" to make operations appear "unprofitable," three toothpaste and soap factories were seized during the same month. The full tide of interventions overcame Cuba's private business in August and early September, when the Cuban Portland Cement Company, Swift and Company, Tropical Gas Company, Continental Can, Moa Bay Mining Company, four shoe factories, and dozens of other businesses changed hands.[35] The July and August interventions terminated in the short but bitter struggle over oil and came in the middle of the developing full-scale economic war between Cuba and the United States. The interventions of the summer of 1960 accentuated the already open and sharp class conflicts within Cuba and the political battle with the United States.

Although the struggle between Cuba and the oil companies did

[35] Moa Bay, a subsidiary of Freeport Sulphur Co., was valued at $75 million. Formed in 1957, enjoying preferential tax treatment, and scheduled to be amortized in only five years, the firm exported processed nickel and cobalt (extracted from iron) to its own refinery in Louisiana. In October, 1959, the government placed a 25 per cent tax on minearl exports and collected a flat fee on properties the company failed to exploit. The government also allowed the company only a peso profit (at a time when the peso was depreciating rapidly in exchange markets).

In December 1959, a labor conflict between a construction firm in the mines and the mining union caused the company to request $13.5 million to complete various construction projects. The government loaned the company $8.1 million, but operations came to a halt sometime in the late spring. For two to three months prior to the intervention, there had been no activity.

not reach a head until June and July, its origins go back to the Petroleum Law of November, 1959, and the Cuban-Soviet oil deal of February, 1960. The Petroleum Law put the three big foreign-owned refineries on notice that the Cuban government intended to play an increasingly larger role in the island's oil business. The law limited exploration concessions and compelled the companies to forfeit any concessions that were not exploited and to pay a 60 per cent royalty on production (55 per cent if the crude was refined in Cuba for export). Although foreigners had spent millions of dollars exploring for oil in Cuba since World War II, domestic production of crude came to less than 1 per cent of total consumption. In the government charges were made that the companies had deliberately sealed wells to protect supplies of crude from their major producing wells abroad. This suspicion probably lay behind the provision of the law that ordered the companies to turn over all of their geological records to the newly created Cuban Petroleum Institute (ICP). The oil law clearly intended to clear the way for total government domination of the exploration and production phase of the industry, and in many respects corresponded to existing statutes in Mexico, Chile, and elsewhere in Latin America.

ICP's job was to explore, exploit, refine, transport, distribute, buy and sell oil and oil products, develop the petro-chemical industry and operate all state-owned and intervened private facilities in all phases of the industry. The foreign companies read the oil law uneasily because it challenged their authority not only in the unprofitable exploration phase of the industry (under the provisions of the law, INRA unsealed six private wells in April, 1960), but also in

---

Freeport operated a subsidiary in Cuba until 1947, the Nicaro Nickel Company, which was owned by the United States government. The management was reorganized in 1952, and the Nicaro plant (reportedly worth $110 million) fell into the hands of the Nickel Processing Company, a firm in which the National Lead Company owned 60 per cent of the shares, the remainder being held by Cubans. Nicaro used ores from mines owned by Freeport. In late 1960, the United States announced that "confiscatory" export taxes forced the closure of the plant.

The above listing by no means exhausts the number of intervened firms and is meant as a more or less representative sample of the reasons for and dates and pace of the seizures.

refining and distribution. In May, in fact, a powerful blow was struck when Cuba declared void the exclusive dealership contracts between the refineries and gas station owners. Even before 1959 was out, the companies could not have failed to have drawn uncomfortable parallels between the Agrarian Reform Institute, which had become a state within a state during the first few months of agrarian reform, and the new Petroleum Institute, which was not only a potential rival, but which was set up to manage the industry in its entirety if circumstances so warranted.

The agreement between the Soviet Union and Cuba, announced on April 1, 1960, was another major challenge to the industry's economic position. The Soviet Union agreed to sell Cuba crude oil considerably below the price charged by the oil monopolies to their Cuban refineries. The companies refused to refine Soviet crude, setting into motion a sequence of events that could have only one outcome. A final letter by the Texas Company (West Indies) Ltd. to the National Bank of Cuba on June 6 reiterated its refusal to handle Soviet oil. During the same month the refineries evacuated the families of their non-Cuban employees and permitted supplies of crude to run down to dangerously low levels. ICP, on its side, began to accumulate crude. At the end of the month, Shell Petroleum Company of Cuba (owned by Canadian Shell, Ltd. of the Royal Dutch Shell group) formally banned further shipments of crude to Cuba and repeated its rejection of Cuba's new oil policy. The Texaco refinery was seized on June 29, and two days later, militia units peacefully took over the Esso (Cuba) Inc. refinery, together with the Shell plant. Within a month, Soviet supplies of crude replaced private supplies.

The oil companies displayed three separate arguments to justify their refusal to refine Soviet oil. They claimed that they were "protected" by Law Decree No. 1758 (November 2, 1954), which was written by the Batista government to encourage the construction of the new refineries, and which was silent on the question of government oil. In the words of the United States Ambassador to Cuba in 1960: "Events and circumstances leading to . . . the construction of the Texaco refinery to 1957 . . . establish that such action was undertaken with the understanding that the companies had the right to supply and refine their own crude oil." [36] The Cubans replied by citing Article 44 of the Law of Combustible Minerals (May 9, 1938), which states that any refinery operating in Cuba is obliged to refine "petroleum for the Nation." The companies retorted that this meant crude oil taken from Cuban soils or waters, and the legal dispute was left at that.

The refineries also claimed that the principle of managerial control would be injured if they bowed to the government's demand. This was a relatively weak argument, because the companies had previously assented to other government controls of one kind or another, and because the logic of this position would mean that Cuba could take no steps to save foreign exchange by finding new sources of cheap crude, in the socialist world or elsewhere.

The basic reason for the companies' intransigence was that compliance with the government's demand would cut deeply into profits. In essence, the Cuban government wanted the refineries to supply their own competitors with no promise of a profit on the transaction. It is for this reason that Shell asserted that it was "unwilling to prejudice existing supply relationships," while for Cuba, a savings of an estimated $20 million annually was in the offing.[37] What had developed was a conflict of interests that might have been compromised under more propitious circumstances. In the context of the Cuban Revolution in the summer of 1960 a compromise was clearly out of the question. The companies fully expected to be taken over sooner or later and decided to force a showdown over the issue of Soviet crude. Had they expected to operate indefinitely in the future, they certainly would have tried to minimize their losses by working out a compromise or, failing that, by bowing to the government's wishes. The issue of Cuba's debt to the refineries tends to confirm this line of reasoning. The companies complained that the Cuban government owed them millions of dollars in blocked foreign exchange and demanded payment. In the past, debts had been

[36] *The Havana Post,* July 6, 1960.
[37] Speech by Premier Castro in *Obra Revolucionaria,* No. 12 (June 25, 1960).

allowed to accumulate, without bringing on a crisis, because they had always been paid. In another context, the outstanding debt in June, 1960, would also have been paid sooner or later, but the oil companies did not expect to be paid. They clearly expected to lose their assets and decided to cut their losses. There is no direct evidence that the intransigence on their part was specifically designed to force United States intervention, although a more moderate interpretation may not be too wide of the mark: "The subsequent refusal . . . to refine Soviet crude oil may be interpreted as a calculated move in collaboration with the [United States] government to precipitate a crisis which would create severe difficulties for the revolution while also providing justification for the impending cut in Cuba's sugar quota. The cut in the quota might otherwise be regarded as 'economic aggression' in contravention of OAS treaties." [38]

Whether or not the Cuban government intended to nationalize the refineries at some future date, the fact that the companies expected to be nationalized shaped events by forcing the showdown. It is easy to understand why they responded in the way that they did. The Revolutionary Government had shown no ritualistic respect for private property in rural Cuba and, under the confiscation and intervention authorities, had steadily acquired manufacturing, transportation, and commercial assets. The class conflicts that emerged in mid-1959 had been intensified by various revolutionary measures, and, in turn, had compelled the government to seize businesses and put into effect increasingly radical political measures. Moreover, the oil companies could hardly have viewed the increasing authority of ICP with equanimity. From this perspective, revolutionary actions in 1959, the most important being the Agrarian Reform Law, sealed their fate one year earlier. The real issue of the oil war, then, may not have been whether or not Cuba had the "right" to demand that the refineries process Soviet oil, but rather how fast socialism would develop in Cuba.

The oil war triggered a far more bitter battle with the United

[38] Maurice Zeitlin and Robert Scheer, *Cuba: Tragedy in Our Hemisphere* (New York, 1963), p. 175.

States and the Cuban middle classes. On July 6, in reply to the seizures of the refineries, President Eisenhower cut back Cuba's assigned share of the United States sugar market in 1960, a move that
had been talked about for months on the mainland and anticipated
by the Cubans. The same day, Cuba's Council of Ministers authorized the nationalization of all United States properties on the
island [39] and, on July 21, the seizure of two of the largest United
States-owned sugar mills. A third mill changed hands the next day,
and the remaining mills were taken over on August 6, together with
the telephone and electric power monopolies. Five weeks later the
Cubans nationalized the three largest United States banks.[40]

The initiative returned to the United States the following month
when an embargo was placed on exports to the island (medical supplies and foodstuffs formally were excepted, but in fact United
States firms refused to fill Cuban orders), and in reply, Cuba nationalized the remaining United States investments (164 companies in
all) on October 24, raising the total value of expropriated United
States properties to about $1.5 billion.[41] Meanwhile, the govern-
ment had nationalized 382 Cuban firms on October 13, including
the sugar industry's remaining 105 mills and the entire banking system, placing all investments of any importance, excepting those in
real estate, retail trade, and agriculture, in the hands of the central
government.[42] It is interesting to note that Law No. 891, ordering
the nationalization of banks, failed to accuse the banks of any eco-

[39] *Gaceta Oficial,* July 7, 1960.

[40] Resolución No. 1 (*Gaceta Oficial,* August 6, 1960) and Resolución No. 2
(*Gaceta Oficial,* September 17, 1960), respectively.

[41] Resolución No. 3 (*Gaceta Oficial,* October 24, 1960). Included were thirty
insurance companies, fifteen importers, eleven hotels, casinos, bars, and cafe-
terias, seventeen chemical firms, sixteen mines and quarries, eight textile firms
and an equal number of basic metal plants, six tobacco exporters, and six food
processors. One or more firms in twenty-two other industrial categories were
nationalized.

[42] Ley No. 890 (*Gaceta Oficial,* October 13, 1960). Included were nineteen
construction firms, eight railroads, thirteen department stores, forty-seven
furniture stores, sixteen rice mills, sixty-one textile plants, seven paper companies, eight container factories, and eighteen distilleries. Also seized were
one or more firms in sixteen other industrial categories.

nomic sabotage or other counterrevolutionary activities; it justified their expropriation solely in terms of the needs of economic planning.

The timing of the nationalizations of United States industrial and other properties were closely synchronized with United States actions against Cuba. But the reasons given for the nationalization of the Cuban enterprises could apply with equal force to the "retaliatory" seizures of United States investments. Some Cuban owners had abandoned their firms, others had slowed down production, and most had reinvested very little of their profits while dangerously expanding business loans. The government also justified nationalization on the grounds that direct controls of the island's productive capacity were required for national economic planning, and that it was necessary to quiet the fears of those private entrepreneurs who were cooperating with the revolution.

The October decrees were the great turning points of the Cuban Revolution; they compelled the government to embark on the path of full-scale socialist economic planning. Overnight, the entire system of reforms and controls placed on private business during 1959–1960 to promote rapid economic development was out of date. From the standpoint of organizing and rationalizing the economic system, the revolution had to begin all over again, and the government retreated somewhat to gain time to consolidate its political position. In what Castro referred to as the "second stage" of the revolution, it was promised that "methods" would not be so drastic.[43] In an attempt to calm the fears of small private business, Castro maintained that the government had no intention of seizing all businesses, and that, unless all other remedies failed, there would be no more interventions at all. He also assured small retailers that the newly nationalized department stores would not price them out of business. The first pledge, apparently sincere at the time it was made, proved to be premature and unrealistic.

A series of confiscations, nationalizations, and purchases widened and deepened the socialist sector of the economy throughout 1961

[43] *Obra Revolucionaria,* No. 27 (October 17, 1960).

and 1962. In May, 1961, thirteen laboratories manufacturing pharmaceutical products were purchased, raising the public share of total output in the industry from 8 to 60 per cent (fourteen firms had already been nationalized and 230 small enterprises remained in private hands).[44] Next month, 97 private bus companies were taken over by the Transport Ministry, and, about the same time, the private schools were nationalized. By the end of 1961, 286 private clubs were being operated by the government as workers' social circles, thousands of automobiles, houses, and other assets had been taken from exiled families, and most of Cuba's urban apartment houses were placed in the hands of the state (which in turn sold equity in them to tenants) by the Urban Reform Law of October 14, 1961.

From the standpoint of the value of production, these measures socialized about 85 per cent of Cuba's industry by the fall of 1961, and, one year later, 90 per cent. Looking at the distribution of workers between the private and state sectors, only 15 per cent of industry, 8 per cent of transport, and 45 per cent of commerce were private in mid-1962, and the entire construction and communications industries were socialized.[45] In December, 1962, when shortages of clothing and other articles had appeared, the final wave of nationalizations swept over the retail and wholesale trade sectors. Over 7,-000 shops throughout Cuba were taken over and grouped under the Ministry of Interior Commerce.[46] Thus, employment in the public sector of commerce rose from 52 per cent in 1962 to 77 per cent in 1963. In the following year it was planned that the figure would be nearly 100 per cent. With this measure, the only nonagricultural productive assets that remained in private hands were small enter-

[44] *Trabajo Cuba*, No. 5 (May 1961), pp. 60–64.

[45] Cuba, JUCEPLAN, Dirección de Estadísticas, *Projecto de Anuario Estadístico* (PAE) (July, 1963), Tables 3.3, 6.11. Within manufacturing and mining, employment in private firms as a proportion of total employment was: mining, petroleum and derivatives, and sugar, zero; nonsugar food products, 43.6 per cent; beverages and tobacco, 23.6 per cent; textiles and leather, 21.9 per cent; chemicals, 5 per cent; construction materials, 4.3 per cent; metals and machinery, 3.6 per cent.

[46] *Ibid.*, Table 9.

prises in manufacturing, chiefly in the bakery,[47] tobacco, and garment industries (which by 1963 were operated on the basis of physical allocation of supplies), and family owned and operated restaurants, service industries, and retail stores. The rapid and relatively uneventful process of expropriation and nationalization had nearly come to an end, and only the middle farmers tempted the government to extend the socialist sector of the economy still further. The task of reorganizing the new social economy had fallen on the Revolutionary Government from the very beginning of the agrarian reform, but by 1961 and 1962 it had replaced the question of ownership of the means of production as the central political issue.

[7]

The discovery of practical and workable modes of industrial organization was relatively rapid and marked by few errors. By mid-1961 nearly all of Cuba's industry was organized along socialist lines, even though as little as twelve months before few people even suspected that the events of July–October, 1960, would be climaxed by the great nationalization decrees. By 1965 the organization of industry was beginning to take its final form, as the government started to establish combines that would be vertically integrated from the production to the distribution stage. There were two reasons why the search for suitable forms of industrial organization, even in those sectors characterized by as many irrationalities as agriculture, was devoid of the false starts and dead ends that partially crippled the revolution's efforts to find a stable and workable mode of agricultural organization. Unlike the agrarian reforms, the major expropriations of industry were compressed within a three-month period; thus, the scope and magnitude of the organizational problem were perceived immediately. Secondly, the nationalization of industry came at a relatively late stage of the revolution—a sizable proportion of the industrial sector was already in public hands, and in the countryside, INRA was already introducing socialist modes of production. By the fall of 1960, the need for a planned economy was evi-

---

[47] *Ibid.*, Table 6.1. One-quarter of food products and 15 per cent of textiles and leather manufacturing remained in private hands.

dent, and the physical basis of a planned socialist economy had to a large extent already been laid down. With the early experience in agriculture fresh in their minds, planners in industry were not compelled to cope with the uncertainties and confusion that faced INRA from the day of its inception.

The revolutionary leadership had from the outset a strong bias towards industrial consolidation and central physical planning of economic resources, and this was another factor that shortened the pause between the nationalization decrees and the final socialist reorganization of industry. There was little or no debate about alternative forms of organization, particularly over the issue of decentralization and "worker control" of industry along Yugoslavian lines. These possibilities were never even remotely considered by the revolutionary leadership, not because they did not conform to the Soviet industrial model, but rather because they were not deemed appropriate to the Cuban scene.

An immediately pressing problem was raising productivity and production, especially in the large small-scale industry sectors of the manufacturing economy. Rationalizing these sectors was one of the most important problems of industrial reorganization. Consolidating production units and firms in these sectors was the obvious, practical response to the problem. By eliminating unproductive work units and production processes, it would be possible to economize on the use of scarce raw materials and labor skills, improve product quality by introducing quality controls, and generally lower costs. It would also be possible to diversify output and make fuller use of installed capacity. To cite one example, the Squibb Company produced 22 items before nationalization; afterwards, the same plant produced about 150 items. It would also be feasible to eliminate wasteful product variety. In 1961, 600 brands and types of oil products were replaced by 35 types; 1,200 raw materials in paint manufacturing were replaced by less than 250 because of the change in the nature of the market; tobacco, beverage, pharmaceutical, paper, and other lists were also simplified. The consolidation movement laid the basis for the future realization of economies of large-scale production, administration, sales, and distribution, advantages that had escaped Cuba because the "typical" manufacturing firm was so small and inefficient. The importance of having a basis for rationing and economizing of administrative and technical personnel was accentuated by the flight of experienced managers and technicians. The United States economic boycott, in much the same way, placed an extra burden on the distribution of spare parts.

Thus, the consolidation movement involved first and foremost the closing down of inefficient plants and the expansion of production in the more efficient units, meanwhile placing the allocation of resources within each industry under a central authority. Throughout 1961 and 1962, thousands of small establishments were merged into consolidated enterprises, which are very similar to the Soviet combine, in that they bring together all plants with the same function under a central administrative authority.

In the island's largest industry, a series of older, antiquated sugar mills were closed down. The first was demolished in December, 1960, its machinery and equipment cannibalized and labor force reallocated. By 1964, at least thirty-five more mills were closed. At one stage, long-run planning envisaged a link between the remaining low-cost mills and a series of factories (using by-products, mainly) which would allow the utilization of the former on a year-round basis. The process of consolidation, merger, and rationalization in other industries left some workers temporarily stranded. In the shoe industry, where about one thousand small sweatshops were consolidated into a handful of units, about eight thousand workers were displaced temporarily in the fall of 1962. (A contributing factor was the shortage and rationing of leather.) Employment was also reduced in textile, cigarette and cigar manufacturing, and a few other branches of manufacture, but rose in more sectors than it fell. Simultaneously, however, involuntary part-time unemployment, seasonal unemployment, and casual labor was largely eliminated by the large expansion of demand for consumer goods, the growth of construction, and the stabilization of markets. In this way, the consolidation movement was not only rational from the standpoint of economic efficiency, but also proved valuable for the mobilization of support for the revolution on the part of the urban proletariat, the majority of whom were employed in small-scale and home industry, where employment had always been unstable, irregular, and uncertain. The consolidation movement also meant placing existing production units within each industry under central administrative control. In industries such as rubber, plastics, and chemicals, the size of the production unit remained unchanged, and only the administrative unit was widened.

Because the local market was relatively small and the absolute size of any given enterprise limited, there was no overriding concern over possible diseconomies of large-scale production in the form of the administrative inefficiencies characteristic of giant industrial combinations in advanced capitalist economies. Quite the contrary, the consolidation of industry laid the basis for internalizing external economies of scale, as well as exploiting internal economies already present. The chief fault of the consolidation movement was that insufficient attention was paid to the transitional problems arising from the abolition of older forms of organization before the new forms were in good working order. This was especially true of the consolidation of the distribution system. The textile industry was, perhaps, the most outstanding example of the benefits of industry-wide planning.[48] Thus, there were in late 1960 many arguments

[48] Textile firms were brought into the socialist sector in three waves: during the 1959–1960 interventions and seizures of Batistiana properties; October, 1960, when Law 890 nationalized sixty-one firms (some of which had already been intervened); late 1961, when fourteen private companies were purchased by the government. Between 9,000 to 10,000 workers were engaged in textile manufacture. The 1953 Census reported 9,707 workers; the Ministry of Industries and Education censuses in 1962 put the total at 9,026 and 9,668 workers, respectively. Employment in the industry failed to make any headway during the 1950's, although there was an advance in production.

Textiles were first encouraged by the 1927 tariff, at a period when the industry was entering the factory stage. Spinning operations quickly fell behind weaving and knitting operations; even in the 1940's yarns made up the bulk of raw material imports. In those days sweatshops produced the majority of Cuba's cotton and other materials. Then World War II curtailed supplies, tariffs were raised, and new units were constructed. The industry, however, remained inefficient. The Reciprocal Trade Agreement with the United States placed a ceiling on the Cuban tariff, and the island's giant neighbor (allied with Cuban importers) even went so far as to fight successfully a planned domestic subsidy to the industry in 1948.

in favor of, and no important arguments against, the consolidation
of industry.

Until the creation of the Ministry of Industries (MININD) in February, 1961, INRA's Department of Industrialization dominated
the nonagricultural, public economy. Created in November, 1959,
the Industrialization Department acquired all of the manufacturing
enterprises seized under the confiscation authorities and intervened
by the Ministry of Labor and other organisms of the government.
Of the 380 Cuban-owned firms nationalized in October, 1960 (Law
No. 890), 126 units, consisting of the largest and most important
properties held by the national bourgeoisie, were handed over to
the department; 150 sugar mills were given to the department's
General Administration of Sugar Mills, and the rest were distributed to the Department of Production and other ministries and state
agencies. A total of eleven state bodies were in control of economic

---

Unlike nearly all other sectors of Cuban manufacturing, there is available
a thorough study of the structure of the textile industry ordered by the Revolutionary Government in 1959 (*Textil, passim*). The most striking fact brought
out by the study was that 67.3 per cent of spindle capacity and 44.9 per cent
of weaving capacity was owned by one firm. Small firms employed 24.4 per
cent of all workers employed in spinning operations and 54.7 per cent of all
workers engaged in weaving. Capital per worker in spinning operations, therefore, was greater in small firms than in the giant of the industry; as for weaving
operations, the ratio was about the same.

Dominated by one giant firm, on the fringe of the industry were one
medium-sized firm (whose capacity was termed "adequate" by the study) and
perhaps one hundred tiny units, nearly all of them highly inefficient. Of Cuba's
total spindle capacity, only 7.5 per cent was installed after 1946; only 29.3
per cent of her loom capacity was constructed after 1946. New spindle and
loom capacity alike were installed in the two largest firms alone; elsewhere in
the industry workers produced textiles with equipment over fifteen years old.

The major problems of the industry (apart from the large size and technical
disparities between firms) were twofold: competition from better quality imports narrowed the domestic market; a lack of domestic raw materials inhibited
the expansion of the industry. These two problems were, of course, interrelated: domestic production as a proportion of demand in 1959 (excluding
jute) came to 43.5 per cent for fibers; 69.6 per cent for spun yarns; 59.6 per
cent for woven cloth; 95.8 per cent for manufactured items (including jute,
the figure for manufactured items was 40.8 per cent). To meet these problems
the following solutions were given top priority: To take up the raw material
slack, the report suggested subsidies for the expansion and diversification (for
varied needed grades of cotton) of cotton farming, and, for the production of
rayon, the expansion of eucalyptus cultivation. Second, emphasis was placed

enterprises of one kind or another. The Industrialization Department and the Sugar Mill Administration, together with the National
Bank, were the most important; these were followed by the National Transport Corporation, the Department of Maritime Development, the Ministry of Public Works, and INRA's Department of
Production. All of these organisms had acquired important industrial, transportation, communications, and other assets before the
great nationalization decrees in the fall of 1960. The significance of
this for the development of socialist-minded administrators, socialist
planning techniques, and general planning orientation should not
be underestimated. For example, on the eve of Resolution No. 3,
which nationalized 166 United States-owned firms on October 24,
1960, the Industrialization Department alone managed over 300
plants (consolidated into fourteen administrative units), of which
only 126 had been acquired earlier in the month under Law 890.

Thus, the department, as well as other arms of the Revolutionary

on raising labor productivity, only 61 per cent of the norm (defined in the
context of experience elsewhere in Latin America) in spinning, and only 44
per cent of the weaving norm. Underutilization of capacity was the major
problem; had capacity been fully employed, the productivity figures would
have risen to 74 per cent and 82 per cent, respectively. Third, the authors of
the study strongly recommended adjustments in the tariff schedule; compared
with other Latin American countries, Cuba was overexposed to international
competition (although the authors do not explicitly take into account experience of high protection elsewhere in Latin America which has hardened older,
inefficient systems of production). The major source of difficulty lay in preferences granted United States imports, since tariffs on imports from other countries appeared to be high enough; on white cotton fabrics, for instance, the
rate on imports from the United States was only 22.8 per cent, while for all
other countries, the schedule was higher (ranging up to 57.2 per cent on imports from Germany).

The income elasticity of demand for textile products in Cuba was relatively
high (1.24 for all products for the island as a whole); the technical problems
involved in adjusting the tariff schedule were minimal; rationalizing the domestic industry would be a simple task. To raise labor productivity and
guarantee raw material supplies, the authors suggested the following: the
consolidation of small firms; one collective bargaining contract for all workers
in the industry, together with industry production norms; rationalization of the
wage structure; the centralization of all aspects of the industry, even to the
degree of putting supplies of cotton and other raw materials directly under
government control. It is highly significant that these radical proposals were
made during the "reformist" period of 1959 by investigators of a "liberal"
persuasion.

Government, was compelled to think in terms of socialist planning well before the majority of Cuba's businesses were actually nationalized. Seen in this light, the purpose of the main nationalization law was just as much to consolidate a revolution already far down the path of socialism, as it was to lay the basis for generalized planning by expropriating Cuba's remaining key business. There was a kind of unstable equilibrium between the private and public sectors which the nationalization decrees resolved.

The new Ministry of Industries (whose first chief was Che Guevara) rapidly acquired physical assets and personnel from a number of other government branches and absorbed outright INRA's Industrialization Department, the Petroleum Institute, the Mining Institute (created in August, 1960, and attached to INRA to manage the mining industry and supervise the few remaining private operations) and the Sugar Mill Administration. This was the last step in the centralization of control of business. On the eve of the revolution the National Bank and Batista's new development institutions shared ownership, and sometimes management, of dozens of newly created businesses. Management of most of these businesses was centralized under INRA's control late in 1959.

Meanwhile, INRA and other branches of the state acquired new assets as a consequence of the revolutionary decrees. All of the industrial assets acquired either before or after were administratively consolidated and placed under the Industries Ministry's control in February, 1961. Despite the centralization of management (or perhaps because of it) Guevara's ministry soon got the reputation as one of Cuba's best-run state organisms. Guevara had the qualities of leadership, the intellectual and political authority, and the key economic command, which he determined to make the most of. The strategic location of the ministry is indicated by its central role in Cuba's all-important foreign trade. In the first half of 1963, MININD sold nearly 95 per cent of the island's exports and took 44 per cent of its imports. (The Ministry of Domestic Commerce and INRA accounted for most of the remainder, 27 per cent and 15 per cent, respectively.) [49]

[49] Vice-ministerio de Economía, *Cuadros Resúmenes, 1er semestre 1963*, Table 12.

Further idea of MININD's importance can be gathered from the number and scope of consolidated enterprises that it managed. In 1963, under the Vice-Ministers of Light Industry and Basic Industry were twenty-eight and eighteen consolidated enterprises respectively.[50] "Light" and "basic" industry were not strictly analogous to consumer and capital goods industry; included in the former, for example, were wood, rubber, and metal containers. The size of existing plants and total investments and the importance of the industry in the national economy basically determined whether an industry was classified as "light" or "basic." Most of the "basic" industries, however, could fairly be termed capital goods industries.

Only in the sugar sector, where the mills were administered by the Vice-Minister of Basic Industries, did INRA resist successfully the growth of Guevara's ministry. A full-scale debate in early 1963 over the question of the management of the cane fields was resolved temporarily in favor of the *status quo;* INRA would continue to manage the cane farms, and MININD would operate the mills. The sugar industry thus remained divided. Had the state-owned cane fields been put under the direction of the mills, given the low level of technical skills and administration which handicapped the latter, more mismanagement undoubtedly would have resulted. Yet by 1965, the Revolutionary Government apparently minimized this problem, because it began to reorganize industry and agriculture into fully integrated combines, each organized around the production of the specific commodity or group of commodities.

MININD was only one, albeit the largest, of Cuba's new industrial complexes. The Ministry of Transport (called earlier the National Transport Cooperation) grew steadily throughout the first four years of the revolution, taking over the functions of the old Civil Aeronautics Commission (dissolved in August, 1960) and ac-

[50] Ministerio de Industrias, "Relación de Empresas Consolidadas pertenecientes al Viceministerios de Industrias Ligeras y de Industrias Básicas" (undated, mimeographed). "Basic" industries were automotive, sugar, electricity, fertilizer, phosphorous metals, non-phosphorous metals, minerals, nickel, paper, petroleum, basic chemicals, salt, agricultural equipment, machine construction, and metals assembly. MININD had two other vice-ministries, Industrial Construction and Economic. The latter administered eight offices: Planning, Supplies, Labor and Salaries, Costs and Prices Finances, Technical, Relations with Private Industry, and Organization.

quiring Cuba's shipping, railroads, and major bus companies. By the end of 1961, for example, the ministry's bus consolidated enterprise managed 3,400 of the island's 4,000 vehicles and had reorganized eighty companies that had been privately owned.[51] By 1962, the new Ministry of Domestic Commerce, created in February, 1961, at the same time that MININD and the Ministry of Foreign Commerce were organized, was operating approximately 8,000 retail outlets, restaurants, hotels, and so on, reorganized into seventeen consolidated enterprises, the largest of which were clothing (3,028 outlets), food stores (1,130 outlets), and hardware stores (1,109 outlets).[52] At the end of 1961, the National Institute of Tourism managed ten consolidated enterprises, which comprised 327 administrative units and 1,085 individual establishments.[53] In October, 1960, the private banking system was put under the National Bank, which was subsequently reorganized in 1963 after coming under attack for its "bureaucratism." The Ministry of Public Works took under its wing the construction firms intervened in 1959 to mid-1960, and finally took over the nineteen major contractors and construction materials firms nationalized under Law 890. In 1962 the value of gross industrial product originating in the key socialist sectors was distributed as follows: MININD, $1,629 million; INRA, $456 million (mostly in foods); Public Works, $54 million (all in construction materials); Transport, $26 million (all in metals and machinery); other, $4.6 million.[54]

[51] "Los problemas del transporte," *Trabajo Cuba*, 2, No. 18 (December, 1961), p. 53.

[52] *PAE*, 1962, Table 9.4.   [53] *Revolución*, September 25, 1961.

[54] *PAE*, 1962, Table 6.4.

[7]

Organized Labor
before and after
the Revolution

[1]

Like the markets for most agricultural, manufacturing, financial, and other commodities and services, the labor market in prerevolutionary Cuba was fragmented, inflexible, and economically irrational. Also like other branches of the political economy, labor was organized into corporatist-oriented interest groups, or economic baronies. As an individual, the worker enjoyed few rights and exercised no power. As a member of a strong union, the worker was secure, well paid, and "privileged."

The leaders of the most powerful unions owed their position not only to their constituencies, but also to Cuba's political bosses and leaders. In the organized sectors of the labor market, as in most other markets, wages were administered, rather than determined by the vicissitudes of the marketplace. Moreover, more often than not, collective bargaining was replaced by government settlement of wage, employment, and other disputes. "Unions had to participate in politics to get what they wanted," MacGaffey and Barnett wrote. "In turn, unions were used by ambitious men to promote their own political careers." [1] After the late 1930's, Cuba's organized labor movement was thus dependent on the government, to the extent that national union leaders were referred to as the government's "labor boss" or "labor chief." The organizations of scientific, engineering, and other professional workers were also extraordinarily powerful, as well as politically dependent, and membership in the

[1] Wyatt MacGaffey and Clifford R. Barnett, *Twentieth Century Cuba* (New York, 1965), p. 179.

177

old Cuba's over two hundred professional associations, or colleges, was mandatory.

Cuba's labor organizations were born only after a long, uphill struggle. Early union activity, dating from about 1865, was significant more for its educational value (labor journalism made its appearance during this period) than for its organizational achievements. With the exception of the tobacco workers, organized into unions in the 1890's and among Martí's staunchest supporters, few of Cuba's workers began to lay a basis for permanent organization until well into the twentieth century. This was particularly true of the sugar workers, who lived under strict labor discipline, and whose every attempt at collective action was ruthlessly crushed.[2] United States occupation of the island following the War of Independence dampened union activity. Only when the great wave of Spanish immigrants introduced the doctrine of anarchosyndicalism into the factories and shops beginning in the first decade of the century did the workers acquire an independent ideology. During World War I, anarchosyndicalist-led workers fought and won many strikes.

With the accession of Machado in 1925, the more militant labor leaders of all political persuasions were ousted and replaced by men more amenable to the needs of the rising Cuban middle classes. The Cuban Communist party was founded in the same year and remained the most durable political party on the island. For the next ten years the island's workers suffered increasing hardships as the Great Depression reduced the Cuban sugar trade to a fraction of earlier levels. Wages dropped disastrously: one sugar company which had paid cane cutters eighty cents daily in 1925 offered only twenty cents in 1933, and wages for cane haulers plummeted to five cents per twelve hour day. In the last days of the Machado dictatorship, labor as a political class was large and potentially very strong, but its economic position hit rock bottom. With intensified organizational activities, led by the Communists in the countryside,

[2] Charles Page, "The Development of Organized Labor in Cuba" (Ph.D. dissertation, University of California, 1950), *passim.*

it was only a matter of time before labor's political role was made to correspond more closely to its economic importance and sheer numbers.

Cuba's working classes were the key element in the 1933 revolution, and the new government was labor oriented. In rural Cuba over thirty sugar mills were seized by the workers, who formed workers' soviets in some of them. By January, 1934, the Communist-led Fourth National Labor Congress claimed over 400,000 members. Union organization was placed on an industrial rather than a craft basis, and various prolabor demands of an economic and social character were made of the government. With the counterrevolution of 1934–1935, which brought an obscure sergeant named Fulgencio Batista to the surface of Cuban politics, the new unions were dissolved, and the general strike of early 1935 was broken. But in a series of decrees culminating in the 1940 Constitution, the Cuban government legally guaranteed union organization and collective bargaining.

During the Popular Front period preceding World War II, Communist policy shifted and the party entered into a pact with Batista. Reformist policies replaced the old revolutionary ideology, partly because the legalization of the party in 1938 brought many nonrevolutionary workers into its ranks, partly because the memory of the defeats of 1935 was still fresh, and partly because of the political needs of the new alliance. Under Communist leadership, the Cuban Confederation of Labor (CTC) was founded in 1939. In the same year, the new National Federation of Sugar Workers was organized.

Unlike many Communist parties in the West, the Cubans followed militant economic policies during the war. In 1940 a 25 per cent wage increase was won by the sugar mill workers; by presidential decree, wages rose 50 per cent, 10 per cent, and 32 per cent in 1942, 1944, and 1945. Meanwhile, the CTC rolled up impressive organizational gains as membership more than doubled between 1944 and 1945. The Communists, "by superior industriousness, devotion, training, and tactical skill—all of which qualities their bitterest enemies emphasized—succeeded in attaining practically complete control of the Cuban labor movement" from 1933 to 1947.[3] Explaining the rise of the CTC, and the role of Lázaro Peña, its first secretary-general, the Christian Reformist Felipe Zapata admitted that the Communist leaders dominated the movement by virtue of their "superior capability, integrity of principle, and moral strength." [4]

A running feud between Peña and Eusebio Mujal Barniol, an official in the Autentico party which ruled Cuba from 1945 to 1952, ended in the practical, if not ideological, victory of the conservative forces in 1947, when the purge of the Communist CTC leaders began. The United States government placed pressure on the Grau government to rid the labor movement of Communist domination.[5] A few local leaders were bought out, and others were won over by dangling high posts in the new rival federation before their eyes; where the existing leadership stood fast, rival unions were formed and supported by the government. Even the strongly anti-Mujal bank workers', telephone employees', and electrical power workers' unions finally gave way. The new "cleansed" CTC received "every kind of cooperation from the Ministry of Labor," but the purge had been accomplished by "opportunistic and demagogic chauvinist rivals." [6]

Meanwhile, the new CTC leadership inherited the legacy from the Communists of militant union "economism," and the government had to insure against a Communist comeback by allowing the new CTC free rein. Thus, the postwar period witnessed further important economic gains by organized labor, eroding the Communists' hold at local levels. Despite these tactics, an estimated 25 per cent of Cuba's organized labor remained pro-Communist.[7] Of 120 sugar mill locals, the Communists retained control of 40. The reason was that the provincial labor unions carried little weight in the alliance between organized urban labor and the state. One-third of the island's work force lived in the Havana area, which was the center of gravity in the political physics of Cuba. Social legislation was in-

[3] International Bank for Reconstruction and Development, Economic and Technical Mission, *Report on Cuba* (Baltimore, 1951), p. 365.
[4] Felipe Zapata, "Esquemas y notas para una historia de la organización obrera en Cuba," *Unidad Gastronómica* (June–November, 1948), p. 13.
[5] Page, *op. cit.*, p. 114.   [6] *Ibid.*, pp. 124, 129.   [7] *Ibid.*, p. 160, n. 39.

differently enforced in the countryside, and urban labor leaders failed to back many grievances filed by their harassed rural-based affiliates. Thus, militant leadership was welcome in many parts of rural Cuba.

While the Communists retained what strength they could in the countryside, confining their activities in the cities to educational and propaganda work, the official CTC further consolidated its power after the Batista coup in 1952. Party loyalties meant very little to Mujal and other labor leaders, who switched their allegiance from the Autenticos to Batista. By 1954 the CTC claimed well over one million members in a total labor force of less than two million. The relationship between the new dictatorship and the CTC was one of give and take, although to cement the "national" alliance and create the political discipline necessary to meet the economic crisis of 1952–1953, Batista was compelled to continue the prolabor policies of his predecessors. The exceptions were related to his attempts to attract new foreign investments by implementing antifeatherbedding and other proefficiency policies. On the Havana busses and the United Railroads these changes went through without a strong protest. In 1955, the sugar companies introduced bulk loading of sugar in ocean shipping, although the union still required that sugar be bagged in the mills. During the recession of 1956, "the unions . . . accepted without protest dismissals on economic grounds." [8]

To survive, the Batista regime required a national consensus. This need constrained the dictator in his attempt to eliminate the labor "problem." The unions were pliable instruments of state policy as long as the government continued to deliver the goods. Although the dictator was quick to move against the unions for political reasons, the "reforms" of union practices merely touched the surface of the problem. In 1955 compulsory check-off of dues was enforced, and the CTC's right to "intervene" its affiliates was strengthened. Strikes with narrow economic aims were almost invariably won by labor. In 1958, a bad year for the island economy, four thousand

[8] United States Bureau of Labor Statistics, *Labor in Cuba* (Washington, 1957), p. 21.

Cuban Telephone Company workers were granted wage increases ranging from $15 to $35 monthly, and the oil workers received raises ranging from 7 to 13 per cent.[9]

Within the government Batista required something like a consensus, as well; as later events showed, there were potentially unreliable elements everywhere, Communists who had somehow managed to retain their posts in various public and quasi-public organisms, Mujalistas whose loyalties changed with every shift in the political wind, democratic unionists now employed by the Ministry of Labor who failed to see that their internal struggles were a lost cause, and sheer opportunists devoid of even formal political coloring. Hence, the way was opened to bribery and corruption on a scale unusual even in Cuba.

Thus, during the second Batista regime the Communists' strength in the labor movement was undermined by the privileged position of the CTC in the national economy, and the system of corruption temporarily pushed the old ideologies out of sight.

[2]

The structure of the Cuban economy determined the character of the work force and the labor market and, indirectly, the uneven development of the labor movement. In agriculture, Cuba's rainfall cycle occasioned large seasonal fluctuations in the supply of sugar and therefore the demand for labor. In 1958, over one-half of the island's rural labor force of 900,000 workers was employed in cane cultivation. During the dead season—June through December—about 400,000 workers were unemployed, the majority of them sugar workers.[10] Wage rates, comparatively low because there were no

[9] S. J. Rundt and Associates, *Rundt's Market Reports*, No. 221.

[10] About one-fourth of the cane labor force worked for two or three months in the coffee harvest, which preceded the *zafra*. Other off-season jobs were available in rice farming, where labor requirements are large from early spring to early fall, and construction. The vast majority of seasonally unemployed workers returned to the family farm, grew subsistence crops on plots furnished by the sugar mills, or eked out a bare subsistence on credits furnished by local stores. According to the only available monthly unemployment data, in late 1958 nearly 30 per cent of the Cuban labor force was unemployed or underemployed (see Appendix B).

important alternative employments, did not compensate cane workers for forced seasonal idleness.[11]

In industry, the structure of the island's manufactures differentiated the work force into three broad layers. First, nearly one-third of the industrial labor force was employed in the sugar mills, where wages were relatively high and stable and employment was steady from year to year. The mill workers formed a proletarian elite in the countryside, even though their annual income was low due to seasonal unemployment. Organized into a strong union and determined to protect their wage rates in order to prevent their annual earnings from falling below the subsistence level, the mill workers successfully resisted the introduction of labor-saving machinery, won wage increases when the price of sugar rose and prevented wage cuts when sugar prices fell, and thus helped to harden the pattern of resource utilization in the sugar industry.[12]

Second, in small-scale, high-cost manufacturing industries and firms (clothing, footwear, and other important industries, as we have seen), wages were low, employment was irregular, and working conditions substandard. By comparison with the advanced sectors, unemployment and underemployment were unusually high. The approximately 150,000 workers (about one-half of the total manufacturing labor force) in these branches of production were without effective labor union representation and government protection. Closed shop and other restrictive union practices prevented these workers from finding employment in the advanced sectors.

Lastly, in the modern, chiefly foreign-owned sector of industry, where technological superiority and monopolistic practices kept prices high and stable and generated handsome profits, workers were well paid and enjoyed secure employment. These semiskilled and skilled "privileged" workers were mainly concentrated in tele-

[11] As we saw in Chapter Four, wages in the sugar sector were fixed by the government. Wage rates were based on the profitability of cane cultivation, the type and amount of work, and the relative bargaining power of the mills, the *colonos*, and the workers. Thus, market forces provided the framework within which wages were determined administratively.

[12] When technological advances reduced days or weeks worked per year, mill workers were compensated with a bonus for "superproduction."

phone and telegraph, electric power, oil refining, tobacco, brewing, banking, and hotel and restaurant industries.[13] Organized into strong, exclusive unions, some of which resembled guilds, were perhaps 225,000 to 300,000 workers, or a maximum of 25 per cent of the nonagricultural labor force.

Labor union policies were oriented or conditioned by economic stagnation and instability and the fear of unemployment and underemployment. The unions enforced strict entry, promotion, transfer, discharge, apprenticeship, training, and other policies affecting employed union members. Some unions refused to admit Cuba's pitifully few technical school graduates except as apprentices, while simultaneously opposing apprenticeship contracts. Many unions successfully opposed mechanization, labor-saving investments, and the rationalization of work processes. In 1953, for example, the cigar workers were able to ban domestic sales of machine-made cigars. On the Havana docks featherbedding raised loading costs up to 800 per cent higher than in Miami. In 1950, a railroad executive estimated that 40 per cent of his payroll was expended for work not done. It was not uncommon for union locals to resist the introduction of machinery in competing factories to insure against a loss of markets. Again, there were cases where employers were allowed to introduce new equipment only on the condition that the displaced workers be retained in the same department. An employer offer to transfer displaced workers to other departments was countered by a demand that new workers be hired.

Government legislation and administrative decisions reinforced restrictive union practices in the "privileged" sector. "The issues that most concern management," MacGaffey and Barnett wrote, "and to which unions were quick to react were precisely those most closely regulated by law, such as rigid job tenure, rigid seniority requirements by the union, make-work rules, and restrictions on

---

[13] Worker consciousness of his "privileged" status was very strong and even survived the nationalization of industry. "It became clear in the course of our interviews," Zeitlin wrote about his experiences in 1962, "that many workers had pronounced self-conceptions of themselves as generally more 'privileged' than other workers—while many, in turn, agreed that there was a distinct group of 'privileged workers' " (Maurice Zeitlin, *Revolutionary Politics and the Cuban Working Class* [Princeton, 1967], p. 115).

mechanization." [14] Perhaps the most powerful union control over management won through political action was the right to permanent employment. Minister of Labor consent was needed for most dismissals, a policy first decreed in 1938 and then embodied in the 1940 Constitution. Another law with serious negative economic effects compelled employers planning to move their operations to low-wage areas to pay the same wages that obtained in high-wage areas. Provision for annual one-month paid vacations and a law that guaranteed forty-eight hours pay for forty-four hours of work raised real wages well over 10 per cent. To spread available work opportunities, the government required employers to hire substitutes for workers on summer vacation, in effect, to hire two work forces.

Fringe benefits added to costs. Pensions for retired workers in the "privileged" sector were high. Although the government failed to implement a provision in the 1940 Constitution for unemployment insurance, "policy seems to be to subsidize labor through mandatory labor legislation, and through tariffs on manufactures and on agricultural products." [15] The aim was to prevent layoffs by forced overstaffing, subsidies, special tax allowances, and government intervention. In effect, the state required that businesses use operational losses as a kind of guaranteed annual income. Enforcement of labor legislation was particularly strong in the large-scale, foreign-owned factories, but completely negligent in small-scale industry.

The economic effects of union restrictive practices and state intervention seriously impeded capitalist development. Most important was the large gap between wages and labor productivity. The British Board of Trade described the wage structure in prerevolutionary Cuba as "one of the highest and most rigid . . . in Latin America." [16] This was hardly an exaggeration. In 1957 real wages in Cuban manufacturing were higher than in any country in the West-

[14] MacGaffey and Barnett, op. cit., p. 185. For the legal framework of Cuban labor see Page, op. cit., passim.; Barbara Ann Walker, "The Labor Policy of the Cuban Government" (M.A. thesis, University of California, 1958), passim.; Pan American Union, Cuba: Statement of the Laws (Washington, 1959), pp. 126–127.

[15] Lowry Nelson, Rural Cuba (Minneapolis, 1950), p. 44.

[16] Great Britain, Board of Trade, Cuba: Economic and Commercial Conditions in Cuba, Overseas Economic Surveys (London, June, 1954), pp. 2–3.

ern Hemisphere, excepting the United States and Canada, and compared favorably with Western European levels. Averaging about $6 for an eight-hour day in manufacturing as a whole, wages in Cuba's sugar mills ranged from over $4 for unskilled workers to $11 for skilled employees.[17] What is more, labor productivity was abysmally low. Real wages in United States manufacturing industries in 1957 were less than double the level in Cuba, but output per employed man in manufacturing was more than four times as great. This disparity between wages and productivity lay behind the endless complaints by Cuban and foreign capitalists about overly rigid seniority practices and job tenure conditions, union make-work practices, and prolabor government policies, and helped to prevent the efficient utilization and allocation of capital. In the eyes of European observers, "the inelasticity of the country's one-crop economy, the high and rigid wage structure, the impossibility of dismissing redundant employees, and the strong opposition of labor to mechanization and other means of reducing costs . . . are additional handicaps from which Cuba suffers in an increasingly competitive world." [18]

Not only was the average wage level out of line with average labor productivity, but also the *structure* of wages failed to correspond with productivity. Interfirm differentials and disparities within occupations were often greater than differentials between industries. Scant available data show that in those industries in which all production units were unionized, the wage spread within a given occupation was much less pronounced than in those industries that were only partially organized (see Table 3). In ten leading companies in the mid-1950's, stenographers earned between $120 and $330 monthly, bilingual secretaries made between $130 and $377 per month, while routine office workers took home between $130 and $389.[19] Thus, the difference between the salaries of the highest-paid and the lowest-paid workers in the same occupation was about three to one. Interindustry differentials were not so marked; the

[17] *Labor in Cuba*, p. 21.
[18] *Cuba: Economic and Commercial Conditions in Cuba*, p. 3.
[19] *Labor in Cuba*, Table 4, p. 20.

difference between average wages in Cuba's five high-wage industries (films, chemicals, textiles, rubber, and optical products) and
those in the five lowest-paying industries (apparel, glass and pot-
tery, tobacco, foods, and wood products) was only about two to
one.[20] Similar irrationalities characterized wage differentials between skilled and unskilled workers. In 1955, for example, nine
leading companies in manufacturing, utilities, and petroleum-refin-
ing paid unskilled workers an average of $.92 hourly, while in the
semiskilled and skilled construction trades wages averaged about
seventy-five cents per hour. Finally, within the firm and a given
category of work, there was also little relationship between wages
and productivity. Many workers commonly preferred piece rates,
but most unions enforced systems of standardized wage payments
in order to enhance their prestige and authority.

The second major economic impact of restrictive practices in the
labor market was reduced labor mobility. Organized labor sealed off
protected industries from pressures emanating from the urban unemployed and from workers in low-wage, small-scale industry.
Immobilities in the labor market in turn hardened the wage structure. Third, there were few incentives for young workers to seek
technical training; in fact, there was even a scarcity of unstandard-
ized, on-the-job training programs outside of the sugar mills. Hence,
Cuba developed a serious shortage of trained, skilled workers.
Fourth, the special kind of "social insurance" programs of the
Cuban government meant that the burden of a general economic
recession was placed arbitrarily on specific employers, rather than
being spread evenly among all producers. Lastly, racial discrimination by foreign and Cuban businesses added to the inefficiencies
and irrationalities in the labor market.[21] Cuba's stagnating economy

[20] Cuba, Ministerio de Hacienda, Instituto de Estudios Financieros, *Trimestre: Suplemento del Directorio Financiero,* 1, No. 1, January–March, 1962,
Table 11, p. 50. The dispersion of annual incomes was not as great as the
dispersion of monthly wages, implying that relatively high wages in seasonal
industries partly offset seasonal unemployment (*Cuba: Economic and Commercial Conditions in Cuba,* pp. 38–39).

[21] There were relatively more Negroes than could be expected on a probability basis in skilled labor trades, unskilled labor, personal services, and some
sectors of the rural labor force. There were relatively less in all other classes of

magnified all of these irrationalities by further distorting the wage and employment structures.

Table 3. Intra-occupational wage differentials in Cuba, 1962 [a]

	Percentage of employed workers		
Hourly wages ($)	Typists [b]	Lathe operators [c]	Sugar mill laborers [c]
Less than .80	.1	18.9	3.8
.81– .90	1.6	19.0	.4
.91–1.00	6.1	7.1	5.8
1.01–1.10	5.3	13.1	2.6
1.11–1.20	14.7	12.3	1.5
1.21–1.30	8.7	18.4	.6
1.31–1.40	20.2	4.1	1.1
1.41–1.50	11.7	1.2	35.3
1.51–1.70	22.1	3.1	31.4
1.71–1.90	6.8	1.8	6.9
Over 1.90	3.7	1.0	10.6
Total	100.0	100.0	100.0

[a] This table shows intra-occupational wage differentials in three occupations for which data are available. Sugar mill laborers were the only fully organized workers. Between 1958 and 1962 intra-occupational differentials changed very little, although interfirm and interindustry differentials changed substantially.

[b] "Bases para la organización de los salarios y sueldos de los trabajadores," *Trabajo Cuba,* Suplemento, 4, No. 9 (June, 1963), p. 5.

[c] Cuba, Ministerio del Trabajo, Centro de Investigación Laboral, personal interview, Antonio Benítez, Subdirector, August 15, 1963.

In sum, in prerevolutionary Cuba there was no labor market in the sense that one exists in the advanced capitalist countries. No market or government pressures worked to rationalize the distorted wage structure to bring wages in line with productivity.[22] Labor

employment (Nelson, *op. cit.,* Table 15, p. 154). Discrimination was reflected in Negro:white income differentials at both low and high incomes (*ibid.,* Table 16, p. 156). The high proportion of Negro skilled workers suggests that the unions discriminated very little, an observation confirmed by the fact that many union leaders were Negroes. In 1959 the revolution gave Negroes privileged hiring status in business firms seized that year which had discriminated in the past.

[22] Union wage policies improved the "privileged" sector at the expense of other workers, who received lower wages and experienced more unemployment,

costs were thus transformed into fixed costs. Production processes lost any possible flexibility, and labor and capital were combined into inefficient "bundles." In town and country, industry and agriculture, finance and commerce, the "labor problem" haunted all attempts to accelerate capitalist economic development.

[3]

The key labor question during the first two years of the revolution was the political control of the unions. As we have seen, government-labor alliances were an established part of the old political economy. Rarely did the CTC follow an independent political line or were CTC leaders free of personal, financial, or political ties with the government in power. With this fact firmly in mind, developments during 1959 and 1960 are more comprehensible.

The fall of the Batista government set into motion two contradictory developments. The Labor Section of the 26th of July Movement was appointed Provisional Committee of the CTC, which was headed by David Salvador. A decree on January 20 gave the new government authority to summarily remove union leaders. Of the twenty-one committee members, sixteen were associated with the 26th of July Movement, and five with the PSP (Communist party). The formal origins of this alliance went back to October, 1958, when the PSP's National Committee for the Defense of Workers Demands and the Democratization of the CTC formed a coalition with the 26th of July's National Workers Front.

---

although widespread featherbedding undoubtedly reduced the employment effect of militant wage policies. High business profits suggest that "privileged" workers did not improve their position at the expense of capitalists. Nor did high wages come out of an expansion of national income; on the contrary, union wage policies helped to inhibit the growth of production. Nor did high wages come out of monopsony profits siphoned out of the labor market, because wages in the privileged sectors were well above competitive levels for a long time. Thus, the conclusion drawn by Wallich for the 1940's no doubt retained its validity in the 1950's: "This pressure [for higher wage rates and job security] probably has increased the tendency toward unemployment which has prevailed steadily except at the peak of the war boom" (Henry C. Wallich, *Monetary Problems of an Export Economy: The Cuban Experience, 1914–1947* [Cambridge, 1950], p. 4).

Simultaneously, a vacuum developed on the factory and shop level. The old Mujalistas had lost moral and political authority, on the one side, and the 26th of July was short of local cadres, on the other. Into the vacuum stepped local Communist unionists, many of whom regained posts they had lost in the purges over ten years earlier. The Communists entered local union politics with impressive credentials. Driven underground by Batista, the party was compelled to return to its working-class constituency and rebuild its strength. Throughout the 1950's it engaged in active organizing campaigns and led a number of strikes, particularly in the countryside. Originally the PSP had opposed Castro's guerilla tactics, but this apparently cost it very little goodwill in its constituencies, which were not directly involved in the military struggle.

The inherent tension between national and local leadership began to dissolve at the end of January when the 26th of July leaders, without referring the question to the workers, removed their five Communist colleagues from the Provisional Committee. Meanwhile, the ORIT (Inter-American Regional Organization of Workers of the ICFTU) had stepped in and "sought to prevent CTC leaders who had held office before December 31, 1958, from becoming victims of political passion." [23] Perhaps this was one reason why second-level and many local leaders were finally spared. Also influencing the situation was the fact that the national 26th of July leadership required allies in the developing struggle against PSP cadres.[24] That the basic motivation of some 26th of July leaders was to protect and consolidate their position by taking the initiative away from the PSP is suggested by the fact that in February, *well before* communism and anticommunism became issues in Cuba, the CTC announced a purge of CTC unionists at the local level, simultaneously kicking off a propaganda campaign for anti-Communist unity within the ranks of labor.[25] This campaign was held in conjunction with a rally during the same month at which Salvador called for a general increase in wages of 20 per cent, reinstatement

[23] *The Cuban Trade Union Movement under the Regime of Dr. Castro,* ORIT-ICFTU special publications (Mexico City, October, 1960), p. 10.
[24] J. P. Morray, *The Second Revolution in Cuba* (New York, 1962), p. 16.
[25] See, for example, *The Havana Post,* February 19, 1959.

of workers fired under the Batista regime, and support for the new government. In this way, the CTC took a "popular" line that could not fail to help its anti-Communist campaign.

The PSP was thus in an unenviable position; the CTC brought many Mujalista local leaders over to their side, raised many economic demands, and conducted a number of important strikes.[26] In this period, more and more controls were being placed on the private economy, and the center of economic gravity was slowly shifting from the private to the public sector, but the economic system remained capitalistic in character. Thus, the PSP could not oppose the CTC on the grounds that the latter was following an "incorrect" or counterrevolutionary wage policy. Quite the contrary, the PSP was compelled to support the CTC's line.

During the spring of 1959, when the CTC had established control over the union electoral apparatus, on the heels of an intensive anti-Communist propaganda campaign, and with PSP candidates absent from many elections, the CTC won complete control of twenty-eight of Cuba's thirty-three federations via the ballot box. Firmly in control for the time being at least, in May twenty of the federation leaders reaffirmed their anticommunism and pledged to defend the rights of private property.[27]

This was a highly significant development, because it came on the eve of the Agrarian Reform Law. In essence, it meant that the CTC moved sharply away from the government's position and established itself as the right wing of the 26th of July Movement. Its line was antisocialist (in that agrarian reform meant the expropriation and partial collectivization of property) as well as anti-Communist. Meanwhile union wage policies were increasingly militating against

[26] Twenty-two sugar mills were struck in February over the issues of hours of work, working conditions, and wages. Castro intervened and requested the sugar workers to postpone action until after the *zafra*. He reasoned that the companies were attempting to provoke a major strike in order to bring down the revolution, and that the bargaining power of the workers would be greater during the next *zafra* when the revolution would be more fully consolidated. The strike ended, but there were many slowdowns. There were also strikes or strike threats in power, oil, banking, hotels, and other industries during this period.

[27] *Ibid.*, May 24, 1959.

economic development, which was the central underlying theme of the revolution.

Thus, the differences between the new CTC leaders and Mujalistas (admitting exceptions in both camps) boiled down to differences in personal integrity and, undoubtedly in some cases, the ability to make a career in the Batista-dominated labor movement. Both groups were wedded to the private property system, antisocialist as well as anti-Communist, and committed ideologically and psychologically to established forms of trade union struggle. Their policies clearly represented a barrier to any attempt to rationalize the labor market or the wage structure.

This narrative provides the backdrop for the story of the rise in PSP influence within the CTC. It does not suffice, however, to explain why the PSP moved into many key leadership roles at Premier Castro's initiative. Three additional considerations should be borne in mind. First, the PSP had a large reservoir of goodwill in many sections of the working class, especially the sugar workers, oil workers, and bank employees, dating back to the days of World War II. Furthermore, many workers were disturbed when the 26th of July leaders formed alliances with second-line Mujalistas, whom they knew to be corrupt. Secondly, the PSP apparently offered Castro the loyalties of disciplined, honest, and perhaps most important, production-and-productivity-minded cadres. Lastly, the generalized "let the government do it" attitude among Cuba's working classes weakened whatever bonds some workers felt with the 26th of July leadership. In this context, it is not difficult to understand how the political revolution on the labor front which pushed the PSP and radicalized 26th of July and Mujalista leaders into the foreground, was consolidated so easily.

On October 16, 1959, Augusto Martínez Sánchez, a staunch supporter of Castro, was appointed Minister of Labor. One month later, a few hours before the Tenth Congress of the CTC was scheduled to begin, he temporarily called it off, undoubtedly because a large majority of the delegates were anti-Communists. Under pressure, however, the suspension was lifted, and two days later, about three thousand delegates, nearly 10 per cent of whom were PSP unionists, met in Havana. Almost immediately, the latter walked out of the congress when three of their colleagues were eliminated from the slate of candidates for the executive committee of the CTC. Bitter quarrels, fights, and near-riot conditions ensued. Castro intervened with a call for a single unity ticket (undoubtedly after putting pressure on those with Batista connections); his prestige was sufficient to put into power a committee of non-Communists, but not anti-Communists, headed by Salvador.

The ultimate resolution of the question of union leadership occurred behind the scenes. In January, 1960, the new executive committee authorized a purge of anti-Communist and counterrevolutionary leaders. Salvador left the country in the same month, and he resigned when he returned in March to learn that leaders of twenty-two of the twenty-eight non-Communist federations had been replaced or had resigned. It could hardly have been an accident that in this period labor had gone "haywire" with their wage demands.[28] Worker reaction to the purges, which went into the lower ranks as the months passed, was of course mixed, but there is little evidence of opposition. In April, for example, the secretary general and other officials of the construction workers' union resigned, but the workers gave Castro a vote of confidence.[29] Although an informal wage freeze was introduced in the spring of 1960, working-class income was rising rapidly with reductions in unemployment and underemployment.

The climax of the shift in leadership came in December, after what Guevara called an "arduous war against the representatives of mujalism, representative of the old CTC gang," [30] when Amaury Fraginals, chief of the powerful electrical workers, and about two dozen followers were dismissed from their posts, although changes in the middle ranks continued well into 1961. Although the PSP old-timer Lázaro Peña was made secretary general of the CTC (now CTC-R) with no opposition at the Eleventh National Congress in

[28] Roger Valdés, "Trade Winds," *The Havana Post,* March 22, 1960.
[29] *The Havana Post,* April 6, 1960. Salvador himself was expelled from the CTC in November, 1960, and jailed in 1961.
[30] Speech on June 18, 1960, *Obra Revolucionaria,* No. 11 (1960).

November, 1961, the majority of Cuba's union officials were not ex-
PSP unionists, but rather "radicalized" leaders from the 26th of July
and Mujalista camps.[31]

[4]

Between the reform of the labor leadership and the reform of the
trade union structure itself half a year passed. A process of merger
and consolidation of local and regional union sections began in the
late summer of 1960, accelerated after the great expropriations in
the fall, and was completed in 1961. Thus, there is a clear historical
link between the movement into socialism and physical planning
and the reorganization of the unions; the latter was in no important
sense independent of the former. From its very inception in February, 1961, MININD sponsored almost continuous conferences
between union leaders and representatives of the consolidated enterprises, and other branches of the socialist sector followed suit.[32]

[31] In the summer of 1962, Maurice Zeitlin described the situation: "Five
members of the thirteen-man Executive Committee of the CTC-R, and eleven
of the Secretaries-General of the twenty-five National labor unions are old
Communists. Most of the 26th of July labor leaders, if my discussions with
some of them are any indication, do not differ noticeably from the Communists
in their thinking [about the fact that stress should be placed on production and
productivity, rather than on the idea of unions as defenders of the workers
against the state bureaucracy]" ("Labor in Cuba," *The Nation* 195, No. 12
[October 20, 1962], p. 241).

[32] Perhaps the first merger was between the port unions in Nuevitas in July,
1960, when the unified maritime-port workers union was formed. One of the
main purposes, and a significant effect, of the merger was to unify the dock
workers lists in order to plan labor needs more rationally. Next month, gastro-
nomic workers in Havana Province merged nine unions into one. In August,
most of Cuba's major hotels were being managed by the government, and the
union mergers complemented this new stewardship. In October, unions in air
transport, metals, mining, and petroleum refining were consolidated. Other
unions followed suit. On the highest level, the number of national federations
was reduced from thirty-three to twenty-five. The largest federations were the
sugar workers (316,000 members), agricultural workers (139,000 members),
tobacco workers (114,000), construction workers (120,000), and commercial
employees (101,000) (Carlos Fernández R., "El XI Congreso Nacional de la
CTC-R," *Cuba Socialista*, 2, No. 6 [February, 1962], pp. 50–51). By the summer of 1962, the agricultural workers union grew to 180,000 members (*Trabajo
Cuba*, 3, No. 9 [May, 1962], p. 9). In 1963, the sugar workers federation was
integrated into the agricultural workers union.

Apart from alterations in the structure and organization of the labor unions, there were also basic changes in their functions. The concept of unions as independent instruments of the working class and the means of workers' control of industry never received serious consideration. The revolution's leaders and the island's top unionists and labor publicists rejected the idea on both ideological and practical grounds. It was believed that workers' control would reduce the authority of the collective and create local pockets of autonomous decision-making, setting one group of workers against another. In a period when the defense of the revolution was paramount, the authority of the collective was thought to be absolute. On practical grounds, the government rejected workers' control because Cuba's major economic problem was development and growth, not an "equitable" distribution of income. Another reason for integrating dependent unions into a central planning structure was that in many sectors the workers were simply not prepared to assume the task of directing the economy.

The intended functions of the new unions were best expressed in the new Law of Union Organization, decreed in August, 1961. According to the preamble, the old labor legislation hampered "the realization of the Government's plans to construct a society in which man does not exploit man." The law ordered the unions to "assist in the fulfillment of the production and development plans of the nation, to promote efficiency, expansion, and utility in social and public services. . . ." [33] Two months later, at the CTC-R Eleventh Congress, the national federations agreed on a series of measures to raise production, productivity, and level of savings. The most important of these was the elimination of union bureaucracy, manifested in dual functions, useless jobs, and an absence of contact with shop conditions. All in all, there were perhaps sixty thousand union functionaries in one capacity or another, the great majority inherited from the old top-heavy and bureaucratized CTC under Batista.[34] Other agreements were to save raw materials and fuel, to eliminate

[33] Ley No. 962, *Gaceta Oficial* (*Extraordinaria*), August 3, 1961.

[34] This was the number of registrants in a course for union personnel. Not all were full-time, paid functionaries.

the automatic nine-day sickness leave and holiday bonuses, to exceed the savings goals set by the 1962 plan, and to maintain the 4 per cent "industrialization" payroll tax while foregoing interest payments.

Union personnel were to work hand in glove with Cuba's industrial, agricultural, and financial managers, but simultaneously were to help to protect workers from administrative abuses. "The unions," Guevara wrote in mid-1961, "must defend the specific and immediate interests of the working class at the level of the enterprise or the factory." [35] This dual and possibly contradictory role was partially resolved with the creation of the grievance commissions. Nevertheless, there was considerable apathy and indifference to union activity among workers. The Labor Procedure Laws provided for the recall of leaders, but it is difficult to know the extent to which leaders have been replaced on the initiative of the workers. Many unionists were replaced in 1962 in the course of the purges of the labor section of the PSP, but this was on the government's initiative. The unions did play an independent role in the areas of managing welfare funds, distributing new and abandoned housing, forming and directing social, cultural, and recreational centers, and providing teachers and other aid for Cuba's many education programs. [36]

[5]
Like the unions, the place of the Ministry of Labor in the new political economy was profoundly modified during the second year of the revolution. During 1959 and part of 1960 the Labor Ministry

[35] Ernesto Guevara, Discusión Colectiva, Decisión y Responsabilidad," *Trabajo Cuba*, 2, No. 9 (July, 1961), pp. 40–47.

[36] Other issues were the question of industrial versus craft unionism and the role of collective bargaining. Both issues were resolved on the basis of production and productivity criteria (Blas Roca and Lazaro Peña, quoted in *Hoy*, September 6, 1962; Ernesto Guevara, quoted in *Revolución*, November 29, 1962). Craft unions were eliminated and workers were organized along industry lines. The government placed more constraints on the collective bargaining process. Workers in general assemblies vote to approve collective agreements hammered out by union representatives and management. The technical advisory councils are invoked in the event of major disagreements. Even in the event of full agreement, the Ministry of Labor must approve all agreements.

extended the victories that workers had won in the past. The law forbidding layoffs was broadened to include agricultural workers, and the six-month waiting period for all workers was eliminated. In these and other ways, the Labor Ministry bound the labor market up more tightly in knots while protecting in theory the interests of the working classes. Some reforms needed no justification: the new Office of Labor Control worked to eliminate the nepotism, favoritism, and racial discrimination that had long been features of employment policies of both the state and many private firms. The Office was particularly successful in eliminating racial discrimination. Meanwhile, the ministry delegated many of its functions to organisms on lower levels in order to get away from the past pattern of excessive centralization.

Following the economic disruptions in the private sector attributable to the increasing hostility of Cuba's business groups to the great reforms of 1959, the structure and functions of the ministry began to undergo a change. A decree in January, 1960, increased the role of the ministry in the intervention process and brought it even more closely into worker-business relations. The occasion was a set of laws passed in 1959 that started an avalanche of labor disputes. The first law permitted the reopening of labor actions decided under Batista's old ministry; a second ordered firms to rehire workers fired during the old regime; a third prohibited discharges for economic reasons. The first two laws were political in character and the third was economically motivated, with the purpose of maintaining production. Under these laws, thousands of new disputes arose and old disputes were reopened. By the summer of 1961, the ministry had accumulated over 112,000 actions, many requiring intervention.[37] Thus, the ministry "radicalized" itself; to settle the disputes, it was given a broader field of action, including the right to seize businesses.

The ministry acquired real power after the nationalization of industry and during the first, hectic months of socialist economic planning. The Second Organic Law of the Ministry of Labor was passed

[37] As reported by Minister of Labor Martínez Sánchez at the Eleventh National Congress of the CTC-R, November, 1961.

at the end of December, 1960, giving labor the authority to distribute jobs and making it an integral part of the planning mechanism. But it was not until April, 1962, that a new subsecretary of planning was created and the Division in Charge of Labor Control acquired the power to direct layoffs and labor mobility and to punish employer violations of labor legislation. In August, the government directed workers to acquire identity cards, and all enterprises received instructions to use the division to fill vacancies. Nevertheless, real control of the labor market, excepting the employment of skilled workers in the urban centers, eluded the ministry. Even *within* major divisions of the Cuban economy there was a noticeable lack of employment planning.

The reason that the ministry was not able to perform its new function lay in a paradox facing the Revolutionary Government. On the one hand, popular socialist government required active working-class support. On the other hand, economic and social development required a self-disciplined, dedicated work force. Thus, the government prepared for the participation of the workers in economic and social planning. "The government," Guevara said in 1961, "cannot dictate norms, make plans, fix goals, without the participation of the people, for, in this case, it would be cold bureaucratic planning." [38] At the same time, the revolution's leaders carried on intensive campaigns against absenteeism and union bureaucracy and in favor of volunteer labor and "socialist competition." Also, within the factories, according to Guevara, "the administrator and the administrative councils are the ones who have sole and absolute responsibility for the fulfillment of the obligations committed to them [by the government]."

Two new labor organizations established by the Ministry of Labor also had this dualistic character. Neither pure working-class organizations nor pure state organisms, the technical advisory coun-

[38] "Discusión Colectiva, Decisión y Responsabilidad," p. 43. A year earlier Guevara referred to the developing "joint administration by workers and the government of each business" (speech on June 18, 1960, *Obra Revolucionaria*, No. 1 [1960]).

cils and the grievance commissions exhibited a contradictory or ambiguous character.

The purpose of the technical advisory councils was to involve the workers more intimately in production. The councils' specific tasks were to develop "emulation" plans in order to fully utilize the workday, improve labor discipline, conserve raw materials, improve working conditions and employment security, and create volunteer work battalions; to formulate production and investment plans; and to obtain the consent and active participation of workers in planning goals laid down by the Central Planning Board.[39]

The ambiguous character of the councils was reflected in a number of ways. First, the workers themselves nominated three "vanguard workers" from each major department, of which the firm's administration chose one. Thus, the administration exercised a semiveto power over the workers' choices. A further ambiguity arose because the administration merely had to consult the councils on questions of production, labor conditions, and so on. Further, the administration was empowered to reject proposals initiated by the councils.

More confusion arose over the question of wages and norms of work. Originally, the councils were given the authority to fix salaries and set norms, to be changed from time to time as technical conditions changed. Bonuses were earned when workers surpassed their norms, to be paid from a fund fed from the net profits of the particular enterprise (which did not fail to encourage real interenterprise competition, particularly in the sugar industry). This was decentralized decision-making of a highly significant type and in effect gave workers the power to fix their own salaries, with the final approval of the Ministry of Labor. There is little evidence of the extent to which the workers attempted to take advantage of this authority, but one can easily imagine the uncertainties and confusion in many shops in the context of the general hold-the-line wage pol-

[39] Rafael Castellanos, "Los Consejos Técnicos Asesores y la Producción Nacional," *Universidad Popular, Economía y Planificación, Segunda Parte,* Universidad Popular, Séptimo Ciclo (June, 1961), pp. 117–119.

icy of 1961–1963. Later, the council's statutes were revised, and national standards, not only with regard to the wage level but also to the wage structure, were laid down in 1963 and fully effected in 1964. In essence, the planning center did not trust to the workers the task of rationalizing the incredibly distorted wage structure the revolution inherited from the old regime. On reflection, in fact, it is difficult to see how the workers, acting *independently* in *local* collectivities, could fail to have made this structure more irrational.

In short, the councils were basically administrative organs resting on a political base: workers' nominations. Administrators and workers alike were thus confused about their basic function. In mid-1962, many workers were not even aware of the existence of the councils in other plants. Nor did many workers set up councils in their own factories. Thus, even though the councils were to initiate collective production decisions, by 1964 they were largely defunct.

As with the technical councils, the grievance commissions had an ambiguous character with regard to their real base. Until the commissions were reorganized in April, 1962, they were made up of workers' representatives, who were elected in secret ballots from each work place. In the reorganized commissions, each unit was comprised of three members, one each from the Ministry of Labor (selected by the administration and workers together) and the firm itself, and the remaining one elected by the workers.[40] The reorganization also involved adding an appeals procedure: when a majority votes against the administration, the latter has no right to appeal, but when the vote goes against a worker, there is no such limit on the grievance procedure.

Two general complaints were increasingly heard throughout 1961: first, that commissions failed to air many grievances; second, they refused to hear appeals of decisions that the workers considered wrong. Evidently the commissions, to which were elected mainly revolutionary militants, felt that bending too much to workers' demands would weaken their authority. Thus, paradoxical as it may seem, the commissions began to represent the workers' interest

[40] "Dos Nuevas Leyes Laborales," *Trabajo Cuba*, 3, No. 10 (June, 1962), pp. 58–62.

more closely after Ministry of Labor and administration representatives took seats on them. Despite this, the general attitude of the workers toward the commissions in 1962 remained passive. Red tape and bureaucracy replaced misdirected local militancy as the source of discontent with the commissions, although by late 1963 they were functioning much better.

The new labor organizations unquestionably failed to arouse the hoped for interest in planning and production. "Today," Adolfo Gilly wrote in October, 1964, "the Cuban population does not yet take part in the solution of fundamental problems of economic planning, except by diffuse social pressure. . . . The workers in general show little interest in discussing the production plan. Since such discussions are confined to their place of work, the plan appears to them as a complete abstraction." The new system of economic decision-making was thus not without its bad side effects; the workers "do not respond to calls for 'production rallies.' " Compounding the problem, "defenders of the system consider their lack of response conclusive proof that the workers do not understand and are not interested in planning problems." [41]

There were many revolutionary organizations bidding for the time and efforts of the workers, however, and in any event the line of identification of the worker with the revolution went directly to Premier Castro through the mass organizations, bypassing the newer shop organizations. The other important factor was the revolutionary leadership's lack of clarity in building these workers' organizations; just how much workers' control would be incorporated into the councils and commissions was apparently never really decided. But it must be stressed that the reorganization of the labor unions themselves paid off, for it laid the basis for improving the relationship between productivity and wages and raising the level of savings.[42]

[41] Adolfo Gilly, "Inside the Cuban Revolution," *Monthly Review*, 16, No. 6 (October, 1964).

[42] In the course of 1960, the unions pledged to freeze wages and raise productivity. The shoe workers promised to end absenteeism and "apathy"; other unions, the airline workers, for example, renounced overtime pay; and the sugar workers finally agreed to the extension of bulk shipments of sugar. All of the

[6]

The foundering and uneven development of the newly constituted unions, Labor Ministry, and the new labor organizations must be placed in the context of the leadership's changing and sometimes unclear theory of the place of the working class in the revolution. It is not an overstatement to say that the new labor policy is not even comprehensible without an understanding of the revolution's ideology. The seeds of this new ideology were contained in the thinking of Premier Castro at least as early as 1959 and germinated quickly as Cuba moved into socialism: "We have to erase ideas of the past from the workers' minds . . . ," so far as attitudes toward work are concerned.[43] This view was a significant addition to that of the first year of the revolution, a passive view which held that workers had

---

unions were involved in a campaign to promote the sale of People's Savings Certificates and Housing Institute bonds.

Beginning in 1962, the unions set target figures for production, productivity, and savings. Also, the unions contributed to the programs of the Ministry of Education that looked to raise the technical level of the Cuban worker. Many false starts and a great deal of confusion marked this period. At the Eleventh CTC-R Congress, Peña attacked some union leaders for failing to set goals or for setting imprecise or timid goals ("Las Secciones Sindicales: Baluartes del Movimiento Obrera," *Trabajo Cuba*, 3, No. 4 [February, 1962], p. 11). The merger and consolidation of the unions raced ahead of the ability of union leaders to take on new responsibilities. The major problems were a lack of competent technical and administrative—as opposed to political—personnel and the struggle during 1961 and early 1962 between the "old" and "new" Communists. Thus, on the one hand there were continuous attacks by the union leaders against bureaucracy in their own organizations, and anarchic organization on the other. Neither was a clear tendency, although Cuba suffered both. At the Eleventh Congress, for example, Peña simultaneously denounced the tendency to concentrate power at the level of the national unions and provincial CTC-R's and condemned anarchic organization defended by others "in the name of antibureaucracy." The attacks continued throughout 1962 and remained in general terms. The unions were chided at the Twenty-sixth National Council of the CTC-R in September for arbitrariness, failure to obey orders from the top, and overidentificaiton with the management of enterprise (*Revolución*, September 2, 1962). In 1963, public attacks became more specific; bureaucracy in the bank workers' union, for example, was a favorite target (Jesús Abascal, "Con el Impulso de los Bancarios," *Trabajo Cuba*, 3, No. 13 [August, 1963], p. 10).

[43] Castro speech to the CTC National Council, *The Havana Post*, September 15, 1959.

merely to postpone or put off wage and other demands. Work—physical, creative, and collective work—was the hallmark of the revolutionary:

It sufficed that Comrade Guevara should have the initiative to launch the campaign to have everyone take part in physical labor, that the idea should catch on on such a scale as we have seen the Cuban people reach, these days, at the height of their creative enthusiasm; we have seen a people raise high the banner of labor, we have seen work resurrected by the people. And that which yesterday was regarded with contempt, that which the aristocracy and the dominant classes taught to regard with scorn, physical labor, is today lifted by the people to the most honorable activity.[44]

The supreme importance finally attached to the idea of *collective* labor is shown in a Castro speech delivered at the height of the economic crises in 1962: "Among the working class there are still many who are individualistic, self-interested, and irresponsible. They live in a world that is not of the revolution. They do not understand the revolution. Therefore, they have to be purged from the working class as a degenerated, negative, corrupt, discredited, and demoralized group." [45] Put positively, "We admire the Soviet man, the new man, the creator of a new society; a magnanimous, fraternal man, free from the selfish characteristics of people of a capitalist society." [46]

The immediate reason for this line of thinking and policy was the disappearance of Cuban capitalism and the discipline of the old wages system, together with the failure of a new socialist discipline to arise spontaneously. In the context of the great stress on production, productivity, and economic development in general, the practical reasons for stressing the virtues of work are not hard to find.

[44] Castro, quoted in *INRA*, 2, No. 3 (March, 1961), p. 50.

[45] Castro, quoted in *El Mundo*, July 18, 1962.

[46] Castro interview with Soviet editors, January 29, 1962, radio broadcast. The idea of the creative worker is perhaps best expressed in a description of the ideal administrator, himself a "worker in the vanguard." He "should be just, conscientious, prudent, with integrity . . . he should combine revolutionary impetuosity with a practical sense" (*Trabajo Cuba*, 2, No. 17 [November, 1961], p. 31).

Moreover, with the advent of economic planning, and the general belief of the revolutionary leadership that planning requires the active consent and participation of the masses of workers, another overriding practical concern rapidly came to the surface. These ideas on work and labor, however, contained far more than an immediate pragmatic content. Work was the cornerstone of economic growth, the only way to construct socialism, under which the working class can abolish itself as a class and through which the path to full communism leads. These were the ideological guidelines for the revolution, first developed in 1962 and later given constant expression and re-emphasis.

It was the theory and practice of "socialist emulation" which tied together in a practical way labor and production. Emulation consisted of "work" and "consciousness," that is, an intensified, more creative individual productive effort together with an emphasis on helping other workers to raise production and productivity. From 1961 to 1964, the idea of socialist competition went through two basic stages. In the first period, which was ended by the economic crisis of the summer and fall of 1962, "social" incentives were emphasized over "material" incentives.[47] In the second stage, there was explicit recognition that material incentives would have to be extended, rationalized, and, at least for the time being, relied on heavily. Meantime, there was no let up on the theme of socialist competition in the original sense of the phrase. During 1961, material incentives were a distant second to social incentives,[48] and even in late 1962, Guevara, for one, insisted that the latter—the "call to duty"—took precedence over the former.[49]

[47] The phrase often used in Cuba was *estímulo moral*. These "moral" or social incentives promote emulation that is "economically disinterested" and thus conform to Marx's original idea of socialist emulation. But competition *between* individual workers, however economically disinterested, departs from Marx's conception.

[48] Author's interview with Ernesto Guevara, Havana, October 9, 1961.

[49] Speech to the graduates of the School of Industrial Administration, radio broadcast, December 22, 1962. In practical terms, socialist competition meant working a full day, saving fuel and materials, maintaining equipment, acquiring new skills—in short, promoting the economically rational use of resources and time. It also involved bettering work conditions, including job security (*Trabajo Cuba*, 2, No. 6 [June, 1961], p. 56).

Socialist emulation was at least a partial failure, and increasing recognition of the high costs of volunteer labor and a growing absenteeism problem,[50] combined with the imperatives of economic

---

The first official steps toward a system of socialist emulation were taken in the summer and fall of 1960. In August, the Ministry of Labor established a system of honorary rewards granted to workers who surpassed certain minimum standards. Shortly after, the government created various Emulation Boards and a Division of Labor Emulation within the Labor Ministry. Even in this early period, however, socialist competition was not devoid of material rewards. Early in 1961, for example, a program was instituted under which Cuba's one hundred best workers were singled out each month for an award and vacation at one of the many new tourist centers.

[50] The first signs of volunteer labor utilitzation appeared in 1959, with the creation of the Organization of Volunteer Workers (absorbed by the CTC-R in August, 1962). This agency supplied workers for emergency tasks in agriculture and transportation. The voluntary labor movement did not really get underway, however, until the sugar harvest of 1962 (see Chapter 8). In the movement the example set by the revolution's leaders has always been paramount. "The only privilege I have," Tirso Saenz, Vice-Minister of Basic Industry, said in 1962, "is the right to work harder than anybody else" (quoted by Samuel Shapiro, *The Nation,* 195, No. 8 [September 22, 1962]). For the revolution, the main disadvantage of volunteer labor is that from a technical point of view labor is misallocated—for example, skilled factory hands cut cane during the harvest. Plans to raise productivity of those who remained in the factories and on the construction projects came too late and were too little (radio broadcast, Lazaro Peña, December 19, 1962). From a political point of view, the movement brought together urban and rural workers, office workers and manual laborers, administrators and leaders, and ordinary people, and hence did much to "cement the worker-peasant alliance." Guevara described the importance of volunteer labor in this way: much more than merely a way to relieve labor bottlenecks, the movement was "a vehicle of union and comprehension between our administrative workers and the manual workers, to prepare the road toward . . . a new stage of society where classes will not exist, and, therefore, there will be no difference between a manual worker and an intellectual worker, between worker and peasant" (speech on August 15, 1964, *Obra Revolucionaria,* No. 21 [1964]).

The other side of the coin was the problem of absenteeism, which hindered production planning until a rational and equitable set of material incentives were developed to complement socialist emulation. Attacks against absenteeism were common during 1961–1962, declined in 1963–1964, and subsequently almost disappeared. At the First Plenary Meeting on Production (Greater Havana area) held in September, 1961, to cite an example, absenteeism was considered to be, after production, Cuba's most important economic problem (*Revolución,* September 25, 1961). Guevara declared in late 1961 that the problem had taken on "alarming characteristics." There were a number of reasons for the phenomenon, most of which were temporary. First, workers

planning, led to the rationalization of material incentives in late 1962. This new policy was basically related to the profound need to bring the wage structure into harmony with labor productivity. In

who came under the most heavy criticism (the hotel and restaurant employees, for example) were employed in industries that temporarily were inactive. Second, a great many street hawkers and ambulatory merchants found factory employment in 1959 and 1960 and retained their street businesses on a part-time basis. Third, the expansion of employment during the first two years of the revolution introduced many younger workers into the factories, and these youths figured importantly in the absentee column (Jaime Gravalosa, "La batalla contra el ausentismo," *Trabajo Cuba,* 2, No. 15 [October, 1961], p. 36). Fourth, the shortage of consumer commodities, especially severe during 1961 and 1962, reduced labor incentives. Last, and most important, was the lingering on of old habits and attitudes toward work. The World Bank unquestionably went too far when it wrote that "the fact that . . . an employee in Cuba cannot be discharged has a ruinous psychological effect on him . . . [destroying] his initiative and incentive" (*Report on Cuba,* p. 148). As Page more moderately put it, however, "Cuban workers are . . . prone to absenteeism" (*op. cit.,* pp. 231–232). In brief, the end of absenteeism as an important social-economic phenomenon depended on the creation of a specifically class consciousness on the part of Cuban workers.

The revolution's policy toward absenteeism went through two phases. In the first phase, absenteeism was considered to be a product of the failure of workers to understand their obligation to contribute to production ("Así actúan las Comisiones de Reclamaciones," *Trabajo Cuba,* 2, No. 18 [December, 1961], p. 46). This was based on the observation that young workers with inadequate attendance records on the job were often militants outside of their places of employment (Gravalosa, *op. cit.,* p. 36). Thus, it was not uncommon for the Labor Ministry to denounce plant administrators for suspending workers without first going to the grievance commissions. In the second phase, which began when the economic situation deteriorated in 1962, official attitudes toward absenteeism changed. Guevara was especially outspoken on the issue, accusing "high people" of contributing to what had become a "national problem" and putting forth the idea of compulsory measures to meet it (*Revolución,* April 16, 1962). These were finally imposed in August and consisted of public admonishments, salary deductions, suspension from work, and similar measures (Ministry of Labor, Resolución No. 5798, August 27, 1962). A month later, President Dorticós spoke of the need to use "utmost revolutionary severity" to meet the problem (*Revolución,* September 10, 1962). In 1963 references to the question were less frequent and job attendance improved notably. The reasons seemed to be related to the effects of the antiabsenteeism campaign itself: the new Social Security Law, which provided incentives for regular employment (Pedro M. Escalona, "Las fábricas se van organizando," *Trabajo Cuba,* 4, No. 13 [August, 1963], p. 3); improvements in the production and distribution of goods; and a general upswing of morale due to the aftermath of the missile crisis and the elimination of many PSP personnel from the revolutionary organizations.

April, 1962, the flaws in the prize system introduced in 1960 were recognized by the Minister of Labor's announcement that "to increase production we will establish emulation on the basis of material stimuli in conformity with present realities." [51] Even with this new dimension added to socialist competition, the results were unsatisfactory; complaints were heard in late 1962 and early 1963 that the program had a bureaucratic character and that there was little mass participation.[52] Thus, led by the unions, themselves following guidelines put down by the Minister of Labor, a formal all-Cuba emulation program got underway in April, 1962. This was preceded by meetings between enterprise administrators and unions, followed by assemblies of production workers during which collective and individual commitments were supposed to be determined. Emulation remained a *personal* commitment, however, and by late 1963, the program was frequently described as "lax"; in agriculture, for example, only 22,000 of over 380,000 workers had committed themselves to it. Not surprisingly, since it was the most revolutionary province, Oriente consistently came ahead of other provinces in national competitions,[53] and it was there that the first volunteer "red battalions" made their appearance in the 1963 *zafra*.

Another, ultimately more important, aspect of the question of material incentives was the attempt to tie regular wage payments more closely to productivity. Material incentives were also used to stimulate workers to improve their technical or professional training and to advance to higher grades. All of the publicity given to the "introduction of material incentives" in early 1963 by no means signified a *lack* of such incentives earlier; it meant merely that existing incentives (wage structures) were historically given and bore little relationship to the needs of rational planning. There was thus a drive to rationalize both the general level of wages and the wage structure. The first goal was partly achieved by a general freeze on money wages beginning in early 1960; in an interview with the author, Minister of Economy Boti considered the rapid increases in wages prior to this time to be a "mistake." The significant features were the self-imposed freeze on salaries in the sugar field beginning

in March, 1960; the many union agreements throughout 1960 to refrain from agitating for higher wages; the renunciation by the Eleventh National CTC-R Congress of the Christmas bonus and some
overtime payments; the $200 monthly maximum wage, applicable to
those earning under that figure in 1962; and, finally, the general
principle of minimum work quotas.

Equally significant were the attempts through 1962–1964 to rationalize the wage *structure*. Instructions for the establishment of
labor norms were published jointly by the Labor Ministry and the
CTC-R in the summer of 1962. Individual jobs and some group
tasks were normed, and the norms measured the labor of the typical, not the best, worker.[54] A timetable for the application of norms
was set down. By the middle of 1963 about two-thirds of the workers in Ministry of Industry plants had been incorporated into the
new system as a result of the efforts of nearly fifteen hundred spe-
cially trained *"normadores."* [55] General assemblies of the workers
themselves discussed and approved the norms. Fighting those who
would resist change on the one hand, and those who would me-
chanically transplant the norms prevailing in the more advanced socialist countries on the other, the Industries Ministry kept up its efforts to rationalize the norms in its own domain.[56]

The need for work norms was, of course, just one half of the
story. Without a system of wage differentials that corresponded to
the norm structure, costly supply surpluses and shortages would be
sure to develop. From 1961 on, there were increasing references to
the "present anarchy of salaries." [57] A Ministry of Labor meeting in
early 1962 stressed the relationship between the "present uneven-

---

[54] *Hoy,* September 6, 1962. The actual technique for arriving at norms was
to raise average production by 10 per cent and reduce average time of work
by the same figure (*El Mundo,* October 12, 1962). Apparently, this technique
was used because productivity in 1962 was unusually low.

[55] Juan González, "La formación del trabajo en la industria cubana," *Nuestra
Industria: Revista Económico,* No. 1, p. 27.

[56] *Ibid.,* pp. 23, 27. Norms were continuously changed because of the ever-
changing supply conditions, that is, the number of available technicians, emergencies arising out of military mobilization, shortages of materials and spare
parts, and so on.

[57] *Ibid.,* p. 22.

ness in the wage scale" and economic development.[58] A foreigner could observe in mid-1962 that the relationship between wages and productivity were tenuous indeed, because wage incentives were not tied to equipment maintenance, product quality, and innovations. According to Guevara, wage differentials were among the most serious problems of the revolution.[59] Late in the same year it was observed that wage spreads in mining ran from $3 to $27 per day, and in manufacturing from $7 to $15 per day (in small and large factories, respectively) for essentially the same work. More significant for the shortage of farm labor, daily wages of construction laborers were roughly double those of agricultural workers.[60] Perhaps even more important, average monthly earnings of the former were more than double that of the latter (see Table 4).[61]

The first formal step in the direction of a national wages policy (apart from the drive to freeze wages at current levels) came when the Constitutional Reform Law of March, 1960 abolished the old National Commission of Minimum Salaries and formulated the principle that wages would be set by "law." [62] Shortly after, the Ministry of Labor was granted the right to regulate salaries, and a subsequent resolution in August implemented this step.[63] But it was not until early in 1962 that a national commission was set up to study the question of rationalizing the existing wage and salary structure.

The general principles that the commission laid down, which provided the basis for a detailed plan of wages and salaries, were two-fold. First, equal pay for equal work, where "equal work" depends not only on the objective task to be performed but also on the quali-

[58] Radio broadcast, February 7, 1962.

[59] Cited by Pedro M. Escalona, "Salarios justos, horarios adecuados, y pagos abreviados," *Trabajo Cuba*, 2, No. 3 (March, 1962), pp. 44–47.

[60] Fidel Castro and others, *Hablan para el Instituto Popular de Chile*, Instituto Popular de Chile (Santiago, Chile, 1962), pp. 54, 74.

[61] In a highly unstable labor market, it is impossible to say whether daily or monthly earnings are more significant in the allocation of labor. In Cuba during 1962 annual earnings in construction would clearly not be the relevant factor. Table 4 shows private and public sector monthly earnings in the main branches of the Cuban economy in 1962.

[62] *Gaceta Oficial*, March 14, 1960.

[63] Resolución No. 16782, *Gaceta Oficial*, August 25, 1960.

fications and effort of the worker.[64] Thus, both workers' ideas of equity and planners' ideas of efficiency were thought to be realized. The second principle was that the new wage structure would not be used as a justification to reduce any worker's current income. All jobs would be classified, and a new salary assigned; if a worker in a given category currently earned more than the scheduled salary, he would retain his present salary. A worker promoted to a higher paying job, which nevertheless was classified as paying less than the individual's present salary, would fail to enjoy a wage increase. In this way the first principle would be fully realized over a number of years; given expected rates of promotion, attrition, and so on, salaries were expected to be leveled out by 1972.[65]

Table 4. Average monthly earnings, 1962

	Socialist sector	Private sector	Total average
Agriculture & related	$ 72	$ 52	$ 60
Agriculture	68	52	58
Cane	67	50	56
Noncane	69	53	59
Cattle	73	53	58
Forestry	92	92	93
Fishing	117	—	117
Other	127	—	127
Industry	167	112	158
Construction	148	—	148
Transportation	206	199	205
Communications	160	—	160
Commerce	121	120	120
Services & administration	96	—	96
Total average	125	66	98

Source: JUCEPLAN Dirección de Estadísticas, *Proyecto de Anuario Estadístico 1962* (July, 1963), Tables 3.7, 5.28.

[64] Escalona, *op. cit.*, p. 44; Guevara, cited in *Revolución,* January 28, 1963.
[65] During 1962 various alternative wage scales were studied and debated, and experiments were conducted with different norm schedules. One plan discussed in April sought to establish twelve salary categories; in the following year this was reduced to eight:

Administrative $65.00 98.60 114.75 134.30 157.25 185.30 218.45 263.50
(monthly salary)

[7]

By 1963-1964 the revolution had begun the difficult task of reorganizing the labor market, rationalizing the wage structure, and laying a basis for the use of social incentives to compliment material incentives. To guide them, Cuban planners had the experiences—the successes as well as the failures—of the Soviet Union and the Eastern European socialist countries. On the Havana docks the elimination of double time pay and the rationalization of the size of work gangs reduced loading and unloading costs up to 50 per cent.[66] A schedule of norms for agricultural workers was published in late 1962 and slowly and sporadically implemented during the following two years. By early 1963, work norms and new wage schedules had been widely applied in mining, and in a dozen industries steps had been taken in this direction. In tobacco manufacturing, for instance, the introduction of work norms generated "violent shocks" in the industry; in one plant employment was reduced by one-fifth (the superfluous workers were sent to basic or technical schools of one kind or another) and casual and part-time employ-

---

Nonadministrative (hourly wage)	$0.48	0.56	0.65	0.76	0.89	1.05	1.23	1.49

Source: "Bases para la organización de los Salarios y Sueldos de los Trabajadores," *Trabajo Cuba* (suplemento), 4, No. 9 (June, 1963), p. 10.

The immediate significance of these new schedules for the general level of wages is not known. In mid-1963, for example, when the wage plan was introduced into the soap industry, most of the workers were unaffected, although a few workers received a raise (*Trabajo Cuba*, 4, No. 10 [June, 1963], p. 5). In mining, rates for lower-paid workers rose considerably (Guevara, cited in *Revolución*, January 28, 1963). In the metals industry, the new schedule was somewhat higher in all categories than rates established in 1960 (*Metal*, May, 1960, p. 7).

Over a longer period, the new schedule undoubtedly inhibited general wage increases untied to increases in productivity. As for the wage structure, there was bound to be an improvement as time passed, despite the fact that it would probably change to counter new problems created in part by the wage schedule and incentive system themselves, that is, a tendency for workers to shift into high-productivity industries, for management to reduce the number of nonproductive workers, for workers and management to overstress physical effort at the expense of technical work, and for workers to labor beyond optimum hours of work.

[66] "Victoria en el Puerto," *Verde Olivo*, 2, No. 17 (April 30, 1961), pp. 56-59.

ment was eliminated, raising income of some "nonprivileged" work-ers and lowering real incomes (if leisure time is included) of "privi-leged" workers in the union sector. All in all, it has been estimated that between 1958 and 1962 actual hours worked by the average Cuban worker rose from 1,854 to 2,554 per year (while hours for which compensation was made remained the same: 2,496 hours an-nually) partly as a consequence of volunteer labor and partly as a result of the abolition of the "forty-four for forty-eight" and the re-duction in holidays and automatic sick leaves.[67]

From the perspective of a working class under capitalism, and certainly from the viewpoint of labor leaders under collective bar-gaining, the general increase in hours of work would hardly be viewed as a net gain. From the standpoint of economic rationality and growth under socialism, however, the same conclusion cannot be so readily drawn. The fact that irrationalities in the labor market were one source of economic stagnation, together with the fact that the revolution's leaders constantly stressed that the working class under socialism must obtain material gains collectively and as a whole, meant that there was both a practical and ideological argu-ment in favor of an intensified productive effort acceptable to the majority of Cuban workers.

The modern, "free" labor market was the outcome of the growth of capitalist markets and the factory system. Where product markets are planned, the idea of "free" labor markets and independent col-lective bargaining must of necessity undergo a transformation. That the elimination of the old labor market and policies condemns the handful of "privileged" workers to lower material standards (at least temporarily) is obvious, although in the case of Cuba every ef-fort seems to have been made to make the transition as inexpensive as possible for the better-off sectors of the working class. If it is true that planned product, capital, and other nonlabor markets necessi-tate planned labor markets (although by no means outright com-pulsion), and if it is true that socialist economic planning in Cuba was considered (realistically so, in our view) necessary to get the economy off dead center, then the reorganization of the labor mar-

[67] *Labor Conditions in Communist Cuba,* Table 3, p. 44.

ket was simply the consequence of the reorganization of the economy. For an understanding of the political transformation of Cuba
during the first crucial years of the revolution, therefore, the basic
changes in labor policies and practices have little explanatory importance. This is important to stress because many students of the
Cuban Revolution (not all of them unsympathetic) interpret labor
"controls" as a means of consolidating and retaining political power,
and thus explain political phenomena by reference to the new labor
policies. This, we believe, is mistaken; in fact, we believe that without an underlying acceptance of the new policies in their general
outline on the basis of a more or less sophisticated knowledge of
their essential *practicality* and, under socialism in a low-income
country, of their *necessity*, the consolidation and deepening of the
political revolution would not have gone so smoothly.

[8]

Agricultural Planning

[1]

Unlike the Russian Bolsheviks and Chinese Communists, the Cuban revolutionaries inherited an economy largely unscathed by civil war. No runaway inflation destroyed confidence in the local currency; the Cuban peso still exchanged at par with the dollar. No large-scale fighting or famine thinned the ranks of the industrial working class. No endless years of war impoverished the city or countryside. Cuba's factories, fields, ports, railroads, and communications remained in good physical working order.

Batista did leave behind a burdensome heritage: a vast backlog of unfulfilled economic and social needs. Immediately, the Revolutionary Government turned its full attention on two of the most pressing, unemployment and the foreign exchange problem. In his Moncada trial speech, Castro had stressed the importance of unemployment when he argued that the rebels based their chance of success on the character of the old society itself, particularly the "700,-000" unemployed. During 1959–1961, he referred again and again to the abolition of unemployment as the most sensitive index of the revolution's success. According to Guevara, the revolution's leadership viewed unemployment as an "acute political problem," but considered the foreign exchange situation "more dangerous, given the enormous dependence of Cuba on foreign trade."[1] Batista had grossly mismanaged and left unprotected Cuba's reserves in an abortive attempt to keep the economy buoyant during the last year

[1] Ernesto Guevara, "The Cuban Economy," *International Affairs,* 40, No. 4 (October, 1964).

of his rule, and from December, 1957, to December, 1958, free reserves declined from $263.4 million to $84.5 million, well below legal requirements.[2]

The new government mounted a two-pronged attack on both the unemployment and balance of payments and exchange reserve problems. First, the agrarian reform was considered the basic precondition for the rational utilization of the land and the diversification of agricultural production. Castro and his top policy-makers hoped that the agrarian reform would lead both to a decline in unemployment and a reduction in the importation of foods and agricultural raw materials, and thus an improvement in the balance of trade. The agrarian reform would thus kill two birds with one stone.

Castro applied similar reasoning to industry. As we will see in detail in the following chapter, the revolution's leaders planned to increase industrial production and employment by widening the local market and restricting imports from the United States via increases in working-class income and indirect and direct controls over foreign trade, respectively. At first the government expected that the expansion of demand would encourage businessmen to utilize excess productive capacity. Later on, Cuba's policy-makers hoped that the pressure on existing capacity would lead to an accelerated volume of new investments.

Finally, Castro expected that agricultural and industrial development would reinforce each other, leading to a cumulative advance of agricultural and industrial production and employment and a decline in imports of both farm commodities and manufactured goods. Cuba would thus solve the employment problem while lessening its dependence on foreign trade and the United States.

[2]

Agricultural planning underwent three general stages, January-December, 1959, early 1960 to 1962–1963, and 1963 on. The first

2 Cuba, Ministerio de Hacienda, *Informe del Ministerio de Hacienda del Gobierno Revolucionario al Consejos de Ministros* (Havana, September 14, 1959), Table No. 12. Guevara reported the decline from $251 million to $77 million (*The Havana Post*, February 6, 1960).

was basically a preparatory phase. On the one hand, Castro popularized the idea of diverting land from sugar into the cultivation of other crops, meanwhile raising cane yields to maintain the volume of sugar production. In April, 1959, for example, he spoke of the need to "eventually" reduce acreage under cane.[3] In May, he argued that irrigation and fertilizers could raise cane yields by 50 per cent.[4] The cane fields remained under private ownership and control, however, and little was done to implement these guidelines.

On the other hand, INRA prepared detailed plans for the expansion of the production of commodities imported from the United States.[5] Top priority was given to rice, oils and fats (pork production), cotton, and beans. All in all, these commodities accounted for nearly $100 million of Cuba's $165 million foreign exchange expenditures on agricultural commodities in 1958.

Bringing domestic production of foods and raw materials up to domestic consumption requirements would not be easy. Self-sufficiency in basic food and raw material crops required that Cuba divert at least 500,000 hectares of land from cane cultivation. In order to maintain the volume of sugar production, cane yields needed to be increased by a minimum of 20 per cent. In addition, self-sufficiency in the production of animal feeds (chiefly, corn) required the diversion of an additional two million hectares, clearly an impossible feat.[6]

The second phase of agricultural planning began in early 1960 and gradually ended between 1962 and 1963. This phase was marked by great boldness and daring, an unlimited confidence in the ability of Cuba's farmers and farm workers, an interpretation of sugar as a passive rather than active force in economic development, and extremely high costs of mistaken policies. Two major policies characterized the second stage.

[3] *The Havana Post*, April 5, 1959.

[4] "¿Qué es la Reforma Agraria?" *Boletín de Divulgación* (INRA), 1, No. 6 (1959), p. 10.

[5] Jacques Chonchol, interview with the author, Havana, June 14, 1960.

[6] The first estimate was made by INRA's Department of Production and Foreign Commerce. The second estimate was made by Francisco Dorta-Duque ("Justificando una reforma agraria," Instituto de Ciencias Sociales, Pontíficia Universidad Gregoriara [Rome], mimeographed, pp. 37–38).

First, INRA ordered the immediate, large-scale diversification of agriculture on both the cane cooperatives and people's farms. The institute hoped to be able to introduce a scientific, mixed agriculture on each of the major production units under its control. Almost overnight, Cuba's farmers and farm workers were expected to create a locally and nationally diversified, expanded agricultural economy of the type that required hundreds of years of development in Western Europe. René Dumont, a French agronomist and influential INRA adviser, put forward an extreme version of this policy. Dumont called for the "liberation" of one-half of the cane cooperative's land, diverting two-fifths for forage crops and three-fifths for food and industrial crops that require peak labor loads during the dead season.

Second, and integral to the first policy, Castro ordered the cooperatives to cut the reserve cane fields during the First People's Zafra of 1961. Of roughly 100,000 *caballerías* of cane, 10,000 *caballerías* were uprooted and earmarked for diversion to other crops. Sugar production rose dramatically, reaching 6.7 million tons, almost 1 million tons above 1960 levels.[7]

INRA made three major errors in the second stage of agricultural planning. First, the institute failed to take enough concrete steps to increase cane yields, thus sharply reducing sugar harvests in 1962 and 1963. Second, INRA did not anticipate that the large-scale, island-wide diversification program would cause a severe labor shortage in the sugar sector and, therefore, lower future cane production still further. Third, institute policy-makers failed to realize fully that

[7] Sugar production in 1959 and 1960 was 5.9 and 5.8 million tons, respectively, somewhat higher than the 1958 volume of 5.7 million tons. In all three years, about 105,000 *caballerías* of land were under cane. Area harvested was 83,100 *caballerías* in 1958; 80,400 *caballerías* in 1959; and 87,300 *caballerías* in 1960. Area harvested in 1961 came to nearly 93,000 *caballerías*. Good rains and the harvesting of the high-yield reserve cane in 1961 more than offset the decline in yields due to deficiencies in the fall plantings in 1959.

Highest yield cane is "fall cane" (sixteen-months growth before the first cut) and cane left standing two seasons. Yields of both types can reach 60–70,000 *arrobas* per *caballería*, although they are often lower. Cane cut year after year will yield 40–45,000 *arrobas* after the first and second cuts; 30–35,000 *arrobas* after the third cut. After seven or eight years, yields fall to 20–25,000 *arrobas*. Spring cane (new seed and twelve months growth) yields 40–45,000 *arrobas* on the first cut.

successful agricultural diversification required large-scale invest-ments in the technical education and training of the rural labor force. Each of these errors must be analyzed in detail.

In the first place, although Castro urged the cane cooperatives and *colonos* to raise cane yields in the fall of 1960, and although the first agricultural plan for 1960–1965 projected an increase of 50 per cent in yields, INRA did not take any concrete steps to implement the plan. On the contrary, there was little new planting and hardly any weeding of the cane. What is more, INRA oriented its credit and investment policies toward other crops. The reason for INRA's neglect of sugar is fourfold.

Perhaps most importantly, from the beginning Castro and the other revolutionary leaders sharply attacked prerevolutionary Cuba's favorite slogan, *"sin azucar no hay pais,"* translated freely, "sugar equals survival." From early 1959, the government discred-ited this old article of faith: "Sugar went hand in hand with eco-nomic stagnation; sugar meant monoculture and economic depend-ence on the United States; sugar was condemned for guilt by asso-ciation with the island's old governing classes." [8] These themes helped to create an antisugar mentality during 1959–1961, encour-aged farmers and workers to neglect the cane, and led to the dete-rioration of the fields. Inevitably, INRA slighted sugar cultivation in favor of other crops.

Second, government leaders at the time discounted the possibility of marketing large quantities of sugar abroad after 1961. The United States withdrew the Cuban quota, prospects for free market sales were dim, and the socialist countries had not at that time made any long-term commitments to buy sugar, although they agreed to purchase four million tons in 1961. Cuba's future relation-ships with the Soviet Union and China were uncertain at the begin-ning of 1961, and Cuba could not anticipate that either country would make long-term purchases in large quantities and at high prices.[9]

[8] James O'Connor, "Cuba: Salvation through Sugar," *The Nation,* 197, No. 11 (October 12, 1963), p. 212.

[9] Fidel Castro, speech quoted in *Hoy,* August 11, 1963. In January, 1964, the Soviet Union and Cuba signed the first long-term sugar agreement.

Third, the neglect of sugar was partly based on the assumption that the industrialization program would save foreign exchange by increasing the production of import-substitute commodities. These expectations proved to be unrealistic, and Cuba reported growing deficits in the balance of trade from 1961 to 1963. Making matters worse, a shortage of imported and locally produced consumer goods turned the terms of trade against private farmers cultivating food crops and thus increased autoconsumption and barter sales.

Last, until 1961, INRA failed to introduce even the most elementary economic accounting procedures. Early institute feasibility studies were concerned more with technical possibilities and requirements than with economic costs and benefits. Not until 1963 did INRA conclude that the relative costs of cultivating an additional hectare of sugar cane were significantly less than the costs of growing rice, corn, beans, and a number of other commodities.[10] In 1964, Guevara explained the mistake: "The entire economic history of Cuba had demonstrated that no other agricultural activity would give such returns as those yielded by the cultivation of sugar cane. At the outset of the revolution many of us were not aware of this basic economic fact, because a fetishistic idea connected sugar with our dependence on imperialism and with the misery in the rural areas, without analyzing the real causes: the relation to the uneven trade balance." [11]

INRA's second major mistake was the failure to anticipate severe labor shortages in the cane fields in 1962 and 1963. To be sure, during the first half of the long 1961 harvest the supply of fieldhands

[10] Carlos Rafael Rodríguez, "El nuevo camino de la agricultura Cubana," *Cuba Socialista,* 3, No. 27 (November, 1963), p. 86. According to INRA's surveys, it would pay to grow cotton and *maní* and the all-important viands (*malanga, boniato,* and yucca) should be grown locally, given the lack of an international market for these items. INRA also concluded that a portion of Cuba's bean-consumption requirements be grown on the island, given the scarcity of this item in international trade. On the other hand, the relative costs of utilizing different grasses, water control, and so on in cattle ranching were not known in 1963 ("Acerca del desarrollo de la Granadería," *Trimestre de Finanzas al Día, Suplemento del directorio financiero,* Instituto de Estudios Financieros del Ministerio de Hacienda, 2, No. 7 [July–September, 1963], pp. 31–46, quotes from six Castro speeches touching on the cattle question in 1963).

[11] Guevara, *op. cit.*

was sufficient, although during the second half local, transitory labor shortages developed. But during the 1962 harvest, the scarcity of labor took on large dimensions. Sparsely populated Camaguey Province alone needed 30,000 volunteer workers. Far fewer regular workers were available for the 1963 harvest. Nearly one-half of Camaguey's 80,000 cane cutters were employed elsewhere.[12] Almost 30 per cent (about 90,000 workers) of Cuba's total cane force was unavailable.[13]

The reason for the labor shortage was twofold. On the one hand, wage rates in the cane fields varied with the amount (or weight) of cane cut and loaded daily.[14] The amount of cane cut thus depended on cane yields, which declined by about one-third from 1961 to 1963. The chief reasons were the harvesting of high-yield reserve cane in 1961, insufficient rainfall in 1961 and 1962, deficient seeding and cultivation of the fields, and damage to the cane by unskilled volunteer labor. The decline in yields thus compelled the cane cutters to work harder in order to maintain a given level of income. Only in those areas where yields were unchanged was there an adequate supply of labor.[15]

The original labor shortage thus set in motion a vicious circle. The use of volunteer labor damaged the crop, contributed to the shortage of professional harvesters, and thus increased the need for more volunteer workers. Probably more important, experienced fieldhands were also unavailable during the off-season months when the fields are weeded and cleaned. Deficient cultivation therefore lowered yields still further, compounding the on-season shortage. These interrelationships caught sugar industry planners offguard.

Employment opportunities opening up on the state farms because

[12] "El partido y la Tercera zafra del pueblo en Camaguey," *Cuba Socialista*, 3, No. 17 (January, 1963), p. 131.

[13] A census taken by the local cane commissions projected a total demand of 352,000 workers and a total supply of 260,000 workers.

[14] In 1963, for example, it was expected that 35 per cent of the harvest labor force would receive an extra 22 cents per 100 *arrobas* if more than 120 *arrobas* were cut daily for fifteen days, and that 50 per cent would receive an extra 32 cents for cutting more than 150 *arrobas* daily. In practice, the percentages were 14 per cent and 17 per cent, respectively.

[15] Author's interview with Gerardo Bernardo, Havana, August 20, 1963.

of the diversification program also contributed to the scarcity of labor in the sugar sector. Indirect evidence is provided by the fact that in 1962 and 1963 the coffee growers also were unable to acquire sufficient harvest laborers.[16] Direct evidence is the expansion of employment on the cattle ranches, rice plantations, and other properties organized into people's farms. Before the revolution, employment on farm units subsequently managed by the people's farms probably did not exceed 50,000 workers. Less than 4,000 workers were employed on the cattle ranches themselves. By the spring of 1962, 120,000 farm laborers had permanent jobs on the *granjas*.[17] Thus, of the 90,000 cane cutters who had abandoned their regular work, probably about 70,000 found employment on the people's farms, where wages were higher, employment steadier, and the type of work less difficult. Most of the remainder of the ex-cane labor force shifted into the construction industry, which was very active in the rural districts. Before the start of the 1962 *zafra*, the CTC-R Eleventh Congress guaranteed that sugar workers would retain their newly acquired construction jobs in the event that they returned to the cane fields for the harvest.[18]

[16] Severo Aguirre, "Ante el tercer aniversario de la reforma agraria," *Cuba Socialista*, 2, No. 9 (May, 1962). The effect of employing volunteer labor was to reduce the quality of the harvest by an estimated 10 per cent.

[17] *Trabajo Cuba*, 3, No. 6 (March, 1962), p. 17. Imperfect censuses show that employment on the *granjas* increased as follows: May, 1961 (96,000); August, 1961 (103,000); August, 1962 (150,000). A small proportion of the expansion was due to the incorporation of more farms into the *granjas*.

[18] The exact distribution of the ex-cane labor force is unknown. INRA's chief himself could only refer to "local sources of employment" that kept Las Villas cane cutters out of the cane fields (Carlos Rafael Rodríguez, "Cuatro Años de Reforma Agraria," *Cuba Socialista*, 3, No. 21 [May, 1963]). The majority of the "disappearing" sugar workers were formerly employed as seasonal laborers by private cane growers. These rootless, homeless workers were the most underpaid of Cuba's rural proletariat and eager to seek out better economic opportunities. Employment on the cane cooperatives organized on the properties of the very largest *colonos* and the great sugar estates did fall off somewhat from 1961 to 1963. There were, for example, complaints by some administrators of the cane farms of labor-pirating by the people's farms. But the estates and largest *colonos* employed a maximum of 25 per cent of the harvest labor force before the revolution, the vast majority of whom became permanent members of the cane farms (Lowry Nelson, *Rural Cuba* [Minneapolis, 1950], Table 20, p. 167, citing the Agricultural Census of 1945). The

The combined effects of the labor shortage and the decision to harvest and uproot the reserve cane fields in 1961 (which itself contributed to the labor shortage, as we have seen) were very serious. From 1961 to 1962, sugar production fell off by 24 per cent. The destruction of the reserve fields reduced the amount of area harvested by 10 per cent and lowered yields by about 5 per cent.[19] Other factors contributing to the decline in production were the absence of experienced workers, a lack of coordination between industry and agriculture, irrationalities in the distribution system, and insufficient rainfall. Over the entire period (1961–1963), output declined by 42 per cent, again due to the decline in area harvested (greater in 1963 than in 1962 because of the failure to maintain a sufficient level of new plantings), a decrease in yields, a scarcity of labor, and drought.[20]

The cane labor shortage adversely affected not only yields, but also reduced the sucrose content of the cane because of the unusually long time required for volunteer labor to transport the cane from the fields to the mills. Furthermore, the volunteer labor pro-

---

small and middle *colonos* grew the bulk of Cuba's sugar and hired most of the island's sugar workers.

The development of a socialized agriculture thus placed private growers in a highly unfavorable competitive position vis à vis the state sector. Yet in an important sense INRA was the author of its own difficulties. Although the institute lacked control over the supply side of the rural labor market, it did exercise control over the demand side. Ministry of Labor resolutions were required before jobs could be obtained on the mushrooming state farms. Although there was little local formal authority to expand employment, the *granjas*, Public Works Ministries, and other branches of the public economy apparently followed independent hiring policies. These uncoordinated actions contributed heavily to the shortage. INRA grossly overestimated the amount of permanent rural employment upon which the *granjas* could draw and underestimated the degrees of mobility of the cane cutters who had previously worked for the private growers. INRA also underestimated the degree to which the high seasonal demand for labor in the cultivation of tobacco, potatoes, yucca, malanga, fruits, and vegetables partially or completely overlapped the sugar *zafra*.

[19] In 1961, 18 per cent of Cuba's cane was over twelve months old (high-yield cane); in 1962 and 1963 high-yield cane amounted to only 8 per cent.

[20] Rainfall declined by 25 per cent from 1960 to 1961, and an additional 13 per cent from 1961 to 1962. Average yields fell from 50,000 *arrobas* per *caballería* in 1961 to 37,200 *arrobas* and 33,000 *arrobas* in 1962 and 1963, respectively.

gram added to transportation and other support costs, as well as disrupting industrial production. All in all, INRA's failure to plan manpower needs, coordinate the hiring policies of the *granjas,* and develop a rational wages policy in the sugar sector entailed extremely high costs.

The Agrarian Reform Institute's third basic error was the attempt to introduce almost overnight a large-scale crop diversification program. Until 1961 the error was not immediately apparent, because INRA at first expanded production by increasing land under cultivation, a policy that did not require an intensification of yields and hence an advanced technical agricultural capability.[21] Between 1959 and 1960 from 100,000 to 200,000 hectares were cleared and cultivated, and an additional 100,000 hectares were cleared.[22] Thus, by the end of 1960, total land under cultivation rose by 5 to 10 per cent.

INRA's new lands policy had some advantages and many disad-

[21] *Agricultural Plan,* p. 2.

[22] In February, 1960, INRA planned to cultivate 75,000 hectares previously unused (Letter, Jacques Chonchol to Thomas Carroll, February 9, 1960). In Núñez Jiménez' March, 1960, report of INRA's activities, it was announced that about 100,000 hectares had been broken, prepared, or seeded. Two months later, INRA announced that about 160,000 new hectares had been plowed, prepared, and sown, but in mid-1960, a private estimate placed the figure at only 115,000 hectares. It is difficult to know which is closer to the truth; in 1962, a high INRA official spoke of the revolution having eliminated maribu land altogether, thus raising cultivable land by over 200,000 hectares (Aguirre, *op. cit.,* p. 40). Most of this land was cleared in 1959–1960.

Two years later, INRA director Rafael Rodríguez estimated that over 400,000 hectares of maribu and forest land were cleared, but that a sizable portion of it was not broken, not to speak of seeded or cultivated (Rodríguez, *op. cit.,* p. 23). Another 10,000 hectares were said to have been drained, the largest part in the Zapata Swamp. A figure for total new cultivated lands given out in early 1963 was 540,000 hectares, but this included lands previously in pasture and planted in cane, and it is uncertain what proportion was brought into use in the post-1960 period.

Impressionistic observations of the operations of the early cooperatives made by the author in the summer of 1960 encourage the view that a sizable amount of new land was actually put to use in this period. It was not at all uncommon to visit a cooperative that had increased lands cultivated by one-quarter to one-half again as much as previously. And in the henequen sector during the same period, 10 per cent of the 1960 crop was grown on previously unused lands. All the above estimates, plans, and sheer guesses leave out the expansion of the private sector.

vantages. On the one side, there was a plentiful supply of farm labor, many thousands of uncultivated hectares, and much pressure to increase food and raw materials production. On the other hand, the costs of clearing *maribú* and forests were extremely high, heavy bulldozer operations frequently destroyed topsoils, and much of the land brought to cultivation was especially subject to erosion. Lastly, expanding the base of the island's extensive agriculture increased transportation and communication costs.

As a consequence, as 1960 wore on, Cuban agricultural planning became increasingly characterized by a combined policy of local diversification, mixed farming, and an all-consuming interest in elevating crop yields. These goals were central to both the first five-year agricultural plan and the government's general projections for the entire economy formulated in 1960 and early 1961.[23] Both plan and projections looked to "progressively" modify INRA's new lands policy in the direction of higher yields.

The agricultural plan envisaged a tripling of fertilizer use, large irrigation and drainage investments, double cropping, better rotations, the use of high quality seeds, and improved soil preparation and cultivation. Planned increases in yields of between 80 and 90 per cent, together with an expansion of land under crops of between 10 to 20 per cent, were expected to double total agricultural production between 1960 and 1965. Target outputs were highest in rice, oils and fats, poultry, and other commodities that were imported in large quantities.

Equally important were plans for a mixed agriculture, in particular the integration of cattle ranching and the cultivation of food and industrial crops. INRA looked to use food by-products—the chaff of the rice plant, for example—as raw materials in the cattle sector. The institute also planned to mix dairy farming, hog breeding, and cane cultivation on the cane cooperatives. Reforestation also figured in INRA's plans, which projected a new Cuban "productive garden." New forests and woods would prevent erosion, provide shade for animals, stand as windbreaks for cultivated fields, and expand

[23] For example, M. Kalecki, "Bosquejo Hipotético del Plan Quinquenal, 1961–1965, para la Economía Cubana" (December, 1960), p. 2.

Cuba's supply of lumber. The Ministry of Agriculture in fact reforested over 14,000 hectares before it was liquidated at the end of 1960. INRA's Department of Reforestation reconstructed nearly 27,000 hectares in 1961, over 28,000 hectares in 1962, and planned to reforest another 54,000 hectares in 1963–1964.[24]

The major burden of the diversification program fell on the people's farms, which INRA hoped would be Cuba's port of entry for a scientific agriculture. The *granjas* were viewed as integral units producing meats, feed grasses, and a wide variety of other crops. INRA planned to put 400,000 hectares in pangola and other high quality grasses, nearly one million hectares into food and other crops, and build up a highly intensive ranching industry.[25] Many individual *granjas* were able to expand production under the impetus of large-scale INRA credits, grants of machinery, and technical aid, although the total amount of land diversified is unknown. The *granjas* had little or no success in elevating crop yields.[26]

INRA also expected the cane cooperatives to rapidly diversify agriculture and expand production. Plans were laid to put the 140,000 hectares diverted from cane in 1961, together with an additional 30,000 hectares of previously uncultivated land, into a wide range of crops. An additional 40,000 hectares were to be planted in pangola and other cover crops. INRA's guiding idea was that sugar cultivation monopolized Cuba's best soil, which was not needed to

[24] Private INRA estimates; JUCEPLAN, Dirección de Estadísticas, Projecto de Anuario Estadístico, 1962 (Havana, July, 1963), Table 5.25.

[25] Cattle policy in the private sector was anti-intensive from the start, mainly for political reasons. An INRA regulation in March, 1960, limited cattle density to one head per hectare on lands that the middle and some large ranchers were allowed to retain. This was clearly highly inefficient from an economic standpoint. INRA was caught in a contradiction, partly of its own making and partly inherent in the situation. Reduced to a formula, intensive ranching plus a sizable private sector equaled a class of well-to-do ranchers. INRA, of course, could not expect the latter to be politically reliable or enthusiastic revolutionaries.

[26] Dozens of personal interviews and a number of field trips back up these observations. The popular literature on individual *granjas* is quite large. Some examples are: *Verde Olivo*, 2, No. 33 (August 20, 1961), pp. 12–15 (on Havana's "Raúl Gómez García"); 2, No. 34 (August 27, 1961), pp. 23–27 (on Pinar del Río's "Benito Juárez").

grow high-yield cane.[27] By late 1961, there were 16,000 hectares in rice, 64,000 in corn, 15,000 in *millo*, 20,000 in beans, 10,000 in oil-producing vegetables, 12,000 in cotton, and 36,000 hectares planted with fruit trees.[28] Much of this land, however, was ill prepared, badly cultivated, and low yield, but in the absence of production statistics, an accurate evaluation of diversification on the cane cooperatives is impossible.

There are four main reasons why INRA's diversification and mixed agricultural program was finally abandoned as a failure. In the first place, local crop diversification was beyond the technical capabilities of INRA planners, agricultural technicians, and the rural labor force. The institute attempted to transform the rural economy from extensive to intensive modes of production, thus placing an enormous burden on the short supply of experienced farm administrators on each of the roughly one thousand state-controlled farms. Thus, inadvertently, INRA created a new economic bottleneck by greatly intensifying mismanagement and administrative disorganization.[29]

The second reason for INRA's failure can be attributed to the United States trade embargo on Cuba. Another reason for the neglect of sugar cane stemmed from the loss of the United States market. Mechanization was seriously hampered by the shortage of spare parts, replacement equipment, and new tractors and other farm machinery. In mid-1961, for example, INRA estimated that over one-third of Cuba's tractors were out of service. Diversification was also held back by a *de facto* ban on United States exports of breeding hens and other poultry and animals.[30] In brief, shortages of im-

---

[27] Alfredo Menéndez Cruz (director of INRA's General Administration of Sugar Mills), quoted in V. Lopez Pellon, "La más Cubana de las zafras," *Bohemia*, 52, No. 50 (December 11, 1960), p. 33.

[28] Jacques Chonchol, "Análisis Crítico de la Reforma Agraria Cubana," *Trimestre Económico*, 30 (I), No. 117 (January–March, 1963), pp. 126–127.

[29] Criticisms were made of insect control in rice and cotton; indiscriminate use of fertilizers; timing of sowing; lack of patient labor in preparing the earth and soil selection techniques. INRA's plans lacked coordination; in 1962, area prepared for root crops exceeded by one-half supplies of seed. Malanga seeds for only 39,000 of 78,000 planned hectares were available.

[30] Chonchol, *op. cit.*, p. 121.

ported equipment and raw materials worsened the entire agricultural situation. Some of the commodities in shortest supply during this period (fats and oils, rice, beans, and others) were previously imported in whole or in part from the United States.

The third reason was INRA's failure to integrate the private agriculture into the structure of the planned rural economy. One problem was inefficient collection practices. Until late 1962, INRA's agents at the island's 130 food collection centers frequently passively awaited the arrival of small farmers with products for sale.[31] Another problem was that working capital and other loans often were not tied to delivery guarantees. Still another was a highly irrational price structure. Until early 1963, for example, price differentials for many crops—differentiating regions, seasons, quality of product, private-state suppliers, and so on—were nonexistent. To cite another example, beef prices were too low relative to those of other stock animals, and the price structure indirectly encouraged low quality beef. Prices thus bore little relation to costs, to a large degree because of the lack of trained or experienced manpower able to differentiate commodities by quality, and the inexperience of the planners themselves. Only in the tobacco and coffee sectors was INRA careful to maintain high prices and an efficient price structure.[32]

There is no evidence that INRA systematically discriminated

[31] Fidel Castro and others, "Hablan para el Instituto Popular de Chile," Instituto Popular de Chile (Santiago, November, 1962), p. 70.

[32] Price structures in the tobacco and coffee sectors were more rational, although guaranteed prices were retained as an umbrella over the inefficient grower. Raw tobacco prices were raised by 25 per cent from 1958–1959 to 1959–1960 (The Havana Post, May 22, 1968), and then retained at the new levels. Partly for this reason, the value of the latter crop was nearly double the former. Tobacco was always the most efficient branch of Cuban agriculture, and the revolution did not change that. INRA sharply limited its experiments in diversification and a mixed agriculture in the tobacco fields of Pinar del Río.

Similarly, in the coffee sector little attempt was made to transform the old agriculture, but rather to make it more efficient. To this end, technical aid and credits were expanded throughout the entire period of agrarian reform. Again, the price structure was left intact. Growers were guaranteed domestic prices up to twice world prices and assigned domestic and export quotas.

against the private farmers in order to finance the expansion of the state farms and industry; quite the contrary, in 1963 the institute raised buying prices across the board, leading to an increase in private commodity sales to INRA of 60 per cent.[33] Neither is there much evidence that before 1963 INRA used its power to price farm commodities to promote diversification, improved crop quality, and a dynamic private sector.

A further difficulty arose with the introduction of physical planning and control. In 1961, ANAP began to set "quotas" and "goals" for its base organizations, but these were mainly broad targets formulated only for the provincial level. These targets were set without any consultation with the farmers themselves until early 1961, and with imperfect consultation in the following two or three years.[34] Perhaps the most important problem was INRA's ambivalence toward the middle farmers, who produced the lion's share of Cuba's food and a sizable share of the island's sugar. As we have seen, not until late 1963, when INRA collectivized the middle sector, were even the preconditions created for the integration of this sector into over-all agricultural planning.[35]

INRA credits constituted the only important link between state and private farming during this period. When private credits dried

[33] This announcement was made by Rafael Rodríguez to the Second ANAP Congress and was reported in *Hoy*, August 10, 1963. An examination of INRA's price schedules confirms this.

[34] *Revolución*, November 20, 1961; January 17, 1962; Jacques Chonchol, "Informe correspondiente," January 31, 1961, manuscript.

[35] From about April, 1962, to the fall of that year, the government did its best to quiet the fears of the middle farmers. In May, for example, Castro announced that medium-sized farms would be returned to their owners if the government "had to" in order to maintain production. Next month, Rafael Rodríguez assured those middle farmers who put idle land to the plow that they would receive "guarantees" against expropriation (author's interview with Gerardo Bernardo, *op. cit.*). Toward the end of the year, however, when the cloud over the island's food situation began to lift, it was once again made clear that the middle sector would eventually be nationalized. The exact timing of the Second Reform, however, came as something of a surprise. As late as August, 1963, *colonos* in Las Villas were being threatened with expropriation in the event that they failed to weed their cane fields (speech by Ovidio Díaz, INRA delegate in Las Villas, reported in *Hoy*, August 3, 1963).

up in 1959–1960, BANFAIC and the various stabilization institutes quickly expanded short-term and long-term loans to private farmers at less than one-half the old rates of interest. Planned ANAP credits in 1961 amounted to $100 million, although actual loans fell well below this figure. ANAP production loans during 1962–1963 came to $137.4 million (of which less than $100 million was recovered), and investment loans totaled $44 million. All in all, 50 per cent of INRA's agricultural credit was channelled into the private sector at interest rates comparable to those charged the state farms.

The final problem facing INRA during the second phase of Cuba's agricultural policy was the breakdown in the distribution system. By late 1960, the larger middlemen who handled commodities both bought and sold by the private and state agricultural sectors were eliminated. During the next two years, the government nationalized the properties of thousands of smaller wholesalers and retailers. INRA, the Ministry of Internal Commerce, and other state organisms charged with distributing raw materials, fuels, machinery, consumer goods, and agricultural commodities had little opportunity to prepare themselves for their new role. The problem of distribution has always been difficult in centrally planned socialist economies, and Cuba, particularly during this phase, was no exception. Some foreign advisers attempted to convince INRA to allow a few middlemen to operate in order to eliminate excess liquidity in the economy and smooth the flow of commodities, but the institute chose the more difficult path of increasing productivity and production and making operative the new state distribution system.

The effects of INRA's policy (or, more accurately, nonpolicy) toward private agriculture were very serious throughout 1961 and 1962. The private farmers increased autoconsumption and expanded roadside and barter sales. In mid-1962, Castro went so far as to say that Cuba's small farmers "reverted to [a] subsistence agriculture." [36] Later in the year, INRA's president asserted that one-third of the island's bean production was not sold to the state because the private market offered two to three times institute prices. Un-

[36] *Obra Revolucionaria*, No. 17 (May 25, 1962).

able and unwilling to move against the small farmers by banning private sales or ordering forced deliveries,[37] too inexperienced to rationalize the private sector, and unable to revive the old system of private credits and marketing arrangements, INRA almost inevitably stumbled through these first years on the basis of trial and error.

[3]

By comparison with the second stage of agricultural planning, the third phase was more cautious, traditional, and realistic. Its two basic features were the revival and expansion of the sugar industry and cattle ranching and the remaking of the crop diversification program under the slogan "national diversification and local specialization." In effect, Cuba decided to pursue the advantages of international specialization and the division of labor within the framework of the world socialist economy.

The Cuban government made the sharp turn from the second to the third stage for three general reasons. First, by 1962–1963, the island received firm long-term commitments from the Soviet Union to purchase large quantities of sugar at high, stable prices. Second, Cuban planners realized that any and all industrialization programs presupposed a high and rising volume of imports of fuels, raw materials, new equipment, and spare parts, and therefore a large expansion of traditional exports. Third, as we have seen, INRA studies pointed up the comparative cost advantages of sugar cane; institute planners concluded that cane yields could not be raised without large-scale investments of real and human capital, and administra-

---

[37] Exceptions occurred during the last half of 1961 and first two months of 1962 when some PSP members holding down local INRA posts alienated many peasants by following a policy of forced sales. After this period, INRA banned neither private sales of official prices nor barter sale nor autoconsumption. Quotas *were* established on cattle ranches in order to prevent a further reduction in the herds (Fidel Castro, *Obra Revolucionaria*, No. 17). In general, INRA recognized that the real solution to food and raw material shortages was to raise productivity and production, not multiply administrative controls on marketing (see: radio speech by Rafael Rodríguez, December 4, 1962; speech by Castro to the Second ANAP Congress, *Hoy*, August 10, 1963; speech by Antero Regaldo to Second ANAP Congress, *Hoy*, August 9, 1963.)

tors, farmers, and workers alike realized that the policy of local diversification was beyond Cuba's present technical capabilities.

The new sugar policy, the keystone of the third phase, emerged in embryonic form in late 1961 when INRA urged the cane cooperatives and *colonos* to replace the ten thousand *caballerías* of cane that were uprooted during the harvest of the same year. A year later, Guevara and other government officials maintained that crops other than sugar were being "overstressed" and warned that the government desired an absolute, although not necessarily a relative, expansion of cane production. In the fall of 1963, Guevara said that the revolution's most important economic error was the neglect of sugar cane. In the same month, Castro announced that cane and cattle would be the foundations of the economy until 1970 and projected a goal of eight to nine million tons of sugar and twelve million head of cattle by that year.

Actual INRA plans were more modest, forecasting a volume of production of between seven and eight million tons. Two alternative schemes were put forward, the first by INRA itself, which was largely controlled by the "old Communists" who did not hesitate to integrate Cuba into the structure of the main socialist economies, and the second by Guevara and others who wanted Cuba to be as self-sufficient as possible. The first group chose to expand land under cane cultivation to about 120,000 *caballerías*. The second group argued for the introduction of a crash program to increase yields and maintained that 80,000 to 90,000 *caballerías* of cane were sufficient and that Cuba needed insurance in the form of high-quality land against possible difficulties encountered under the new system of international specialization. The revolutionary leadership eventually hammered out a compromise. INRA would shoot for seven million tons of cane grown on 103,000 *caballerías*. Plans were laid to raise yields in the state and private sectors to 60,000 and 40,000 *arrobas* per *caballería*, respectively.[38]

[38] *Informe Central*, Reunión Nacional de Producción Agrícola, Rafael Francia Mestre, Jefe, Depto. Producción, June, 1963. See also, "La Reunión Nacional de Producción Agrícola," p. 46. I place Guevara in the anti-INRA camp on the basis of his speech to the National Sugar Plenary in December, 1962 (radio broadcast, December 20, 1962), in which he projected a doubling of yields

With these aims clearly in mind, INRA mounted a multiple attack on the problem of sugar cane. A "six points" slogan popularized new, efficient cultivation practices.[39] Restraints on the wage demands of the Agricultural Workers Union, a rise in raw cane prices during the 1963 harvest, and more technical help and volunteer labor to clean the fields were designed to strengthen the small *colono*. INRA introduced work norms in the mills and cane fields in order to establish a rational system of individual and group material incentives and thus reawaken the interest of professional cane cutters in harvest work. A beginning was made in programming the harvest in order to economize on labor and plan other harvests to dovetail with the *zafra*. Finally, INRA increased prices paid to *colonos* during the 1964 *zafra*.[40]

Probably more important in the long run, INRA recognized that the diversification and construction programs, together with the agrarian reform, permanently changed the distribution and composition of the rural labor force. Thus, the Ministry of Industries, INRA, and other organisms placed special emphasis on the mechanization of the harvest, the most labor-intensive aspect of sugar production.[41] "There is no other solution to the labor problem,"

---

from 40–80,000 *arrobas* per *caballería* by the end of the decade. He stressed the importance of 100 per cent mechanization, intensified irrigation and use of fertilizer, and high-yield strains.

[39] The "six points" were: no burning of the cane; the elimination of the savannas; the extermination of the borer; 100 per cent fulfillment of seeding plans; the full utilization of existing irrigation facilities; the maintenance of clean paths between the fields year round.

[40] For cane prices see Oscar Duyos, "Los problemas actuales del acopio y los precios de compra de los productos agrícolas," *Cuba Socialista*, 4, No. 33 (May, 1964), p. 75.

[41] In 1963 and 1964 volunteer labor fell off, chiefly because local cane commissioners ceased recruiting high-paid industrial, construction, and other labor. INRA raised wages in 1963 and again in 1964, but this did not reduce the need for volunteer labor. Thus, government leaders continually denounced rural *"vagos incorregibles"* and the CTC-R issued appeals for "permanent volunteers" in early 1963. Also, the Rebel Army assigned more volunteers to the 1963 and 1964 *zafras*.

Experiments in 1963 showed that 4,000 cutting machines and an equal number of loaders could bring in one-half of a normal harvest. Over 600 machines (1,000 machines had been planned) were used with varying success in Camaguey in that year. For 1964, INRA counted on 3,500 machines.

Castro said in mid-1962. Experiments during the 1963 harvest, however, revealed that mechanization was inefficient in areas where yields were low. Thus, on the one hand, an end to the labor shortage required that at least one-half of the harvest be mechanized; on the other hand, mechanization required that INRA fertilize a minimum of 50,000 *caballerías* and irrigate at least 25,000 *caballerías*. The need for large quantities of foreign exchange, a rising import bill, technical possibilities in the industry, and the labor shortage thus all combined to push Cuba in the direction of a highly intensive cane agriculture.

By the 1964 harvest, the persistent decline in area under cultivation, yields, and production was brought to a halt.[42] Had the hurricane of October, 1963, not seriously damaged the eastern cane fields, production would no doubt have risen 20 to 25 per cent above 1963 levels. And 1965 was an excellent year by the best prerevolutionary standards. As we will see in the next chapter, the long-run prospects of agriculture depended on the success of the new industrialization program: the production of chemical fertilizers, pumping equipment, and other requirements for a high-yield, intensive agriculture.

The second feature of this phase of Cuban agricultural planning was the turnabout from the local self-sufficiency, farm-by-farm diversification policies of 1960–1961. INRA also abandoned the Western European model of a mixed agriculture and adopted the methods common to much of Soviet and United States agriculture: local and regional specialization and national diversification. To this end,

[42] Total spring and fall new seedings in 1962 were limited to 5,500 *caballerías*, less than one-third planned levels, chiefly because of the labor shortage. Another 7,400 *caballerías* of replacement cane was seeded ("Cuatro Años de Reforma Agraria," p. 21). In 1963, only 5,900 additional *caballerías* were planted, a large but unknown portion of which was destroyed by the hurricane in October. Planned seeded area in the spring of 1963 came to 6,000 *caballerías*, but by June, only 2,700 *caballerías* were sown (Rafael Francia Mestre, "La Reunión Nacional de Producción Agrícola," *Cuba Socialista*, 3, No. 23 [July, 1963], p. 46). More fertilizers and insecticides were used, and the new Organization for the Improvement of Sugar Production established seed banks and attempted to eliminate undesirable cane varieties. In the summer and fall of 1963, there was more weeding of the fields and, with a newly organized state sector and improved relations between the small growers and INRA, the harvest was conducted more rationally in nearly every aspect.

INRA formulated plans for large-scale, mechanized, specialized, high-yield operations in the cultivation of kenaf, henequen, vegetable oils, tobacco, tomatoes, cattle feed, and other crops, as well as sugar cane. Most of these were, of course, traditional crops, but INRA intended to cultivate them in an entirely nontraditional manner. The institute planned to diversify Cuban agriculture more slowly, applying new techniques in the sugar and cattle sectors to raise land and labor productivity, and then gradually to transfer technology and physical resources to other crops without lowering production in the traditional spheres. The judgment of the interrelationships between sugar and other crops that we made when the third stage was introduced still stands:

Cuba's soils will not yield eight million tons of sugar until far-reaching technical improvements are introduced in her mills and fields. These new techniques—cultivation practices, rational use of fertilizers, insecticides and irrigation methods and equipment, mechanical harvesting and deliveries to the mill—can and will be spread into other branches of the island's agriculture. Far from handicapping the revolution's diversification program—which continues to make slow headway—close attention to sugar can be put to good use elsewhere in the rural economy. . . . Sooner or later, scientific agriculture must be systematically introduced in Cuba; it may very well be correct to begin in the sugar fields.[43]

The three final goals of the new course in agriculture, announced in 1964 and put into practice in subsequent years, were: a reduction in rice, cotton, and other crops in which Cuba failed to have a comparative advantage; self-sufficiency in root crops, dairy products, and poultry; and the generation of tobacco, coffee, and citrus fruit surpluses for export.

[4]

The sharp, but not unexpected, turn in agricultural planning in 1963 left three features of agricultural planning unaffected, except with regard to emphasis. Cuban agriculture needed water, fertilizer,

---

[43] O'Connor, op. cit., p. 228. The new techniques necessary to advance cattle production—chiefly the intensified use of artificial pastures and artificial insemination to raise the genetic quality of Cuba's cattle herds—also have utility in other branches of livestock production.

and farm equipment in both the second and third stages. First, INRA steadily pushed forward with its large-scale capital spending program for irrigation, required because Cuban rainfall is highly seasonal and unevenly distributed, and because before the revolution only 10 per cent of total cultivated area was irrigated. Castro and INRA were aware that an agriculture that depends on rainfall is an "insecure, risky agriculture" in Cuba. To cite an example, non-irrigated rice fields in Las Villas yielded twice as much when rainfall was adequate, but only one-half that of the irrigated rice farms in Oriente.[44]

With few exceptions, irrigation projects under way in 1961–1962 were small scale, inexpensive, and yielded quick benefits. INRA's foreign agricultural experts stressed local projects, small drainage basins, and advised against large dam projects, a policy that was reversed when Cuba's water shortage became acute in 1963–1964. In August, 1962, after months of drought and full realization of the real scope of the agricultural problem, the Council of Ministers established the National Institute of Water Resources (INRH). The institute drew on three kinds of resources: the local experiences of the Ministry of Public Works, prerevolutionary studies of Cuba's water supplies, and over one hundred Soviet specialists and $15 million in grants for equipment and expenses. Work began immediately on Cuba's five largest rivers. The institute tied its water control plans to Ministry of Communications and Industries programs to expand the supply of electrical energy, and thus shifted the emphasis to large-scale, multipurpose projects. INRH took over the five-year water plan (1961–1965) originally formulated by the Ministry of Public Works, which called for doubling irrigated farmland (to over 400,000 hectares), placed main emphasis on seventeen multipurpose projects, and diverted more water resources to sugar and cattle away from other sectors, in particular, rice cultivation.[45]

[44] Material for the discussion that follows was drawn from: speech by Faustino Pérez, reported in *Hoy*, August 11, 1963; speech by Fidel Castro, *Obra Revolucionaria*, No. 17, May 25, 1962; *Revolución*, January, 1963; private sources in INRA.

[45] A simple, but telling, calculation indicates the abundant fruits that irrigation investments can yield Cuba. The cost of these projects (allocated to irrigation alone) was a maximum of $150 million. Costs per hectare were thus $750.

Second, INRA stressed increased use of fertilizer and insecticide during both the second and third phases of agricultural planning. Total fertilizer consumption in 1959–1960 averaged about 300,000 tons annually—roughly equal to the 1957–1958 average—of which nearly one-half was consumed in cane cultivation.[46] The institute planned to double fertilizer use by 1962 and increase consumption by almost fourfold by 1965. In fact, total consumption was only 470,000 tons in 1962. Shortages compelled INRA to reduce planned 1965 consumption to one million tons and, as we will see, forced Cuban planners to reorient investment policies in 1963.[47]

Finally, INRA continued to push forward its policy of mechanization. Even during the second phase, the institute spent nearly $100 million on farm equipment, chiefly imported supplies (while expending a paltry $2.7 million on food and raw material processing industry.) Nevertheless, Cuba could claim little more than 12,000 tractors in 1962, and imports of farm equipment were increased.[48] More important, in 1962–1963, INRA allocated more machinery to the people's farms. Despite the undeniable fact that there was a pressing need to mechanize the *granjas* (because labor in relation to available land was relatively scarce), the people's farms had at their disposal an average of only one tractor for each 216 cultivated hectares in 1961, compared with the all-Cuba average of one tractor per 258 hectares.[49]

The value of output per hectare exceeded $200 (in 1959–1960, an estimated 2,374,668 hectares were under cultivation, and in 1958, total value of agricultural production [excluding meat and dairying] was $493.8 million). Thus, if irrigation can double average yields, water investments can be amortized in a little over three years.

[46] Agricultural Supplies Section, Department of Production, INRA.

[47] *Informe Sobre el Plan de 1963*, JUCEPLAN (Havana, December 27, 1962), mimeographed, p. 73.

[48] PAE, 1962, Table 5.7. The exact number was 12,300, but many of these were temporarily out of operation. Two thousand of these were located in the machine service stations which mainly served the private sector, although originally they had been set up to service the early cooperatives. Another 4,500 (over 3,500 of which were new) were in the *granjas del pueblo* (the largest of which had their own repair shops), and 2,200 were located on the cane farms. The rest were in the private sector; this fact also may have been behind the Second Agrarian Reform of 1963–1964.

[49] INRA never ceased to emphasize other policies that looked to raise yields. These included the use of quality seed (in 1961, only two farms comprising a

[5]

Some observers have interpreted the false steps and shortcomings we have discussed in Chapter Five and the present chapter—unremitting organizational changes, planning mistakes and misjudgements, and the largely unqualified failure of the second stage—as signs of the basic irrationality of Cuban socialism. In fact, nothing could be further from the truth. For one thing, it cannot be stressed too much that the agrarian revolution was rational in the negative sense that the prerevolutionary agriculture was irrational. For another thing, the revolution's general line of agricultural planning—investments in land and labor oriented toward raising cane and cattle yields and liberating land for crop diversification—has endured all the twists and turns of specific agricultural policy. Again, much of the blame for ineffectual agricultural planning must be placed at the doorstep of mistaken industrial planning (see Chapter 9).

Finally, the Cuban Revolution, including the agrarian reform, brought about a qualitative change in Cuba's resource base, in fact, a redefinition of the very meaning of "economic resources." For this reason, experimentation, change, the emergence of unforeseen difficulties, and more experimentation were inevitable. Policy innovation, assimilation, and transformation do not condemn Cuban socialism, but rather testify to the deep-going character of the rural revolution.

The two resources that underwent the most basic qualitative changes were organization and manpower. Both are extremely valuable; both are important chiefly for their qualitative aspects. And both must be harmonized with other resources in the context of the demands that the society places on the resource base as a whole. Before the revolution, rural organization was sufficient for the demands placed on it by a stagnating economy, and rural manpower was adequate within the framework of an extensive, backward agriculture.

After the revolution, the United States embargo, the redistribution of income, the flight of the middle class, and the determination

---

total of less than one thousand hectares were producing seeds), emphasis on better soil preparation, and the introduction of efficient crop rotations (in 1962, more than a dozen major rotation studies were in progress).

to promote agricultural development, all basically changed the character of commodity demand. Nothing less than an intensive, scientific, high-productivity agriculture was required. Suddenly, a manpower base that had been adequate was now completely inadequate. More important, the prevailing modes of rural organization were eliminated almost altogether by the agrarian reform.

Thus, changes in agricultural planning interpenetrated changes in organization at almost every point. Inexperience, "subjectivism," and the lack of central controls all temporarily combined to undermine economic planning by contributing to the failure to develop an adequate statistics-collection, evaluation, and control arm.[50] Great gaps in INRA's knowledge about what was actually happening in the countryside in turn created an unrealistic sense of well-being bordering on euphoria. Only by 1963, for example, did INRA have accurate data on food stocks in state warehouses. Tightening up central direction of the rural economy inevitably revealed many shortcomings and mistakes, especially the lack of realism in the second phase of planning.

Again, the labor shortage and the need to allocate scarce machinery rationally meant that it was necessary for the cane farms to estimate their manpower needs accurately. Good estimates of labor productivity were thus essential, but such estimates were not possible until machinery and supplies were in fact allocated. Thus, INRA could not plan rationally until it could plan agriculture *as a whole*. Not until 1964 was INRA well enough staffed to conduct an accurate census of local manpower and the stock of farm equipment. Changes in planning goals therefore went hand in hand with the centralization of the formation of these goals.

The most basic point of interpenetration of planning and organization came in late 1963. The new course of "local specialization and national diversification" depended on a new rural organization. Hitherto, the top-heavy, bureaucratic General Administrations of

---

[50] Throughout 1962 and 1963, scores of critical articles, speeches, and reports appeared in Cuba and denounced the appointment of unqualified personnel to key posts, "subjectivism," and so on. For one typical example, see "Ante el Tercer Aniversario de la Reforma Agraria," pp. 44–46.

Cane Farms and People's Farms exercised considerable control over the finances, supplies, investment, and production of local farm units. In 1964, the General Administrations were replaced by Basic Agricultural-Livestock Production Groups which provided economic and technical direction for the *granjas*, and the cane and people's farms were reorganized into economic and geographic enclaves. The *granjas* acquired more local autonomy, particularly in connection with financing. Furthermore, they were enlarged in area in order to obtain the full benefits from local specialization with little danger of administrative inefficiencies arising from large-scale units. Meanwhile, other branches of the rural planning organization were administratively decentralized. In 1964, for instance, INRA reconstituted its National Purchasing Corporations on a regional basis with a considerable degree of local autonomy. In short, INRA drew the conclusion that a policy of local specialization required administrative decentralization. Thus, the postrevolutionary rural organization came full circle between 1959–1960 and 1964. Organized first on the basis of local autonomy and reorganized on the basis of central autonomy, Cuban agriculture was reorganized again on the basis of local autonomy, at a higher level of technical and economic capability.

[9]

Industrial Planning

[1]
Like agricultural planning, the first goal of industrial planning was to solve the two key political-economic problems inherited by the Revolutionary Government in 1959: unemployment and the shortage of foreign exchange. At first, Cuba's leaders failed to formulate any precise industrial plans. According to Guevara, the first year of the revolution "passed without the government coming to grips with the central question of our economy: what line should we adopt and how intensely should we follow it." [1] Yet, also like agricultural planning, the government introduced a *general* program that sought to simultaneously expand both employment and the production of previously imported commodities.

There were two basic phases of this program. In the first phase, the government hoped to encourage Cuban businessmen to utilize idle productive capacity and hence increase employment by widening and deepening the national market. Two approaches were adopted. First, the government placed progressively tighter controls on foreign trade, in particular imports from the United States. Neither the reformers nor the revolutionaries within the 26th of July Movement questioned Martí's slogan: "The country which buys is the one which commands, and the country which sells is the one which obeys"; nor did either group have any doubts that the United States "bought" and Cuba "sold."

Second, the government redistributed income in favor of low-in-

[1] Ernesto Guevara, "Tareas industriales de la Revolución en los años venidores," *Cuba Socialista*, 2, No. 7 (March, 1962).

come farmers and workers and hence expanded the mass of domestic purchasing power. Private associations and public agencies also mounted extensive "buy Cuban" publicity campaigns and expositions of Cuban products, and generally appealed to nationalist sentiment. The results of the first phase were positive. Cuban businessmen responded favorably to the array of incentives held out by the government. Production rose in textiles, footwear, food processing, and other industries. Following the agrarian reform, however, the business classes became more and more politically wary of the Revolutionary Government and gradually withdrew their economic cooperation.

In the second phase, the government aimed to *enlarge* productive capacity by modernization and expansion investments concentrated in import-substitute industries. Until late 1959, Cuban planners attempted to encourage new *private* investment by trade, tax, and other indirect policies. But the hostility of the United States to the revolution, the agrarian reform, and the general radicalization of the revolution all combined to reduce private investment to a minimum. Private business spokesmen—for example, the influential daily *Diario de la Marina*—cautioned the government against barter agreements with other countries and opposed attempts to promote import-substitute investments in the context of developing materials shortages and inflationary pressures. Finally, the business classes and the Revolutionary Government were totally disenchanted with one another. Increasingly throughout 1960, the government itself invested in nationalized and newly constructed state-owned enterprises and economic infrastructure. By the end of the year Cuba had a socialist economy, having monopolized the major means of production.

[2]

The first phase of Cuban industrial planning began shortly after the Revolutionary Government took power and reached its peak early in 1960. During that period, the government employed nearly every weapon in the arsenal of nationalist trade policy—tariffs, import quotas and licenses, and exchange rationing and blocking—in order to create a favorable climate for Cuban manufacturers. In February, 1959, the National Bank introduced a system of import licensing covering about two hundred consumer commodities. In the spring a series of Treasury Ministry rulings reduced the number of duty-free commodity imports. In July the Customs House was reorganized, all matters relating to tariffs were centralized, and government control over foreign trade was tightened. Next month, tariffs were increased on a wide range of commodities, and in September surcharges of 30 to 100 per cent were levied on goods included in the import licensing list. By early 1960 import quotas were in effect on nearly all farm commodities.

Meanwhile, foreign exchange policy was tightened up. In February, 1959, the National Bank restricted dollar remittances abroad and hard currency expenditures on travel and consumer durable good purchases.[2] In the summer the bank began to restrict profit remittances, and in September the Monetary Stabilization Fund placed stiff controls on the import and export of gold. The burden of the new regulations and controls fell on United States exporters, whose Cuban sales declined because of new surcharges on commodities normally imported from the United States, quota reductions, and the elimination in whole or in part of United States tariff preferences.

Despite the controls, the balance of payments situation steadily worsened. Between 1958 and 1959, United States exports to Cuba fell by $108 million; nevertheless, in January, 1960, the Monetary Stabilization Fund held only $35.4 million in real reserves—an all-time low—most of which were commercial arrears.[3] There were a number of reasons for the deterioration of Cuba's payments balance. For one thing, during most of 1959 the National Bank granted import licenses quite freely and failed to vigorously enforce the new trade controls. Secondly, the expansion of wages and incomes during 1959 caused an increase in the demand for imported commodi-

[2] *The Havana Post,* February 12, 1959.

[3] Reprint of Jorge Freyne, "La supeditación del comercio exterior de Cuba al bloque soviético," *Cuadernos,* No. 55 (December, 1961), Table I, p. 15, citing a confidential National Bank of Cuba report.

ties and a growing capital flight drained the island of even more hard currency. Last, dollar inflows were sharply reduced due to a decline in sugar prices and the progressive drying up of private foreign investments and supplier credits granted to Cuban importers.

As 1960 wore on, the National Bank, taken over by the revolutionary wing of the 26th of July Movement in late 1959, progressively increased restrictions on imports and the use of foreign exchange. In March, the government designated INRA's Foreign Trade and Production Department sole importer and exporter of a variety of agricultural commodities. In April the Monetary Stabilization Fund placed controls on the repatriation of dollars by United States employees in Cuba, and the Ministry of Commerce established the Bank for Cuban Foreign Trade as monopoly importer for all government agencies.[4] In July the bank also began to monopolize trade in a wide range of consumer and capital goods.[5] The Foreign Trade Bank marked the intermediary stage between a "reformed" Cuban capitalism subject to indirect government controls, and centrally planned socialism. The final stage came in March, 1961, when the Council of Ministers granted the new Ministry of Foreign Commerce a complete monopoly of foreign trade.

More and tighter controls of trade and currency movements reversed the tide, and the Foreign Trade Bank steadily built up reserves to a peak of $175 million in August, 1960. Imports from the United States fell from $458.5 million in 1959 to $281.5 million in 1960, partly because of a conscious attempt to diversify import sources, partly because of the production of import substitutes in Cuba, but mainly because of across-the-board restrictions on all imports, particularly consumer durable goods and other nonessentials.[6] In effect, a policy of limiting imports to encourage the utiliza-

[4] *The Havana Post*, April 29, 1960.

[5] See, for example, Ministry of Commerce, Resolución No. 295, *Gaceta Oficial*, No. 137, July 18, 1960.

[6] For example, rice imports from the United States fell from $36 million to $17 million between 1959 and 1960 following new barter agreements between Cuba and other countries. Imports of textile products fell from $15.2 million to $7.9 million between January–June, 1959, to the first six months of 1960 because of an expansion of textile production and a reduction in the demand for luxury imports.

tion of domestic excess industrial capacity became a policy of limiting all but the most essential imports.

The government's determination to build up foreign exchange reserves constituted an important source of friction between businessmen and the revolutionaries who were now completely in charge of most of Cuba's government agencies and private organizations. In January, 1960, the Cuban Chamber of Commerce demanded that the National Bank modify Monetary Stabilization Fund rules in order to facilitate payments for imports.[7] In March the National Association of Cuban Industrialists began a systematic effort to help its members acquire import licenses.[8] Complaints about the new foreign economic policies became louder and more frequent throughout the spring and summer, but the government failed to pay them much heed. The government's position was that businessmen had enjoyed very loose credits in the past, were not used to the new controls and procedures, and, in any event, failed to sympathize with the revolution's development plans and new import priorities.[9] Moreover, the National Bank was increasingly reluctant to grant concessions that might make it possible for businessmen to liquidate their idle dollar balances. To be sure, in July, 1960, the government simplified procedures for importers and custom brokers, but it was clear by then that private enterprise would no longer orient Cuba's trade policy and import structure.

The second approach to the problem of unemployment and foreign currency reserves was to redistribute income. The hoped-for effect was twofold. First, income redistribution would reduce consumption of high-income groups and thus lower the demand for luxury imports, paving the way for a shift in the composition of imports in favor of raw materials and capital goods. Second, income

[7] Import licenses were good for ninety days. The Chamber wanted this changed to six months to one year, depending on the type of commodity. The Chamber also requested priorities to favor imports of needed raw materials, machinery, and parts, permits putting different goods covered by different licenses together in one shipment, and a leeway of 10 per cent on commodity prices billed the same day of shipment so that exporters would cease to protect themselves by fixing higher prices.

[8] *The Havana Post,* March 24, 1960.

[9] Author's interview with National Bank officials, July 12, 1960.

redistribution would widen and deepen the domestic market, encourage the utilization of idle capacity, and lay the basis for realizing economies of large-scale production. Another advantage was that Cuba's incomes policy during the first two years of the revolution laid down the political basis for high investment ratios in years to come. By 1961, Cuban planners were under little or no pressure to increase consumption—in particular, social outlays, which absorbed perhaps 60 per cent of the government budget in 1959–1960 —and hence could put an ever rising share of total product into productive investments. The danger of the policy was the strong possibility of disinvestment, inventory drains, and inflationary pressures. Moreover, income redistribution caused a basic change in the *composition* of demand and thus helped to create bottlenecks in both the production and distribution systems.

The Revolutionary Government focused on the advantages and ignored the dangers. Partly owing to wage increases and partly owing to an expansion of employment (in turn arising from earlier increases in local demand), total money wages rose from about $550 million during the first nine months of 1958 to over $1 billion during the corresponding period in 1961. The prevailing level of unemployment in fact placed a ceiling on the expansion of real wages because the increased output of goods and services was mainly absorbed by rural workers, whose annual incomes were rising. From January, 1958, to January, 1961, the proportion of the employed labor force earning more than $75 monthly in urban districts rose from 51.5 per cent to 60.8 per cent and in rural districts from 27.2 per cent to 34.2 per cent (see Table 5). All in all, between 1958 and 1961 there was an increase in real income for perhaps 80 per cent of the Cuban labor force on the order of 30 to 40 per cent, due roughly in equal parts to an expansion of output and income redistribution.

[3]

The second phase of industrial planning, in which the government sought to enlarge Cuba's productive capacity, overlapped the first phase. In effect, there were two subphases: first, the period between early and late 1959 when the government attempted to pro-

Table 5. Monthly income of employed labor force, urban and rural, 1958–1961—percentage of employed labor force earning $75 monthly or more

Date	Urban	Rural	Date	Urban	Rural
1958–Feb	51.5%	27.2%	1959–Oct	56.9%	25.2%
Mar	51.1	28.3	Nov	56.6	27.9
Apr	51.0	28.8	Dec	57.2	29.1
May	50.7	23.2			
Jun	50.1	20.7	1960–Jan	58.0	31.3
Jul	49.8	19.3	Feb	59.5	39.1
Aug	48.9	19.0	Mar	60.4	44.2
Sep	49.7	18.7	Apr	60.7	43.0
Oct	49.9	21.9	May	60.2	35.0
Nov	49.9	26.3	Jun	59.4	30.3
Dec	50.8	24.9	Jul	58.8	29.2
			Aug	58.4	27.1
1959–Jan	51.2	25.0	Sep	58.4	27.4
Feb	51.6	27.9	Oct	59.2	27.1
Mar	51.4	33.3	Nov	59.8	29.9
Apr	52.9	34.2	Dec	60.8	31.2
May	53.6	33.2			
Jun	54.9	28.7	1961–Jan	60.8	34.2
Jul	55.2	28.4	Feb	61.2	39.5
Aug	56.2	26.4	Mar	62.2	42.5
Sep	55.7	25.7			

Source: February, 1958, to December, 1958: Consejo Nacional de Economía, Departamento Econometría, *Empleo y Desempleo en La Fuerza Trabajadora.* January, 1959, to March, 1961: Oficina Nacional de los Censos Demográficos y Electorales, *Encuesta sobre Empleo, Sub-empleo y Desempleo.*

mote new private investments and, second, the subsequent period when private investments gave way to state investments.

Government agencies employed a wide range of instruments in order to promote new private capital accumulation, in particular, tax reform. The most important of the many tax laws passed during the first two years of the revolution was the Tax Reform Law of July, 1959. The main purpose of the law was to completely overhaul the tax structure in order to smooth the path for private capital accumulation and raise revenues for government investments in social overhead capital. On the one hand, personal consumption of middle-class and well-to-do Cubans was reduced by new taxes on luxury goods and services ranging from 10 to 30 per cent, a flat 3 per cent income tax, increases in inheritance, real estate, and personal property taxes, and a 40 per cent profits tax which discriminated in favor of reinvested earnings. On the other hand, the tax structure was simplified by reducing the total number of taxes from over 150 to 20. Capital taxes were lowered or eliminated altogether, and the principle of accelerated depreciation (with carry back-or-forward loss provisions) was introduced. At the same time, kickbacks to tax and customs officials were suppressed, tax loopholes were removed, and tax collections were rigorously enforced.

Thus, the Reform Law sought to absorb property and other unearned income and reduce middle-class consumption in order to increase government revenues, while encouraging new industries, modernization investments, regional diversification, and a shift in agriculture away from sugar.[10] The reform remained in force until August, 1960, when the government revised profits and some excise taxes upward and introduced a progressive income tax.[11]

The government also attempted to encourage private investments via its new controls over foreign trade and foreign exchange. Late in 1959, for example, in processing applications for new industries requiring imported equipment, the National Bank gave top priority to plants manufacturing raw materials to supply established enterprises that converted imported raw materials, and low priority to new conversion plants utilizing Cuban raw materials.

The great majority of new private investment projects were begun in 1959 when flexible trade controls, tax reform, and the rise in local purchasing power created a hothouse atmosphere in which private capital could flourish. New investment projects fell into two

[10] The profits tax base rate of 40 per cent was reduced by 25 per cent for all businesses located outside of Havana Province, all nonsugar manufacturing industry, and all agricultural, mining, and fishing industries.

[11] Incomes of single and married persons up to $200 monthly and $3,600 yearly, respectively, were exempted. Law No. 863 (August 30, 1960) retained the 3 per cent rate for incomes up to $600 per year. The maximum rate was 67 per cent, on that portion of income in excess of $40,000 annually.

general categories. First, there were import-substitute industries directly influenced by the new controls and the expansion of the local market. BANFAIC, BANDES, and other government agencies, together with private associations such as the National Union of Foodstuffs Importers, sponsored projects in chemicals, plywood, glass, tricot cloth, and other industries.[12] Second, there were new projects which were expected to meet the expansion of demand arising from the agrarian reform, for example, food-processing plants, a unit to prepare cotton seed for oil extraction, and so on.

Few new projects in either category were actually started, and none were completed by the original promoters. By the spring of 1960, the flow of private capital was reduced to a trickle. Despite the efforts of some members of Cuban manufacturing groups to "integrate" themselves into the new reformed economy, the revolutionary measures of 1959–1960 almost certainly reduced total private investment spending.

[4]

Both the reformers and the revolutionaries within the 26th of July Movement desired industrialization, but the latter did not believe that private industry was able or willing to do the job. The basic reason was the increasing disenchantment among the middle classes growing out of the agrarian reform law, the deterioration of relations with the United States, the elimination of many class privileges and prerogatives, and the growing sense that the revolution was increasingly oriented toward the poorer farmers and workers. Thus, the revolutionary leadership placed more and more faith in mixed private-public and state enterprise.

Throughout 1960 and 1961, industrialization was held to be the answer not only to Cuba's foreign exchange and unemployment problems, but also the only path to "economic freedom," the "road to collective well-being in the age of economic empires." [13] Ambi-

[12] *The Havana Post,* January 19, 1960; January 24, 1960; January 31, 1960; February 28, 1960; and March 27, 1960.

[13] Speeches by Guevara on May 20, 1960, and June 18, 1960, reproduced in *Obra Revolucionaria,* No. 6 (1960); No. 11 (1960).

tious but very general plans were made for new and expansion investments in steel, chemicals, petroleum, minerals, construction materials, electrical power, vehicles, and other heavy industries. The government's leadership mentioned "plans," "projects," and "needs" for a wide range of light capital goods and consumer goods industries. In April, 1961, Minister of Industries Guevara looked forward to the construction of an "industrial state" inside a "few years." [14]

Expectedly, industrialization figured centrally in the 1962 Economic Plan, socialist Cuba's first real plan. The political-economic goals of the plan were threefold.[15] First, it aimed at a high and stable level of sugar exports sold at stable, "satisfactory" prices. This was considered important for two reasons: planned industrial investments required planned imports of raw materials and capital goods, which in turn required high, stable export earnings; and planned, full-time utilization of resources depended on predictable export earnings because cross-elasticities of supply between imports and home-produced goods were low.

Second, the plan aimed to diversify Cuba's exports, in particular, to expand exports of raw and processed minerals. The third goal was to acquire the full cooperation of the major socialist countries. This was the key to the first two goals. Cooperation meant not only development loans and aid and technical assistance, but also guarantees of favorable, stable prices for Cuba's sugar and other exports. Cuba's first plan was therefore mainly oriented by the need for outside direct and indirect financing.

The plan divided total production between consumption and investment in the proportion of 73 per cent and 27 per cent. Two-thirds of investment was allocated to productive investment (industry, transport, mining, communications, and so on) and one-third to unproductive investment (health, education, housing, etc.), roughly the same proportion that prevailed during 1961. In the short term, the government gave the development of siderurgical, machinery,

[14] Speech by Guevara, television, April 30, 1961.
[15] The outlines of the 1962 plan were described by Minister of Economy Regino Boti in *Cuba Socialista*, I, No. 4 (December, 1961).

and metals-processing industries highest priority. In the long run, metallurgy, sugar, chemistry, electronics, and shipbuilding received heaviest emphasis. Large-scale, integrated industrial construction was postponed until 1965–1970.

The 1962 Plan was at best a "paper plan." Actual balances were worked out within and between major economic sectors, but these balances failed to reflect real input-output relations because of a highly unrealistic appraisal of the resources of inputs necessary to attain planned output goals. In addition, the policy of diversifying exports as a mode of import financing was quickly dropped in favor of the more "strategic" aim of import substitute industrialization.[16] Lastly, as we have seen, agricultural planning was in a highly primitive state, as reflected in the plan's goal to make Cuba self-sufficient in foodstuffs by the end of 1962.

Industrial planning during the following two years was considerably more realistic. Cuba's planners narrowed the range of projected investments and modified the general orientation of investments. On the one hand, the long list of planned capital projects made public in 1960–1961 was shortened. For example, plans for an automotive plant, a siderurgical complex, and other heavy investments were postponed indefinitely. On the other hand, the government reoriented investment policy by placing strongest emphasis on agricultural machinery and irrigation equipment, chemical fertilizers, petroleum, textiles, and sugar milling. Cuba thus became the first socialist country in history to choose to industrialize via an expansion of agriculture.

Other plans scheduled mineral, tropical fruits, and other traditional exports, together with electronics and other nontraditional exports, for expansion in the medium and long run. Another change consisted of the relative decline in "unproductive" investments: expenditures on health, education, and housing. Unproductive capital outlays fell from 34 per cent of total investments in 1961 to 27 per cent and 21.4 per cent in 1962 and 1963, respectively.[17] Finally, the

[16] Author's interview with Ernesto Guevara, September 3, 1961.

[17] After the increase in wages, probably the single most important source of new spending from late 1959 to late 1960 or early 1961 were government

government continued to stress maritime (including fishing equipment) and electric power investments.[18]

The government formulated more modest investment programs and reoriented investment policy after 1962 for two basic reasons. First, the import-substitute industrialization policy of 1959–1961 had the effect of increasing (rather than decreasing) Cuba's de-

---

expenditures on education, health, and housing. Particularly during the first two years of the revolution, advancements in these areas far outweighed progress toward industrialization. An exhaustive description of Cuba's educational system during this period is given by Richard Jolly in Dudley Seers, editor, *Cuba: The Economic and Social Revolution* (Chapel Hill, North Carolina, 1964). The salient features of this system are the elimination of illiteracy; the rapid expansion of the primary school programs and enrollments; the relative neglect of secondary education; the expansion of higher education; and throughout the whole system, a new stress on technical, scientific, administrative education at the expense of "liberal arts" programs. The great emphasis the Revolutionary Government placed on education was due to a combination of related factors. First, the Cuban labor force, especially the rural labor force, was comparatively unskilled and untrained. Second, prerevolutionary Cuba's educational system grossly neglected technical-scientific education at all levels. Third, the flight into exile of many scientific-managerial-technical personnel handicapped Cuban planning and economic progress. Fourth, and most important, the revolutionary organizational changes in industry, agriculture, and other branches of the economy dramatically revealed Cuba's woeful inadequacies in the area of skilled manpower. Workers were asked to perform tasks that they were not prepared to perform and that they never had had to perform before. The shortage of skilled manpower was thus to a large degree *relative* to needs and requirements of the new Cuba, not of the old, which did not place a high premium on trained labor.

[18] Investments in maritime activities (especially fishing) and electric power rose steadily from 1960 to 1964. Cuba has four basic power networks. The major network, centered in Havana and running eastward to Oriente, had a capacity of about 440,000 kilowatts in 1962. The Southern and Northern Oriente networks could generate about 50,000 and 15,000 kilowatts, respectively. The Pinar del Río complex in the far west had a capacity of 10,000 kilowatts.

Completed in 1964–1965 were four power stations at Mariel in Pinar del Río with a total capacity of 200,000 kilowatts. One hundred thousand kilowatts were added to the Southern Oriente network as a result of the construction of two plants at Rente (near Santiago). The enlargement of the Matanzas station added another 37,500 kilowatts to the major Occidental network. In construction in 1965 were five more units with a total capacity of 330,000 kilowatts. Thus, by 1967 or 1968 it was planned that Cuba's power capacity would double ("Nuevas plantas y más kilowatts," *Trabajo Cuba*, 4, No. 6 [April, 1963]; various interviews).

pendence on imported capital goods, fuels, and materials. Far from generating more foreign exchange, after late 1960, Cuba's industrial policies placed a large drain on exchange reserves. This was partly the result of mistaken cost and price calculations. For example, some new investments required so much imported raw materials that the Cubans could have saved foreign exchange by importing the final commodities. The basic problem was not faulty planning, however, but rather the lack of integration of the prerevolutionary national economy. Structural economic changes needed to integrate the national economy required a shift in productive resources from the export sector to the domestic industrial sector, where imports in relation to production are relatively high.[19] The rapid expansion of industrial investments thus resulted in a large increase in imports without a corresponding rise in exports. In 1964, for example, imports constituted over 15 per cent of the value of industrial production. The Ministry of Industries 1963 production plan was 84 per cent fulfilled, but the import plan was only 70 per cent fulfilled.[20] Ministry planners were thus compelled to cut back production and investment plans because of the shortage of needed imports.[21]

The second reason that the government reoriented its industrial policy is closely related to the first. The inability or unwillingness of the Soviet Union to extend large-scale, long-term, low-interest balance of payments credits (or their equivalent in the form of machinery and supplies) compelled the Cubans to focus their efforts on export expansion. As we know, a significant growth of exports required large-scale sugar and cattle investments in land and labor, that is, expenditures on chemical fertilizers, artificial cattle feed, machinery repair, pumping and other irrigation equipment, electric power, and, last but not least, technical agricultural education.

[19] In other Latin American countries making an effort to industrialize, one major bottleneck is also the rise in the import coefficient as a result of the shift from export to home industrial production.

[20] Guevara, speech on February 25, 1964, reproduced in *Obra Revolucionaria*, No. 7 (1964).

[21] According to Guevara (*ibid.*), another problem was the "immense burden of [the larger] factories which are still in poor operating condition because the equipment has deteriorated rapidly, and we do not have the specialized technical equipment to replace it."

Thus, the government decided to stress the development of the sugar and cattle industries, together with nickel mining, through 1970. To this end, the Cubans signed an agreement with the Soviet Union in 1964 that guaranteed sugar sales at prices "much above" the world market average. In 1965, Guevara anticipated that the Soviet Union would industrialize Cuba in return for deliveries of fixed quantities of primary and other products at specified prices, and that the two countries would "begin a new era of authentic international division of labor based not on the history of what has been done until now but on the future history of what can be done." [22]

[5]
Overly ambitious, unrealistic, costly, and "subjectivistic" industrial planning during the period 1960–1963 was basically due to the backwardness of Cuba's economic planning organization, methodology, and techniques. It is therefore to the development of the planning machinery which we now turn.

Cuba's first real planning authority, the Central Planning Board (JUCEPLAN), was created in March, 1960, to coordinate policies of various governmental bodies and to "orient" private business. JUCEPLAN's legal authority also extended to fixing investment priorities, raw material needs, production goals, and other over-all economic priorities and needs. In effect, JUCEPLAN constituted the technical economic arm of the Council of Ministers. Even though Cuba at that time was a capitalist economy and was broadly integrated by market forces, the orientation of most members of the board was towards direct, not indirect planning. The basic reason was that most of the ministers who made up JUCEPLAN (and the heads of INRA and the National Bank) were at that time directly planning dozens of enterprises that had been acquired by their ministries during 1959 and early 1960. The thinking of the board reflected the outlook of its members, which in turn was molded by very common experiences. Thus, from the beginning JUCEPLAN concerned itself less with fiscal, monetary, tariff, tax, and other indi-

[22] Speech in Algiers to the Afro-Asian Solidarity Conference, February, 1965, published in *Nuestra Industria*, 3, No. 13 (June, 1965).

rect planning policies and more with the direct, physical allocation of materials, supplies, and other economic resources.

Nevertheless, JUCEPLAN's first important achievement was the formulation of a six-months budget, Cuba's first complete, published budget since 1937. Despite the dissolution in March of the old National Planning Commission and National Planning Board and the transfer of the functions and personnel of the National Finance Agency and National Economic Council to JUCEPLAN in the summer, the Central Planning Board had few planners and fewer technical bases for direct planning. Furthermore, during this early period of the consolidation of revolutionary power, INRA and many other new or reformed government organisms were highly decentralized and autonomous.

In 1961 the Council of Ministers reorganized JUCEPLAN into five directorates: Central, Balances, Agriculture, Industry and Transport, and Domestic Commerce and Construction. The most important result of this change was that INRA lost some of its autonomy. A new agency, the Coordination, Execution, and Inspection Board (JUCEI), was also created to coordinate, inspect, and exercise "vigilance" over state policy at the local and provincial levels. In practice, this meant ironing out problems of work duplication, eliminating hoarding of scarce raw materials, and organizing volunteer labor. In Raúl Castro's words, "JUCEI does not supplant any authority [but] helps the other authorities." According to JUCEI's president in Havana Province, the board's purpose was to eliminate "personalism and capricious individual decision-making" that was the consequence of the disorganized mixed economy of 1960 and the *"guerrillerismo"* of the revolution's leaders and cadres.[23]

JUCEPLAN's next accomplishment, with the aid of JUCEI, was the completion of a number of studies of specific industries and branches of the economy in late 1960 and 1961. None of these studies, not even Chonchol's detailed investigation of agriculture, were plans, but rather general projections or guides to planning. This was

[23] José A. Naranjo, JUCEI president in Havana Province, quoted in *Revolución*, October 2, 1961.

also true of the first outlines for over-all economic plans drawn up by Kalecki and Bettelheim.[24] Guevara rightly gauged the significance of these projections when he said that the "rough draft" that served as the 1961 plan was "isolated from the masses" and "assumed optimum conditions of supply and technical personnel for attaining maximum output."

[24] The first attempts to draw up outlines for an over-all economic plan were made after the great expropriations in the fall of 1960. A Czech mission arrived in Havana in October, 1960, and produced a short, general memo on planning techniques which was circulated early in 1961 (*Informe final sobre los resultados del trabajo del grupo de expertos sobre los problemas de planificación, financiamento y organización de la economía nacional* [Havana, undated], mimeographed, 15 pp.). Published more rapidly was M. Kalecki's "Sketch for the Five-Year Plan, 1961–1965," which was finished in December, 1960 (*Bosquejo Hipotético del Plan Quinquenal, 1961–1965, para la Economía Cubana* ([Havana, December, 1960], mimeographed, 58 pp.). Kalecki's work was a series of optimistic projections of sugar exports, investments, and so on, and then a working out of the implications of these projections for transport, commerce, wage levels, etc. The general basis for estimating production goals was the expected expansion of the internal market because of population growth and anticipated increases in per capita income. Kalecki's outline was thus based on an evaluation of demand conditions to the near complete exclusion of supply conditions.

Kalecki projected an annual rate of growth of total production and consumption of 13 per cent and 10 per cent (or 7.5 per cent per capita) per year, respectively, over the period 1961–1965. Sugar exports were required to expand by 60 per cent (or to 9.4 million tons) by 1965, mainly via an expansion of output by raising yields. Kalecki's idea was correct, but the productive inputs for such an effort were simply not available.

The sketch also projected a substantial across-the-board increase in the output of other agricultural commodities, which was clearly unrealistic with regard to food crops, since the private sector would not be integrated into the planned agriculture until much later. Industrial production was to rise by 144 per cent, chiefly by the utilization of excess capacity in the traditional wage goods industries and transportation. Emphasis was placed on metal products and machinery, paper products, textiles, and minerals, in that order of importance. The notion of comparative advantage figured in Kalecki's thinking, but the post-1964 concept of the export sector orienting investments in industry was absent, at least in an explicit form. All in all, electrical power production and metals and machinery were to receive the lion's share of new investments, 42 per cent of the total.

Appearing some months after Kalecki's work was Charles Bettelheim's "Model for the 1962–1965 Plan" (*Modelo Esquemático del Plan Quinquenal, 1961–1965, para la Economía Cubana* [Havana, August, 1961], mimeographed).

March, 1961, when the Ministry of Industries and other new economics ministries were created and JUCEPLAN reorganized, marked an important division between early local planning and

---

Like Kalecki's outline, Bettelheim's model was also based on an expansion of sugar production to 9.5 million tons in 1965. Bettelheim understood, however, that an annual rate of expansion of total output and consumption of 16.7 per cent and 10.7 per cent yearly, respectively, would require much greater dependence on imported capital goods and raw materials. He thus stressed the importance of sugar sales to the socialist countries that would provide a more or less guaranteed market at stable prices. He also projected investment needs that came to roughly twice those put forth by Kalecki and consequently recognized that Cuba would not only have to expand exports at the rapid rate of 15 per cent yearly, but also would have to rely heavily on foreign loans and aid. While Kalecki saw the Cuban economy as self-sufficient by 1965, Bettelheim predicted that the balance of payments could not reach an equilibrium until 1965–1970. Surprisingly, Bettelheim's projections for total agricultural output exceeded Kalecki's, as they were based on estimates of very high income elasticities of demand for foods and industrial crops. Little was said, however, of the availability of the productive inputs needed for agricultural expansion.

Bettelheim's model was apparently meant to be the first outline for the first Cuban plan of 1962. Whatever the case, Bettelheim incorporated revisions into his model, bringing it into closer harmony with the 1962 plan, which appeared shortly after (*Notas complementarias sobre los Cuadros Recapitulativos* [Havana, September 28, 1961], mimeographed). One change reflects the new interest in siderurgy and the "rapid industrialization" line put forth by Cuban leaders in 1961. In the revision, import requirements of metals and metal products were thus reduced. Another change reduced projected housing investments and gave "unproductive" investments a weight of 30 per cent in total capital formation. A third and surprising change was the *increase* in projections of total production. This change is explicable only in the context of the paucity of reliable statistics for 1961 and is mentioned to point up the tremendous importance of the "data problem."

It is interesting to compare the actual structure of the economy in 1961 with the projected 1965 structure. The share of cane production in total production was to fall from 10.3 per cent to 8.1 per cent. Non-sugar cane farm output was to be reduced from 23.8 to 20.3 per cent of total output. Industry's share was to remain constant at about 51 per cent, although sugar production was to give way relatively to non-sugar industrial products. The significance of this is that in the first (paper) attempts at planning, the Cubans envisaged an *absolute* increase in cane and sugar production, but a *relative* decrease. The new agricultural policy of 1961 departed from this line in that it looked to both an absolute and relative rise in cane output. It should be emphasized that the goal of 8 to 10 million tons of sugar production annually figured in *every* step in the development of Cuban planning. What changed drastically were the estimates of the productive inputs required to reach this goal.

general national planning. As the year wore on, physical and monetary balances were drawn up for specific sectors of the economy,
using Soviet planning techniques. JUCEPLAN's next accomplishment was the formulation of the 1962 plan.[25] Only in September,

[25] Central physical planning in Cuba was based on Soviet planning methods.
First, the party sets the general political-economic goals of the plan, including
the rate of growth of total product, total investment, the utilization level of
existing productive capacity, and so on. Project evaluation in investment
planning was by and large highly pragmatic until at least 1964. No single
criterion was used to the exclusion of others, although the degree to which a
project would substitute for imported goods continued to have top priority. In
addition, JUCEPLAN seemed to have drifted steadily in the direction of more
capital-intensive projects in an effort to minimize the quantity of the labor
input per unit of output.

These political-economic goals are then quantified by JUCEPLAN and
published in the form of "control figures." On the basis of these data, the
consolidated enterprises and production centers elaborate the plan in detail.
There are eight sets of control figures: production, supplies, deliveries, investment, labor force, costs, financial, and new products. Each set of control figures
contains a subset. The production plan, for example, comprises four subsets:
value of output, physical output, productive capacity, and the relevant norms
or indices (e.g., yields per hectare in the agricultural production plan). The
supply plan contains a similar number of subsets: material balances, supplies
of raw materials and services, destination of output, and consumption norms
(e.g., fertilizer consumption per hectare). The financial plan balances monetary
supply and demand. These control figures constitute roughly five hundred
key items, representing about 95 per cent of the island's necessities in consumption and production.

At the level of the production center the control figures are discussed by the
management and work force under the direction of the local party and labor
union unit. Once approved, the figures return to JUCEPLAN via the consolidated enterprises, which in turn make contracts with other consolidated enterprises on the basis of the figures. At every step of the way, the data are modified
and, finally, coordinated. Meantime, trade protocols with other governments
are the first step in the fulfillment of foreign trade requirements. Subsequently,
the plan is approved by the Council of Ministers and thus becomes the law of
the land.

This overly simplified and schematic description necessarily misses the rich
details of the Cuban planning experience. Despite many changes, control of
the planning machinery has remained firmly with the center. Although the
Cuban economic planning literature is replete with phrases such as "the plan is
the work of all" and "the plan is a profoundly democratic process," and although government leaders hammer away at the theme that the workers must
not be content to be merely "spectators" but rather "actors" in the drama, the
fact remains that the role of the workers is narrowly confined.

1962, was there completed even a preliminary version of a long-run plan (1962–1965). To quote a leading JUCEPLAN official, "the 1962 plan permitted the firms and ministries to begin to exercise, although still at modest levels, central direction and planning of the economy." Throughout 1962, however, JUCEPLAN and the ministries, frequently working independently, were compelled to make "permanent revisions" of the plan.

Meanwhile, as foreign economists and technicians were helping the Cubans draw up preliminary economic plans and outlines, the government instituted a crash program to train planning cadres, to distill the past experiences of administrators and technicians into coherent guidelines, and to introduce the rudiments of Soviet planning methods to Cubans. Dozens of conferences at the local, provincial, and national levels were organized to provide a minimum of knowledge about planning techniques. MININD's planning conference in June, 1961, for example, consisted of a series of lectures which conveyed the barest information about costing, balancing, and other essentials of physical planning. The conferences culminated in a general meeting of consolidated enterprise directors and labor union and technical advisory council representatives in November, who agreed on the major tasks for the coming year, that is, raising productivity, perfecting administration, acquiring and spreading technical skills, and deepening revolutionary consciousness.

In practice, Cuba was able neither to get a workable long-term plan off the ground until 1964 nor to crash train a capable corps of planners. The invasion at the Bay of Pigs, constant military mobilization, Castro's struggle with the PSP, mounting shortages, agricultural failures, and other crises or near-crises created emergency conditions in 1962. In March of that year, the Council of Ministers created a special, superplanning authority comprising Rodríguez, Guevara, and Dorticós, whose task was to formulate immediate emergency policies to overcome the shortages. Not until the following year did the group of three begin to find a way out of the near economic chaos of 1961–1962. As for the 1962 plan itself, the island lacked the administrative capacity, data, techniques, and machinery to make the plan work. "We were all such amateurs, so ignorant at the beginning," Castro told Herbert Mathews in 1963. "But we did learn and are still learning the hard way." [26]

[6]

The most important problems of planning in Cuba between 1960 and 1964 were threefold: first, the problem of acquiring good economic data and the skills to use them; second, the problem of administration; third, the problem of centralized versus decentralized management.

The first problem was the lack of adequate planning statistics. Cuban statistics, Juan Noyola wrote, "were the most incomplete and deficient in Latin America." [27] Moreover, the kinds of available economic data were far more useful in a regulated capitalist economy than in a physically planned socialist economy. Furthermore, the flow of many of the statistical series that were available to JUCEPLAN dried up as 1960 wore on, as private organizations and agencies collected and evaluated much of the island's economic data.

A few examples will indicate the chaotic state of data collection and evaluation during this period. In 1961, various government organisms conducted population, agricultural, industrial, and housing censuses, but these were very crude and incomplete, and they did not provide the kind of regularly reported information required by the planners. Only in mid-1962 did the Ministry of Labor set up procedures for the regular reporting of hours of work, wages, prices, and so on. Again, the first reliable agricultural data, excepting information on the main export crops and new specialities such as cotton, were not available until early 1963, when INRA began to circulate internal memoranda listing changes in state-owned commodity inventories.[28] Before 1963, Cuba's planners did not have manpower

[26] Herbert Matthews, *Return to Cuba* (New York, 1963).

[27] "Aspectos Económicos de la Revolución Cubana," *Cuadernos de Ciencias Sociales y Económicas,* Comisión Nacional Cubana de la UNESCO, No. 1 (1961), p. 18.

[28] Perhaps the most important "data problem" was in the area of cost and financial management. On the first cooperatives there was an almost total absence of cost accounting. The concept of "expenditures," for example, was

"inventory" charts for the agricultural sector, and not until 1964 did JUCEPLAN complete a census of available fixed capital in industry, transport, and other branches of the economy.

Of even more significance, JUCEPLAN knew little about the actual economic costs and benefits of investment projects. In mid-1963, Guevara said that Cuba was still a long way off from adequate planning and execution of investments.[29] Even by 1964, JUCEPLAN was not able to compute rational depreciation rates in order to price investments efficiently, systematically attack the severe spare parts problem, incorporate into planning a clear notion of the utilization level of fixed plant, and, in general, allocate capital between various branches of industry in a clearly rational manner. The lack of efficient allocation of investments and other resources was particularly important in Cuba, because Castro did not choose the "forced-draft industrialization" path that would rapidly reproduce capital resources.

The second problem, closely related to the first, was one of administration. In the first place, perhaps as many as one-half of Cuba's technical personnel were in exile by mid-1961. In early 1964, according to Guevara, the majority of administrators and techni-

_____

limited to wage payments. Nor was there a regularized flow of funds from and to the operating unit. Financing was on an *ad hoc*, catch-as-catch-can basis. In the sugar sector adequate cost estimates were lacking until 1962, and not until the following year were costs allocated by individual product.

The flow of funds between state organisms and both the private and state agriculture was uneven and uncoordinated. By 1962, however, the Treasury Ministry was advising INRA on financial matters, and next year the finances of the state sector were being put on a sound basis. Each operating unit was divided into "fields" and "lots," and the cost of land preparation, planting, and so on was computed in terms of labor time. Physical goals were set and funds requested after the cost studies were made. Cash was then allocated to each operating unit from a "special income account," a common fund of each *granja*. Proceeds from sales to INRA's Commercial Department were then deposited back into the income account. In this way, the cost-income relationship was theoretically determined for each crop and operating unit, although control of investment policy lay with the general administrations. In practice, throughout 1962–1963 complaints were made that the state sector suffered from "financial mismanagement." The main reason apparently was the failure of local administrators to maintain the level of labor productivity.

[29] Speech on April 30, 1963, reproduced in *Obra Revolucionaria*, No. 12 (1963).

cians were ex-workers,[30] some of whom qualified for their posts only on the basis of political criteria. In 1963 the great majority of government statistical offices were staffed with ex-accountants and bookkeepers, due to a severe shortage of trained statisticians.

Moreover, Cuba did not even begin to solve the problem of a correct administrative style until 1964. In a penetrating article published in February, 1963, Guevara pointed out that Cuba had passed through two distinct administrative phases: first, the *"guerrillerismo"* stage; second, the phase he termed "bureaucratism."

The first extended through 1960–1961, when solutions to administrative problems were left to the free will of the individual administrators.[31] This resulted in a great deal of friction, conflicting orders and counterorders, different interpretations of the law, the lack of delegation of authority, the inability to organize work routinely, and so on. Guevara wrote that in 1961 the Council of Ministers realized that it was necessary to reorganize the state apparatus "following the planning methods of our sister Socialist countries." Quickly, the Cubans fell into the opposite error, that is, excessive bureaucracy. State organisms were overly centralized, curtailing the initiative of the administrators. According to Guevara, the basic reason was the lack of middle cadres and local and provincial administrative structures. Some local cadres kept pace with the turtle-like central administrative structure; others were more impatient and acted without regard for central administration. Hence, more and more control was lodged with the center. Briefly, there were neither central "correct or timely directives" nor local "spontaneous actions"; administration as such tended to grind to a halt. Guevara's solution was to instill the idea into Cuban administrators that maximum mobilization was required at all times, so that Cuba could reap the benefits of active, creative, and intelligent administration, which was forthcoming during the missile crisis of October, 1962.[32]

[30] Speech on February 25, 1964, reproduced in *Obra Revolucionaria*, No. 7 (1964).

[31] Reproduced in *Obra Revolucionaria*, No. 8 (1963).

[32] The following quotation indicates Castro's own response to the administration problem in a speech delivered January 2, 1965: "What fault must we eradicate? You would say bureaucratism? Then we are in absolute agreement. But how are we going to do this? By creating unemployment, laying off people?

In summary, until 1964 there was little coordination of the flow of information from one state organism to another, there was a lack of control and uniformity in the collection of information, which placed temporal and spatial comparisons on a very unsure footing, and there was no rational administrative structure or style. Perhaps the most trenchant comment came from Rafael Rodríguez: the virtue of the 1964 plan compared with the 1963 plan, he said, was that the former was ready in January, 1964. The fundamental reason was the transition from a capitalist to a socialist society and the change-over from an economy integrated into the structure of the United States economy to an economy more integrated internally. These transformations placed a tremendous burden on the island's hard-pressed administrative infrastructure. The burden was particularly heavy because, while the Cuban leaders developed a clear understanding of the limits and problems of economic and social development in the old society, until 1963, when they decided to specialize in sugar and cattle, they did not have a clear theory of how to develop a socialist export economy.

The third problem, intimately related to the second, concerned the modes of financing industry and agriculture, but in actuality ran much deeper than any mere technical issue. The problem touched to the core of the nature of the Cuban economic structure, indeed, to a controversy that concerned the meaning of the revolution itself.

Two opposing ideas of financing were put forth: first, centralized financing or "budgetary control"; second, "self-financing," which is the standard method employed in the Soviet Union and Eastern Europe.[33] Centralized financing, championed by Guevara, in es-

No! We must not do it that way. . . . It would not be correct; it would not be just; because, gentlemen, if we are going to lay off anyone, we should begin by laying ourselves off first of all, because we are the ones who created bureaucratism. Certainly, bureaucratism came from the past, but in some cases we developed it, and in others we didn't fight it in an effective way."

[33] Defending centralized financing were Guevara, Minister of Finance Luis Alvarez Ron, and the Belgium Marxist economist E. Mandel. Arrayed against them were Rafael Rodríguez, Minister of Foreign Trade A. Mora, and the French Marxist economist Charles Bettelheim. The key articles and papers in the debate are: Ernesto Guevara, "On Production Costs," *Nuestra Industria*

sence means the adaption of the system of economic accounting prevailing in a single enterprise to the Cuban economy as a whole. The banks extend interest-free credit to the individual enterprise in accordance with the national budget. "The enterprises run according to the system of a unified budget," DeSantis has written, "are . . . fairly rigidly inserted into the plan. Each of them is viewed as a *part* of a larger productive mechanism (the public sector as a whole) and the bank's role is a purely accounting one." Goods move between enterprises on the basis of physical plans, and the banks are "merely cash registers which keep track of these movements." As Guevara said, "The enterprise does not have its own capital, and consequently its income is reintegrated into the national budget." The profitability criteria is absent and the enterprise is instructed to fulfill fixed physical targets. "There is however rigid financial control over the *Empresas Consolidadas*," DeSantis continued, "whose task is to coordinate the accounts of the individual enterprises in a given sector." Finally, the worker's material incentives are confined to overtime.

In the postsocialist Cuban economy there was from the beginning an inherent bias in favor of centralized financing. The bank accounts of the firms nationalized in 1960 were placed in a Centralized Fund under the control of INRA's Department of Production. This was an emergency measure rendered necessary by the absence of alternative financing plans and machinery. Later, when the private banking system and the National Bank were consolidated, cen-

Económica, 1, No. 1 (June, 1963); "On the Concept of Value: A Reply to Some Statements on the Subject," *Nuestra Industria Económica*, 1, No. 3 (October, 1963); "Socialist Planning: Its Significance," *Cuba Socialista*, 4, No. 34 (June, 1964); Luis Alvarez Ron, "Financing as a Method of Political Development," *Nuestra Industria, Revista Económica*, No. 1, pp. 17–18; Ernest Mandel, "Market Categories in the Period of Transition," *Nuestra Industria Económica*, 2, No. 1 (June, 1964); A. Mora, "Concerning the Question of the Functioning of the Law of Value in the Cuban Economy at the Present Time," *Comercio Exterior*, June, 1963; Charles Bettelheim, "Forms and Methods of Socialist Planning and the Level of Development of the Productive Force," *Cuba Socialista*, 4, No. 32 (April, 1964). All of the above articles are cited in an excellent critical summary of the key issues in the debate by Sergio DeSantis, "The Economic Debate in Cuba," *International Socialist Journal*, 2, No. 10 (August, 1965).

tralized financing was elevated to the status of a general principle when the fund was transferred to the National Budget and the short and long-term financing of industry was turned over to the Treasury Ministry. A great deal of anarchy remained in the field of economic finance, however, and the Treasury's Budgetary Law of late 1962 was a step toward eliminating it. The law further centralized Cuba's finances, "putting the majority of the national income into the national budget," according to Treasury Minister Luis Alvarez Ron. The Treasury established one central, and six provincial, budgets and abolished the existing system of multiple budgets.

The opposing view, held by Rodríguez, Mora, and others, favored the self-financing of enterprises, or decentralized finance. Self-financing is a system under which loans are made to the individual enterprises and paid back with interest. The banks are the "nerve centers" of the network of financial controls. As DeSantis described the system,

enterprises running under the system of autonomous financing are juridically independent; they have considerable financial independence in their economic activities; the basis of their activity is profitability . . . Their management is . . . indirectly controlled by the credit institutions; the central bodies only exercise overall financial control. Products are traded between enterprises on an ordinary market basis so that products acquire the character of "goods" even within the public sector. Lastly, labor remuneration is largely on the basis of piece-rates; great importance is given to material stimuli.

In practice, self-financing developed within INRA-controlled enterprises and farms in a more or less haphazard way. In 1962, INRA's director, Rafael Rodríguez, gave the system his stamp of approval.

The defenders of self-financing put forth two pragmatic arguments in its favor: first, that their method provided for the use of material incentives, while centralized financing did not; second, that their system led to fewer bureaucratic tendencies. These pragmatic points were theoretically rooted. According to Mora and Charles Bettelheim, economic adviser to Cuba from France, although the Cuban state exercises juridical ownership over the public sector, it cannot exercise actual control; that is to say, the economic structure is not in fact "a single great state enterprise." Ownership of the means of production confers control only when capital is highly concentrated and centralized, as in an advanced capitalist economy. Large-scale, integrated enterprise is *not* the dominant form of economic organization in Cuba.

It follows, according to this line of thinking, that prices should be set by the market, although they must be modified in accordance with the sociopolitical priorities of the revolution. To put it another way, this school believes that it is impossible to abolish the Law of Value (*i.e.*, the relationship between the limited existing resources and man's growing needs) until the gap between economic resources and needs is closed. Hence, juridically independent enterprises, self-financing, and the integration of the economy by the market is the correct method of planning. Finally, according to Bettelheim, the basic cause of JUCEPLAN's administrative problems—excessive bureaucracy—is its false conception of the economic structure and the financial system appropriate to Cuba. JUCEPLAN's real lack of economic control leads to more and more regulations and therefore more bureaucracy.

In his defense of centralized financing, Guevara conceded that his system does not permit the full use of material incentives and may tend toward bureaucracy. Nevertheless, he argued that centralized management not only can work efficiently, but "*is the mode of being of socialist society*, its definitive category and the point at which man's conscience finally manages to synthesize and direct the economy toward its goal, which is the full liberation of humanity within the framework of communal society [italics added]."

Guevara agreed that Cubans are not in fact a part of the same interrelated physical network, but only a monetary one. He also admitted that large-scale, integrated enterprises are not characteristic of the Cuban economy. Nevertheless, he asserted that Cuba is a small island with good communications and transportation and that self-financing is unnecessary for efficient planning. Moreover, he said that Cuba is a micro-unit in the world economy, an export economy, whose internal prices must bear a close relationship with international prices, even at the expense of a lack of correspondence between prices and costs internally. Prices must thus be determined administratively, not by supply and demand conditions within Cuba. Guevara thus believed in the idea of decentralization on a *world* scale.

His other line of analysis placed key emphasis on "consciousness," a shared sense of working together toward common goals. He argued that the transition from capitalism to socialism "distorts" the Law of Value and "makes it rather difficult to use it intelligently." Furthermore, he pointed out that under socialism there is (or should be) a tendency for the Law of Value to disappear, and that it is the task of revolutionary consciousness to hurry this tendency along. He stressed that the struggle to eliminate market values and to usher in communism is a day-to-day battle and must begin at once. In effect, he said that centralized management and financing means planning by all the people for all the people. As a staunch defender of social incentives over material incentives, he insisted that self-financing would tend to set enterprise against enterprise, divide the working class, and make it extremely difficult to develop a "high collective consciousness" among the workers. DeSantis summed up the debate correctly when he wrote that "behind the confrontation between the system of a unified budget and the system of independent financing, the controversy had one main preoccupation; the clash between a mainly economic conception of socialist development and an all-round revolutionary one." As of early 1964, the issue remained unresolved.

[7]

In conclusion, we summarize and evaluate the results of Cuban industrial planning during the period 1959–1963. This five-year period naturally falls into two subperiods: first, 1959–1960, when the economy was basically integrated by market forces; second, 1961–1963, when the economy was subject to increasing control by the Cuban planners.

As we know, the first accomplishment of industrial planning in the earlier period was the building-up of foreign exchange reserves to approximately $175 million by mid-1960. To be sure, this accomplishment was mainly owing to general restrictions on imports of consumer durable goods and other nonessential commodities and services. But it was also caused by an expansion of import substitute production, arising from expanding demand, freer credits, the utilization of idle industrial productive capacity, and a reduction in unemployment and underemployment.

According to official estimates, industrial production rose by 17 per cent and 29 per cent in 1959 and 1960, respectively.[34] These estimates probably overstate the rise in production, due to the absence of hard data and a central statistical collection agency during this period. There is corroborative evidence, however, that 1959 was in nearly every respect a better year industrially than 1958. National Bank estimates show sharp increases in the production of electric power, beverages, tobacco products, containers, tires, rubber footwear, oil products, and other commodities, and a decline in only one listed commodity, cement.

Supplementary data for 1960 are largely unavailable, due to the break in the established data-collection system during that year. It is difficult to believe that industrial output rose by nearly 30 per cent in the context of damaging stoppages in mining, tire and tube, textile, paint, detergent, and glass container production, and of the bitter economic war between Cuban and foreign businessmen and the United States government, on the one hand, and the Revolutionary Government, on the other. Isolated evidence does point to strong gains in other sectors, however, most notably, pharmaceuticals,[35] oil products,[36] beverages, tobacco products, and probably textiles.

The second accomplishment of industrial planning between 1959

[34] Juan Noyola, "La Revolución Cubana y sus Efectos en el Desarrollo Económico," *Trimestre Económico*, 28, No. 3 (July–September, 1961). The figures include sugar production, but the distortion if any is not great, since neither 1959 nor 1960 were unusually good or bad years.

In August, 1963, the author attempted to supplement production data for the years 1959–1963 by collecting output figures from each consolidated enterprise. A lack of time and funds prevented the completion of the project.

[35] *Trabajo Cuba*, 2, No. 5 (May, 1961), pp. 60–64. In the thirteen leading firms the value of output rose by 26.6 per cent, while prices were stable or declining.

[36] The Cuban Petroleum Institute produced 24.9 million barrels of petroleum products in 1959 and 26.8 million in 1960.

and 1960 was the expansion of employment. Appendix B provides a detailed analysis of changes in employment, unemployment, and underemployment in Cuba during this period. In summary, between the fall of 1958 and the fall of 1960, the total unemployment rate dropped from 15 per cent to 12 per cent. More significant, the official rate of underemployment in November of 1958, 1959, and 1960 was 28 per cent, 26 per cent, and 25 per cent, respectively. That these changes grossly underestimate the real decline in underemployment is suggested by data drawn from Zeitlin's sample of Cuban industrial workers.[37] As of the summer of 1962, 86 per cent of the workers who were employed less than six months annually before the revolution were employed ten or more months, and 78 per cent of the workers who were employed between seven and nine months prior to 1959 were working for ten months or more afterwards. These gains were partly offset by the increase in underemployment of those workers who were on the job for ten months or more before the revolution.

In short, the Revolutionary Government during the first two years of the revolution—hardly a propitious time for economic planning—made a good beginning in the direction of solving the two problems that the government itself considered crucial, foreign exchange and unemployment. To be sure, government planners paid a price for this success: severe inflationary pressures building up within the island. Any summary evaluation of industrial planning would be incomplete without at least brief mention of the inflation problem.

A number of factors combined to generate inflationary pressures. First, as we know, private spending steadily mounted through 1959–1960, because of wage increases and reductions in unemployment and underemployment. Private wages and salaries paid in the first eight months of 1958, 1959, and 1960 were $494.8 million, $577.2 million, and $741.5 million, respectively.[38] Rent and other price reductions added to the expansion of private purchasing power. Second, between 1959 and 1960 the government tightened

---

[37] Maurice Zeitlin, *Revolutionary Politics and the Cuban Working Class* (Princeton, 1967), Table 2.6, p. 60.

[38] *Cuba, Económica and Financiera*, 35, Nos. 413–415 (August, September, 1960), p. 4.

up on imports, reducing outlets for the expenditure of new purchasing power. Third, inventories were increasingly depleted, and excess capacity steadily reduced. Finally, and perhaps most importantly, the government budget showed larger and larger deficits. In fiscal year 1959–1960, the deficit was on the order of $290 million.[39] The combination of these inflationary forces was much more powerful than the countervailing trends, specifically, the relatively modest expansion of private and public industrial and other production.

The government was thus compelled to extend price controls into nearly every sector of the economy. At first, price controls on basic foods, drugs, and other necessities were designed to preserve the rising standard of living of the poorer peasants and workers.[40] These first controls thus constituted a kind of selective anti-inflationary policy. As time wore on, however, price controls were placed on nearly every item entering into internal commodity trade. In addition to price controls, government agencies also restricted the expansion of private credit, as well as taking a number of minor anti-inflationary steps.[41] There was, however, no easy cure for the sup-

---

[39] According to PAE, 1962, the Cuban government budget for 1957–1962, in millions of pesos, was as follows:

	1957–58	1958–59	1959–60	1961	1962 (est.)
Income	$403.5	$395.8	$401.4	$ 734.7	$1,103.1
Expenditures	364.6	441.3	690.0	1,468.2	1,252.6

[40] In January, 1959, the Commerce Ministry was authorized to retain commodities in the event that inspections revealed price or weight infractions. The prices of domestically produced and imported drugs were lowered in March. In May prices of staple foodstuffs were frozen, and 10 per cent and 20 per cent ceilings on profit margins of wholesalers and retailers, respectively, were decreed. Official prices had already been established on milk, rice, bread, and beef products. The May law added to the list butter, pork, potatoes, cheese, and other items, including consumer goods such as soap. In September prices of a wide range of imports were frozen, as well as more home produced goods. In December children's foods and other items were added to the list. Prices were also raised on some commodities to protect living standards; for example, the National Tobacco Federation and the tobacco workers voted to raise wages and final product prices in February. In May, Castro personally announced a 22.5–28 per cent increase in raw tobacco prices. (Sources are chiefly the *Official Gazette* for 1959 and 1960. Ministry of Commerce resolutions were the legal authority for the vast majority of price controls.)

[41] The total supply of money began to rise at an increasingly rapid rate from July, 1959, until about a year later, when the rate of increase fell off as a

pressed inflation; even in 1963, after significant price increases on most commodities, excessive purchasing power in the hands of the population remained very high.

During the next period, 1961–1963, the accomplishments of industrial planning consisted of the continual utilization of previously idle capacity and the construction of new productive facilities, both of which contributed to a rise in industrial production.

As of early 1964, Cuba had completed twenty-two new industrial plants and had thirty-eight more under construction, most of them near completion.[42] From 1959 to 1961, new facilities were limited chiefly to small-scale consumer goods factories, and only seven plants were completed, mainly because of the halt in private investment. In 1961–1962 the government finished twelve more plants, and in 1963, three additional factories. Of the thirty-eight additional units under construction in early 1964, the great majority of them were well over 50 per cent finished. Twenty plants were metals or machinery units manufacturing small tools, machine parts, molds and dies, items such as pressure washers and ball bearings, and so on. Next in importance were eight plants classified as "chemicals," which included plastics, plywood, superphosphates, electrodes, and insulin. There were also three mineral-processing units, a similar number of factories producing construction materials, and one textile and food-processing plant each. The investments begun in 1961–1962 thus had a definite character: they were relatively small-scale, integrated units manufacturing a highly diverse selection of capital goods or intermediate goods and materials.

---

consequence of a decline in private credits and a tightening of public spending. Of total new credits created in 1959, the government accounted for about three-quarters; in 1960, nearly all. This should not be interpreted to mean that the government failed to try to tap new and old sources of savings, or that all public spending in this period was potentially inflationary. A number of new measures opened up fresh sources of financing: the demonetization of 500 and 1,000 peso notes; "taxes" levied by the Ministry for the Recovery of Stolen State Property; private donations to INRA; and the 4 per cent "industrialization tax" on wages and salaries.

[42] Sources for these estimates are *PAE*, 1962, Tables 7.5, 7.6; various speeches at the 1961 Production Conference; *Nuestra Industria*, 4, No. 1 (January, 1964).

As we have seen, however, Cuba's industrialization lacked direction and over-all rationality. Of these facilities, few were in themselves ill-conceived or badly planned. Each could satisfy one or more of the standard economic tests; every one of them produced an import substitute or utilized some local raw materials. Compared with prerevolutionary industry, these facilities were relatively inte-

Table 6. Cuban industrial production (excluding sugar)— percentage change from the previous year

Sector	1959	1960	1962	1963 planned	1963	1964 planned
Mining			+21	+97	+6	+35
Metals and machinery			+23	+47	+2	+22
Construction materials			+9	+22	−8	+24
Petroleum products			+11	+16	+1	+3
Chemicals			+30	+26	+11	+40
Textiles and leather products			+7	+38	+22	+19
Food			+4	+15	+10	+14
Beverages and tobacco			−4	+27	+9	+12
Electricity			−7	+17	+3	+8
Other			+71	+27	−2	+28
Total Industrial Production	+17	+29	+12 [a]	+27	+8 [b]	+19

Sources: 1962 and 1963 planned: Cuba, JUCEPLAN, *Informe Sobre el Plan de 1963* (Havana, December 27, 1962), p. 26.

1963 and 1964 planned: Cuba, JUCEPLAN, *Informe Sobre las cifras de control para la elaboracion del Plan de 1964* (Havana, June 25, 1963), p. 28.

1959 and 1960: Juan Noyola, "La Revolución Cubana y sus Efectos en el Desarrollo Económico," *Trimestre Económico*, 28, No. 3 (July–September, 1961). Figures for 1959 and 1960 include sugar output, but the distortion is not great, since these were neither unusually good nor bad years.

[a] The value of Gross Industrial Output in 1962 was 15 per cent higher than in 1961 (PAE, 1962, Table 6.1). Thus, prices rose on the order of 3 per cent.

[b] Preliminary estimate based on first six months of 1963. Later data show that production goals were surpassed in leather products, tanneries, paints, matches, cigarettes and cigars, and were nearly met in beer and malts, ferrous metals, twisted tobacco, flour and paper. As the actual vs. planned totals imply, the production plan was only about 84 per cent fulfilled ("Analisis de la ejecucion del plan de 1963 en el Ministerio de Industrias," *Nuestra Industria, Revista Económica*, 2, No. 6 (April, 1964).

grated. As a whole, however, Cuba's investment policy lacked general direction, an underlying rationality. On the one hand, Cuban planners hesitated to place too much emphasis on heavy industry because of the limited Cuban market. On the other hand, they could not defend a policy which looked to produce locally the thousands of consumer items that Cuba previously imported from the United States. As we have seen, the new agricultural and industrial investment policies of 1963–1964 were an attempt to solve this problem.

The effect of the fuller utilization of existing industrial capacity and the construction of new factories on production itself is summarized in Table 6.

With neither a plan nor planning machinery, and having inherited the problems created by "economic sabotage" in 1960, the island must have witnessed a decline in industrial production in 1961, perhaps of a fairly large magnitude. There are absolutely no reliable statistics for this year; there are only impressionistic data which universally support the view that a wide range of shortages appeared: soap, corks, razor blades, bottle openers, bottles, toothpaste, and other items. The roots of the shortages were complex and impossible to untangle: demand for wage goods had risen rapidly in 1960 and a little more in 1961, and in some sectors increases in supplies were insufficient; the embargo deprived Cuba of materials and spare parts and thus was a contributing factor; the economy was operated neither along market principles nor the lines of a planned economy and, inevitably, was characterized by many temporary irrationalities. Finally, there was the problem of distribution.

The basic change in the distribution system was the substitution of state purchasing and marketing agencies for the old system of brokers, speculators, warehousemen, wholesalers, and retailers. The nationalization of distribution extended over a four-year period (1959–1962), gaining maximum momentum in late 1960 and 1961. One can imagine the adequacy of the "supply" of efficient distribution facilities provided by the private sector from 1959 to mid-1960, and by the public sector by 1964. On the other side, the "demand" for distribution facilities fluctuated widely, being greatest, as it turned out, at precisely the moment when the "supply" was smallest, in 1961–1962. In this period, when production bottlenecks were most severe, extra stocks and a careful inventory policy were required. To take another example, the administrators of Cuba's distribution facilities should have estimated the extra demand for one commodity given a decline in the production of another (where the two are substitutes). But distribution, just nationalized, was most irrational at the moment when it was required to be most rational.

The first major change in distribution was the creation of the people's stores, of which there were 1,400 by March, 1960, the vast majority in the rural districts. A few were newly constructed, the rest were set up in existing farm buildings, expropriated and purchased company and other stores. Another 500 or so were added, together with over 75 warehouses, by March, 1961. The people's stores were designed to bring basic commodities within reach of the small peasants and rural workers. Their one flaw was that the first outlets on the early cooperatives were reserved for cooperative members, leading to some commodity speculation. The second step was the construction of 60 new rural commercial centers and a number of supermarkets during 1960; 150 more were planned for 1961, but, like other projects, materials shortages reduced the number actually completed to a handful. It is difficult to assess the degree to which all of these new outlets displaced private business. By mid-1961, sales were running at an annual rate of $150 million to over 400,000 "customers" (families), with an average sale of $375. Thus, about one-fifth of Cuba's rural families probably utilized the new facilities.

The government continued to attempt to rationalize distribution throughout 1960–1964. Wholesale operations were consolidated, urban middlemen were eliminated, hundreds of new farm and market roads were constructed, and refrigeration facilities were rapidly expanded. But problems piled up faster than new plans could be realized. INRA, for example, took over the central market in Havana in the spring of 1961, when production bottlenecks were narrowing, and it was not until many months later that the market began to function at all smoothly. To take another instance, in the fall of 1961 intermediate warehouses were bypassed in order to reduce the costs of distribution, and foods (and food products) distributed to hotels and restaurants were delivered directly from INRA warehouses. This shift temporarily worsened the situation. Bottlenecks, together with rigidities in distribution, created an active black market, which, in turn, placed a larger burden on the distribution system.[43] Large-scale speculation was eradicated by the summer of the year, but "informal" black markets dotted the urban centers well into 1962. It was not until July, 1962, for example, that an attempt was made to displace Cuba's ambulant merchants (many of whom were small-scale speculators).[44] The soap situation illustrates in microcosm the economic history of this period. A lack of raw materials previously imported from the United States created production difficulties, but the simplification of production lists resulted in small increases in output. Nevertheless, demand rose faster than supply, and, what was worse, expectations as to future supplies were very unfavorable. This created the conditions for a flourishing black market whose flames were fed further by "political" hoarding by counterrevolutionaries.

By 1962, as our table shows, Cuban industry had recovered somewhat, although probably not reaching 1960 levels until 1963. One exception to the 1962 recovery was transport, where the capital stock declined steadily. One-quarter of the island's busses were out of operation for want of spare parts late in 1961. Only one-half of Cuba's 1,400 railroad passenger cars were functioning in 1962 (although the number of passengers carried rose somewhat) [45] and total freight traffic fell by almost 15 per cent from 1961 to 1962.[46] The difficulties blocking efficient planning, however, were still severe, as a comparison of planned and actual production for 1963, shown in Table 5, reveals. Planned output for 1964 was put at 29 per cent and 19 per cent above 1962 and 1963 levels, respectively. Taking the former year as the base, the Central Planning Board

[43] See, for example, Castro's speeches of March 13 and 15, 1961.
[44] Displaced merchants were given subsidies and promises of eventual jobs.
[45] "El transporte terrestre," *Trabajo Cuba,* 3, No. 12 (July, 1962), p. 19.
[46] *PAE,* 1962, Table 8.1.

(JUCEPLAN) counted on increases of 5 per cent and 24 per cent in productivity and employment, respectively.[47] On the performance of Cuban industry in 1963, these targets (one could hardly term them "plans") were no doubt overestimates; industrial production in 1964 was probably no more than 8 to 10 per cent higher than 1963. There would be mainly the problem of reviving those sectors —metals and machinery, construction materials, and petroleum products—which lagged behind in 1963, and which, unlike chemicals, would not receive special emphasis under the "new" economic policy announced in the summer of 1963. As for mining operations, technical developments chiefly would determine the future of the industry. Planned 1964 and 1965 outputs were considerably higher than actual 1963 levels, and while nickel and manganese production seemed satisfactory, by late 1963, Cuba, with the aid of Soviet technicians, still had failed to discover an economical separation process for iron.

[8]

What of the basic problems of industrial planning that remained after the adoption of the "new course" in 1963–1964? A broad view of Cuba's planning system reveals that any substantial improvement in economic planning would hinge on a redefinition of the island's administrative-political structure and the introduction of some form of workers' self-management. These steps would clarify the questions of political representation and power, and economic decision-making.

On the one hand, perhaps the most forbidding barrier to better, more efficient economic and administrative coordination and regionally balanced processes of capital formation is the lack of a territorial administrative structure.[48] Municipal government, along the lines of those in advanced capitalist countries, was simply unknown in the old Cuba, and a largely neglected issue in the new. Decades of systematic rigging of local elections, of overly centralized govern-

---

[47] *1964 Plan*, p. 69.

[48] René Saladrigas, "Criterios para una reestructuración político-administrativa de Cuba," *Cuba Socialista*, 3, No. 17 (January, 1963), pp. 42, 44.

ment (the central government took well over 90 per cent of total tax revenues) and the corresponding "Havana mentality," and of foreign domination or control of internal affairs, all reduced local government to the status of poor orphan. In 1959–1960 the decentralization of the ministries of Education and Labor turned over certain functions to local authorities and helped to remedy this state of affairs. But a broad attack on the problem has never been mounted. Thus, INRA, MINCIN, JUCEI, and other organisms arbitrarily created their own local administrations. Post-1959 Cuba in effect developed numerous local governments that overlapped with regard to territory and function. Only their structures were distinct. The only territorial division maintained in common was the province. Thus, economic plans drawn up by separate ministries were made compatible only on the national and provincial levels. In essence, a total restructuring of Cuba's economic, administrative, and political units—in short, total integration—was required.

Before the island's political units could be restructured, a second problem would have to be resolved: political representation. Two questions are at issue here: first, the question of the personal political relationships among the handful of men who lead the revolution; second, that of local self-management or self-government. The former has importance for the final investment and other priorities laid down at the beginning of the planning year. As Cuban planning actually works, JUCEPLAN's authority is restricted to more or less technical questions (narrowly defined), and the minister with the most authority and prestige is most likely to obtain approval for his projects, economic or socioeconomic rationality notwithstanding. This is one explanation of the relative neglect of transportation, to take one instance, and the favorable position of the Ministry of Industries. Yet so long as Cuba remains at the center of continual international political crises, it is difficult to imagine the original key revolutionary figures divesting themselves of their *de facto* authority.

Less difficult to foresee is the introduction of some form of worker self-management. It needs repeating that the debate over the issue of budgetary control as opposed to self-financing did not revolve around the question of workers' self-government. This has never been a central public issue in revolutionary Cuba. Yet the great stress placed on economic and social equality and a unified working class necessarily inhibits the systematic introduction of market socialism along Yugoslavian lines or the use of material incentives to the degree of the Soviet and Eastern European experience. On the other side, the fact that Cuban workers have little or nothing to say about the general contours of the plan and are restricted in their participation to their small "arc" of the plan will continue to mean a general lack of interest in matters relating to planning, investment, and production, and will continue to restrict support for the revolution to participation in the militia and the mass organizations. There is no way out of this dilemma but to introduce working systems of worker self-government that would reach right up into the Council of Ministers itself. Such a course would represent a sharp departure from practices in other socialist economies and a fundamental contribution on Cuba's part to the theory and practice of socialism.

Yet the political-administrative integration of Cuba with or without workers' self-management is not sufficient without local economic integration. The crucial fact remains that Cuba is an export economy. Most of the island's economic resources are still oriented to primary product exports; many of Cuba's physical facilities, such as harbors, dock facilities, warehouses, and transportation networks, are still oriented to the old United States-Cuban trade, and most of the island's industrial equipment is North American in origin. It will take decades to completely correct this situation. Of even greater importance, Cuba still does not have anything resembling a balanced industrial-agricultural structure. Cuba's economic dependence on the European countries can only increase. "Socialism in one island" effectively means "socialism in one industry" of the world capitalist system.

For Cuba, therefore, the state of revolutionary struggles elsewhere in Latin and Central America is not only a matter of burning political concern; in the last analysis, it is a matter of winning total economic independence from the large powers. In short, in the absence of a Caribbean or Latin American Socialist Commonwealth, which would provide the basis for the planned allocation of economic resources over the region as a whole with the aim of dramatically improving the material and social condition of the Latin peoples, Cuba will no doubt remain an export economy, albeit a progressive one from the standpoint of the majority of Cubans.

[10]

The Political Economy
of Cuban Socialism

[1]

In the preceding chapters we have put forth two major theses. First, we have seen that Cuban economic stagnation and underdevelopment before 1959 was attributable to the cartelization of agriculture, monopolistic industrial organization and practices, and the subordination of the Cuban economy to the United States economy. Historically, Cuban governments attempted to apply political solutions to economic problems, but in the context of the balance of forces of the island's economic classes and interest groups, state economic policy was by and large nonproductive, wasteful, and corrupt. State economic policy therefore intensified the all-pervasive economic inefficiencies and irrationalities characteristic of the private sector. In short, Cuban capitalism as a whole was an irrational economic system.

Second, it was shown that the leaders of the Cuban Revolution were aware of the major economic problems, together with the general technical or practical solutions to these problems. Of far more significance, the revolutionaries were willing to carry out these solutions in practice, no matter what the political repercussions or implications. While they were not at first ideologically committed to socialism, their attitude toward private property in land and the means of production was highly pragmatic. They were prepared to "do whatever needed to be done" to promote on-going social and economic development, even if this meant the rapid nationalization of land and industry and the introduction of socialist planning. Thus, the revolution developed within narrow historical limits; given the goals of the revolution's leaders, the choices open to them at crucial moments were few.

Placed in this frame of reference, the emergence of a socialist revolution between 1959 and 1961 is easily comprehended. Socialism was both *possible* and *suitable* for closely related reasons. Socialism was possible because of the composition and character of Cuba's economic classes. Cuba's middle classes were relatively large compared with many other Latin American countries but were small in comparison with Cuba's urban and rural proletariat and small farmers. Fragmented, dependent, and demoralized, the middle classes were unable to systematically employ state power for their own ends. Cuban governments and the state bureaucracy were made up of timeservers, opportunists, and thieves. For these reasons, there was no significant organized resistance to the rapid socialization of the Cuban economy.

Related to this was the fact that large numbers of people, including manufacturers, well-to-do farmers, merchants, and other groups within the local middle classes, were dissatisfied with the old Cuba and failed to withhold support for many original Revolutionary Government measures that sought to get the economy off dead center. In the heat of the social revolution it was difficult for many Cubans to distinguish between reform measures and policies that went to the heart of the prevailing property relationships. For these reasons the Revolutionary Government had near unanimous support until the political initiative had shifted altogether to the revolutionaries, that is, until it was too late to even attempt to salvage Cuban capitalism.

Socialism was suitable and desirable for Cuba because of the failure of Cuban capitalism, the decades of social and economic backwardness. Cuba's socioeconomic institutions were political by-products of the composition, outlook, and balance of class forces. It is in this sense that what was possible merges into what was desirable, and it was this synthesis that gives Cuban socialism the air of inevitability.

[2]

In this chapter we take up the politics of Cuban socialism, the specific process by which a revolutionary guerrilla army and a broad-based, nonideological political movement were transformed into a Marxist-Leninist socialist party. Early in 1959, the Revolutionary Government consisted of a nineteen-man Cabinet, the National Bank and other key economic command posts, and the Rebel Army. Quasi-public institutions included the labor unions, the various professional associations, the farmers' organizations, and a number of student groups. By early 1960 only five of the original nineteen Cabinet members remained or were retained in their posts.[1] Revolutionaries replaced reformers in the National Bank and other economic agencies. The Rebel Army purged itself of anti-Communist elements. Leadership of the trade unions was in the hands of revolutionaries in the 26th of July Movement and Communists. Finally, in the professional, farmer, student, and other associations a struggle for control raged between revolutionaries and reformers. We explore the causes and consequences of these political changes in terms of the frame of reference we have established in the rest of this work.

The basic source of these political conflicts was the issue of ownership and control of private property in the means of production, and the uses to which private property could and should be put. No one within either the revolutionary or reform camp perceived the revolutionary process in exactly the same way at any given moment, nor could anyone's perceptions fail to change as the revolution progressed, but the issue of private property above all others determined whether or not these perceptions were acted upon and the direction these actions took. Cuban society divided along class lines over this issue, and this division was reproduced in the Revolutionary Government, the private associations, and state agencies.

The struggle over the proper role of private property in the revolution incorporated four distinct tendencies of varying force. In the first place, a small minority of Cubans and foreigners who collaborated with (or were sympathetic to) the political revolution against

---

[1] These were Regino Boti, Raúl Cepero Bonilla, Osvaldo Dorticós, Augusto Martínez Sánchez, and Armando Hart.

Batista marooned themselves on the tiny island of absolute property rights in the surging ocean of reform, regulation, and protection that first swept over Cuba in the 1930's. As we know, corporatism, or political capitalism, found ideological expression in the 1940 Constitution and was implemented extensively during the 1940's and 1950's. In the first months of 1959, more reforms and controls were imposed on the economy and quickly alienated this group from Revolutionary Government goals and policy. These businessmen and executives welcomed the elimination of graft and corruption, which penalized efficient business operations, and the end of the Batista terror, which improved the climate for foreign and local investors. They were cool or hostile to other changes that the government ushered in during the first half of 1959.[2] Wedded either to *laissez faire* principles or to the principle of autonomy of operations in local or foreign business operations, this section of the middle classes was disturbed by the main course of events from the moment the dictatorship fell. At no time, however, did this group figure importantly in the revolutionary process within Cuba. These men were in a position similar to those monarchists in 1850 who saw in Napoleon III the possibility of returning to a past historical era but whose aspirations history itself had already made irrelevant.

In the second place, the vast majority of the middle classes who identified with or joined the 26th of July Movement or the Civic Resistance Movement—politicians, businessmen, professionals, editors, and others—accepted and defended the system of private property, conceived of the revolution's main problem as the alleviation rather than the meeting of pressing social needs, and sought to ameliorate rather than eliminate social antagonisms. Many were disinterested reformers, most were openly anti-Communist, and nearly all identified themselves with Western democracy. Politically insecure, this large, amorphous group had neither an independent political base nor the confidence of Castro and his guerrillas. These men, however, were molded by a tradition of political capitalism which gave to private property considerable *social* content or meaning. Examples included the "permanency rights" won by the cane growers,

---

[2] This judgment is based on extensive personal contacts in Cuba, but nevertheless is still meant to be provisional.

permanent job rights acquired by organized labor, and the "obligation" of the government to intervene or seize nonoperational firms (see below).

These reformers played a role in the revolution during 1959 and early 1960 as government planners and technicians and spokesmen for various middle-class groups. Many of them were radicalized by their personal revolutionary experiences, including Castro's obviously sincere interest in improving the social and economic condition of the masses of Cubans, the resistance of many businessmen and others to government policy, and the negative stance of the United States toward the revolution. Most of them, however, fell out with the revolution over the property issue (for example, the agrarian reform, the urban reform, the seizures of business, and the nationalization of industry) and over the break in relations with the United States. Only then did they raise specifically political issues and denounce the revolution for its "illegality" and "unconstitutionality." In the first months of 1959, the reformers accepted with few reservations the trials of Batistiano "war criminals," the modifications of the Constitution, the dissolution of Congress, the purge and reorganization of the judiciary, the postponement of elections, and the transfer of legislative power to the Council of Ministers.

Thirdly, there was the PSP (Communist party). Throughout most of 1957–1958, the PSP's official position on the guerrilla struggle was either negative or standoffish. Legalized in early 1959, most of the party's energies in the first half of that year apparently went into the struggle with the 26th of July unionists over the control of the labor unions. Only in the last half of 1959 did Castro ally himself with the PSP.

The PSP was ideologically committed to the abolition of the private property system, but the party had a "go slow" attitude at crucial stages of the revolution. The party at first opposed the collective features of the agrarian reform and apparently warned Castro not to move too hastily during the period of mass expropriation of industry late in 1960. The PSP's opposition to deep-going socialist policies was probably due to tactical considerations and fear and timidity in roughly equal proportions.

Lastly, there were the revolutionaries under the leadership of

Castro. The key revolutionaries were the Granma guerrillas, the leaders of the urban underground, the survivors of the Moncada attack in 1953, and the leaders of the Student Directorate. The revolutionaries accepted Castro's leadership without question, enjoyed absolute political initiative in 1959, and have retained initiative and power down to the present. Of the survivors of the Granma landing, only one man, Ifigenio Almenjeiro, was not in a government post in 1964. It cannot be stressed too much that during the entire course of the revolution, the agreement of Castro, and thus the other revolutionaries, was the key factor in acquiring support for any program put forth by any other group.

The revolutionaries held two basic beliefs that distinguished them from the other groups and individuals: first, the belief in armed struggle; second, the belief in carrying out their program no matter what the consequences. In particular, the revolutionaries were the only organized group in Cuba unwilling to limit the "attack" on private property during 1959–1960 to placing more restraints and conditions on its use. Neither "leftist" nor "reformist" ideological binds hampered the revolutionaries' political effectiveness. On the one hand, many of them suspected PSP's motives and had little use for Communist strategy or tactics. On the other hand, they also had reservations about the reformers' willingness to "do what needed to be done." Although many of the reformers supported the war against Batista, the revolutionaries were aware that the middle-class professional and other organizations had sought a negotiated solution to the struggle, partly to end the bloodshed as soon as possible and partly to cut the ground out from under the guerrillas.

Nor did the revolutionaries allow themselves to get bogged down in "correct" procedure or excessive legality. The seizure of business was carried out in keeping with the practical, day-to-day exigencies of the revolution, not in accordance with established, traditional, or legal procedures. In effect, Castro and the revolutionaries defined as "subversive" any right-wing or left-wing position or policy that was nonpragmatic. Again, Castro had and maintained the political initiative from the very beginning and thus personally exercised influence on the scope and pace of the revolution. In particular, the division between reformers and revolutionaries that arose over the property issue was neither avoided nor allowed to develop too fast and get out of hand.[3]

[3]

The first and most important major attack on private property was the Agrarian Reform Law of May, 1959. We have seen that the mill owners, the large farmers, and the ranchers responded unfavorably to many specific provisions of the law, although they confined their opposition to press statements, manifestoes, and demonstrations. Those moderates in the Cabinet who identified with rural propertied classes considered the law to be the first and most significant "betrayal" of the revolution. In the words of one reformer, the Agrarian Reform Law "subverted" the existing property relations.[4] For their part, the revolutionaries saw the agrarian reform as the revolution's basic law. How and why did these widely different interpretations of the reform arise?

One of the tributaries of the Agrarian Reform Law was Law No. 3, decreed by the Rebel Army on October 10, 1958, and co-authored by the moderate Sori Marin, Minister of Agriculture in 1959.[5] Article 2 promised all farm operators cultivating fewer than 27.2 hectares a plot of land of at least that size free of charge. As we know, this provision was incorporated into the May, 1959, Agrarian Reform Law, and where contiguous land was available it was implemented. Article 6 of the October decree provided expropriated landowners with compensation and was also contained in the May, 1959, law, although, with a handful of exceptions, it was not complied with. Nowhere does the October law deal seriously with the related prob-

---

[3] A split between a *unified* 26th of July Movement and the PSP, with Fidel coming out finally in favor of the latter, is sheer fiction. The 26th of July Movement did have a program, but it was made up of a highly diversified group of men and women, and it was not a "movement" in the sense of organization, regular meetings, discipline, etc. In effect, Castro made the 26th of July Movement important when he formed the militia in the spring of 1960.

[4] Aurleliano Sánchez Arango, "Situación de los campesinos y obreros dentre de la reforma agraria," *Cuadernos*, No. 47 (Paris, 1961), p. 37.

[5] Ley No. 3, October 10, 1958, Departamento Legal, Sección Asesoría de las Delegaciones de Zonas Reforma Agraria (Havana, 1959).

lems of foreign properties or the latifundium. The vague reference to these issues in the Introduction raised more questions than it could answer.[6]

Reformers and revolutionaries came to an agreement on Law No. 3 for fundamentally different reasons. The former threw their weight behind it because it gave private property greater social content by providing that Cuba's *minifundistas* be brought up to the "basic minimum" of 27.2 hectares and because it strengthened private agriculture. The reformers also accepted the law because it failed to make explicit the fate of the plantations and giant ranches. The guerrillas favored the law because its provisions were appropriate to the conditions of the small Oriente tenant farmer. The Rebel Army championed their cause against Batista's Rural Guard, exploitative middlemen, and local landowners and, in turn, depended on the goodwill of the peasants.

The response of the two groups to the May, 1959, decree was thus bound to be widely divergent. Law No. 3 was written with the condition of a small sector of Cuban agriculture in mind. The Agrarian Reform Law was written with the aim of reorganizing the entire rural political economy. The former was wholly pro-property rights and pro-small farming. The latter was necessarily more radical, because the Oriente peasants were not "typical" Cuban farmers and their properties were not "typical" farms. The three important radical aspects were the provisions that limited the size of the plantations and ranches,[7] encouraged the formation of rural cooperatives,

---

[6] According to the introduction to the law: "It will be the task of the future government of the Republic to dictate an additional law to fulfill Article 90 [treating the latifundium] of the 1940 Constitution." It is true that the Cuban Constitution of 1940 established a legal basis for limiting the amount of land that any individual could own. Article 90 is similarly vague, and consequently any reference to it may be considered devoid of any real content. Article 90 merely "permitted the fixing by law of the maximum amount of land to be held by a person or entity" and stated that means shall be taken to "restrictively limit the acquisition and possession of land by foreign persons and companies and . . . to revert the land to Cubans." See "Agrarian Revolution in Cuba," *Foreign Agriculture,* Foreign Agricultural Service, U.S. Department of Agriculture, 24 (March, 1960), p. 5.

[7] As we saw, this step was authorized by the 1940 Constitution, but ignored in practice. Until 1959, there were apparently only five cases in which the government expropriated estate land ("Agrarian Revolution in Cuba," pp. 5–6).

and created INRA, the powerful state-within-a-state. Guevara and Raúl Castro (not to speak of the Communists) at first opposed the collective aspect of the law, although other radicals anticipated this aspect some months earlier.[8] As we know, many national 26th of July labor union leaders also opposed the law. For many reformers, the agrarian reform's attack on private property was the breaking point. Cabinet members holding the State, Agriculture, Public Welfare, and Interior portfolios resigned in protest; they were replaced partly by revolutionaries and partly by anti-Communist reformers who supported the law.

The second important crisis in the division between reformers and revolutionaries came in the last half of 1959. As we have seen, the implementation of the Agrarian Reform Law was more deep-going than the law itself, particularly with regard to the cattle ranches. In the summer of 1959, Major Huber Matos, a Rebel Army officer who had not fought with the guerrillas but who supplied them with reinforcements and arms, was INRA's chief in the cattle province of Camaguey. Matos was a militant anti-Communist and also apparently did not support, much less initiate, many aspects of the Agrarian Reform Law. These were especially relevant in Camaguey, which was dominated by a relatively few large ranches and plantations; the basic question was the appropriate mode of collective exploitation of the land, not whether the land should be worked privately or cooperatively. Moreover, Matos' position was particularly sensitive because, as we have seen, Camaguey was faced with a serious economic "crisis of demand." By all accounts, Matos failed to carry out the reform law and devoted much of his time to anti-Communist education and propaganda within the Rebel Army. "In August, 1959," one scholar has written, "the writer was informed in a conversation with an agronomist working under the Point IV program of the U.S. Government in Cuba, of the obvious disorganization of the agrarian reform program . . . in Camaguey.

[8] Regino Boti, Minister of Economy until 1964, then acting Minister of Commerce, came out for the "collective exploitation" of the land (*The Havana Post*, February 27, 1959). Boti seemed always to anticipate later developments: In April, 1960, he said that free enterprise prior to 1959 "did not produce the desired results and thus the Revolutionary Government will follow whatever system is necessary for the good of the country" (*ibid.*, April 12, 1960).

. . . Several months passed before anything happened; at the end of October, 1959, Huber Matos . . . was summarily removed by Fidel Castro, thrown into prison, and charged with blocking the agrarian reform." [9] In summary, Matos' anti-Communism and anti-agrarian reform policies made a showdown between himself and Castro inevitable.

A storm broke over Cuba as a result of Matos' arrest. According to Felipe Pazos, moderate National Bank head until November, 1959, Castro threw away his "right crutch" when he arrested Matos, leaving only his "left crutch," the Communists.[10] Before 1959 ended, three radicals moved into the Sugar Stabilization Institute, the island's key economic command post, and Manuel Ray (Public Works Minister) and Faustino Perez (Minister for the Recovery of Stolen State Property) were replaced by revolutionaries Osmani Cienfuegos and Navy Captain Rolando Diaz. Some reformers and moderates stayed with the revolution until well into 1960. Rufo Lopez Fresquet, for example, did not resign from his position as Minister of the Treasury until March, 1960. Defections of appointed government officials, especially those in the foreign service, were increasingly frequent through mid- and late 1960. By early 1961, however, nearly all of the reformers and anti-Communists had either resigned, been dismissed, or been radicalized by the revolution. Their only strength was minor officials in various state offices, which, according to Guevara, had been given out "haphazardly" in 1959–1960.[11]

[9] Thomas Mathews, "The Agrarian Reform in Cuba and Puerto Rico," *Revista de Ciencias Sociales*, Número Especial sobre el Caribe, 4, No. 1 (March, 1960), p. 122. All the facts of the Matos case have not been disclosed.

[10] Author's interview, June 6, 1962. Pazos failed to understand that the developing worker-peasant alliance meant that Castro would eventually not need any crutch at all.

[11] Ernesto Guevara, "The Cadre: Backbone of the Revolution," *Cuba Socialista*, 2, No. 13 (1962), reprinted in John Gerassi, editor, *Venceremos: the writings and speeches of Che Guevara* (New York, 1968). Key revolutionaries in power (if not official posts) from the beginning were Fidel and Raúl Castro, Juan Almeida (the latter two in control of the Armed Forces and Army, respectively), Núñez Jiménez (INRA), Armando Hart, and Dorticós. "Right-wing" reformers replaced in mid-1959 included Roberto Agramonte (State), Humberto Sori Marín (Agriculture), Elena Mederos (Public Welfare), Dr.

[4]

During the last half of 1959 and 1960 the reformers increasingly attempted to make "Communists in government" the leading political issue in Cuba. As Zeitlin and Scheer have written: "When the interests of [the middle] classes were threatened by Castro's economic policies, they began searching for the specter behind their discomfort; it was they who first identified the revolution with Communism—and by so doing gave substance to the Communist claim that accusations of 'Communism' were merely a guise for attacks on the revolution itself." [12]

The origins of the alliance between Castro's revolutionaries and the Communists are plain. As a result of the negative reactions of government officials, labor leaders, and Cabinet members to the Agrarian Reform Law, Castro lost most of the faith he retained in the nonrevolutionary camp. Always suspicious of the reformers, Castro said that he "needed" the Communists, who were "truly revolutionary, loyal, honest, and trained." In March, 1960, Castro told the Cuban people, "The Communists, Marxists, Leftists are in accord with revolutionary law. I am not to blame for that. I am not to blame that the American companies and large landowners are against our reform program." [13] In a nutshell, the defection of many moderate officials and cadres in the second half of 1959 nar-

---

Julio Martínez Páez (Public Health), and Luis Oriando Rodríguez (Interior). Key "left-wing" reformers who either joined the government in mid-1959 or were associated with public agencies from the start were Pedro Miret Prieto (Agriculture), Rufo López Fresquet (Treasury), and Felipe Pazos (National Bank). The key revolutionary who remained out of the government until November, 1959, when he took the helm of the National Bank, was Guevara.

[12] Maurice Zeitlin and Robert Scheer, *Cuba: Tragedy in Our Hemisphere* (New York, 1963), p. 8.

[13] *The Havana Post*, March 29, 1960. It should be pointed out that the revolution inherited a handful of PSP members who had retained posts in Batista's government. Oscar Pino Santos, who had been public relations director of the old National Economic Council, and Edwardo Santos Rios, subdirector of BANFAIC, to take the two most important cases, finally ended up employed by INRA. Little significance should attach to these moves; thousands of lower- and middle-level personnel in the old state bureaucracy (including those who failed to exhibit an anti-Batista record) and the old labor movement joined the revolutionary camp.

rowed the Revolutionary Government's political base and compelled Castro to seek "truly revolutionary" allies in the PSP. As Castro frequently maintained, those who complained about the rapid pace of the revolution were themselves partly responsible for it.

In July, 1961, the 26th of July Movement, the PSP, the Revolutionary Directorate (a student organization), and minor revolutionary groups fused into the Integrated Revolutionary Organization (ORI). The purpose of ORI was to prepare the way for a united socialist party, the United Party of the Socialist Revolution (PURS). The PSP rapidly took control of ORI and began to dominate the mass revolutionary organizations: the Revolutionary Defense Committees, the Young Rebels, and the Cuban Women's Federation. The exact motives of the PSP and the precise relationships between Anibal Escalante and other Communists who attempted to monopolize power within the ORI and the rest of the PSP leadership is still unclear. What is certain is that Castro's faith in the PSP, together with the shortage of 26th of July political cadres and the extreme economic and political decentralization of the political economy, provided the preconditions for a "takeover" of ORI.

It is also uncertain when Castro became aware of the Escalante group's motives. His public statements on the question offer little help. In an interview on January 29, 1962, for example, he spoke approvingly of the fact that the "influence and prestige of the ORI are growing daily in all mass organizations and generally in the country's life." A few days later, however, the Second Declaration of Havana denounced "sectarianism, dogmatism, a lack of broadness in analyzing each social layer." No doubt partly as insurance, the PSP-edited *Cuba Socialista* reprinted in its February, 1962, issue a section from the CPUSSR XXII Congress Program attacking sectarianism. Then, very quickly, in two speeches on March 13 and 26, Castro brought the whole question out into the open. The purge of Escalante's cadres began immediately. One after the other, Communists in the Escalante wing of the PSP were fired from their positions in ORI, JUCEI, INRA, the labor unions, and other agencies and associations and replaced by 26th of July revolutionaries. Moreover, there was a reappearance of high 26th of July personnel who had resigned in protest against Escalante's maneuverings, or who had been replaced for taking an intransigent anti-Escalante position.

Subsequently, of the key older PSP leaders, only Carlos Rafael Rodríguez survived without a loss of stature, undoubtedly because of his early support for the guerrilla struggle and lack of association with Escalante. About a second PSP leader, Lázaro Peña, who remained in control of the Cuban Workers Federation (Revolutionary), Gilly wrote in 1964: "You have only to live for a time in Cuba, participate in the Revolution's activities, and be in daily contact with the Cuban people to learn of the one leader who enjoys the unanimous opposition of the Cuban workers . . . Lázaro Peña." [14] Of the remaining old PSP directors of the ORI, only Blas Roca, long-time leader of the PSP, held (or holds) a top leadership post. Six other old Communists were directors of the ORI, but they were in a minority. Firmly in control were ten 26th of July radicals who were actively involved in the guerrilla war or the underground and five other non-Communists who were active in either the military or political struggle against the old dictatorship. [15] In 1964, when PURS was formally launched, a directorate of six men governed the party. With the exception of Blas Roca, whose actual authority was progressively reduced, all of the party leaders were 26th of July revolutionaries.

There were two basic reasons why Castro was able to easily dislodge the Escalante wing of the PSP from the ORI, that is, why the Communists posed no real threat to Castro's leadership. In the first

[14] "Inside the Cuban Revolution," *Monthly Review*, 16, No. 6 (October, 1964), p. 13. This was as much for his *role* as labor leader as it was for his PSP post; Zeitlin's sample shows that only 16 per cent of Cuba's workers were downright hostile to the Communists, while 17 per cent were "indifferent," and the great majority, 60 per cent, were "friendly." The rest, or 7 per cent, were party members.

[15] The other Communists were César Escalante, Severo Aguirre, Flavio Bravo, Manuel Luzardo, Joaquín Ordoquí, and Ramón Calcines. The ten revolutionaries consisted of the Castros, Guevara, Almeida, Valdés, Guillerno García, Sergio del Valle, and Augusto Martínez Sánchez (all rural guerrillas); Armando Hart and his wife, Haydee Santamaría, were urban underground leaders. The remaining five directors were Osvaldo Dorticós, Emilio Aragonés, Osmani Cienfuegos, Raúl Curbelo, and Faurre Chomón (head of the old Revolutionary Directorate).

place, Castro was careful to keep the Rebel Army, the People's Militia, and the police completely independent of ORI. The original Granma guerrillas continued to control the organizations that monopolized the means of coercion. Raúl Castro remained Minister of Armed Forces, Juan Almeida remained Commander-in-Chief of the Army, and Ramiro Valdés continued to head up the Interior Ministry. Moreover, the Escalante group failed to make any headway at the top. With two exceptions, all of the ministers in power in October, 1960, were still in their posts one year later.[16] Thus, when Castro opened the doors of the revolution to the PSP, he undoubtedly was confident that the party would not try to seize the initiative away from his 26th of July group and, in the event that they made the attempt, that he would be able to deal with them with little difficulty. In retrospect, this was a completely realistic assessment.

In the second place, Castro's men were far ahead of the party as a revolutionary force, both in terms of economic and social policy and in terms of developing a revolutionary cadre. The party was intent on capturing key posts in the mass organizations; Castro was intent on deepening the revolutionary process. In this sense, the PSP failed to provide any competition for Castro's group. For these two reasons, Castro was confident that he could make use of the Communists in late 1959–1960 without any serious danger either to his own leadership or the revolution itself. In fact, Castro's own constituency was being forged more rapidly than he himself was probably aware, and in retrospect his heavy reliance on the PSP in 1960–1961 may have been unnecessary. To sum up, Castro used the PSP when he felt that the reformers were subverting the revolution; he dislodged the PSP from control of ORI when he felt that *they* were subverting the revolution.

[5]

As we have seen, with the alliance between the revolutionaries and the Communists in late 1959–1960, many moderates defected

---

[16] Mario Escalona Reguera (Public Health) and Julio Camacho Aguilera (Transport) were replaced by José R. Machado Ventura and Omar Fernández Cañizares, respectively. During this period, three ministries (State, Social Welfare, and Agriculture) were eliminated.

from the revolution. From their perspective, it was perfectly plain that if the revolution was becoming more "socialistic" and if the Communists were taking an active part in governing Cuba, then the Communists must be "taking over." That the revolution would have become more radical with or without the Communists, and that as a result the Communists were being used by Castro rather than vice versa, apparently occurred to few.

Nevertheless, a great many moderates, including businessmen, professionals, and others, remained supporters of the revolution despite the cries of "Communists in government." This support was probably decisive in late 1959 and most of 1960, that is, in the period *before* Castro was able to develop a firm worker-peasant alliance, a large-scale militia, and, in general, a solid base in the masses. For this reason, it will be useful to explore the causes of middle-class support for Castro until the nationalization of industry and the complete falling out with the United States in late 1960.

In the first place, most Cubans viewed Castro as the liberator, a Martí or Bolivar, who promised to end the tyranny, clean up corruption, and put Cuba on an independent, progressive path. Second, there were many economic and social policies that reformers and revolutionaries could agree on. One example is the Fiscal Reform Law of 1959 that was drawn up by a tax reform commission headed by moderate López Fresquet. The law was firmly backed by the radicals, as well as by conservative groups, for example, the National Association of Cuban Industrialists, which reaffirmed its support of the law at a banquet in August, 1959. Most moderates also supported the law that cut rents by 50 per cent, because it could be interpreted as reform legislation which drastically altered the rates of return on alternative investments and hence would channel capital away from residential construction and into productive investments. For the revolutionaries, the rent law was political gold. Moreover, it opened the way for the intervention or seizure or some construction firms that failed to make the changeover from residential to other construction or that failed to obtain contracts from private business. These are two of many examples of new policies that were supported by many moderates and revolutionaries alike.

Third, it was difficult for the reformers to distinguish between the intervention of business and socialism itself, that is, between the temporary and permanent seizure of private capital. The reason was that government takeover of financially troubled enterprises in order to pay wages and other outstanding obligations was established practice in prerevolutionary Cuba. Under a decree promulgated in 1934, the Ministry of Labor was empowered to recommend intervention to the President of the Republic, who in turn was authorized to appoint delegates with the power to seize private enterprise in order to force compliance with any Ministry of Labor ruling. Another decree in 1938 authorized government seizure to rehire workers who were illegally discharged. A third authority in 1942 paved the way for intervention of business in order to maintain production, and thus anticipated actual practices in 1959–1960. A final decree authorized the Superior Labor Council to take over firms to enforce compliance with council decisions.[17] Under these decrees and laws, there were at least one hundred interventions prior to 1952, although in the years of the last Batista dictatorship there were only a handful.[18] To be sure, prior to 1959, government takeover was aimed primarily at erasing financial deficits and bringing government prestige to bear on especially troublesome labor disputes, while after 1959 seizure was motivated by the desire to use Treasury funds to make nonoperational firms operational. But the revolutionaries were taking pragmatic, not ideological positions on intervention and thus could count on considerable moderate support.

A fourth related reason many nonrevolutionaries did not defect from the revolution after the radical alliance with the PSP was that until well into 1960, leading radicals repeatedly assured the moderates that the Revolutionary Government had no intention of leading Cuba into socialism, and defection meant exile. In the second month of the revolution, Guevara asserted that Cuba was "about to

[17] These decrees and laws are Decree-Law No. 251, Decree No. 798, Law-Agreement No. 5, and Decree No. 1893, respectively (United States Bureau of Labor Statistics, *Labor in Cuba* [Washington, 1957], p. 11; The American Chamber of Commerce of Cuba, *Cuba, Facts and Figures* [Havana, April, 1957), pp. 64–65].

[18] Cuba, *Anuario Estadístico Azucarero, 1953* (Havana, 1954).

enter into an era of full capitalism." [19] One year later, he said that "Cuba blends state-owned concerns, private U.S. and Cuban investments under strict government control, and Russian equipment and know-how." In the same month, INRA director Captain Núñez Jiménez assured Cubans that the government "does not intend to assume operation of the sugar industry." [20]

These assurances were partly credible for four reasons, despite the fact that the government owned or managed a considerable share of Cuban agriculture and industry. First, sophisticated moderates were aware that the PSP was committed to a go-slow policy and had no intention of jumping dramatically into full socialism. Second, the reformers dominated BANDES, BANFAIC, the National Bank, the Ministry of Agriculture, and many other state agencies until late 1959 and early 1960 and hence were in a position to extend help and encouragement to private industry. Third, a break with the United States was still unthinkable. Fourth, the revolutionaries backed up their words with deeds. For example, in January, 1960, intervention was lifted from five Santiago bus lines after they completed what the government considered to be necessary equipment repairs. In February, Cuba's second largest flour mill (Molinera Oriental, S.A.) was freed from a $1 million obligation to BANDES incurred in 1956 and was placed by the National Bank in private hands. Nevertheless, the future of private enterprise was writ large in an announcement by Castro in the same month that the Revolutionary Government planned to invest over $150 million in state-owned and managed industry.[21] For the private promoter and investor, this announcement must have been a severe blow, signifying that new investment resources, especially foreign exchange for imports of capital goods and raw materials, would be increasingly difficult to obtain.

Fifth, many moderates did not withhold their support from the leadership even when it was clear that economic and social policy had a collectivist or socialist content because there was a general awareness that "something needed to be done." Related to this atti-

[19] The Havana Post, February 13, 1960.   [20] Ibid., February 21, 1960.
[21] Ibid., February 26, 1960.

tude was the general feeling that the Revolutionary Government was honest in the handling of public funds, sincere in its largely successful attempt to eradicate racial discrimination, and functioned with a minimum of physical coercion and an absence of police torture, and in general was a far more humane regime than the Batista dictatorship. In a sense, this attitude expressed a class guilt: many individuals within the middle class partly blamed themselves for Cuba's past economic stagnation and economic and social underdevelopment. Thus, even as late as the summer of 1960, they did not want to be considered active counterrevolutionaries, even as they were increasingly troubled by the revolution's direction.[22]

Last, as we know, the moderates and revolutionaries shared a pronationalist, in particular, a pro-national economic development, point of view. In fact, moderates such as Felipe Pazos dominated those institutions that in 1959 attempted to reduce Cuba's dependence on the United States, a policy that this country condemned in the United Nations in October, 1960, when it accused Cuba of "artificially" reducing imports from United States suppliers.[23] Thus, in a very real sense the attempt by the moderates to conserve foreign exchange, generate a larger number of import-substitute industries, and diversify trade directly contributed to United States hostility to the revolution, and hence to their own subsequent defections.

The reason is that the economic and diplomatic war with the United States during the last half of 1960 was the great dividing line for the majority of the moderates, although the explosion of the munitions ship La Cobre in the spring of the year was seen by the revolutionaries as the key event in United States-Cuban relations and, in fact, spurred the development of the militia. Even though both moderates and revolutionaries wanted to speed Cuban national development, from the beginning they did not share a com-

[22] The government was highly impatient with the hemming and hawing of this group. "As for those traitors who haven't yet jumped from the ship of the Revolution," President Dorticós said in July, 1960, on the occasion of the resignation of Cuba's Ambassador to West Germany, "let them do it and do it quickly so that we can proceed ahead better without that unnecessary weight" (ibid., July 12, 1960).

[23] Reprinted in The New York Times, October 15, 1960.

mon line on United States influence and foreign investments. Castro's position was that foreign investments helped Cuba only under certain restrictive conditions. Moderate Lopez Fresquet believed that foreign investments not only provided Cuba with scarce foreign exchange but also with "democratic ideals." [24]

In practice, foreign capital inflows came to a halt between January and April, 1959.[25] Then Felipe Pazos announced that foreign investments were again entering Cuba.[26] Until late in the fall of 1959, the moderates' sanguine view of the role of foreign capital prevailed, but subsequently the government's line hardened, going through three distinct stages. In December, 1959 the National Bank announced that only nonagricultural United States investments would be welcome. In February, 1960, Guevara took the position that foreign participation in new "basic industries" would be limited to minority ownership in mixed (private-public) companies, even though he left room for alternative possibilities. "If foreign investments," he said, "are made in keeping with our needs and following our indications, then that's a different story." [27] But by the fall of the year, this line was altogether changed. Foreign capital was considered to be completely unwelcome, and only in "exceptional" cases would the government consider mixed companies with majority shares in the hands of private Cuban capital.[28]

Thus, the revolutionaries expected and did not dread the economic war with the United States during the latter half of 1960, while the moderates considered it the breaking point. Open diplomatic and economic warfare sharply stepped up the rate of emigration, pushed many of those who remained on the island into the counterrevolutionary camp, and even alienated those business elements competitive with United States capital and economic interests. Even the "left moderates" either identified with and respected

---

[24] *The Havana Post,* January 11, 1959.   [25] *Ibid.,* March 22, 1959.
[26] *Ibid.,* April 29, 1959.
[27] Cited in *Diario de la Marina,* February 4, 1960; *The Havana Post,* February 6, 1960.
[28] According to Dr. Boti at the Third Plenary Session of the meeting of the Inter-American Economic and Social Council in Bogotá, Colombia, September 7, 1960.

or feared the United States. During the period in which Cuba maintained formal relations with the United States the moderates hesitated to step into the counterrevolutionary arena. One of the reasons that the revolutionaries easily retained the political initiative therefore was that United States policy tended to reduce to a minimum active internal hostility to the Revolutionary Government.

As we know, from the revolutionaries' point of view, the United States was a different case. They were extremely sensitive to the historic role of the United States in Cuba and were anxious to dispel any impression that they were necessarily as politically dependent as three generations of predecessors. As we know, Castro believed that "foreign interests" should not be permitted in Cuba unless their operations benefited the island. "The trouble is," he said in February, 1959, "that foreign interests are used to getting what they want." He charged that the United States Ambassador had been running Cuba and announced that "we must be free economically." [29] Later on, the seizure of foreign properties was partly justified by references to Cuba's "economic independence." [30] In brief, the radicals considered the elimination of the foreign "monopolies" a precondition for national economic and political independence.[31]

This line of reasoning was no doubt correct, as far as it went. But the question arose, in the absence of large-scale private foreign investment, how could Cuba finance a development program? As we have seen, the original 26th of July program stressed the possibility of mobilizing domestic savings for productive investments. But as 1959 wore on, due to the reaction of the business classes to the agrarian reform and other new government policies, this was obviously unrealistic. In May, 1959, Castro himself said that an attempt to mobilize domestic savings sufficient to finance a large-scale development program would be "impractical and dangerous." [32]

[29] Quoted in *The Havana Post*, February 3 and 4, 1959.

[30] For an example, see *Trabajo Cuba*, 1, No. 4 (August, 1960), citing a speech by Martínez Sánchez.

[31] Guevara speech, cited in *The Havana Post*, March 22, 1960.

[32] At the May, 1959, OAS economic conference in Buenos Aires, Castro said that Cuba wanted expanded trade and loans with no strings attached to replace private direct investments and to supplement current domestic savings.

Cuba thus was dependent on public foreign loans and credits for developmental financing.

This line of analysis sheds some light on the four-cornered relationship between the revolutionaries, the reformers, the United States, and the Soviet Union during the first half of 1960. Many reformers remained in political limbo and waited for the United States to make a decisive move. Meanwhile, the revolutionaries placed the most negative interpretations possible on United States policy decisions during 1959–1960. As a consequence, the United States would not offer Cuba loans and credits, nor would the revolutionaries accept financing with any strings attached.

The Soviet Union finally filled the vacuum. Following the Mikoyan visit to Cuba in February, 1960, Cuba obtained Soviet credits and a favorable trade agreement. In turn, this gave more ammunition to the anti-Communists, particularly because the prerevolutionary government did not even have formal relations with the Soviet Union. Meanwhile, the United States expressed increasingly grave doubts about the Revolutionary Government. The Agrarian Reform Law met with official disfavor. In January, 1960, Ambassador Phillip W. Bonsul announced that the United States sympathized with the "ideals and aspirations" of the revolution, but warned that social progress "is not divorced from due consideration towards the rights of private North American interests who, in general, have made a constructive contribution to Cuba." [33] In the same month, Vice-President Nixon threatened that expropriation without compensation would have serious repercussions in Congress and implied that the United States might cut Cuba's sugar quota. This line was echoed in Congress and given wide currency in the United States press.

Increasingly bitter charges and countercharges were thrown back and forth between Cuba and the United States during the first half of 1960. Relations between the two countries inevitably deteriorated to the point of no return when it became clear that neither side would alter its assumptions concerning the respective motives and goals of the other. When the economic war in the summer of the year concluded with the nationalization of foreign and Cuban in-

[33] Quoted in *The Havana Post,* January 24, 1960.

dustry and the end of diplomatic relations with the United States, the moderates cut their final bonds with the revolutionaries. Meantime, the Soviet Union quietly supported Cuba at every turn. In sum, Castro was determined to push through policies that did not respect what the United States considered to be its "legitimate interests." The United States failed to accept these policies in a spirit of mutual respect and equality. The moderates believed that the break with the United States was suicidal. Hence, Cuba reoriented itself to the East, and the United States increased its support of the counter-revolutionaries, intensifying the civil war with the sides drawn up along class lines.[34] This is the basic meaning of Guevara's remark to the author in late 1961 to the effect that the "United States made us socialists."

[34] The Cubans offered to negotiate differences in a note of January 27, 1960. The offer was reopened on February 22, 1960, and on subsequent dates. The following provision was attached: "The Revolutionary Government wishes to make clear that the renewal and subsequent course of such negotiations must necessarily depend on the government or the Congress of your country not taking unilateral measures which would prejudice the results of the above-mentioned negotiations, or that might be prejudicial to the economy or the people of Cuba" ("Let the Philosophy of Plunder Disappear and War will Disappear," Address by Fidel Castro, Fifteenth Session of the General Assembly of the United Nations [Havana, 1962], pp. 30–31). It is difficult to believe that Cuba expected the U.S. to take the offer seriously; plans were then being made for the sugar cooperatives, which would be formed on U.S. properties that at the time remained in U.S. hands. Preparations had been made for the cut in the sugar quota early in the spring, and in the middle of the oil war, the Sugar Workers Federation announced that the workers were ready and willing to run the sugar mills when the government was ready to nationalize them. The United States clearly expected the total expropriations of the sugar industry. For this reason, the blows traded from July through October should not be viewed as a *causal* sequence of any real importance.

One bright ray in the gloomy drama was a statement by President Eisenhower on March 16, 1960 (*The Havana Post*, March 17, 1960) in which he promised not to punish Cubans or the Cuban government in any way. Perhaps because of this, the quota cut was rationalized in the following manner: "Cuba's sugar commitments to Communist bloc countries under barter trade agreements and hostility toward the United States created doubts as to the wisdom of relying on Cuba for sugar. *Therefore* [author's italics], in July, 1960 the U.S. government cut Cuba's sugar quota for the remainder of the year by 700,000 short tons" (*Foreign Agriculture*, U.S. Department of Agriculture, Foreign Agricultural Service [December, 1961], p. 9). Cuba's crop in 1961 was the highest in recent history and had to be bartered under new agreements with the socialist and other countries.

[6]

By the summer of 1960, the Revolutionary Government acquired productive assets in a number of ways. The agrarian reform placed Cuba's best soils at INRA's disposal. Economic sabotage and crises compelled the government to take over many businesses and properties. Prerevolutionary government *de facto* ownership of assets became *de jure* ownership after 1959. The government confiscated the properties of many Batistianos. Finally, many assets fell into the government's hands as a result of uncoordinated "reformist" policies. Thus, key sectors of the economy were under state control before the nationalization decrees of the late summer and fall of the year.

There was little political resistance to the forward thrust of the radical leadership in its steady acquisition of productive assets. Subsequently, socialism was consolidated quickly and peacefully, both with regard to economic and political reorganization. The reason for these two developments was twofold. First, as we have seen, many moderates did not desert the revolution until a relatively late date. It was not until the period between November, 1960, and mid-1961, after relations between the U.S. and Cuba had completely deteriorated, that the main exile force—the mass of businessmen, executives, and professionals—left the island.[35] Prior to this period, the great majority of the exiles came from the upper classes —the big ranchers, planters, mill owners, and businessmen (January through October, 1960)—and from the old political and military castes—army officers, Batista political associates, top government employees, and businessmen intimate with the official family (early in 1959).

Second, Castro meanwhile was winning support from the lower socioeconomic classes. The moral authority of the government was extremely high, and the nearly unanimously supported confiscations undermined respect for private property in the public mind. More specifically, the drive to develop rural cooperatives and state farms

[35] Letter to the author, J. Arthur Lazell, Deputy Director, Department of Health, Education, and Welfare, Social Security Administration, U.S. Cuban Refugee Program, May 10, 1962. In late 1961 and early 1962, exiles from the "lower economic classes" increased, but middle-class refugees still predominated (Lazell letter to author, February 9, 1962).

in sugar, cattle, fishing, and rice industries and the proliferation of people's stores improved incomes and material standards for thousands of rural workers and peasants, strengthening their allegiance to the government. In February, 1959, only 27.9 per cent and 51.6 per cent of the rural and urban labor forces, respectively, earned $75 per month or more. In February, 1960 and 1961, the figure had jumped to 39.1 per cent (rural) and 59.5 per cent (urban), and 39.5 per cent (rural) and 61.2 per cent (urban), respectively. Meanwhile, total unemployment and underemployment (*i.e.*, part-time work by the day or week), excluding seasonal unemployment, had dropped from 29.6 per cent of the labor force in January, 1959, to 20.9 per cent in January, 1961 (see Appendix B). Beginning in late January, 1959, rural health and educational programs won more support for the radicals, particularly among the isolated and forgotten marginal farmers in Oriente. Tobacco growers and other small farmers were attracted to the new government by readily available cheap credits, machinery, and technical help, and the abolition of rental payments. Furthermore, they welcomed the ouster of the middle and large farmers and ranchers from the leadership of the rural associations. Even with the rise in autoconsumption and roadside and barter sales of foodstuffs during 1961–1962, the government refrained from taking any but the most moderate measures against the small farmers.

Meanwhile, a base among the urban workers was developing, hurried along by the sympathy of a large number of workers to socialist and Communist ideas, owing to three decades of PSP educational and propaganda work in the cities and countryside. As we know, underemployment and seasonal unemployment were steadily reduced through 1959–1961. Zeitlin's studies show a dramatic reduction of casual and seasonal unemployment and a strong correlation between the degree of support of the revolution and prerevolutionary employment status. Additional evidence that the reduction or elimination of regular and irregular part-time unemployment generated much support for the new government is provided by the Catholic University sample study of rural Cuba in 1958. Asked to list their needs and problems in order of importance, nearly three-quarters of those sampled placed "sources of work" first on the list.

In addition, in 1959 and during the first two or three months of 1960, there were many wage increases and contract renegotiations favoring the workers.[36] For the permanently unemployed there were increased subsidies, and plans drawn up to abolish urban unemployment altogether were given wide publicity. The interests of the revolution were identified with those of the Cuban people, and the interests of the people were increasingly those of the workers. These were the identifications and equalities implicit in the rhetoric and analysis of the revolutionary leadership. The process of the interventions, which required active worker participation, the formation of the militia in 1960, and the first rough stabs at planning in 1961, when workers were asked to share the responsibilities and burdens of development, all helped bring the workers closer to the revolution. When the private clubs were seized, workers' clubs were organized on their premises. From a negative standpoint, the demand for elections, the reconstruction of the party system, a speedy end to "revolutionary law" and a return to an independent judiciary, and the insistence on caution in any relationships with the Soviet Union, all originated in middle-class fear and discontent and were echoed very faintly in working-class circles. This is not surprising, for the workers, if they did not react favorably to the Batista coup of 1952, which eliminated "formal" democracy, were not especially hostile to it.

As moderate, middle-class, and professional support narrowed, the revolution's worker and peasant base thus broadened. The revo-

---

[36] There were dozens of new collective agreements in 1959 that incorporated wage increases. New minimum wage scales in the leather and shoe industry reportedly raised labor costs by 100 per cent. A 12 per cent increase in the wages of cane cutters was decreed for the 1959 *zafra*. The Labor Ministry decreed a 20 per cent increase for textile workers in one of Cuba's largest plants, while the National Association of Textile Manufacturers and the Federation of Textile and Needle Industry Workers came to an agreement over higher minimum wages for the industry as a whole. Meanwhile, in March, 1959, minimum wages for civil servants were increased, and INRA, INIT, INAV, and other new state organisms were following independent wage policies, often competing for labor among themselves. Even in late 1959 and early 1960, union leaders were pushing for higher wages, and in some cases second-round increases.

lution also grew stronger because its leadership, cadres, and militants were more tried, tested, and loyal. A year after the Revolutionary Government came to power, Jean-Paul Sartre asked the leaders "questions about their lives, about the evolution of their thought. All of them told me that the Revolution had pulled them much further than their original positions. Violent clashes had occurred and they had to confront severe realities: some of their old friends had not followed the movement; others, reluctantly in the beginning, had become *radicalized*."[37] Not a single survivor of the Moncada attack or the invasion of 1956 defected; compared with the urban revolutionaries, they underwent a more severe test of their "revolutionary-mindedness," and they felt more personal loyalty to Castro. Sartre was referring to the reactions of the revolutionaries to United States foreign policy ("By trying to crush the Revolution, the enemy allowed it to convert itself into what it was"[38]) and failed to see the more powerful revolutionary dynamic taking place within Cuba, but his words apply equally well to the second phenomenon.

It was, in fact, this radicalization in the course of, and as a consequence of, the policies taken to promote economic and social development which is the practical link between our main theses and "what men actually did." Men made the revolution, and the revolution made men (Castro has characterized the revolution as a "schoolroom"). Both are true. The precise relationship between the "revolution" and the "revolutionaries" can never be known; in the careers of some, we can trace a straight line leftward; in those of others, there were discrete changes and reversals. (For example, Minister of Communications Enrique Otulski dropped out of sight when he was replaced as early as June, 1960, by Rolando Curbela, later revealed to be a CIA agent, but returned to a position of authority after the purges in 1962.) But each transformed the other within the framework of the needs and desires to get the social economy off dead center and the objective possibilities of accomplishing this; there were concrete needs; there was a general awareness of the retarding effects of the old forms of organization; there was a plethora

[37] Jean Paul Sartre, *Sartre on Cuba* (New York, 1961), p. 151.
[38] *Ibid.*, p. 152.

of "nonideological" practical advice; there were objective possibilities of reorganizing the social economy. The revolution was a process that followed its own internal logic and ultimately stamped out its own ideology.

These tendencies were continuous processes with apparently no sharp divisions. As each group of defections changed the make-up of the Cabinet and the government agencies, the power of local INRA chiefs and other revolutionary functionaries was reduced. Revolutionary power was thus centralized at the same time that the class base of the regime was changing. By 1961 the radical leadership publicly and openly proclaimed a worker-peasant alliance, which, whether consciously planned or not, was forming from the very beginning. In this alliance the pivotal group was the sugar mill workers, whose long traditions of revolutionary politics and militant unionism meant that they understood organization, the power of a collective effort, and the importance of strong leadership. Nearly 100,000 strong, they were not confined geographically, and this gave a national character to revolutionary strength. As evidence of their revolutionary consciousness, the mill workers walked off with most of the 1962 National Emulation Prizes awarded by the Cuban Workers Confederation (CTC-R).[39] Further, the leadership relied most heavily on the mill workers in national emergencies. Guevara referred to them as the "most combative, class-conscious working group."[40] Early in 1960, Castro said that Cuba's sugar mills would be converted into fortresses in case of attack, and that the mill workers militia should be the "best organized, trained, and disciplined."[41] By mid-1961, over one-half of the cane cooperatives 122,000 members (and well over one-half of the able-bodied males) were in the militia.[42] These workers thus represented roughly one-third of the militia's entire strength at the time.

As the revolution's social base changed and as the sifting-out process within the government centralized and consolidated the power

[39] *Trabajo Cuba*, 4, No. 2 (February, 1963), p. 3.
[40] Guevara speech on June 18, 1960, *Obra Revolucionaria*, No. 11 (1960).
[41] Quoted in *The Havana Post*, March 29, 1960.
[42] Antonio Núñez Jiménez, *In the Second Year of Agrarian Reform* (Havana, 1961), pp. 10–12.

of the revolutionaries, a politically stable socialism rapidly emerged. This was reflected in changing policies of compensation for expropriated properties [43] and in the changing language and perspective of the radical leadership (see below). It is difficult to assess the degree to which this was the end product of conscious policy; in one sense, it "just happened," the product of forces set in motion in 1959. What is certain is that the reformers and moderates did not have a center of power from which to compete with the revolution-

[43] There would be few important *domestic* political implications unfavorable to the government arising out of the agrarian reform, since so few landowners were actually affected. Because a relatively few people and corporations owned the majority of Cuba's farmland, compensation payments would have very few political advantages (in the sense of staving off any potential threat to radical rule), but would lower Cuba's potential investable economic surplus.

The government apparently failed to realize this early in the game. Castro said in mid-1959 that the reform would cost $300 million in compensation payments. Concrete steps were taken to compensate owners: Law No. 576 (*Gaceta Oficial*, September 30, 1959) directed the issue of $100 million in twenty year, 4½ per cent bonds to pay for land taken under the reform. Earlier, INRA was given the authority to substitute other bonds that circulated in the world market if expropriated owners wished them (*ibid., Resolución* No. 19, September 1, 1959). Land valuations were based on declared values of properties for tax purposes. Real market values, of course, were higher.

Early in 1960 the first bonds were approved by the Tribunal of Accounts and submitted to the National Bank for delivery to owners INRA had bought out (*The Havana Post*, January 14, 1960). As the class war in Cuba developed during the second half of 1959 and early 1960, the question of compensation receded to the background, and it became clear that the revolution's authority would not be undermined if rural property owners went uncompensated. Few bonds were issued; few cash payments were made. In a report on March 17, 1960, INRA director Jiménez said that nearly $7 million compensation had been paid in bonds (all in Agrarian Reform Bonds, which were not negotiable except at a big discount), and over $2 million had been paid in cash. Since 476,000 hectares were purchased, this would come to about $20 per (undervalued) hectare.

Another source places the amount of compensation at only about $7 million, as of December 20, 1960, months after the Jiménez report (letter, February 2, 1962, Chonchol to Carroll); $5.6 million was in bonds, and $1.3 million in cash. Whatever figures are correct, these comparisons strongly imply that few if any payments were made after March, 1960.

Prior to July, 1960, the government moved much more carefully against U.S. properties compared with Cuban lands. So far as the latter were concerned, physical seizure usually preceded the implementation of legal processes (letter, February 9, 1960, Chonchol to Carroll). The government's attitude changed

aries. Even if they had had equal access and means of power, it is improbable that they would have been able to compete successfully, because Castro was the only sure source of power and authority, and the moderates had no chance to control him. Furthermore, Cuban capitalism had already been "reformed" into a state of stagnation. The total impact of economic reform in 1959 to early 1960 was to impair the market mechanism still further.[44] Moreover, a re-

sharply in the context of its economic war with the U.S. So far as the expropriated sugar lands were concerned, the Cubans offered 2 to 3 per cent, thirty-to-fifty-year bonds to be amortized with 25 per cent of dollar earnings by sales of sugar to the United States of over 3 million long Spanish tons per year, at a price no less than 5.75 cents. This would hardly satisfy the U.S. property owners.

Where the domestic implications of noncompensated expropriations would be very unfavorable to the government, adequate payments were arranged. This was the case with the Urban Reform Law, which provided for income of up to $600 per month to former owners of apartment houses and other properties, as well as with the 1962 law authorizing the expropriation of retail stores, under which 10 per cent of a company's assets was paid at once and the rest in 120 monthly installments. In both cases, large numbers of people were affected by the law, seven thousand families by the latter. The Second Agrarian Reform, which affected even more families, also provided compensation.

The Cuban experience suggests a normative political economy of compensation. On a political level, compensation payments tend to inhibit the counterrevolution; from the standpoint of economic development needs, they tend to keep some potentially valuable people in the country. The negative effects can be measured by the loss in potential investable economic surplus. These factors must be balanced out before any rational decision is possible.

Other things being equal, how much compensation a country can "afford" depends on the contribution of expropriated earnings to the growth of national product. If in the old system the expropriated earnings were spent on capitalist consumption and/or repatriated abroad, then the new government can "afford" more compensation. That is, the future growth rate of national product will be higher, and the necessary effective "tax rate" on the rest of the population needed to pay the expropriated capitalists will be lower. If, on the other hand, capitalist earnings were previously invested productively, then the country can "afford" to pay out less compensation. Ironically, then, it pays a new government to compensate "bad" capitalists (who previously used their earnings unproductively) and to refrain from compensating "good" capitalists, assuming a *given* political threat in the case of failure to pay any compensation.

[44] From an economic perspective, the new controls and reforms (including the vastly increased state expenditures on social investments) had a twofold impact on the operation of the private economy. These can be perhaps best be visualized as a stream with two opposing currents, one running in favor of

formed capitalism failed because Cuba lacked a sizable class of reformed *capitalists*. New and *authentic* reforms cut into the existing
power structure and were the mainspring of more or less sharp class
conflicts, simultaneously provoking the hostility of the United

---

private business and one running against. On the one hand, the successes of
the private economy from 1959 to mid-1960 can be placed mainly at the door
of public policy, which did not exclude cajoling and threats of intervention or
even outright expropriation. To take a key example, the expansion of agricultural output during this period was partly due to the fact that landowners
anticipated that idle and inefficiently utilized lands would be expropriated,
although the greater part of the expansion must be due to the new favorable
credit and marketing conditions and to the decline of competition from imports.
In this and other ways (foreign trade, tax, monetary, public expenditure, and
other indirect and direct policies) the government jolted the private economy
into a good short-term economic performance.

On the other hand, the positive effects of the reforms were more or less
rapidly offset by (or transformed into) negative effects. As state control went
deeper, market regulations multiplied and taxes rose, foreign trade fell more
and more into the hands of the National Bank, more cooperatives were formed
on public lands, and more firms were confiscated or intervened, the ability of
the economy to function well as a *market* economy was impaired. As time went
on, the labor situation became more contradictory and created a profits squeeze,
and the direction the economy was taking became increasingly unclear and the
goals of economic planning were confused. Last but not least, as the composition of the Revolutionary Government changed, business became increasingly
confused as to the real source of state power, and this reacted unfavorably on
expectations and, ultimately, production and investment.

Moreover, the public sector as such collided more and more frequently with
the private sector. The government controlled a large share of Cuba's agriculture and industry, which was being operated more on the basis of crude
planning principles than on market relationships. Subsidies to state agriculture
won thousands of farm workers away from private agriculture; housing subsidies
meant that state construction firms and private firms engaged in public housing
programs could lure workers away from agriculture, some parts of industry,
and the remaining sectors of the construction industry; the planned expansion
of state agriculture meant that fewer materials and less foreign exchange were
available to private farmers and private manufacturers; the emphasis on increasing production in the confiscated and intervened firms compelled the state
to heavily subsidize these firms, placing private-owned competitors in an unfavorable position. In short, the whole system of priorities (unplanned and
uncoordinated as they were) which emphasized agricultural diversification,
industrial crops, import substitution and export diversification, which de-
emphasized imports of consumer goods, particularly consumer durables, and
investments in "luxury" fields (including housing), prejudiced the future of
large segments of the private sector. In this sense, Cuban reformed capitalism

States, compelling the moderates to take sides. Those who sided with the "revolution" could no longer be considered "moderate"; this was the irony of the reformist position in 1959–1960, and this was their own personal tragedy.[45]

as it developed in 1959 and early 1960 was economically unstable, without fixed reference points, in disequilibrium. It is impossible to say whether or not the market mechanism would have broken down and transformed itself into full socialism for this reason alone, that is, had the struggle with the United States not broken out into the open from July to October. It is certain, however, that this was a powerful tendency which, in the context of the hostility of the middle classes at home, would in the absence of a turnabout by the revolution's leaders, sooner or later be realized.

It must be added, of course, that one cannot definitely prove that this tendency was not *planned* by the radicals in power, although this thesis requires, to put it mildly, putting aside simple common sense. More realistic is the thesis that the economic and political imperatives arose naturally out of a situation whose outcome few foresaw; that an uncompromising determination (by men with few ideological preconceptions) to get the Cuban economy and society off dead center led to the turning point of October, 1960. The available evidence certainly supports this view, and our analysis in subsequent chapters confirms it. Even by mid-1960, the government was apparently inclined to continue to operate the economy along mixed, reformist lines. There was, first of all, a serious shortage of state managerial personnel, planners, and politically tested and reliable administrators. The revolutionary leadership had also given repeated assurances that there was an important role for private enterprise in Cuba's future. The National Bank was making an effort to untangle some of the new trade, foreign exchange, and monetary regulations that had been baffling private businessmen. The Labor Census of April, 1960, had not, as many had anticipated, turned out to be the beginnings of a "directed" labor force. Large sums were being spent to attract tourists and to revive the faltering U.S. tourist business. As late as July, 1960, the Minister of Economy was working on a new corporation income tax; three months later, there were no corporations left in Cuba. In that summer seemingly no one was prepared to grapple with the profound problems of operating a socialist economy on the basis of the direct allocation of resources.

[45] This is illustrated very clearly by the lack of any coherent realistic program supported by any sizable body of exile thought. Most of the manifestoes turned out by exile groups shy away from any issue, problem, or policy with a strong class content. Given the class structure and distribution of political power, given the strong redistributive quality of public policies, and given Cuba's major economic problems, it is easy to understand why exile programs are either unrealistically reactionary, or vapid, overly abstract, and fail to come to grips with real problems. In the first category was the program of Manuel Antonio de Varona's Democratic Revolutionary Front, which was organized in Mexico in June, 1960. The FRD's manifesto looked to "reduce state inter-

[7]

The lack of a fixed ideological position by the revolutionary leadership until 1961 and the interplay between ideology and practice since then makes Cuba unique in the socialist world. "Revolution," Sartre wrote, "is a *praxis* which forges its ideas in action. . . . Cuban leaders do not ignore [ideologies]. They simply do not make use of them." [46] In Guevara's words, "revolutionary theory, as the expression of a social truth, surpasses any declaration of it; that is to say, even if the theory is not known, the revolution can succeed if historical reality is interpreted correctly and if the forces involved are utilized correctly." [47]

The reasons why the revolutionaries finally put practice first and ideology second were threefold. In the first place, the liberal-reform ideology in Cuba was nearly totally bankrupt. It offered no credible explanation for the failures of Cuban capitalism, nor did it hold out any promise for the future.[48] Secondly, the Communist, or official Marxist, ideology was also unable to come to grips with the Cuban reality, mainly because it placed excessive faith in the ability of the national middle classes to develop the economy and to win Cuba's

---

vention [in the economy] to the barest minimum, offer solid guarantees to property owners, to free enterprise and to national and foreign investment. . . ."

[46] Sartre, *op. cit.*, p. 149.

[47] "Notes for the Study of the Ideology of the Cuban Revolution," *Verde Olivo*, 1, No. 3 (October 8, 1960), pp. 10–14.

[48] For example, Felipe Pazos, a well-known moderate, wrote after going into exile: "The economic and social tensions . . . that gave rise to the original non-Communist revolution . . . were not those of poverty and extreme inequity." This judgment clearly has validity, as far as it goes. But he continues, "Economic stagnation, chronic unemployment, corruption, and frustration— these seem to me to have played the largest part in bringing about the revolution." But this explains nothing; there is no theory of stagnation, and no explicit realization that corruption, frustration, and unemployment were secondary causes which obscured the real problems of the island. Like all reformers, whether democratic-minded such as himself, or crude opportunists such as Mujal, or for that matter, such as Batista himself, Pazos shied away from analyses of market and political structures and the explosive implications of such analysis. Thus, liberal thought and reform remedies concocted from the theories of reformed capitalism in advanced industrial countries were totally bankrupt as applied to Cuba; liberal theory in Cuba was little more than pure rhetoric.

independence from the United States. Thus, it was characterized by a cautious, go-slow attitude, class collaborationist policies, and overdependence on the experiences of the Soviet Union, China, and other countries.[49]

Most important, the guerrillas themselves quickly learned that the rudimentary ideas on politics and revolution that they originally held were false and dangerous. As Guevara wrote, "Before the landing of the 'Granma,' a mentality predominated that, to some degree, might be called 'subjectivist;' blind confidence in the power to liquidate the Batista regime by a swift, armed uprising combined with spontaneous revolutionary strikes, and the subsequent fall of the dictator."[50] This problem was solved as the guerrillas began to learn the realities of peasant life in the Sierras. Guevara wrote:

To the *campesinos*, the bestialities of the army and all the persecutions would not be sufficient to put an end to the guerrilla war, even though the army was certainly capable of liquidating *campesinos'* homes, crops, and families. To take refuge with those in hiding was a good solution. In turn, the guerrilla fighters learned the necessity, each time more pointed, of winning the *campesino* masses, for which, obviously, they had to be offered something they desired very much. And there was nothing a *campesino* sought more than land.[51]

After January, 1959, however, the revolutionaries still lacked a revolutionary ideology that corresponded with social forces and conditions in Cuba as a whole. Even the father of the "revolution be-

---

[49] For example, the PSP opposed the collective features of the agrarian reform because the party believed that Cuba, like all other socialist countries, would have to go through the "stage" of land redistribution to the peasant and individual ownership. In fact, in Cuba the seeds of a collective, planned rural economy were planted simultaneously with the transformation of land ownership.

[50] Ernesto Guevara, "We are Practical Revolutionaries," in John Gerassi, editor, *Venceremos* (New York, 1968), p. 122.

[51] Ernesto Guevara, *The Revolutionary War* (Havana, 1967). "People in the Sierra grow like wild flowers, unattended. Then they fade away, constantly busy at a thankless task. It is due to our daily contact with these people and their problems that we became firmly convinced of the need for a definite change in the life of our people. The idea of an agrarian reform became crystal clear, and Communism with the people ceased to be mere theory, to become an integral part of ourselves."

trayed" thesis, Theodore Draper, wrote that "when Fidel Castro entered Havana . . . no one knew what he was going to do. It is doubtful whether he himself knew, except in the most general terms." [52] This actively squares with Castro's own self-evaluation, frankly expressed in his famous "Marxist-Leninist" speech of December 1, 1961:

We were like a man with a vocation for music. But a man's vocation for music does not grant him the right to call himself a musician if he has not studied musical theory. When we started our revolutionary struggle, we already had some knowledge of Marxism-Leninism and we were in sympathy with it. But, by virtue of this, we could not call ourselves Marxists-Leninists. . . . We were apprentice revolutionaries.[53]

Thus, early in January, 1959, Castro called the revolution "not a socialistic . . . but a democratic and national revolution." In May, before the agrarian reform began to set class against class, Castro referred to the revolution as neither capitalist nor socialist, but "humanistic." But the widening and deepening of the revolution changed the leadership's "explanations" of events to the Cuban people and the outside world. Accumulating practical experience, maintaining a firmness of objective, and retaining close relationships with the people, the revolutionaries at first trained themselves to deal with *effects*—economic stagnation and underdevelopment, social backwardness, political ineptitude and corruption—not with *causes*. But remedying effects soon led them into causes: the land problem, low industrial productivity, an inefficient wage structure, the absence of adequate education and health facilities, and dependency on the United States, all were rooted in Cuban capitalist

[52] Theodore Draper, "The Runaway Revolution," *The Reporter*, 22 (May 12, 1960).

[53] Radio interview, Moscow Domestic Service, January 29, 1962. Nearly a year before, Castro said that the revolution was "feeble at first, especially from the ideological standpoint . . . we were all surrounded by a veritable sea of prejudice and falsehood . . . the true Revolution had to . . . disclose the truth and reveal it to the people. Those were the days when all the means of information were in the hands of the most reactionary elements of the country . . . it was necessary to advance carefully and safely; that is why we always appealed to the confidence which the people had in us."

society. Thus, from concrete experiences, certain generalizations were made, and these in turn became the outline of a new ideology —Cuban socialism.

The word "socialism" was apparently first used to describe Cuba's aims by a non-PSP leader, the Secretary-General of the Federation of Bank Employees, early in 1960. The phrase "United States imperialism" was applied in June, 1960, to describe the tactics of the oil companies.[54] A "national" revolution became an "anti-imperialist" revolution. "The most important thing which we have achieved as a result of the revolution," Castro said in January, 1962, "is national liberation, full national sovereignty. Cuba has been freed from the tutelage of U.S. imperialism."[55] Meanwhile, expressions such as "authentic democracy" and "democratic revolution" gave way to "collective discussion" and "democratic centralism."

At the Eleventh CTC-R Congress in November, 1961, Castro said that the revolution was "of the humble, by the humble, and for the humble." Based on this essentially empirical observation, he termed the Revolutionary Government "the government of the working class and the peasant class." Thus, he related the facts to an ideology, and next month he acknowledged his debt to "Marxism-Leninism" and described himself as a "Marxist-Leninist." Far from signifying that he had become a puppet of the PSP and the Soviet Union, his purpose was to dispel that very notion by making explicit the fact that his views shifted in accordance with the class reactions and responses to practical economic and social measures.

Marxism-Leninism in Cuba became a process, not a dogma. It was first of all based on principled positions on basic objectives, for example, in the area of foreign policy toward both the United States and the Soviet Union. Second, it was based on the principle of "allowing everything within the revolution, nothing outside of it." This has resulted in a critical and practical outlook and simplicity of spirit inside Cuba that permeates nearly all revolutionary institutions and practices. In the cultural field, for example, a Cuban journal put the following question to the best-known younger Cuban

[54] J. P. Morray, *The Second Revolution in Cuba* (New York, 1962), p. 102.
[55] Radio interview, January 29, 1962.

writers: "What is the function of the writer in the Revolution?" The most common answer was "to write." [56] Another reflection has been the attempts by the radical leadership to explain economic and political relationships to the people in essentially analytical, nondemagogic, even if frequently oversimplified, terms.

Lastly, Cuban Marxism-Leninism was based on the assumption that Cuban workers and peasants, as well as the leadership, had already acquired the virtues, strengths, and morality of "socialist man." Superficially this assumption appears to be a mere confusion between "what is" and "what ought to be." For example, Castro said in 1962 that "it is clear that every day we understand better, and every day we know, or ought to know better, how to push forward the Revolution." [57] In reality, most revolutionary institutions were organized on the basis of this assumption, which was also grounded in the ideas, actions, and behavior of Castro, Guevara, and the other key revolutionary leaders who, in fact, were (and are) virtuous men. For these reasons, Herbert Mathews' summing-up on Cuba is essentially correct: "The Cuban Revolution moves, and it is *Cuban*. No interpretation that lacks the feel of the Revolution, the emotions, the impulses, the hopes, the fears, can be anything but inspired guesswork at best." [58]

[56] "Conversatorio con los jóvenes autores," *Casa de las Américas*, 4, Nos. 22–23 (Havana, January–April), 1964.

[57] *Obra Revolucionaria*, No. 17 (May 25, 1962).

[58] Herbert Mathews, *Return to Cuba* (New York, 1963).

[11]

Postscript

As mentioned in the Preface, the following observations about the evolution of Cuban socialism since 1964 are based on secondhand material.

First, it must be stressed that Cuban socialism has survived for positive rather than negative reasons. Castro, unlike Stalin, has not sealed his country off from the rest of the world, thus consolidating support because of ignorance of alternative economic and political systems. In fact, the shoe has been on the other foot. Cuba welcomes contacts and visitors from abroad and periodically organizes conferences to make and develop contacts with Third World, European, and other citizens. The United States, on the other hand, has introduced and systematically enforces a policy of "isolating" and harassing Cuba by CIA-organized raids and pressure on Canada and Europe not to trade with the island. Again, the revolution has not survived, like some Eastern European revolutions, because of the presence of the Red Army. Similarities between the Cuban Revolution and the Eastern European countries that reflect unfavorably on Cuba have been largely the figment of the imagination of Cuban exiles.

Second, the economic situation has not improved in a regular, cumulative manner, but remains spotty. Nearly every month some commodities are put on ration and others are taken off. Increasingly, more commodities are placed on the "free" list, for example, many health services, lower and higher education, many cultural and recreational events, housing, public telephone service, and some transportation services. As a friend of mine who recently visited Cuba put it, "Money is more and more useless, because there is very little to buy with it except essentials." He continued, "I wouldn't be surprised if by 1975 Cuba jumps into full communism."

Whatever the future holds, it should be remembered that Cuba's drive for social and economic development revealed the inefficiencies and irrationalities of the old society such as a book could never do; if the new socialist organization had not been accompanied by waste and inefficiency, this would have implied that the old organization and society was not the retardative force that we have argued it was. The Cuban government continues to try to resolve the contradiction between actual and potential progress by large-scale, continuing investments in technical and other education, health, land, and other backward spheres of the old society. The education budget in 1966–1967 was roughly 330 million pesos, or about four times as large as Batista's education budget.

Third, Cubans today accept socialism fully, and many are prepared to die defending their system. Five years ago, Gilly wrote that "it is not quite four years since capitalism disappeared from Cuba. But already no Cubans—I refer to the Cuban people, not to that tiny vestigial minority whose eyes are still on the capitalist past and their lost privileges, real or imaginary—even fleetingly thinks of a sugar cane plantation or a factory or a ship as something that can be the property of one person or a group of persons rather than social property." The support that the Cuban masses continue to give Castro, their willingness to mobilize to defend the revolution, and their day-to-day activities in the factories, farms, and schools is sufficient testimony to their strong sense of identification with the events of 1959–1969.

Fourth, Castro himself remains *the* "institution" of the revolution. He led a movement that destroyed nearly all of the old institutions, including the old labor unions, and in their place there was nothing except Fidel himself. "Leadership," wrote G. D. H. Cole, "is essential to make a class an effective agent of social development. But if classes need constructive leadership, leaders are nothing unless they are able to place themselves at the head of forces upon which the objective situation confers the opportunity of real power."[1] This brief quote catches the situation in Cuba from just the right perspective. Castro is the "institution" because he has provided ongoing constructive leadership. And it is highly significant that mass demands for formal democratic procedures have been noticeably absent in Cuba.

The basic reason, I believe, is that Castro is able to read the mood of the average Cuban, understand it, and act upon it. When he fails to do this, informal pressure, sometimes in the form of passive resistance, builds up in the population at large. Observers have seen and felt this in nearly every sphere of Cuban life, for example, in the nature of the organizational changes in agriculture and the cooperatives of landowning peasants, in the new "communes" made up of the youth, in the university, and elsewhere. Outsiders fail to understand that a great deal of what gets done in Cuba is accomplished voluntarily, without the mediation of the government rules and firm guidelines. This is particularly true in education, art, literature, film-making, and other cultural fields. The position that Guevara summed up as long ago as 1961 still holds to this day:

In general terms, it may be said that a political power which is attentive to the needs of the majority of the people must be in constant communication with the people and must know how to express what the people, with their many mouths, only hint at. How to achieve this is a practical task which will take us some time. In any event, the present revolutionary period must still persist for some time, and it is not possible to talk of structural reorganization while the threat of war still haunts our island.[2]

Perhaps of greatest significance in the long run, the revolution has continued to broaden and deepen, penetrating into all spheres of civil society. In domestic policy, youth have become the new revolutionary force, the leaders of the volunteer brigades, and spearhead of ultracollective experiments in social organization such as the agricultural-oriented program in the "Isle of Youth" (officially, the Isle of Pines). Finally, what is one of the most far-reaching de-

[1] G. D. H. Cole, *The Meaning of Marxism* (London, 1950), p. 50.
[2] "Cuba and the U.S.," *Monthly Review*, 13, No. 5 (September, 1961), p. 224.

velopments of all, and certainly one of the greatest domestic upheavals in the history of Cuban society, the liberation of women in economic, political, and social life has cut deeply into centuries-old Spanish traditions of male superiority, indeed, the older definitions of masculinity itself.

In foreign policy, Cuba has accepted the implications of the slogan "What is the history of Cuba except the history of Latin America?" But besides offering moral and material support for armed revolutionary struggle in Latin America, Cuba closely identifies with North Vietnam, the National Liberation Front, and other revolutionary countries, movements, and currents around the world, including the black liberation movement in the United States.

Appendix A

The Statistics
of Rural Revolution

Between June, 1959, and July, 1963, the Institute of Agrarian Reform (INRA) redistributed over 4.6 million hectares of land (about 46 per cent of Cuba's total farmland) to state-run agricultural units and small private farmers. Another 1.4 million hectares of sugar land was expropriated, confiscated, or purchased (raising the total to about 6 million hectares); the management remained in the hands of the same farmers.

Table A–I shows the allocation of these properties between the public and private sectors in the summer of 1963. Between May, 1961, and July, 1963, little land was nationalized or redistributed. On the former date, the cane farms (then termed cane cooperatives) incorporated 809,454 hectares, while the people's farms comprised 2,433,449 hectares; [1] in two years they had been enlarged by 100,000 and 400,000 hectares, respectively, partly at the expense of farmers who had abandoned their properties, but mainly from tracts of land which INRA had expropriated earlier and had failed to distribute.

According to Table A–I, about 1.38 million hectares of sugar land were assigned to *colonos* cultivating between two and five *caballerías* and the cane farms. Total sugar land owned privately amounted to just over two million hectares in 1962.[2] Given that the cane farms alone comprised about 904,000 hectares in 1963, total sugar land in the public and private sector reached 2.9 million hectares. In 1953

[1] "La reforma agraria cubana" (II parte), p. 41.
[2] "Cuatro Años de Reforma Agraria," p. 16.

Table A–I. Distribution of nationalized farmland in Cuba, July, 1963

Assignment	Area (in hectares)	Percentage
To Private Sector	883,000	19.0
Tenants (under two *cab.* farms) [a]	480,000	8.8
Tenants (two-five *cab.* farms) [b]	475,000	10.2
To Public Sector	3,768,300	81.0
Cane farms [c]	903,700	19.9
People's farms [c]	2,844,600	61.1
Henequen farms	20,000	
Total	4,651,300	100.0

[a] Jacques Chonchul, "La reforma agraria Cubana" (II parte), *Panorama Económico*, Santiago, Chile, No. 228 (March, 1962), p. 41. Following the 1946 Agricultural Census, about 85,000 tenants of various kinds farmed less than two *caballerías* of land. By 1959 there were probably over 100,000 farms in this category; INRA's chief in 1963 placed the total at 120,000, although this is certainly an overestimate (Carlos Rafael Rodríguez, "Cuatro Años de Reforma Agraria," *Cuba Socialista*, 2, No. 21, [May, 1963], pp. 9–10).

In 1962, about 50,000 sugar growers, the great majority of them tenants, worked less than two *caballerías* each. Given that nearly 32,000 titles were awarded to tenants operating farms that comprised less than two *caballerías* (few of these were sugar farms), at least 20,000 small farmers failed to receive titles.

Yet none of these farmers, nor any of the small *colonos*, pay rent any longer. In one sense, therefore, the land operated by these two groups should be included under "expropriated" land. The small sugar growers worked 581,100 hectares ("Cuatro Años de Reforma Agraria," p. 16) and the second group operated a total of 272,000 hectares (assuming an average of one *caballería* per farm, the all-Cuba average for farms comprising less than two *caballerías*). Including this area, the amount of "expropriated" lands comes to 5,504,400 hectares, or 55 per cent of the island's farmland.

[b] Resolution No. 251 (March 23, 1961) gave all tenant *colonos* cultivating between two and five *caballerías* of land the opportunity to purchase up to five *caballerías* at $400 per *caballería* (the first two *caballerías* were received free). The director of INRA, in May, 1961, said that "many thousands of peasants are benefiting from the application of this Resolution" (Antonio Núñez Jiménez, *Informe al pueblo sobre dos años de reforma agraria*, May 17, 1961, p. 2).

In 1962, there were about 11,000 *colonos* cultivating from two to five *caballerías* for a total of about 475,000 hectares ("Cuatro Años de Reforma Agraria," p. 16). We assume all 475,000 hectares were distributed in accordance with Resolution No. 251.

[c] *Proyecto de Anuario Estadístico, 1962*, Dirección de Estadísticas, JUCEPLAN (Havana, July, 1963), Table 5.1. It is possible that an addi-

the great sugar companies controlled nearly 2.8 million hectares; [3] *colonos* who *owned* their own land, then, counted a total of 100,000 hectares. INRA took the rest (2.8 million hectares) away from the big sugar companies and banks. Thus, 1.4 million hectares (total seized land less area distributed to small *colonos* and cane farms and other state units) of expropriated land failed to be distributed in the sense that the thousands of remaining *colonos* were not given explicit private property rights. Nor were any changes made in regard to *colono* payments to the mills during harvests. Apart from the abolition of rents, the legal status of these farmers is not significantly different from that before the revolution.

Tables A–I and A–II may be summarized as follows: Nearly all of the land in the island's sugar sector was expropriated; of these 2.8 million hectares, over 900,000 hectares (land formerly operated directly by the mills, together with some acreage taken from large *colonos*) were incorporated into the state cane farms. About 475,000 hectares were given to or purchased by *colonos* operating units of between two and five *caballerías* in size. Other *colonos* retained the remainder, or 1,425,000 hectares.

All of the land expropriated in Cuba's cattle sector was assigned to the state-run people's farms, as were all expropriated properties in other nonsugar sectors, excepting 408,000 hectares given to small private farmers. All of Cuba's large operating farm units were assigned to the public sector, which in 1963 comprised over 3.7 million hectares. An absolute minimum of two million hectares of these public lands were, before the revolution, in very large farms (1.1

tional 171,900 hectares in *fincas estatales* (reported in "Cuatro Años de Reforma Agraria," p. 9)— transitory form of rural organization—should be included in land allocated to the public sector. The *Anuario* makes no mention of *fincas estatales*.

Carlos Rafael Rodríguez wrote in May that there were only 887,300 hectares in cane farms, not 903,700 hectares, as the *Anuario* reported in July. The disparity is probably due to the fact that a few *colonos* who had neglected their fields, or who had abandoned their properties, were expropriated after the 1963 *zafra*. In the case of the amount of land assigned the people's farms, there is only a minor disparity between the two sources.

[3] The mills owned over 1.9 million hectares; the rest was leased (U.S. Department of Commerce, Bureau of Foreign Commerce, *Investment in Cuba* [Washington, 1956], p. 32). Even in 1958, the mills leased 500,000 hectares ("La reforma agraria en Cuba," Table 9, p. 450).

Table A–II. Nationalized farmland, by commodity, number of farms, and owners in Cuba, 1959–1963

Principal commodity (in 1959)	Area expropriated, confiscated or purchased (in hectares)	No. farms	No. owners
Sugar [a]	2,800,000	3,129	83
Cattle [b]	1,100,000	900	631
Henequen [c]	20,000	14	14
Rice, tobacco, etc. [d]	2,152,600	ca. 5,000	2,159
Total [e]	6,072,600	ca. 9,043	2,887

[a] Of the 2.8 million hectares of sugar land, 1,261,587 hectares, in 596 U.S.-owned farms, were expropriated on July 6, 1960. Three months later, on October 13, 1960, the Cuban Council of Ministers authorized the expropriation of an additional 910,547 hectares in 2,537 Cuban and foreign sugar farms. These two decrees (Nos. 851 and 890) handed INRA a total of 2,172,134 hectares (*Informe al pueblo,* p. 5). It is noteworthy that thirteen U.S. and nine Cuban sugar companies controlled 1,173,015 hectares and 620,005 hectares of this area, respectively. In fact, 2.2 million hectares is an overestimate of the amount of seized *sugar* land under the two above authorities. Some of the farms taken over on July 6 were planted in other crops, and a considerable proportion was grazing land. Since this land was a substitute in production for sugar, we have included it under sugar. It also should be noted that the number of *sugar* farms expropriated is overestimated. The remaining .6 million hectares (2.8 minus 2.2) was expropriated, confiscated, or purchased under other authorities.

The number of owners is underestimated, since a few large *colonos* (owners) and banks had their properties taken over. The island's 161 mills, which owned or controlled nearly all of Cuba's cane land, were owned by eighty-three corporations.

"Administration cane" used to account for a maximum of 20 per cent of Cuba's total production. In 1962, the cane cooperatives grew 34 per cent of the total (Alfredo Menéndez Cruz, "Problemas de la industria azucarera," *Cuba Socialista,* 2, No. 12 [August, 1962], p. 7). In 1963 the cane farms (the old cane cooperatives) grew 40 per cent of the total ("Cuatro Años de Reforma Agraria," p. 16). It follows, therefore, that a maximum of 20 per cent of Cuba's sugar was grown by expropriated, large *colonos.* As an indication of how much *colono* land was seized and collectivized, this figure has two serious drawbacks. First, the mills held more idle land than the big planters; even though they may have delivered 20 per cent of total output as "administration cane," they directly held more than 20 per cent of Cuba's cane land. Second, the mills often grew cane in the name of one or more *colonos;* thus, their real share of total output was larger.

million hectares in cattle ranches, and over 900,000 hectares in mill-operated cane farms). Probably an additional 500,000 to 700,000 hectares were previously in large rice, potato, and other farms. Thus, perhaps one million hectares were in small farms (owned by large property holders) prior to 1959 and were subsequently expropriated and incorporated into people's farms.

Table A–II also discloses that a relatively small proportion of the island's farms were expropriated or purchased—a little more than 5 per cent. Fewer farmers lost all or a portion of their properties—

ᵇ According to official sources, 900 ranches were expropriated (*Informe al pueblo*, p. 22). We have confirmed this estimate in the following manner: In 1952, on the 1,058 largest Cuban ranches, there were 1,098,651 head of cattle (*Investment in Cuba*, p. 39). From 1952–1960, the total number of cattle in Cuba grew from 4,032,615 (*ibid.*) to 5,100,000 ("La reforma agraria cubana" [I parte], p. 20). Supposing that large ranches grew at the same rate as the total cattle industry—a reasonable assumption given that the big ranches were complements in production to other farms—then the 1,058 biggest units had 26 per cent more head (or, 1,384,300 total head) than in 1952.

As of May, 1961, INRA had assigned 1,154,428 head to the people's farms and cane cooperatives. Most if not all of these cattle were taken from the 1,058 largest ranches. Therefore, the official figure of 900 expropriated ranches appears quite reasonable. Some of the remaining head (over 200,000, less slaughtered cattle in 1960 and early 1961) were retained by the 150 or so big ranches which escaped seizure; the rest were retained by the unknown number of expropriated ranchers who were allowed to keep 30 to 50 hectares of pasture land.

As for the amount of pasture land taken (excepting land allowed to revert to pasture when the sugar market was off, already included under "sugar" land), official sources place the total at 50,000 *caballerías*, or about 680,000 hectares (*Informe al pueblo*, p. 22). This is certainly mistaken. Nearly one million hectares were expropriated in 1959 alone, the majority in Camaguey Province.

Furthermore, given that 1,154,428 head were expropriated, the official estimate, if correct, would signify that cattle density per hectare on expropriated ranches was about double the national average. This is incorrect, for two reasons: First, the largest cattle ranches were notoriously extensive in character. Second, the big ranches were allowed to keep fourteen head per *caballería* on the 30 to 50 *caballerías* some were allowed to retain. This figure roughly reflected the then current density, working out to about one animal per hectare. Since 1,154,428 head were seized, the new government must have divested the ranchers of about the same amount of land. Since some of INRA's cattle were donated to the public sector by private individuals, we have placed the figure a bit lower—at 1.1 million hectares.

only 2,887 of roughly 165,000–170,000 farm operators. Of Cuba's approximately 60,000 farm *owners*, a mere 5 per cent lost their lands. From the standpoint of the amount of land expropriated or purchased—over 6 million hectares, or more than 60 per cent of the

---

There were certainly no more than 631 owners; of the first 400 ranches seized, there were only 131 owners (*The Havana Post,* June 26, 1959).

c Six of these farms were purchased in December, 1959 (*Havana Post,* December 20, 1959). The rest were probably bought in January, 1960 (*Informe al pueblo,* p. 20).

d Area expropriated was computed as follows: The people's farms comprised 2,844,600 hectares. An additional 408,000 hectares were allocated to new title-holders. Of these 3,252,600 hectares, we know 1,100,000 came from the old cattle sector. The rest must have come from other sectors.

Number of farms expropriated computed as follows: The 1946 Census placed the number of farms comprising more than 30 *caballerías* at 4,423. INRA estimated on the basis of a census that 3,602 farms over 30 *caballerías* in size were subject to expropriation under the Agrarian Reform Law. The total number of farms of that size lies somewhere between these two figures: Some large farms escaped seizure, but during the period 1946–1959, some large farms were divided into smaller units. We suppose that there were about 4,000 large farms.

In 1963, 592 farms of over 30 *caballerías* remained in private hands ("Cuatro Años de Reforma Agraria," pp. 9–10). About 3,400 large farms must therefore have been expropriated. A few of these were sugar farms and ranches. On the other hand, some farms comprising less than 30 *caballerías* (owned by large units) were expropriated. Adjusting for these factors, very roughly 5,000 farms outside of sugar and cattle were seized. This guess roughly corresponds to an early INRA estimate (made without benefit of a census) of 4,128 farms comprising on the average more than 30 *caballerías*. These farms were outside of the sugar and cattle sectors. Both of these figures are underestimated by the degree to which area in sugar and number of farms are overestimated.

As for the number of owners: 2,873 persons or corporations owned farms in excess of 30 *caballerías* in size. Adding owners of henequen farms, 2,887 owners were expropriated. Subtracting sugar, cattle, and henequen owners, 2,159 rice, tobacco, etc. owners were expropriated. This is a minimum figure: A few persons or corporations who owned two or more units comprising on the average *less* than 30 *caballerías,* but which amounted to more than 30 *caballerías* in the aggregate, were also expropriated. This is partially, but probably not wholly, offset by the fact that a few owner-operators of units incorporating over 30 *caballerías* were allowed to keep their farms.

e Total of final column is estimated above.

island's total farmland—the rural revolution in Cuba was as thoroughgoing as any in history. Table A–III shows the size distribution of cane farms and other farms in the private sector in 1961–1962.

Table A–III. Size distribution of farms, private sector, in Cuba, 1961–62 [a]

Size of farm	Number of farms		Total area (hectares)	
(*caballerías*)	Cane farms	Total	Cane farms	Total
30 and over	116	592	63,763	377,456
20–30	652	1,456	222,890	507,551
10–20	1,658	3,105	319,695	610,320
5–10	3,433	6,062	332,683	607,532
2–5	10,972⎱ 154,703		473,838⎱ 2,348,150	
Under 2	49,513⎰		581,101⎰	
Total	56,344	165,918	1,993,970	4,451,009

[a] "Cuatro Años de Reforma Agraria," pp. 9–10, 16. Total farms and area from August, 1961 cattle census, which is incomplete. Cane farms and area from data collected during 1962 *zafra*.

Tables A–IV and A–V give available data on the two main forms of public agriculture in 1961.

Table A–IV. Distribution of cane cooperatives, by size, province, number of members and workers, May, 1961

Province	No. agrup.	No. coop.	Area (hec.)	Area per coop. (hec.)	No. memb.	No. event.	Aver. no. memb. & event.	Aver. hec. per wkr.
Pinar del Río	2	29	30,641	1,057	4,682	1,607	217	4.9
Havana	3	29	31,036	1,070	4,121	1,364	189	5.7
Matanzas	4	62	67,892	1,095	8,406	1,993	168	6.5
Las Villas	10	125	120,450	965	17,979	6,391	195	4.9
Camaguey	14	168	252,724	1,504	32,598	11,673	264	5.7
Oriente	13	209	306,705	1,467	54,662	23,586	374	3.9
Total	46	622	809,448	1,301	122,448	46,614	272	4.8

Source: Administración General de las Cañeras Cooperativas.

Table A–V. Distribution of people's farms, by size, province, number of workers (May, 1961)

			Number of workers		Hectares per worker	
		Area	Aver. area			
Province	No.	(hec.)	per farm	Permanent	Total	Permanent	Total
Pinar del Río	29	328,012	11,311	4,007	21,741	81.9	15.1
Havana	23	172,048	7,506	2,947	5,663	58.6	30.5
Matanzas	11	106,232	9,657	3,006	9,096	35.3	11.7
Las Villas	41	328,522	8,013	4,341	9,883	75.7	33.2
Camaguey	58	700,162	12,072	4,344	12,110	161.2	57.8
Oriente	105	797,873	7,672	8,676	38,005 [a]	92.0	21.0
Total	267	2,432,849	9,148	27,321	96,498	89.1	25.2

Source: Administración General de las Granjas del Pueblo.

[a] The large number of temporary workers in Oriente and, thus, the relatively small ratio of hectares per all workers, are because the *granja* construction program in Oriente was in full swing in May, and the number of temporary employees was temporarily swelled by thousands of construction workers.

Table A–VI. Organization of Cuban agriculture, by public and private sectors in May, 1961

Sector	No. of farm units	Area (in hectares)	Average area	Percentage of total area
I. Socialized Sector				
A. Cane Cooperatives [a]	622	809,448	1,301	8.0%
B. *Granjas del Pueblo* [b]	266	2,433,449	9,149	24.2
C. Cooperatives				
1. Henequen [c]	11	20,000	1,730	0.2
Total	899	3,262,897		32.4
II. ANAP [d]				
A. Sugar	67,238 [e]	1,085,906 [g]	16	10.8
B. Other	84,854 [f]	1,330,094 [g]	16	13.2
III. Private Sector				
A. Sugar	6,238 [e]	1,014,261 [g]	161	10.1
B. Other	6,988 [f]	3,375,892 [g]	103	33.5
Total (II & III)	165,318	6,806,153		67.6
GRAND TOTAL	166,217	10,069,050		100.0

Sources:

[a] "*La reforma agraria cubana*" (III parte), p. 101. Note that there are only

Table A–VI summarizes the organization of the new agriculture as of May, 1961. Until the Second Agrarian Reform, the new rural structure remained fundamentally unchanged; some exceptions are noted in the source notes.

---

622 cooperatives. Reference to Table A–II reveals that 3,129 sugar farms were expropriated. It will be recalled that the latter figure is somewhat of an overestimate. But the major disparity is due to the fact that many mills had scattered plots which the cane cooperatives consolidated. The administrative unit in most cases, however, remained unchanged: the offices of some of the cooperatives were located in provincial towns, coordinating a number of units.

ᵇ *Ibid.*, pp. 97–98.

ᶜ *Informe al pueblo*, p. 20.

ᵈ ANAP comprises all farms of less than five *caballerías* of land. By August, 1963, 4,429 farms comprising 3,527 *caballerías* were in production cooperatives, and 46,133 farms on 32,364 *caballerías* were in credit cooperatives. There was a considerable amount of overlap between the two.

ᵉ Alfredo Menéndez Cruz, "Problemas de la industria azucarera," *Cuba Socialista*, 2, No. 12 (August, 1962), Table I, pp. 1–2.

ᶠ Residual. According to Chonchol, *op. cit.*, p. 102, there were 150,000 ANAP members. I have estimated the nonsugar private sector as follows (this confirms the Chonchol figure): Assuming that the percentage of sugar farms under five *caballerías* is equal to the percentage of total farms under five *caballerías*, 92 per cent of the island's sugar farms were under five *caballerías*. Of all Cuba's farms, 152,092 comprised five *caballerías* or less; subtracting sugar farms, we are left with 84,854 farms. This leaves 6,988 farms in other crops than sugar comprising five *caballerías* or more each.

Of the 84,854 nonsugar ANAP farms, 20,000 were under coffee, 20,000 were under tobacco, 3,000–4,000 under potatoes, and the rest under other crops and grazing cattle.

ᵍ We know that there were 1,085,906 hectares in ANAP sugar farms. Supposing that the area in farms comprising less than five *caballerías* expanded at the same rate as that in the total number of farms from 1945–1959 (or 24 per cent), there were 2,416,000 hectares in ANAP farms in 1961. Thus, there were 1,330,094 hectares in "other" farms.

We know that there were 1,014,261 hectares in sugar farms outside of ANAP. Thus III.B is the residual.

Appendix B

The Labor Force,
Employment, and Unemployment
in Cuba, 1957–1961

The Labor Force

In this appendix we estimate the main dimensions of the Cuban labor force in 1960 and describe the trend of employment and unemployment from January, 1957, through March, 1961 (and, more tentatively, in 1962 and 1963). We offer these data as guidelines for students of the postrevolutionary Cuban economy. Few of the data have been published or made public inside or outside of Cuba.

There are two sets of statistics of employment and unemployment in April, 1960. The first source is the *Labor Census* (vol. 1 and 2), *Distribution and Characteristics of the Labor Force,* edited by the Ministry of Labor of the Revolutionary Government, March 30, 1962, Havana. The Labor Census was taken during the week of April 18–24, 1960, when every Cuban worker and employer was required to register with the Labor Ministry.[1] The second source is the monthly *Employment and Unemployment in the Labor Force,* National Economic Council, Department of Economics, Havana, computed on the basis of a stratified sample of five thousand households. Most of these series begin in January, 1957, and end in December, 1958, but similar sample data for the period January, 1959, through March, 1961, are available in the monthly *Investigation of Employment, Underemployment and Unemployment,* National Office of Population and Electoral Censuses. The benchmark year for these series was 1953, the date of Cuba's last previous population

---

[1] These figures were kindly provided by Professor Maurice Zeitlin of the Sociology Department of the University of Wisconsin, who obtained them while doing field work in Cuba in 1962.

census. For this reason, one should be chary about using these data uncritically.[2]

The disparities between the two sources are shown in Table B–I. If there had been a complete census of the population which the investigation sampled, the probability is over 95 per cent that there would have been a difference of less than 55,000 between the census and the sample figures for the total labor force. At first glance one might be tempted to accept the census figure of the total labor force as reliable since the difference between the two sources is only 54,493 persons. But Table B–I reveals that the two figures are roughly similar because there are large offsetting errors in their components. The sample estimate of the employed male labor force is 220,000 over that of the census figure. The census figure of the unemployed female labor force exceeds the sample figure by nearly 134,000. Similarly, the former places the employed female labor force and the unemployed male labor force higher than the latter. How can one reconcile the two sources? A good beginning is to enumerate the ambiguities in the census and the definitional differences between the census and sample series.

Table B–I. Cuban labor force (excluding proprietors), by sex and employment status, April, 1960

	(1) Labor census (April 18–24, 1960)	(2) Sample data (April, 1960)	(3) Difference (1) − (2)
Total labor force	2,318,493	2,264,000	54,493
Male	1,827,302	1,945,000	−117,698
Female	491,191	319,000	172,191
Employed	1,826,472	2,010,000	183,528
Male	1,500,857	1,723,000	−222,143
Female	325,615	287,000	38,615
Unemployed	472,021	253,630	218,391
Male	306,445	221,730	84,715
Female	165,576	31,900	133,676

[2] These data were obtained by the author during a visit to Cuba in late 1961. To our knowledge, there is only one manuscript copy of recent numbers of the *Investigation* (apart from ours) in existence.

First of all, the census definition of the labor force itself is somewhat muddy. Article 3 of the census provides a relatively *objective* definition of the labor force: "All persons 14 years old or more who are capable of effectively doing some manual or intellectual work." But Article 8 not only excludes students, housewives, institutionalized and incapacitated persons, pensioners, and unremunerated houseworkers employed less than fifteen hours weekly, but also "those able to work, but who do not have to work for their necessities." This introduces a *subjective* note into the definition. Some Cubans who were not seeking employment undoubtedly registered with an eye to Article 3. Others, *rentiers*, for example, who might have accepted employment, may have taken their cue from Article 8 and failed to register. The investigation, on the other hand, duplicates the subjective approach used in the United States and includes in the labor force anyone who *says* he is able to work and actively seeking work. At once we are up against definitional differences.

Second, the census and sample series incorporate different definitions of "unemployed persons." In the first place, the census includes unpaid family workers employed more than (as well as less than) fifteen hours weekly; in the sample, these workers are counted as "employed." For another thing, the census penalizes those workers who fail to register by placing their names on the bottom of an employment list used to fill future openings (Article 19). Thus, many persons undoubtedly registered who intended to enter the labor force some time in the *future*. These persons clearly should not have been counted as members of the unemployed labor force at the time of the census. It is impossible to estimate with any precise accuracy how many individuals were in this category, but the number was not small, since 121,081 persons (over 25 per cent of all "unemployed" workers reported by the census) were new entries in the labor force. The normal number of new entries in any given year is about 28,000.

For these reasons the sample unemployment data are clearly more accurate than the census unemployment data; future members of the labor force and unpaid family workers employed fifteen hours or more weekly are eliminated in the sample series.

In April, 1960, according to the sample series, 5.7 per cent of total employment (or 114,570 workers) fell into the latter category. These workers should be included in the census count of "employed persons," raising this figure to 1,941,042, and narrowing the gap between the sample and the census count. Some (probably over one-half) of these unpaid family workers, however, are women. For this reason, by reallocating unpaid family workers we *widen* the disparity between the census and sample figures of female employed by an unknown degree.

Do we have a firm basis for choosing between the census and sample figures of total employment? To use the (revised) census figure of 1,941,042 persons, we must explain why the sample overestimates male employment and underestimates female employment. As for the latter, the sample undoubtedly missed many partially and fully employed females in retail trade, domestic service, and agriculture. It is impossible to check this against the census, though, since that source fails to include an occupational distribution of employment by sex. As for male employment, the sample data fail to reflect emigration. Moreover, the sample data include persons who remained in Cuba but were not cooperating with the new government (ex-military personnel, ex-public officials and functionaries, and others). For these reasons we favor the (revised) census employment figures.

Although we know that the sample unemployment data are more realistic than the census data, one qualification should be made. The census shows 165,576 unemployed females; the sample figure is 31,900. After deducting female unpaid family workers from the census count (undoubtedly more than 50,000), a sizable disparity still exists between the two sources. Can this gap be explained on the theory that it represents individuals making up the future labor force? Unfortunately, the answer is no. Of the 165,576 female unemployed (census count), 62,773 failed to report their last occupation, or were new entries. Most unpaid family workers were undoubtedly included in this category; this group also incorporates the "future" labor force. Excluding (no doubt, wrongly) *all* 62,773 of these women still leaves a gap of about 70,000 between the two sources.

To conclude: We place the employed labor force at roughly 1,-

940,000 persons in April, 1960. According to the sample series, the unemployed labor force came to 253,630. But this figure underestimates female unemployed (and perhaps some male unemployed, as well) by an unknown amount. Our discussion above suggests that the total figure should be closer to 300,000, however. The total labor force (excluding proprietors) in April, 1960, was therefore in the neighborhood of 2,240,000. This estimate exceeds the sample estimate but falls below the census count.

An accurate count of the Cuban labor force should include proprietors. According to the census, there were 131,408 employers and self-employed in April, 1960. The total labor force numbered therefore 2,371,408 persons, about 55 per cent of the population fourteen years old or over.

Employment and Unemployment, 1957–1964

The rhythm of employment and unemployment in Cuba from January, 1957, to March, 1961, is shown in Table B–II. Conclusions regarding *absolute* changes in these figures, as we know, must be used with caution, but the data probably reflect more or less accurately relative movements.

From January-March, 1959, to January-March, 1961, the Cuban labor force grew by 1.6 per cent, while total employment rose by 9.6 per cent. Total employment, however, was somewhat low in the first confused months of 1959. The data show that by early 1960 employment had reached the early 1958 level; 1959 was thus a year of recovery. From 1960 to 1961 employment continued to grow faster than the labor force; first quarter employment was up 2.8 per cent, while the labor force expanded by only 1.1 per cent.

Some of the increase in employment was undoubtedly temporary, as the 1961 sugar harvest was unusually high (due chiefly to the cutting of reserve cane fields).

Probably more significant, total employment in November, 1960, was only 24,000 less than in March, 1960 (always a peak month for employment because of the sugar harvest). The difference in 1957 amounted to 84,000 workers; in 1958, 213,000 workers; and in 1959, 68,000. Comparing March employment highs with August or Sep-

Table B–II. Employment and unemployment in Cuba, January, 1957, to March, 1961 (in thousands)

Date	(1) Labor force	(2) Employ- ment	(3) Unemploy- ment	(4) Underem- ployment	(5) Rate of un- and under- employment (3) + (4) / (1)
1957 Jan	2,211	1,932	279		
Mar	2,205	2,005	200		
May	2,214	1,967	247		
Jul	2,219	1,903	316		
Sep	2,219	1,895	324		
Nov	2,212	1,921	291		
1958 Jan	2,208	2,012	196		
Mar	2,211	2,057	154		
May	2,204	1,973	231		
Jul	2,209	1,939	270		
Sep	2,234	1,934	300		
Nov	2,216	1,844	372	247	28.0%
1959 Jan	2,234	1,863	371	290	29.6
Mar	2,255	2,021	234	245	21.2
May	2,245	1,962	283	261	24.2
Jul	2,254	1,915	339	276	27.3
Sep	2,258	1,898	360	276	28.2
Nov	2,257	1,953	304	284	26.1
1960 Jan	2,251	2,029	222	290	21.9
Mar	2,261	2,051	210	217	18.9
May	2,273	1,967	306	264	25.1
Jul	2,293	1,971	322	302	27.2
Sep	2,297	1,997	300	289	25.6
Nov	2,296	2,027	269	296	24.6
1961 Jan	2,279	2,063	216	260	20.9
Mar	2,284	2,132	152	200	15.4

tember lows reveals the same pattern: a great deal of seasonal unemployment (greatest from May to November) was clearly wiped out in 1960 in the course of the agricultural diversification program.

Beginning in November, 1958, a series on underemployment became available. Through March, 1961, there was no clear change in the series, putting aside the unusual seasonal low associated with the big 1961 sugar harvest. The reason is that reductions in underemployment in some sectors of the economy, notably agriculture (where the series fails to pick up all seasonal unemployment), textiles, clothing, tobacco, beverages, and some other manufacturing sectors were to a significant degree offset by a rise in underemployment in construction (in Havana), mining, and the tertiary sector. In the first two sectors of the latter, hours worked per week dropped, while total hours worked per week remained largely unchanged.

A number of signs point to the conclusion that the employment situation improved most of all in agriculture. First, the employment rate in the agricultural provinces was more favorable than in Havana Province. In Oriente and Camaguey, for example, the unemployment rate moved as follows:

	1957	1958	1959	1960	1961
First three months	10.2%	8.5	17.9	11.3	8.5
Last three months	16.9%	23.8	20.5	14.4	

Second, there was a steady decline in the percentage of the employed labor force working for families without pay (the majority of these workers were in agriculture):

	1957	1958	1959	1960	1961
First three months	7.7%	8.0	7.1	6.5	5.3
Last three months	9.0%	7.1	7.4	6.3	

Third, we must consider the composition of employment and unemployment by occupation and industry. The percentage of employed workers in agricultural *occupations* was as follows:

	1957	1958	1959	1960	1961
First three months	40.6%	41.5	38.4	38.9	38.5
Last three months	40.0%	35.4	37.1	37.8	

The percentage of total unemployed workers in agricultural *industries* was:

	1957	1958	1959	1960	1961
First three months	27.9%	32.3	30.5	32.2	23.5
Last three months	46.2%	45.4	43.8	37.3	

And the percentage of total unemployed workers in agricultural *occupations* was:

	1957	1958	1959	1960	1961
First three months	29.5%	32.6	31.2	32.0	23.5
Last three months	45.8%	46.2	43.6	36.9	

We interpret these figures as follows: From the last three months of 1957 and 1958 to 1960, agricultural unemployment (whether measured by industry or occupation) to total unemployment fell on the order of 20 per cent. There was an increasingly smaller proportion of unemployed agricultural workers to other unemployed workers. Meanwhile, there was little or no change in the proportion of total *employed* workers in agriculture (1957–1958 to 1960, last three months). Thus full-time agricultural employment did not change very much compared with employment elsewhere, while relatively more unemployment in agriculture was liquidated.[3] It follows that there was a shift of workers from agriculture to other sectors (mainly public construction). By early 1962, Cuba's Industries' Minister could write that unemployment in the countryside had been "ended."

Although March, 1961, was the last month for which sample data were collected, the Central Planning Board circulated internally estimates of employment and unemployment for 1962 and 1963. These estimates were gathered from the various ministries and the Agrarian Reform Institute during a period in which there were no systematic and comprehensive statistical services available to the board. Thus, available data for these two years are useful only as indicators of the general direction and rough order of magnitude of change. According to the Planning Board, unemployment and underemployment were down to an estimated 140,000 persons in 1962, nearly all of them urban workers.[4] In the same year the labor force

[3] These figures disprove statements by Cuban exiles to the effect that agricultural unemployment rose during this period. See, for example, Felipe Pazos, "Desarrollo insuficient y deparperacion económica," *Cuadernos, Suplemento, Cuba, 1961,* No. 47 (Paris, March–April, 1961), p. 52.

[4] Cuba, JUCEPLAN, *Informe sobre las cifras de control para la elaboración del plan de 1964,* June 25, 1963 (mimeo), p. 64.

had contracted to just under 2.1 million persons, mainly as a consequence of emigration but partly due to a small movement from commercial to subsistence agriculture.[5] The employed labor force was thus on the order of 1.95 million people. The decline in the employed labor force due to emigration was apparently offset by new jobs for new entries into the labor force together with a reduction in the number of unemployed workers. One year later, in 1963, unemployment and underemployment rose slightly to 150,000.[6]

In 1964 it was planned to raise the level of employment by 200,-000 over 1962 (and 210,000 over the 1963 level). This required that the Planning Board eliminate existing unemployment altogether and create jobs for all new labor force entries as well. The board projected the entire expansion in the socialist sector of the economy, looking to raise employment by 55,000 in manufacturing and mining.[7] The remainder of the expansion was planned to originate in agriculture, public services (education, health, and so on), communications and transport. In construction, finance, and trade it was expected that the level of employment would remain stable. Although there are no available data for 1964, it is doubtful that planned goals were entirely met, although, because 1964 was a year of economic expansion, the plan was probably at least partly fulfilled.

[5] Cuba, JUCEPLAN, Dirección de Estadísticas, *Proyecto de Anuario Estadístico 1962*, July, 1963 (mimeo), Tables 3.2, 3.3.
[6] *Plan, 1964, op. cit.*   [7] *Ibid.*, p. 69.

Index

Agrarian Reform Law (1959), 40,
 90-91, 119, 133, 285-287
 and cattle ranchers, 96-99
 class conflict, 46-49
 and people's farms, 113-118
 see also INRA
Agrarian Reform Law (1963), 129-
 130
Agriculture
 cooperatives in, 105-113
 diversification, 224-228, 233-234
 irrigation for, 235
 specialization, 83-84
 unemployment, 214-215
Agriculture and Industrial Development Bank (BANFAIC), 78,
 132-133
Army, see Rebel Army

Batista, Fulgencio, 2, 29-33
 agricultural programs, 77-81
 corruption system, 149-151
 economic goals, 7, 144-147
 U.S. withdraws support, 2
Bay of Pigs (1961), 40

Castro, Fidel, 11, 37-41
 and agrarian reform, 100
 and agricultural planning, 215
 "betrayal of revolution," 3-5, 9
 on collective labor, 203
 and communism, 289-290
 on foreign interests, 298
 lower-class support, 301-302
 Marxism-Leninism, 312-313
 middle-class support, 293
 and middle farmers, 127-128

and ORI, 290
 on property confiscation, 167
 purge of ORI, 291-292
 support of coffee farmers, 76
Castro, Raúl, 8, 254
Cattle ranching, 57, 69-71
 and agrarian reform, 96-99
Central Planning Board
 (JUCEPLÁN), 253-260
Communist Party of Cuba (PCC),
 283-284
 and the CTC, 180-182, 190-192
 and the ORI, 290
Cuban Confederation of Labor
 (CTC), 189-193, 179-182
Cuban nationalism, 27-31, 52-53
Cuban Petroleum Institute (ICP),
 161
Cuban Revolution, 41-53
Cuban Sugar Stabilization Institute
 (ICEA), 85

Dorticós, Osvaldo, 40

Economic and Social Development
 Bank (BANDES), 79
Economic and Social Development
 Program, 145
Escalante, Anibal, 290
 see also ORI

Five Year Agricultural Plan, 73

General Agreement on Tariffs and
 Trade (1947), 144
Great Depression, 18, 27

337

Guevara, Ernesto, 8
and foreign investments, 297
friend of Castro, 38
on industrial planning, 261, 265-266
on labor, 198
qualities of, 174
on revolution, 310-311
on sugar, 219
on unemployment, 214
on unions, 196
Gutierrez, Gustavo, 48

Immigration, 13, 15
Industry
consolidation of, 169-171
industrialization, 248-253, 271-275
nationalization of, 155-168
see also individual industries
Integrated Revolutionary Organization (ORI), 290

Labor
absenteeism, 205-206
Law of Union Organization, 195
material incentives, 207
political control of unions, 177, 189, 195
prerevolutionary organizations, 6-7, 178-189
volunteer labor, 205
wages, 208-210
see also Ministry of Labor

Machado, Gerardo, 27, 28, 178
Magoon, Charles, 48
Martí, José, 37
Matos, Huber, 40-41, 287
Mining industry, 153-155
Ministry of Industries (MININD), 172, 175-176
and union leadership, 194
Ministry of Labor, 196-201
Mujal, Eusebio, 48, 180

National Association of Small Farmers (ANAP), 121-127
National Institute of Agrarian Reform (INRA), 91-96, 130-133
and agricultural planning, 217-239
and cattle ranchers, 97-99

and cane cooperatives, 105-113
and small farmers, 120-127

Oil industry, 160-165

Pais, Frank, 43
Pazos, Felipe, 288
Peña, Lázaro, 180, 291
Prerevolutionary Cuba
capitalist structure, 6, 11, 16-17
dependence on United States, 25-26
income, 17-19, 58
nonagricultural economy, 136-141
Pujol, Raúl, 43

Rebel army, 2, 8, 43
and agrarian reform, 90-91
and INRA, 130-131
Rodríquez, Carlos Rafael, 128-129
on industrial planning, 262
Russia, see Soviet Union

Sánchez, Augusto Martínez, 192
Soviet Union
and crude oil, 162
support for Cuba, 299
Sugar Coordination Law (1937), 68
Sugar industry
backwardness of production, 62-66
economic stagnation, 218
labor shortage, 219-223
rents and profits, 66-69
sugar quota system, 26, 30, 59-62

Tax Reform Law (1959), 246-247
26th of July Movement, 38, 39, 41, 43-46, 52, 54

United States
prerevolutionary Cuban policies, 19-25
and Cuban oil, 164-165
economic war with Cuba, 296-300
limits Cuban industry, 86-89
Reciprocal Trade Agreement (1934), 25-26
Sugar Acts of 1948, 1951, 26
Urrutia, Manuel, 40

War of Independence, 13, 20

Zapata, Felipe, 180